Librarians Are Whispering:

"Informative, entertaining and useful, Ackerman's book will be popular with all customers who like to write. Hands down the best book on screenwriting I've ever read."

—Carl Birkmeyer, Media Services Manager, Baltimore County, MD, Public Library

"The practical and informative lessons in this well-written book will allow anyone from the novice to the experienced writer to write their own screenplay. Ackerman's entertaining and informative guide is sure to be popular with customers."

—Kathy Coster, Scottsdale, AZ, Public Library

"*Write Screenplays That Sell* is more than a guidebook for aspiring screenwriters, although it is certainly that. As accessible as a conversation with a trusted mentor, it provides the training that innate talent needs to be productive. In the process, it constructively weaves the elements of the art and the science of film writing into a work that will be invaluable to new or experienced screenwriters, as well as a source of fascination to film buffs who would never dream of writing a screenplay, but enjoy learning as much as they can about the medium they love."

—Sally Decker Smith, Indian Trails Public Library, Wheeling, IL

"Hal Ackerman's book is comprehensive in its approach to teaching screenwriting. His background as a successful screenwriter and his experience as a teacher work together as he breaks the process into logical lessons. He has identified skills that can be taught, and created exercises that writers can use to hone those skills. Plotting, characterization, writing dialogue—all are addressed as Ackerman teaches fundamentals and identifies potential pitfalls. This book will help budding screenwriters who need lessons, tips and encouragement."

—Jane Eickhoff, Associate Director, Harford County, MD, Public Library

Write Screenplays That Sell

the Ackerman Way

Write Screenplays That Sell

the Ackerman Way

Hal Ackerman

Published by
Tallfellow® Press, Inc.
9454 Wilshire Blvd
Beverly Hills, CA 90212
www.Tallfellow.com

ISBN: 978-1-931290-65-4

Printed in USA
10 9 8 7 6 5 4 3 2 1

Contents

Prologue

By Pamela Gray

When I was a student in Hal Ackerman's graduate screenwriting class at UCLA, I dreamed of someday breaking through that seemingly impenetrable wall between aspiring and professional screenwriters. Now that I'm on the other side of that wall, I'm privy to an insider's secret: a blank computer screen, following the words FADE IN, is just as terrifying as it was before I got paid to stare at it. In fact, that screen can be even more daunting now that the "imagined" readers over my shoulder are actual studio executives, directors and producers with the power to humiliate and fire me. When I became a working screenwriter, the old adage "You take yourself with you wherever you go" once again proved to be true: My inner demons traveled right along with me as I passed through the wall. *(What makes you think YOU can write this screenplay? THIS is the script that will show the world that you're a fraud! They will NEVER make this movie—and if by some miracle they do, Anthony Lane's gonna have a FIELD day tearing you apart!)*

Not that I'm complaining. It is a privilege to be a paid screenwriter, wrestling with inner and outer demons, rather than an unemployed one. My point, however, is that I don't believe "success" erases the challenges inherent in the creative process. A paycheck does not make the writing flow effortlessly, an agent does not resolve your second-act problems, and produced credits do not miraculously eliminate on-the-nose dialogue. Screenwriting is a craft, and we only become better screenwriters if we practice our skills on a consistent basis, pay attention to the lessons we learn from each script we write, and continue to integrate the wisdom and guidance of special teachers who cross our path. Hal Ackerman was that teacher for me.

I'm very pleased that Hal has written a screenwriting book, because now others can benefit from his teaching. Hal cares about his students and sincerely wants them to succeed. With humor and compassion, along with concrete, intelligent exercises and suggestions, he guides his students to do their best possible work—and then, of course, tells them to "do it better."

I still start each project with an Ackerman Scenogram and find it to be the most useful structuring tool I've tried. Remembering back to a rigorous class exercise in which we analyzed, on index cards, every scene in David Mamet's *House of Games*, years later I still ask myself, "What does each character want in this scene? What do I, as the writer, want?" And I have never forgotten the contract Hal made each student sign on the first day of class: we had to promise to put conflict into every scene we wrote. I've since been in script meetings where producers or executives make suggestions for scenes without conflict in them. When I tell them there must be conflict in every scene and they disagree, I'm never quite sure how to explain that I signed this contract back in 1991...

Perhaps the most valuable gift I received from Hal was my understanding and appreciation of the rewriting process. I laugh when I think back to his pushing me to write a third draft of *The Blouse Man*, a screenplay I wrote as his student. (I still consider Hal my *Blouse Man* midwife.) It just didn't seem possible that there was any work left to do and, frankly, I found Hal's insistence rather annoying. By the time the film, which became *A Walk on the Moon*, wrapped, I had a five-foot-high stack of drafts.

So why does that blank screen after FADE IN make us feel frightened? Because we're about to embark on a journey and we don't know if we're up to it. We don't know if we're prepared or if we've packed the right clothes. We're not even sure we *deserve* to take this trip. And what will happen? Will we get lost? Get food poisoning? Malaria? Will we be pickpocketed? Hijacked? At the same time, we're also terribly excited. We want to plunge in recklessly—forget maps and itineraries—it's an adventure! Let's just follow our instincts! Whether you experience the post–FADE IN adrenaline rush as fear or excitement, it doesn't hurt to take along a guidebook. If reckless plunging leads to second-act chaos, if you're standing at an intersection and don't know where north is, if it turns out that every time you journey forward, you wind up right back where you started—or if you suddenly realize you're not even sure how to begin—take a deep breath and open Hal Ackerman's guidebook. Keep it along for the trip until it's time to FADE OUT. And then read it again before the next trip.

Pamela Gray's credits include A Walk on the Moon, *starring Diane Lane and Viggo Mortensen*, Conviction, *starring Hilary Swank and Sam Rockwell, and* Music of the Heart, *starring Meryl Streep. She's written an adaptation of Liane Moriarty's bestseller,* The Husband's Secret, *for CBS Films, and used three Ackerman Scenograms to help structure a story of three interconnected women. Pamela has adapted* A Walk on the Moon *into a musical which will debut at American Conservatory Theater (A.C.T.) in San Francisco in 2018. (And Hal's notes, annoyingly similar to the ones he gave her twenty-five years earlier, were brilliant.)*

Prologue

By Nicole Riegel

On one of my first days of UCLA's MFA Screenwriting Program, I sat in a packed room with savvy, talented, competitive writers who were pitching stories about aliens, space, monsters, werewolves and global takeovers. The stories had big, sweeping moments of action and huge set pieces. Everyone wrapped their pitch with the standard "it's this meets that" summary that so many in the film business use. For example, "It's *Jurassic Park* meets *Titanic*!" And there I was, a soldier from southern Ohio sitting in the back of the classroom holding a story about trapped coal miners in West Virginia. There was no moment in my story where the miners realized they were being hunted by terrifying creatures. I could, however, tell you the desires of these trapped men. I knew their secrets. I knew that this chapter of their lives was the one that would cement the core of their character beyond the last page. I loved my characters unconditionally because they were among those that raised me.

As I proceeded to peddle my story of blue-collar men from Appalachia, I saw some yawns. I think one person was sleeping. But after I finished and I looked from blank stare to blank stare, Hal turned to me with a big grin on his face. He decided to give me a shot and put me in his class. One thing became very clear to me after that pitch session, and that was that my voice was not the same as the others. I was obsessed, and still am, with coal miners, factory workers, waitresses, soldiers and ranchers. I found the lives and faces of my youth in the American Midwest endlessly fascinating, and Hal was the first person to encourage me in telling their stories in a long line of discouragement.

A week later I found myself in Hal's classroom and he continued to rigorously pick at my characters. Hal questioned everything. Where did they grow up? Why were they walking into a room instead of storming into it? What was their motivation for asking a question of another character, and was I sure that was the way they would ask it? He examined their every word and action under a microscope. The following year I moved on from coal miners to the riveting lives of garbage workers. Boy, my career was going places. Once again, Hal picked at their every decision. At the core of the story was a broken marriage and Hal questioned me to death about why one of the characters wanted the divorce. He rejected every response I gave to him, raising his voice each time he had to ask me again. I remember feeling like I might throw my pages at him and walk out the door. It became so heated that I finally snapped back, "Because she doesn't love him anymore!" There it was. Hal calmed down and said, "That's the truth in that relationship. That's what the scene is about. That's what this character has been carrying."

From that point on I was prepared to walk into any room and immediately answer any question posed to me about my characters, from events that pre-dated those in the script and long after the words, "The End."

That preparedness has served me well over the years and acted as a sturdy foundation for my growth as a writer. As time passed, I found that some of my stories were too complex to tell in the span of two hours. A key skill to develop is being able to determine where your story lives, and sometimes that home is television. On one occasion, preparedness met opportunity and I found myself at the other end of a job offer from Julia-Louis Dreyfus and HBO to adapt a book titled *Soldier Girls* into a mini-series. The story was one that I felt particularly ready to tackle, one about three impoverished women from Indiana who joined the National Guard. I'm not sure I'd ever been so nervous, as I was tasked to lead a writers' room in tandem with the producer in my very first television job. On the first day I felt like I was back at my first pitch in Hal's 434 class, except this time I was armed with the tools I needed to succeed. I questioned every single character, picked apart their actions, words, and mannerisms until we could feel them in the room with us. The job wasn't done until we could predict the characters' behavior down to the smallest nuance.

We built full, complex, messy lives in the *Soldier Girls* room, and I give a lot of credit for that to Hal. He embraced an uncommon voice, and his foresight helped shape me into the writer I have become.

With so many people telling artists what it takes to be "successful," it can feel like it's hard to know where to turn, and whose advice will lead you down the right path. Hal is someone I know from first-hand experience can lead you down that path. Allow him to push and question you. If you get to a point where you feel stupid because you can't answer his questions, it's okay, because now you know where to do more digging. Be receptive, and when it hurts and you feel like the village idiot, dust yourself off and walk back into the room the next week because that's what writing a film or show is all about.

This book is titled *Screenplays That Sell*, but I have never met a writer whose sole aim was to make money and "sell" who is happy and working consistently. Hal understands this, and that is why he is in a unique place to give such advice. He is the reason why the first thing I do when writing something new is to figure out who my characters are, and then let them guide me through their story. I have every reason to believe that's what sells.

NICOLE RIEGEL IS THE WRITER AND CO-PRODUCER OF THE HBO MINI-SERIES SOLDIER GIRLS *WITH JULIA-LOUIS DREYFUS. SHE IS CURRENTLY ADAPTING THE PLAY* GROUNDED *STARRING ANNE HATHAWAY FOR SIDNEY KIMMEL ENTERTAINMENT AND ENTERTAINMENT 360. SHE*

WAS FEATURED ON THE 2013 BLACKLIST AND WAS A 2014 SUNDANCE WRITING LAB FELLOW FOR HER SCRIPT LYNCH.

Acknowledgments

The summer I was 20, I was working the midnight–to–eight a.m. shift at a midtown hotel. At the same time I was heading home, six million New Yorkers were on their way to work. Several thousand of them got out at the Herald Square subway stop, Broadway and 34th Street. On one particular morning I looked at their adult faces. They were dead. Or angry. Or resigned. Or numb. They weren't happy. I realized that this was the way they would feel for the next eight hours at work, plus the ride home. And that this comprised the great majority of their day. They'd be up for another hour or two after dinner, and then get up at six the next morning and start all over again.

It wasn't quite a Scarlett O'Hara moment. I did not say, "As God is my witness, I'll never be hungry again." But I did make a promise to myself that I would try to work at something that made me happy for as long as I could get away with it.

A few decades later, so far, so good.

I'm a freelance writer and a screenwriting professor in what is likely the best screenwriting department in the world. I wake up every day knowing I'll be doing something I love.

Besides the respect and love I have for him as a friend and teacher, I have immeasurable gratitude to Richard Walter for bringing me to UCLA. And the same in equal measure to Pamela Hunter's husband, Professor Lew, for keeping me there. Thanks to all the student commandos whose enthusiasm and zeal and honesty and desire have been my constant and enduring inspiration.

For their valuable editorial and research aid on this book, great thanks to Dave Johnson and Marc Arneson, both of whom I predict will be at podiums within a very few years. The same thanks and predictions go to Julie Ann Sipos and Jonnell Lennon. Thanks, also, to Paul Schaefer for the graphic aid.

There is a Zen koan that says, "It is a poor teacher whose students do not surpass him." Among my own UCLA students who have made sure through their successes that I am a good teacher, whose scripts written in my classes have been significant factors in propelling their careers in feature film and mutely in television, are Felicia Henderson, Sacha Gervasi, Allison Anders, Travis Fine, Nicole Riegel, Jessica Dube, Steven Canals, Heather Marion, Kit Steinkellner, Barbara Curry, Susan Arneson, Jonell Lennon, Amy Aniobi, Matt Wheeler. I know that teachers and parents are not supposed to have favorites, but Pamela Gray's underrated and underadvertised *A Walk on the Moon* will someday find the audience it deserves.

These triumphs have been publicly celebrated, but I am equally proud of many unheralded writers, some of whom may find the limelight soon and some who may not, but all of whom made significant breakthroughs in their writing. And when that happens, there is no amount of public acclaim to equal that inner feeling of elation.

Continue, all of you, to be brilliant.

PART ONE

Before You Can Be a Screenwriter

CHAPTER 1

Can Writing Be Taught?

There is an opinion widely held among intelligent people that a nascent artist either has talent or does not. And that in the presence of talent, teaching is either irrelevant or harmful, and that in its absence, teaching is wasted. It is the cult of the natural. After all, did Mozart go to Juilliard? Did Carnegie need an MBA to run a steel empire? Edison had only three months of formal schooling. Shakespeare attended no writing seminars. The American author Flannery O'Connor, when asked whether universities stifled creative writers, replied, "Not enough."

It is unarguably true that every field of human endeavor is graced with certain individuals who are gifted with such an abundance of natural talent that, for them, teaching is as necessary as a second appendix. And on the other end of the spectrum, there are people with so little aptitude, who are so limited in imagination, so undisciplined and lacking in stamina that the best teaching in the world will have no effect on them.

While it is true that talent cannot be taught, people with talent can be taught. You cannot teach an athlete to have a 48-inch vertical leap, like Michael Jordan had in his prime, but the game of basketball can be taught, both its essential skills and the deeper levels of the game that separate the abundantly talented from those who achieve greatness. Let us not forget that Stravinsky had his Nadia Boulanger, as did Bernstein. Tennessee Williams came out of the Iowa Writing Project, as did Flannery O'Connor, David Milch and John Irving. Despite the orange-tinged tweets emanating from the current occupant of the White House, education is far from a terrible thing. During the three decades I have taught at UCLA, our screenwriting program has launched a tidal wave of successful and influential writers, a small sample of which include David Koepp, Audrey Wells, The Michaels — Werb and Colleary, Billy Ray, Shane Black, Dustin Lance Black (no relation), Alexander Payne and that Francis Coppola fellow; not to mention our newest generation of writers who are staffing and running the rooms of hugely successful television shows.

More than a dozen screenplays written in my own seminar classes have become produced feature films, many more than that number have been bought or optioned and an equal number have won major contests and awards. My UCLA colleagues share similar successes, as do writing instructors in our sister colleges and universities.

The Serenity Prayer reminds us that there are things we can control and things we cannot. We cannot control how people will respond to our work. We can control the degree of effort, commitment, dedication and desire we direct toward making ourselves the best writers we can become.

Faced with the certain knowledge that we will never be as good as (fill in the name of your hero), we have two clear choices. One is to break all our pencils, throw the Underwood out the window, trade in the Mac for a power saw, and never try. The other, as Anne Lamott suggests in *Bird by Bird*—the best book I've ever read about writing—is to "do it anyway."

This book is written for people who choose No. 2. I hope you will learn from it—not merely screenplay terminology or how to properly label each moving part—but also how to make each of the parts, and then how to make them better. And to know, if it isn't better, why it isn't better and how to make it better. And then, how to make it better than that.

I make this promise to my students at the beginning of each new term, and I make it to you: **Ten weeks from today, you will be better screenwriters than you are right now**.

How *much* better depends not on the amount of innate talent you come in with, but rather on the **level of commitment** you are willing to put out. **Stamina** is important. Writing is harder than it looks. It takes time. It is wearying. It's easy to get tired, both in the short run—in the writing of an individual screenplay—and, in the larger sense, in the marathon run of a writer's creative life.

You've seen all of those weight-loss infomercials on TV, with their guaranteed shortcuts. You have probably figured out by now that there are no shortcuts. The same is true of becoming a better writer. This book contains many exercises devoted to working the specific writer's "muscle groups." You have to go to the writers gym every day, do all the reps, all the crunches, all the thrusts, all the weight. And after all that, there is no guarantee that you will become Mr. or Ms. Universe.

It takes faith. Physicists have proven that given the weight and mass of a bumblebee and the surface tensile strength of its wings, it is physically impossible for it to fly. And yet it can. We are bumblebees. We have to do the impossible, to make something exist that previously did not and which, without our effort, would never exist.

Each of us must maintain the ridiculous, arrogant, stupid, illogical, but utter and unshakable belief in ourselves that we can do this; that we can create a story with believable characters involved in circumstances that are entertaining and exciting and enlightening of the human condition.

The ability to see one's own shortcomings. Before we were writers, we were people. And before we were big people, we were much smaller people surrounded by bigger people. And those people told us what kind of a world it was. It was a world that derided people for their mistakes, that rewarded only success, that mistook delayed success for failure, that saw only the risk of shame and embarrassment in taking chances and of having one's hopes and deficiencies exposed naked to the world.

How are we going to respond to criticism of our work? How do *you* respond? What latent disability has been cast upon your ability to listen? To what degree have you already internalized the expected criticism and lashed yourself with it? Where does the idea of "perfection" fit in your cosmology? How fearful are you that the best you have done is the best that you can ever do?

Flexibility, emotional muscle, curiosity, courage to explore, delight in the process. These are some of the underdeveloped "muscle groups" we will work in our writers gym, in addition to the skills specific to the craft of screenwriting.

And of course there is talent, which, like beauty, is a gift. It is a gift often squandered. Talent must accompany a work ethic that doesn't take "good enough" for granted. I have never met any writer talented enough to be lazy.

Are you guaranteed, if you do everything this books asks, that you will become a David Koepp or Nicole Holofcener? A Farrelly brother? A Coen brother? A Wachowski sister? A Polish brother? Yes, absolutely!!

No, of course not. Success begins at the point where luck meets preparation. So let's do what we can to be ready.

WRITERS GYM EXERCISES

Write a Rant

What is the thing or person that irks you most? Lawn

sprinklers that spot your car? TV ads? War? Politics? People who apply makeup while driving?

Write a furious diatribe against it. Attack it. Lacerate it. Vent your spleen. This will be the document that ends the thing that you hate.

When you have finished, write PART 2. With equal commitment, honesty, depth, passion and insight, be an advocate for the issue you have just attacked. (If it was a person, write his or her character piece about *you.*) You need to write characters who disagree with your points of view, and write them convincingly. Someday you might have to write two brilliant closing statements by two passionate lawyers. You'll be ready.

CHAPTER 2

A Word or Two About the Writer's Life and the Industry We Love

Screenwriting is unique in the arts. It is the only medium where the writer's original material is looked upon as a mere suggestion. The spurious notion that film is a "director's medium" is so widely accepted that it is barely questioned. How that has come to be true is a study in successful marketing and brainwashing. There certainly is not the slightest bit of creative logic behind it. Leonard Bernstein did not rewrite Beethoven. He played all the notes. He did not say, "Does it have to be a hymn? Does it have to be to joy?"

Any argument put forward justifying the auteur myth breaks down when we look at television. Television is no different than cinema in any meaningful way except that the screens are smaller (and even that distinction is disappearing as TV screens get bigger and movie screens shrink). Television is now known as a writer's medium.

Stay for the final credits of any film. The last item onscreen will read: "For purposes of copyright, the author of this screenplay is…" and the next word will not be the screenwriter's name. It will be the name of the film company. Once a film is made, we do not own the copyright. This business practice allows film companies to hire and fire us at will, and makes every screenwriter a whore, however high priced.

By contrast, the Dramatists Guild's Minimum Basic Agreement—the document that exists between producing entities and playwrights—forbids any changes from being made to the writer's text without consent and prohibits shared writing credit being claimed by anyone making solicited or unsolicited contributions.

So why aren't we all writing plays?

Look at next weekend's movie box-office grosses. The nationwide audience on the first weekend for any reasonably successful film exceeds the total number of people who saw all of Shakespeare's plays during his lifetime. The situation is even worse for writers of prose fiction. As in any field, there are a few superstars making stratobucks, but brilliant writers who publish stories in literary journals in order to make a modest living need merely to write and sell ten short stories every day.

The film business dangles that big, bright shining bauble, the possibility of riches and fame, in front of us. With possibility comes hope, and with hope, delusion. Let's say it once. Financial success and popular recognition will *never* be mathematically probable. Enough new screenplays are registered at the Writers Guild by January 19 of any given year to satisfy the full slate of films that will be made and released that year.

For those of you who haven't fainted yet, the employment situation is not quite as bleak as that. For better or for worse (you decide), nearly every film employs the services, and sometimes the very highly priced services, of a large number of writers, some of whom are credited onscreen and others who are not.

The January 19 statistic also does not take into account all the many, many, many, many original screenplays purchased or optioned each year but not made, nor all the assigned (and often highly paid) adaptations of existing works of fiction, nonfiction and theater that are commissioned but not made. Purchasers do not like to advertise how many failed ventures they invest money and time in, but the ratio of films made to projects receiving any financial development is, conservatively, 1 to 1,000.

It also does not include that great Golden Goose, television. Scores of writers are employed through network and cable, long-form and short-form, fiction- and reality-based writing for television. Thousands more are re-compensated in the form of royalties and residuals.

There are livings to be made.

How does your work get the best shot it can possibly get? How can you make your work good enough to get into the ballgame, to get the encouragement or attention that might lead to its getting bought, which may lead to its getting made, or to your getting hired to write something on assignment?

How can you get good enough? How can you be a better writer three months from now than you are right now? And how can you be a better writer three months after that?

You're standing on a ladder. Your ability is on one rung and your aspirations to how well you would like to write are several rungs higher. Each script you write with full commitment will allow you to climb a rung or two. But that very act will also raise the level of your aspirations. There will always be a disparity between how good you are and how good you can imagine yourself being. Your aspirations will nearly always be out of the reach of your ability to attain them, but this is the irritation in the oyster that creates the pearl.

A classic *Honeymooners* episode called "Young Man with a Horn" has Ralph Kramden struggling through the entire show to hit a high note on his cornet. But it keeps eluding him as the cornet squeaks horribly, making his eyes bulge and his face turn red. At the climax of the story, he picks up the instrument for one last try. And this time, waveringly for a moment, he reaches the note. And the triumphant last line is, "Well, that's a piece of it, Alice."

All that work for just a piece of it. Is it worth it? Prudent friends or family members might think not. The only relevant question is: Do you? Are you willing to pay the price? Make no mistake; there will be a price to pay. It will be a long road (one hopes) whose ultimate destination at this moment is unknown. There will be more moments of frustration than of celebration. If getting just "a piece of it" is all you can hope for, will that be reward enough for you?

What you can't know until you have experienced it is how good it feels. Hitting a piece of that note. Writing one true line. A scene that takes an unexpected, unplanned turn into a depth you've never explored. There are few areas of human endeavor that reach down into our deepest souls. Love. War. Art. Athletics. War is too dangerous, so let's cut that out, and love comes only to the lucky. That leaves athletics and art, and brings us back to the notion of the writers gym.

Would you decide one day to build a house by hand, possessing only the lumber and tools you happen to be shouldering at that moment? Or, mesmerized by the beauty of a figure skater, would you buy a costume and a pair of blades and think you could compete in the Olympics? Skaters, gymnasts, concert pianists—all of them put in their twelve-hour days and six-day weeks tooling the machinery of their bodies into implements of their craft. Should a writer do any less?

Let's not kid ourselves. We are competing in the screenwriting Olympiad. Buying this book is like buying a membership in that writers gym. It contains instructions for using the apparatus that will hone and strengthen and develop all the specific muscle groups of screenwriting: **story structure (The Big Picture), scene writing (The Small Picture), narrative and descriptive writing and dialogue**. In addition, there are discussions of the Short Film, research, rewrites, and living the writer's life.

You don't lose weight by purchasing a membership or buying cool-looking workout clothes. *Looking* at those machines will not take any inches off your flabby waist or add a centimeter to your spindly triceps. You've got to work them. You've got to show up every day and get sweaty. This book is not an electric stimulator that gives your abs the equivalent workout of a thousand crunches. It is not a miracle diet that promises results without exercise or restraint. **Writing is harder than it looks.**

Do you remember the fable about the shoemaker who set all his leather out on his workbench at night, and returned in the morning to find all the shoes and boots mended by elves? I have tried that. I have stacked all my rough notes alongside my computer screen and gone to sleep in hopes that the following morning I would find that the elves had turned them into five brilliant pages.

But no. The sad and lovely truth, my friends, is this: WE ARE THE ELVES.

WHY YOU NEED THIS BOOK

The phrase "Wow, wouldn't that be a great idea for a screenplay" has propelled many writers to jump into a script with no more forethought than what a pair of teenagers gives to raising a child as they tear each other's clothes off. Procreators and writers both trust that the purity of their spontaneous eruption will contain within its nucleus all the nourishment and guidance needed for a healthy outcome. Judging by the vast numbers of messed-up kids and crappy screenplays, I'd have to say maybe not.

We all know how to write the English language. We have all been possessed of the brilliant lightbulb of an idea. We believe that these two items in the presence of expensive formatting software are all the materials necessary to produce a good screenplay.

If only there was a recipe! Two pounds thin fillet. Half a cup of grated onions. A teaspoon of salt. Bake in a 350° oven for 27 minutes.

But alas, no, that is not the way the creative process works. And therein lies the essential schizophrenia facing the screenwriter in Hollywood. *We* want to make each one by hand. *They* want them manufactured uniformly. With the increasing corporate ownership of film studios, the corporate ethos is being imposed on their movie "product." Notions of branding, of the niche marketplace, are the concerns imposed on that product, one which the screenwriter still feels is a work of passion.

An executive at McDonald's once declared that their corporate goal was to make a McDonald's meal in Austin, Texas, taste exactly the same as anywhere in the world. They have an elaborate 20-step process for making their french fries that begins with the exact size and weight and shape of the potatoes, and those steps are adhered to in every franchise from Boston to Bangkok. Studio executives salivate at the thought of being able to exercise such precise control over the operation, and to be able to perfectly predict the resulting product!

But where in the pantry do you look for a dash of humor, a pinch of compassion, a cup of insight? Where do you read how much to put in when it says "season to taste"? Are the ingredients fresh? How long should it bake?

Writers want to say what's never been said. Executives want what they've already heard. The majority of produced screenplays are the genetically impaired results of the crossbreeding of those two species. Do you doubt it? Open the Sunday entertainment section. Check out the ads for all the movies playing. How many of them would you consider going to? Of those you've seen, how many have disappointed you?

For the duration of our time together, we are going to suspend our disbelief about the industry. We are going to believe we are priming ourselves to practice our craft in an industry where crap does not rule, where quality is not an impediment, and where the joyful pursuit of excellence is a worthy aspiration. I want to feel confident that when you are asked to reach for greatness, you'll be ready.

My own screenwriting guru is Napoleon Bonaparte. When he was asked to define his military strategy, his reply was, "If you wish to take Vienna, *take Vienna!*"

How does that anthem apply on our battlefield? It means don't be timid. Take chances. Spread your wings. Even the smallest film is larger than the largest life. Rip your chest open. A little wider. Reach down inside. A little deeper. Fear not. Take Vienna.

WRITERS GYM EXERCISE

Self-Portrait/Writers Anthem

Visual artists do self-portraits. Writers write about why they write. Why do you write? What are your goals, professionally and personally? Write your anthem. Why *you* write. What do you hope to get from the process, from the result?

If you don't go shopping for it, it won't be in your basket.

CHAPTER 3

Why We Don't Write

IMMUTABLE RULE #1: In order to have written a screenplay, you first must actually WRITE a screenplay. All the words. All 110 pages. It's frightening. No wonder every writer does his or her best to avoid it. You know the writer's proverb: "Never put off 'till tomorrow what you can put off to next week." There are countless good reasons for procrastinating. Some are socially meaningful, like feeding the homeless. Washing graffiti off buildings. Working an extra shift.

On the first day of class I pass out index cards and ask my students to write down what they do to procrastinate. Here is a partial list from a recent group:

Research. Clean house. Practice trombone. Surf the Net. Watch TV. Hang out with friends. E-mail. Play video games. See movies. Shop. Make phone calls. Build things. Think about writing. Talk about writing. Network. Give up. Raise children. Read screenplays. Drink. Drive. Draw. Have sex. Chain smoke. Run. Play tennis, handball, racquetball. Work out. Nap. Daydream. Organize closets. Defrost refrigerator. Make lists. Do yoga. Play music. Groom the dog. Fall in love. Fall out of love.

WRITE.

When we scrape just under the surface, we will likely find one dominant reason to procrastinate. We're afraid we're not good enough and that our inadequacies will be exposed. The fear of humiliation, of being judged deficient, can be paralyzing. If we never really take the shot, we can always harbor the belief that we would have been good at it if we'd only had the time. To spin the old adage, "Nothing ventured, nothing lost."

But of course a great deal *is* lost if nothing is ventured.

Start with everything you might have written if you'd taken the chance. If you're like every other writer, a lot of it would have been garbage. Some part of it might not have completely sucked. And maybe one tiny fragment of it might have been halfway decent. Would you not count that as something of value, lost?

But there is more.

Vince Lombardi, the legendary coach of the Green Bay Packers, said that the greatest feeling is to give everything you have on the field and win. What he is less known for saying is the second part: that the second greatest feeling is to give everything you have on the field and lose. The point here is giving it your all.

Make a point of watching a baby who is learning to stand and walk. Count how many times it falls on its butt. Guess what? So did you. Ultimately, though, it did not stop you. You persevered. Getting up and getting there was a stronger drive than the sum total of everything that deterred you, including the pull of gravity and the weight of derision. No one ever learned to ride a bike, ice skate, rollerblade or surf without wiping out a hundred times.

Sometime during our emotional development, through the combined diligent efforts of parents, teachers and members of the opposite gender, *falling* became synonymous with *failing*. We became self-conscious, susceptible to the judgment of others and to the even harsher preemptive judgment we place on ourselves.

We all know the alphabet; we can all read and make shopping lists and write letters. It seems like a very short hop from there to creative writing, and that, unlike music or portraiture, it should be something we should be capable of doing. But we secretly dread that what we have to say is not profound enough, not funny enough, not original enough, not beautiful enough, not interesting enough, not *enough* to warrant anyone's attention. We fear the double-edged blade of derision and exposure. There are many possible responses to this, and I've ranked them in my own ascending order of preference:

1. Surrender to the fear and never give it a shot.
2. Deaden the fear with massive quantities of drugs and alcohol.
3. Create other reasons to avoid doing your best as a hedge and an excuse.
4. Accept that you might indeed suck. And strive to do your best anyway.

Falling is not failing. It is an unavoidable step in the process. It's the only possible way of ever getting to where you suck less. The sooner you start making the baby mistakes, the sooner you progress to more sophisticated mistakes.

WRITERS GYM EXERCISE

What are the five most common things you do to avoid writing? Write them down. Estimate the amount of time those activities occupy.

Whose disapproval do you most dread? Imagine sending those people to the vacation paradise of their dreams, an all-expense-paid ten-week vacation. For the duration of the next piece you write, they will be having such a good time that they will not be peering over your shoulder, telling you by word or facial expression that what you have done is not good enough.

CHAPTER 4
Why We Write

Name ten screenwriters who are not also directors.

Would you recognize Dustin Lance Black if you saw him on the street? How about Diablo Cody? Both wrote Academy Award-winning screenplays (*Milk* and *Juno*).

Okay, so it's not for the fame.

You all know that Steven Spielberg directed *Schindler's List*. Ten points if you know who wrote the screenplay. Bonus ten if you know who wrote the book on which the screenplay was based.

Okay, so it's not for the notoriety.

So, what's left? The money? That must be it. Writers working at guild-sanctioned jobs are ridiculously overpaid. A million bucks for a *screenplay?* Forty grand for a 30-minute TV episode? That's stealing! Plus residuals (200 to 300 percent if the show is successful), plus more money if the show goes into syndication. If you're also a producer, add royalties.

What percentage of writers do you imagine grabs that brass ring? Guess again. Nope, lower still. Edgar Allan Poe earned about $43 during his writing life. And that's more than the majority of aspiring screenwriters earn. Take the total lifetime earnings of Writers Guild members, *including* the most successful, then divide that amount by the number of lifetime hours spent writing. It'll average out to roughly 84 cents per hour.

And yet...

Think of the thousands of people writing and the millions of hours they spend on their novels and screenplays, poetry and prose, *without ever selling them.* Why in the world would they be doing that? Are they all masochists? Now think about how other kinds of people ply their trade simply for the love of it. How many freelance proctologists do you know?

The reason that most of us write is corny, it's sentimental, it's tragically unhip, but it's the truth. We do it because it's what we want to do.

I won't go so far as to say that it makes us *happy* (*none* of us would be so superficial as to be *happy*), but it makes us feel different. Better in some way. A lot of writers have written passionate pieces on why they write. Allen Ginsberg immediately comes to mind. (You might find him interesting to read the next time you run out of the usual ways to procrastinate.)

There is no great mystique about "the writer's life." Writers do the same things everybody else does day to day, except we do them more clumsily. We do our laundry, run errands, make car payments, kiss up to bosses, buy stocks, go to the movies, ride the bus, try to stay healthy, fear death, raise children, go out to eat, try to meet somebody, play ball. But our eyes are not on the pavement of the road. We are traversing more than one highway. We are simultaneously engaged in physical reality and in alternate mental versions of the same event. We are constantly processing reality as *Yeah, but what if?*

Our brains are little pots of fertile soil and the universe is constantly raining down seeds. Ideas, notions, little chimes ringing, story possibilities, understandings of moments. You see a grown son and his aging mother arguing ferociously at a curbside—she not wanting to get in the car, he berating her, threatening to leave her there. He is cruel to her. Maybe you see a vision of that same scene between them when he was five and she was threatening to leave *him*.

In a furniture store you overhear a forty-year-old man and woman arguing over the purchase of a lamp to go in her teenage daughter's room. He says the deal was that if he moved in, the daughter would go live at her father's. You hear no more, but you create alternate realities of the woman buying the lamp, sending the man packing, or the woman surrendering. You want to look in their shopping cart. That lamp is their life.

Writers listen for harmonies; civilians hear melody alone. For them the facades of ordinary situations are opaque, and they see what is there to be seen. Writers are attracted to translucence. We start with nothing but an idea, an agitation, a compulsion, an irritation. That, plus a bumblebee's faith that it can fly.

Declaring yourself a writer takes courage. Doctors and real estate agents are given a shingle to hang out in front of their offices validating their entrance into the profession. We have to hang our own shingle. There is no governing body. There is no test, no final exam, no grades, nothing to study for, no way to know when we're ready except when we ordain it so.

We're all given a certain capacity for understanding the human condition, some more than others. That's the "art" part. And that factor is out of our power. What is within our power is how much of our potential we develop. Remember, 90 percent of 60 is more than 50 percent of 100.

It takes stamina. Or obsession. It takes belief in one's self or its equally valuable partner, self-delusion. It takes resilience in the face of defeat, which some may call masochism. It takes courage. There's no other word for it. It takes courage to enter into a life-and-death battle with no knowledge of the outcome.

The next time you go to the movies, look at the names of all the hundreds of job titles and the thousands of people who hold them. Every single one of those jobs comes with an instruction manual. Every job except ours. Our job is to write it. It's called the screenplay.

If it is your desire to be a screenwriter, here are THE TWO MOST IMPORTANT RULES to follow. Without doing this, everything else in this book is merely theoretical.

The second most important thing to do is to make a writing schedule for yourself.

Let it conform to the true rhythms and constraints of your life. If you are a single mother with two young children, it would not be realistic to think you could write from nine to four every day. Be realistic. Do not be one of those people who make 37 impossibly idealistic New Year's resolutions, thinking they seem holy to the rest of the world, but transparently giving themselves a license to fail.

I'd suggest you block out no less than 90 minutes per session, especially if it takes half an hour of ritual digression to get you into it. The more regular the activity, the more quickly it becomes habitual. Think of a watercourse carving a riverbed over eons. You want to etch writing into the soul of your day.

Post the schedule in your writing space. They tell insomniacs to do nothing in bed except sleep—not to eat or read or watch TV there. Maybe you can do the same with your writing space; do nothing else there but write. There is something positive to be said for conditioned responses. As you enter your workspace, you get into work mode, like an athlete taking the field or an actor the stage. It's putting on the game face. It's getting ready to rumble.

So, the second most important thing is to make a writing schedule.

AND THE *MOST* IMPORTANT THING: STICK TO IT.

You can use pencil, typewriter, quill and foolscap, or DSL with eight trillion megabytes. But put the tush on the cush.

WRITERS GYM EXERCISES

Write out your writing schedule. This is not theoretical. Do it.

Now.

Rule Breaking

In a series of one-line (or, at most, two-line) impressions, make a litany of all the times you broke the rules: lied, cheated, stole, set fire, pilfered, prevaricated, deceived. For example: "Poisoned my sister's goldfish. Enjoyed it." Or, "Took joyrides in the family car at age fourteen while parents were in hospital." (There are some great examples of Eavesdropper Scenes in an appendix at the back of this book.)

Extract the juiciest of all those incidents. Write it as a story, in prose. However long it takes—one page, ten pages. How would you adapt it to a screen story? Make a running order of the scenes. Would you need to invent other scenes to dramatize events that were not mentioned in the prose version?

CHAPTER 5

What a Screenplay Isn't

Picture two beakers of clear, transparent liquid on a table. The chemical formula for the contents of each beaker is written on an index card. The card in front of beaker No. 1 bears the familiar symbol for water, H_2O. Two parts hydrogen, one part oxygen. The card in front of beaker No. 2 bears the formula H_2O_2. We are thirsty. Which to drink?

We know that H_20 is water. What does our intuition tell us about the mystery formula H_2O_2? Is it two glasses of water? Oxygen being a good thing, we would logically predict that the enhanced oxygen content would enhance the water. Atoms being small particles, we might surmise that the degree of difference between the mystery substance and water would be miniscule. Superoxygenated water—maybe some pricey new concoction that trendy Hollywood people drink? Shall we drink it and see?

No, let us not do that! Because H_20_2 is not designer water. H_20_2 is hydrogen peroxide, an antiseptic used to cleanse and heal skin wounds. Its label contains severe warnings against getting it in your eyes or swallowing it. We buy it in drugstores in a diluted solution. Swallow it at full strength and it'll kill you. Who would predict that the addition of *one tiny atom* of life-sustaining oxygen to a molecule of life-sustaining water would yield a toxic substance? And what is the point of this analogy?

Your screenplay is a water molecule. Do not let it become hydrogen peroxide.

Let's look at the most common "extra molecules of oxygen" as they apply to screenwriting. You may be surprised. You may become irate at hearing the techniques that you consider essential to the way you write being described as transgressions. Remember, we're not talking about adding poison to water. That would be obvious, and we'd have no reason to defend the practice. We're talking about oxygen.

The most commonly made hyperadditions to screenplays are, ironically, the things that make many movie scenes great; which is to say, the specific way they are acted and directed. We mistakenly try to write the finished movie on the page—to re-create (or actually precreate) on the page exactly what will appear on screen. Every nuance of character expression. The subtle reaction shots. The inflection and cadence with which each character speaks a line. The fluctuations of light and shadow. The placement and movement of the cameras and their continuing relationship with the subject. The music. The costume, the hair. The visual effects, the backstory and interior thoughts of the characters as revealed in well-described facial expressions and hand gestures.

What we have described here is not a screenplay, but its close-blood cousin, THE SHOOTING SCRIPT.

PRECEPT #1: A Screenplay Is Not a Shooting Script.

A screenplay and a Shooting Script (like water and hydrogen peroxide) have two profoundly different reasons for their existence. **A SCREENPLAY is an instrument for telling a story. A SHOOTING SCRIPT is a blueprint for the production of a motion picture.**

Do you see any similarity in those two verbal phrases? 1. Tell a story.

2. Produce a motion picture.

No, they are different activities. They require different instruments.

Below are two short scenes in SHOOTING SCRIPT form. They are followed by the same two scenes pared down to SCREENPLAY form.

AS A SELF-CORRECTING EXERCISE, READ THE FIRST VERSION OF THE SCENES AND REMOVE ALL EXTRANEOUS CLUTTER. WRITE A CLEAN, EDITED VERSION OF THE SCENE. THEN COMPARE YOUR EDITED VERSION WITH THE CLEANED-UP VERSION IN THIS BOOK THAT FOLLOWS.

EXHIBIT A: SHOOTING SCRIPT VERSION (HYDROGEN PEROXIDE)

1. EXT. – MAIN STREET MERTSBORO, INDIANA, – A SUMMER NIGHT

ESTABLISHING SHOT:

The town looks like a Norman Rockwell cover for the Saturday Evening Post.

AM CAR RADIO BUBBLEGUM MUSIC OVER

WIDE SHOT – CAMERA ON INSERT CAR cruises slowly with a 1963 FORD, a PAIR OF YOUNG LOVERS in the front seat.

INSERT LICENSE PLATE – Indiana, 1969

2. EXT. – DRUG STORE

WIDE – as the Ford cruises past.

3. INT. – FORD

TWO SHOT

As the bowling alley goes by in the background:

LINDY MACDANIEL (21) snuggles close. She is a dream of a girl-next-door, bright and pretty. And very much in love with —

REVERSE ANGLE favoring

JOHN WILSON. A character Jimmy Stewart would have played. Huck Finn mixed with Andy Hardy. As they pass the skating rink —

CLOSE ON LINDY as she smiles dreamily at John.

CLOSE ON JOHN-He pauses with a very serious look. Then he breaks into a smile. Just kidding!

WIDE – As the Ford drives by, CAMERA stops on the big sign in front of Mertsboro High. It reads: MERTSBORO HIGH - HOME OF THE FIGHTING BISON

EXT. – SKATING RINK – MOMENTS LATER

The Ford rolls past the skating rink.

INT. – FORD-TWO SHOT THROUGH WINDSHIELD

Lindy holds John's hand and twirls his hair with one finger.

LINDY
Do you remember the time that —?

JOHN
Splat. I remember.

ECU – Of Lindy's eyes tearing up.

JOHN'S EYES – are moist too at the thought of the nostalgia of the shared memory.

DISSOLVE TO:

4. EXT. – A PEACH ORCHARD–NIGHT

IN THE SKY: A FULL MOON beams down on the quiet world.

DOLLY SHOT – Leading John and Lindy as they walk through the orchard. The Ford is parked in the background.

JOHN'S POV – Of ripening peaches glowing in the moonlight.

INSERT CLOSE ON a peach.

JOHN – plucks a peach. He takes a bite and savors it, testing it like a real peach expert. He suddenly tosses it away.

JOHN

Not ripe yet. Another week.

CLOSE ON LINDY-She looks at John, thinking over his words.

LINDY

Like us.

JOHN – Looks at her for a long beat, saying nothing.

EXT. – ORCHARD-EDGE OF HILL

MEDIUM WIDE – They emerge at the edge of a hill.

LINDY and JOHN'S POV – Of the few lights of Mertsboro.

LINDY AND JOHN – She rests dreamily in his arms.

LINDY

Everything will look so different when we get back.

JOHN
Nothing's changed here in fifty years.
What's gonna be so different?

LINDY
We will.

JOHN
No...

TIGHT TWO SHOT

LINDY
(glances into his eyes)
It's our last night as kids.

JOHN
We're only getting married.

ECU – Of John's hand closing over Lindy's. CAMERA sees her ENGAGEMENT RING.

EXHIBIT B: PARED DOWN SCREENPLAY VERSION (WATER)

EXT. – MAIN STREET, MERTSBORO, INDIANA – A SUMMER NIGHT

The town looks like a Norman Rockwell cover for the Saturday Evening Post.

A 1963 FORD cruises slowly. Its LICENSE PLATE and the AM bubblegum MUSIC say INDIANA, 1969.

INT. – FORD

A pair of young lovers takes a sentimental ride, passing the DRUGSTORE, HIGH SCHOOL, BOWLING ALLEY.

LINDY MACDANIEL (21) snuggles close. She is a dream of a girl-next-door, bright and pretty. And very much in love with —

JOHN WILSON (same age). A character Jimmy Stewart would have played. Huck Finn mixed with Andy Hardy. As they pass the skating rink —

LINDY
Do you remember the time that —?

JOHN
Splat. I remember.

They dissolve in unbearable nostalgia of the shared memory.

EXT. – A PEACH ORCHARD – NIGHT

The Ford is parked under a canopy of trees. John and Lindy walk through the orchard. Ripening PEACHES glow in the light of the full moon.

John plucks a peach and tosses it away after a bite.

JOHN
Not ripe yet. Another week.

LINDY
Like us.

They emerge at the edge of a hill, looking out at the few lights of Mertsboro. Lindy rests dreamily in his arms.

LINDY
Everything will look so different when we get back.

JOHN
Nothing's changed here in fifty years. What's gonna be so different?

LINDY
We will.

```
                    JOHN
          No...

                    LINDY
          It's our last night as kids.

                    JOHN
          We're only getting married.
```

SIMILARITIES

Observe the similarities between screenplay and Shooting Script.

- Each consists of SCENES. Each scene designation begins with a SLUGLINE denoting the scene location.
- Narrative action is written in the same format in both.
- In each, the speakers' names and the dialogue are indented on the page.

DIFFERENCES

Look how clean and unencumbered, how sparsely furnished with only the essentials, the screenplay page is. It looks like a Japanese garden. Now, look how busy the Shooting Script is. There's stuff all over the place, like five teenagers living in the same room.

- Sluglines are numbered.
- There are many camera directions.
- Cuts and new angles have been inserted.
- Set description is elaborated upon.
- Parenthetical direction is given to the actors.

What else do you notice?

The most common, rampant, endemic error that screenwriters make is trying to put too much of the Shooting Script into the screenplay, that is, trying to direct the movie on the page: decorating the sets, casting the roles, designing the soundtrack, possibly catering lunch. This is a noble and visionary enterprise, but the effort is utterly misplaced.

When you employ in your screenplay the devices that are appropriate to a Shooting Script, what you *think* you are doing is writing your movie on paper exactly how you see it on screen. But what a professional reader will see is a neophyte amateur trying to direct on the page.

Furthermore, all the pages it takes for you to write the things you mistakenly think you need—and you will be surprised to discover how many pages that will be, 10, 20—all those pages are no longer doing the thing they *need* to do, which is tell the story. There will be 20 pages LESS of story. And since even a good first draft usually gets about 70 percent of the story, yours will be far less than that, and you won't even know it.

But even an unschooled reader, while perhaps not having the vocabulary or experience to diagnose the reasons *why*, will find the writing too dense, hard to read, and overly technical. It will overwhelm the one thing that you want to be seen: THE STORY. A reader will have to chop through the underbrush with a machete to get to your story.

Your dear friends, parents, teachers, and other loved ones may choose to do that hard work. But a professional reader will not be as forgiving. With all those other scripts that need to be read, yours will fall by the wayside.

GOLDEN GUIDING PRINCIPLE #1:

A screenplay is an instrument for telling a story through a series of scenes that describe what an audience will see and hear, but **not the manner in which they will be seen and heard.**

Okay, so a screenplay is not a Shooting Script. What else is it not?

PRECEPT #2: A Screenplay Is Not a Novel

A screenplay most certainly does contain passages of narrative prose in its descriptions of action, setting and character. However, in a novel or shorter forms of prose fiction, the words are all the reader gets. Hence, the descriptions must be complete. But that old house you so lavishly describe in your novel does not require *or warrant* the same level of detailed description in a screenplay. Your purpose in writing description in a screenplay is different than what is required in a novel. Your written description need only be minimal and impressionistic.

Here's an example of novelistic writing that may mistakenly appear in a screenplay.

VANESSA (37) stands in the doorway with a nostalgic look in her eye. The fresh after-the-rain smell off the prairie, redolent with clover and new hope, evokes fond memories of her maiden aunt, who graduated third in her class at Vassar in 1937, and Vanessa wonders what her aunt would do in a situation like the one she is in, whether she'd sell or resist.

Nice writing. Rich with sensory imagery. Evocative. And what an interesting woman her aunt sounds like. But how much of that passage would properly be in a screenplay? Take a bow if you said, "VANESSA (37) stands in the doorway looking nostalgically at the prairie."

GOLDEN GUIDING PRINCIPLE #1:

Whatever information you provide must be done in a way that the **viewing audience** will be able to **see or hear**.

An audience in the theater cannot know what is felt, surmised, thought, decided, remembered, forgotten. Unlike a novel, a screenplay provides no direct link between the reader and the character's thoughts and history. Private jokes, asides and hip references are, for the most part, seen as big flashing lights spelling AMATEUR.

Of course you are tempted to ignore this piece of advice. You've read the Internet sites. You know that what's-his-name did that very thing in his spec script that just sold for $1.9 mil. Why shouldn't *you* express your individuality by doing it, too? Right?

Wrong.

Two important principles to remember here:

1. In screenwriting (alas, as in the rest of life), two very different sets of rules apply. One is for writers who have already sold a screenplay for a million dollars. Everything in this book is for the rest of us.

2. You do not express your individuality by imitating someone else's breakthrough. Of course we all want to imbue our screenplays with our own individual voice. We want there to be a signature, like Mozart had, like Van Gogh or David Mamet. But we must do it WITHIN the parameters, with terse and vivid descriptions. With dialogue rhythms. With individual and vivid characters and a world that you make real for your readers. Do it in the startling and energetic way that evokes your world realistically. Not with snazzola.

PRECEPT #3: A Screenplay Is Not a Stage Play

The differences between writing for the stage and writing for the screen are profound, far beyond even the mere cosmetic differences such as using exterior scenes and car chases. The way a screen story and a stage story are **conceived and executed** are different down to their genetic code. Writing a screen story is probably closer to writing opera. It's large enough to be understood even if you don't speak the language.

Even dialogue, the most noticeable shared aspect of screenplays and stage plays, is *used* differently in each. Dialogue serves different existential **functions**. In both, it is the utterances of characters, but in theater, *dialogue* is the principal storytelling device. In film, *event* is the principal storytelling device.

Theater is a medium for the spoken word. Films are moving pictures.

There are many things that a screenplay is not. But what it is, when it is functioning at maximum capacity, is a marvelously elegant, tightly fitted mechanism capable of doing many things at the same time.

WRITERS GYM EXERCISES

On a blank sheet of paper, write down every movie shot you know. See if you can come up with 15 or 20 different shots. The more arcane and stylish, the better (wide angle, POV, crane shot, zoom in, tilt). Look lovingly over your completed list. Hold the paper high above your head in your right hand. Grasp the top edge of the paper firmly with your left hand and pull down hard. REPEAT 10 TIMES until the list is completely shredded. You will never need those words again in any script you write.

Do the exact same exercise for **facial expressions, hand gestures, beats (he waits three beats before speaking) and delineations of tones of voice**.

In the last script or scene you wrote, find the first 10 VERBS that you wrote. Replace each with a more VIVID VERB. See how many adverbs and adjectives this allows you to delete.

CHAPTER 6
What a Screenplay Is

Simply stated, a screenplay is a written device of roughly 110 pages whose function is to **tell a story** using the cinematic conventions of scene settings, narrative description, action and dialogue. It must adhere, with some permissible variations in style, to a predetermined length and be written in acceptable *screenplay format.*

Length:

Unlike other forms of literature, the length of filmed entertainment is an inherent finite consideration. A novel can be 1100 or 110 pages. A poem can be 12 lines, or 3, or 12 cantos or 3 books. Stage plays can be six hours or six minutes.

Though there are notable exceptions to every statement ever made, for the most part, feature-length will be in the neighborhood of 105 to 118 pages. The rare feature film may be as short as 85 minutes, and longer epics occasionally exceed three hours. But most mainstream pictures, where marketing departments have far more say in the determination of the product than one would think necessary, run much closer to 90 to 100 minutes.

This means that the length of your submitted screenplay should conform to those parameters. Suspicions will arise if it weighs in at less than 95 pages. Deep breaths will be drawn if it exceeds 130.

The current generation of aspiring screenwriters has a greater awareness of screenplays as text than any previous group. If you feel deficient or underexposed in this area, you must address that weakness. Read many screenplays, good ones and less than good ones.

Format:

With the increasing availability of formatting software, the basic mechanics can be engineered for you. (The studio executive's dream fantasy is coming closer to reality: a script that will "write itself.") But even in this most mechanical of operations, there are grace notes you can employ so that you can enhance and not merely execute your work through a creative and effective use of format.

Do not foolishly interpret this as a license to play games with format and tailor it to your own purposes. Your goal is not to show that you can reinvent the form, but that you can function well within it. Once you become a well-known and sought-after writer, everything changes. You are rewarded for indulgences. You are imitated for the same quirks of individuality that you previously had been scolded for. But until that happy time arrives, there are some rules you should follow.

Yes, I did say "rules." There are people who dismiss the limitation and lack of freedom that rules impose on creativity and assert that rules are made to be broken. Rules are not made to be broken any more than dishes are. You may, perchance, break them. But remember Bob Dylan's line: "To live outside the law you must be honest." It means that if we reject society's rules, we still must hold ourselves personally accountable to an alternate morality.

And that is equally true of writing. Most creative laws are broken out of carelessness or laziness or a writer's subconscious panic that, unless his or her work is presented in a bizarre and individual manner, it will appear ordinary. It is painful and frustrating to hold ourselves accountable to the truth that two unfairly different sets of rules apply: the more lax and indulgent set of rules to the "haves," the more stringent to the rest of us. If we want to get into group

No. 1 it is important that we recognize what is expected of our work while we are still peons.

RULE #1: A screenplay should look like a screenplay and read like a screenplay.

That seems pretty obvious, doesn't it? Yet a lot of alleged screenplays do not demonstrate in a convincing manner that the writer knew what a screenplay was meant to look like. Remember, you are a vendor. You are bringing your goods to a marketplace filled with many other vendors. If you were selling peaches, you'd want to be sure that what you carry to market looks, smells and tastes like peaches. Why would somebody who doesn't know you take the chance buying your peaches if they look like asparagus?

Our impressions of the world are built on perception. So let us commit to *creating the perception* among potential buyers that our product is credible. Let's make the thing *look and read* like a screenplay.

Imagine a situation where a reader likes your script, sees some interesting dialogue, a very interesting character, and an arresting premise. But your format is a little off. There are a number of typos, and it's 134 pages long (with wide margins and smaller type, so it's really 146 pages, he or she notices). And there are some cutesy little asides written to the reader, just like UCLA screenwriting graduate Shane Black did in *Lethal Weapon*.

Should he or she pass this one up the ladder to the boss? Risk the possibility of it being thrown back as amateurish and thereby jeopardize a great job? The door to success has a narrow slit, and scripts that pass through must do so on the wings of enthusiasm.

Nobody really knows what's good anyway. If there are ten scripts on the table and only one can be bought, would this young, eager executive want to be the advocate of a bruised, misshapen peach? Why should anyone risk taking a chance on a writer who has not done everything possible to enhance his or her opportunity? The great likelihood is that script will be sent to the place where paper is given a new life. (Maybe that newly recycled paper will find its way into the script of a writer who takes his or her craft more seriously. Or would that be too ironic?)

The first rule I learned as a waiter when I was 19 applies to writing as well. **Make it look nice for the customers.** Make it **look and read** like a screenplay.

Let's deconstruct and label the moving parts of the scene we played with in the previous chapter.

EXT. – MERTSBORO, INDIANA – A SUMMER NIGHT **(1)**

The town looks like a Norman Rockwell cover for the Saturday Evening Post. **(2)**

A 1963 FORD **(3)**

cruises slowly. Its LICENSE PLATE and the AM bubblegum MUSIC say INDIANA, 1969. **(4)**

INT. – FORD

A pair of young lovers takes a sentimental ride, passing the DRUGSTORE, HIGH SCHOOL, BOWLING ALLEY. **(5)**

LINDY MACDANIEL (21) **(6)** snuggles close. She is a dream of a girl-next-door, bright and pretty. And very much in love with —

JOHN WILSON. A character Jimmy Stewart would have played. Huck Finn mixed with Andy Hardy. As they pass the skating rink —

LINDY **(7)**
Do you remember the time that — ? **(8)**

JOHN **(9)**
Splat. I remember.

They dissolve in unbearable nostalgia of the

shared memory.

(1) Every scene begins with a SLUGLINE, written in all CAPS, that announces the most basic location of the scene and whether it is **INT**erior or **EXT**erior. Whether it is the first scene or the 49th, the existence of a new slugline tells the reader that the story has moved to a new distinct place and/or time.

Double-spacing down from the SLUG, we get to

(2) NARRATIVE DESCRIPTION. Here we may **(5) describe the setting** in more detail, **(6) introduce NEW CHARACTERS** (their names are capitalized the first time they are mentioned), and **(4) orchestrate narrative action.**

CHARACTER DESCRIPTION

We'll discuss character description in detail later because this is a real trouble spot for writers, a place where far too much verbiage is often used for too little effect. Demographic age group (mid-20s) and body type is often enough. We don't need an exact description of a mole on the left cheek. Unless the story is ABOUT a similar birthmark that appears on different people; then yes, you would write it.

But all your characters are not going to possess a statistically unlikely characteristic. Describe what your character is **doing**.

GOLDEN RULE OF CHARACTER: Who we are is revealed in what we do.

DESCRIPTION OF PLACE

Notice in the scene above that the description of the locale is done quite economically. It does NOT describe all the buildings or the street in minute detail, but only enough to give the idea and the feeling of the place.

A screenplay is not the final product. It's a step toward a film. The function of description is to place the audience in the world using few words with evocative details. Every sentence makes a picture.

1. Is it a clear, vivid, specific image?

2. Does it evoke a feeling?

GOLDEN RULE OF ACTION #1:* In describing action, don't let it take longer to read than it would take to do on screen.

Writing incomplete sentences is perfectly acceptable if you are describing action.

```
LEAPING OVER THE FORT

And running on his one good leg, RENEGADE
crouches and fires.

Three villains fall.

Ren whirls.

Rolls.

Another burst of gunfire.

More victims die.
```

A great way to avoid excessive writing about camera movement while still directing the reader's inner eye to see that picture is through judicious use of the **(3) SUBSLUGLINE**. This is a smaller part of the master shot.

In our MERTSBORO example, the Slugline guides the reader's eye from a full wide-angle view down to a tighter shot of the car. It effectively says:

```
CUT TO:

INSERT CLOSE UP: THE FORD.
```

*You're not counting wrong. They're all Rule #1.

But it does so without all the jargon and verbiage. Its function is to isolate smaller parts of full scenes in the way we just observed. It is also used most effectively as a way of INTERCUTTING between two separate but related parts of a scene sequence; for instance, a chase.

If our little John and Lindy scene became an action sequence with the couple being chased by bikers, it might look like this:

```
THE BIKERS
mount up on their HARLEYS and tear ass after
them.

JOHN AND LINDY
see them coming. John floors it. They careen out
of town. Just ahead of them—

THE DRAWBRIDGE
Begins to open

JOHN AND LINDY
Race past the stop sign.

                 LINDY
    John, no!

THE BIKERS
Loom close in their rear-view mirror.

THE BRIDGE
Rises
```

(And so on.)

Using the **Subslug** eliminates the need for all the CUT TO's and allows the sequence to read more coherently. It takes 10 wasted lines out of the script and creates the fast-moving rhythm that is so important in an action scene. Notice that the narrative action that follows the actual SUBSLUG is on the next line, but the sentence continues as though it were one continuous line of prose.

Returning now to the original scene:

FORMATTING CHARACTER DESCRIPTION

The first time any character appears in narrative description, the name is FULLY CAPITALIZED, and age range and character type are given. Maybe it's a little too lean in this example. Better to err on that side, though. You want to give your readers a vivid, impressionistic image of the characters. In my teaching, I've read the following nice, colorful descriptions: "A fire hydrant with a mustache." "When potbellies were handed out, he got into line twice." Don't overly concern yourself with their attire unless it *defines character.* In Alan Ball's *American Beauty*, Lester says about his wife, "See the way the handle on those pruning shears matches her gardening clogs? That's not an accident." It becomes more than a fashion statement. Its being true, and his noticing it, say a great deal about who the characters are.

A great film of the 1970s is *Walkabout* (screenplay by Edward Bond, based on a novel by James Vance Marshall). The story is about two very civilized kids lost in the Australian Outback. It is an integral part of the story that they are wearing their private-school uniforms. It is not a mere decorative costuming choice. They are civilized city kids lost in the primitive wilderness.

Next, our scene has some dialogue. Whenever a character speaks, the NAME **(7)** and the words we select to be spoken **(8)** are indented on the page.

Speaker's Name (7)

Don't call people with important jobs by their first names if that is not how they would be known in the performance of their work. Call your detective INSPECTOR CASSIDY, not BOBBY. The senator isn't JIM, the governor isn't KAREN. First names are okay for bartenders, young characters or your main characters who appear throughout the script. Don't let character names sound too similar. No Betty and

Bethany. No Joan and Joanna. It gets readers confused.

If they're minor characters, it's fine to name them for their characteristics: SCARFACE THUG, BRUNETTE BIMBETTE, GIMPY WAITER, FRECKLE-FACED KID, FIRST COP, SECOND COP.

On the page, the first letter of the first name of every speaker of dialogue is placed in the same column. The name is capitalized, and we single-space to the dialogue (or parenthetical) that follows.

The convention is to DOUBLE-SPACE to the speaker's name from whatever preceded it, whether it was narrative description or another line of dialogue. SINGLE-SPACE from the speaker's name to the spoken dialogue.

Dialogue (8)

When characters speak, we must write down the words we wish them to utter. It does not suffice to write THEY HAVE A CONVERSATION ABOUT AARON'S GIRLFRIEND, BETTY. You must write that conversation.

Dialogue is single-spaced. It starts an inch to the left of the character name. It ends about that far to the right. Less is almost always better. The best dialogue is often the dialogue not written.

If a parenthetical **(9)** is used, it goes on its OWN LINE, even if it comes in the midst of dialogue. (In play scripts, parentheticals are placed on the same line as dialogue and the dialogue then continues.) Writers misuse parentheticals to direct the actors to deliver a line in a certain way (Softly) (Loudly) (After a count of three). They are called the "wrylys" because a frequent direction is (Wryly). As in:

```
                KRAMER
        (Wryly)
    Oh, I suppose you're not.
```

Take to heart these two words regarding parentheticals. **Don't use'em.** The result we hope for is to get a specific line reading from an actor. The first thing that actors do when they see them is cross them out. So, there's *that*. And worse, writing them is like eating salted potato chips. Once we take the first bite, we can't stop. The script gets cluttered. Resist the urge.

We misuse **parentheticals** for the same reason we use camera angles. We are trying to direct the scene on the page. If you notice a lot of parentheticals appearing (a lot means more than one per page), think of it as a symptom of an illness. Your scene has a fever. It's usually a sign that the scene lacks real energy and you're trying to inject it with steroids.

An appropriate use of parentheticals is in a scene that has several characters, and a specific remark is being addressed to one of them.

```
                    GUN-WIELDING THUG
          Hold it.
             (To his partner)
          That means you, too.
```

There are several other oft-used conventions that populate the pages of a screenplay. One that does not appear in our Mertsboro example is a VOICE OVER. This is a narrative voice spoken during the scene by a character who does not appear visually. It is often used as a storytelling device from a pure narrator: it can be the voice of a character in the story at a different stage of life, a reminiscence in old age of a story taking place in the character's youth, or a device to reveal a character's inner thoughts.

We designate Voice Over with the letters VO placed alongside the speaker's name, often—though not always—in parentheses. VO is differentiated from its close cousins OC and OS, which stand for OFF CAMERA and OFF SCREEN, respectively. These are voices of characters who are physically present, just out of camera's reach at the moment. Our scene is in the living room and somebody calls out from the kitchen, for example.

What do you do when you're stuck with a format question that none of your guides explains?

Remember the full definition of a screenplay. It is an instrument for *the telling of a story.* The technology has changed since those early cave dwellers told the humorous and tragic tales of war and the hunt. But that's all that has changed. It's still all about spinning the yarn. Let this tenet always be your guide.

GOLDEN GUIDING PRINCIPLE #1:

You are telling a story, not shooting the movie. Say what you need to say in as unobtrusive a manner as possible.

It might have been the philosopher Spinoza who divided humanity into two essential groups: those who do not know proper screenplay format, and those who do. Our goal for this chapter is to move you into group 2.

But looking like a screenplay is not enough. It's the starting point. In all things there are the mechanics and there is the magic. The *mechanics* here are about making it *look* like a screenplay. The magic is making it *read* like one.

When a screenplay is working, it carries you through as though you are on a luge, able to see only to the next hairpin turn, but carried on a fast, thrilling ride coming inevitably to one conclusion that you never could have seen at the start.

There are many learnable skills attendant to this pursuit. Among them are creating character, writing dialogue, writing narrative action and making scenes work. We examine these in great detail in Part Three, The Small Picture, Scene Writing.

But a screenplay cannot exist outside of the story it is telling. Thus, before we can discuss anything else, we must deal with the most elusive soul of all, and that is STORY.

WRITERS GYM EXERCISES

Read a professional screenplay this week. Read two more in the genre of the screenplay that you will be writing next.

Study format guides.

Acquire a professionally written screenplay. This is going to sound odd and like busywork. (But does 30 minutes on a Stairmaster sound intellectually stimulating?) RETYPE the script. Do not photocopy it. Retype every word. Make sure it looks exactly like the original.

The benefits of this exercise are subliminal. Certain inner boundaries are established that trigger subtle alarms when, in your own writing, you exceed them. Think of an invisible electric fence that confines a rambunctious dog.

CHAPTER 7

What Story Isn't

Has this ever happened to you? In the middle of a conversation about a crazy breakup or twisted romance, or on a day where everything goes impossibly wrong, or when an absolutely bizarre coincidence occurs, your mind suddenly erupts with exhilaration and you exclaim, **"Wow! Wouldn't this be a great idea for a movie?!"**

In the throes of creative frenzy, you leap to your workstation and start pounding the keys. In two days you have written 20 pages! A week later your page count has reached...24. And a month later you're stuck at 25. Why are you bogged down?

Listen carefully, my friends. Sometimes the answer to the question "Wouldn't this be a great idea for a movie?" is NO, it would not. More often that idea would be a great idea for an anecdote, or a sequence within a story, or a skit about an idea that seemed at first like a great idea for a movie but petered out after 20 pages.

How often have you been at a family dinner or an office gathering where someone is urged to tell that story about going to the supermarket, or that time they forgot to change the clocks back, or the time the car got stuck in the snow, and then you listened to the person recount in excruciating detail every event or every unedited word of dialogue? Or listened to them omit important elements, or tell them at the wrong time, or entirely miss the point? And if they got the order right, would *that* be a story?

Is a story merely the **accurate account of a (true or invented) narrative sequence of events?** This happens, then that happens, then this, then that? Obviously, if that were true, film studios would be pillaging footage from Kmart surveillance cameras, slicing it into two-hour segments, and charging 10 bucks to see it.

So a story is something other than a mere sequence of events. But what?

Next to true love, the commodity writers most often think they have but do not is STORY. We may have a piece of it, a wisp of it, a few moments of it, a feeling of what it would be like if we had all of it. And because we have no idea how it got there in the first place, we trust that all the things we think of afterward are part of it.

Story is the most intrinsic and most mysterious and elusive element. It is quicksilver, a reflection of moonlight on water. It is the talisman that writers are most expected to have. We are, after all, *storytellers*, aren't we? Isn't that what it says on the back of our label?

Coming up with a story, a full story, not just a premise for a story or a circumstance for a story, or an idea or a notion about a story, is by far far far far far far and away the hardest part of screenwriting. I will not be violating any confidences if I reveal that in my 30 years at UCLA, working with the most gifted young (and not so young) screenwriters and in private consultations with working writers, a vast majority of their story ideas, at first telling, have been vague, meandering and fragmentary, with barely enough meat on them to fill a three-minute trailer, much less a 100-minute feature film. So you're in good company.

Don't despair. And don't delude yourself into thinking that you have more story than you really do. A frequent occurrence in students' initial two-page treatments is that the first page and a half describes the opening three scenes in excruciating detail. Then the last half-page blows past the rest of the story.

I love it when I see the phrases "a coming of age" story or "a fish out of water" story. As though either of those labels said anything about WHO was coming of age or what age he or she was coming of, or who he or she was before and who he or she will be after, and what motivated him or her and what threatened him or her, and all the eight trillion things that make a character an individual.

I have a cartoon taped to my door depicting two math professors contemplating a long, complex mathematical equation one of them has written on the chalkboard: X's and Y's, squares and cube roots, divided and multiplied. At the center there are parentheses with the words "Somehow a miracle occurs," and then the equation continues. The caption reads, "I think you need to be a little more specific in step number two."

Writers often fall into the same pit of hope and generality. Smile if you've ever written one of these: "And so, by a series of exciting events, the unwilling hero gets enmeshed in the caper and learns about trust." Or, "In a series of crazy, wacky experiences, our hero gets deeper and deeper into trouble." Or, "After some painful interactions with men she finally empowers herself."

These writers are saying what their story is ***about***, but they are not telling the ***story***. What they don't know yet, and what they discover in writing the two-page story outline and getting reactions from their classmates, is that they don't know it yet. What *are* those exciting events that enmesh the unwilling hero into the caper? What *does* he or she learn about trust? And of greater importance, what are the circumstances that bring him or her to the necessity of action and, through that, to the possibility of learning about trust? And at what cost, willing or unwilling?

It is these specific experiences that are the story. It is our job to find them. To invent them, concoct them, remember them, distort them, combine them. And then to write them.

Yes, *that*.

Mozart could not tell his audience "something in three-quarter time in the key of A-flat minor," and then expect them to fill in the gaps. You would not be kept warm in winter by "something long and woolen." You would need to have a coat. Made out of real material in every square inch. A farmer would not bring a bushel to the fruit stand filled with "about peaches." He has to bring peaches! And we have to bring the events of the story. We are the elves. Somehow a miracle *does not* occur.

SAD FACT OF LIFE #1: There are no miracles other than those that we create.

As the poet Wallace Stevens wrote, "There is no emperor but the emperor of ice cream."

So how do we create them, these stories, these miracles of flight?

Thelonius Monk said, "Talking about music is like dancing about architecture." Defining story is nearly as elusive. What is a story to you? If you had to explain what a story was to someone who didn't know, what would you say? It has a beginning, a middle and an end? Okay…It's something about people? Yeah. There's conflict? A theme. A moral? Sure, maybe. But have you left something out? Something vital, perhaps? Maybe something that makes all the difference in the world?

In one of the classic episodes of *Seinfeld*, George is selling, first to Jerry and later to the NBC network executive, the idea of a TV series about nothing. "You got up today and went to work. That's a story. You waited on line for an hour at a restaurant to get seated. That's a story." The network executive was a little dubious. What about you? What do you think? Are either of those a story? This is not a rhetorical question. I want you to answer it. And not just yes or no. Why do you think so, or think not? What are *your* criteria?

If you were standing on a freeway overpass watching thousands of vehicles passing below you, could you theoretically drop a camera and microphone down into any one of those cars at any moment and find a story? There are people. They have a destination, a future and a past. There is likely to be dialogue. Story? Yes? No?

Could you carry a picture frame with you on the street, call "Freeze!" at any moment, and apply the word *story* to any arbitrary combination of people who happened to be caught inside the frame at that moment?

What criteria do you consciously or unconsciously apply? Do you apply any standards at all? Could a story be anything that happens to happen? Yes? No? Why? Don't look on this page for an answer. This page is looking to *you* for an answer. This page is not going to write a story. You are. What does it have to be? What do you have to write for it to be a story?

Here is a partial list of elements that are commonly mistaken for story, but which in themselves are NOT story.

Biography
Psychology
Mythology
Astrology
All of the -ologies
All of the -ographies
Dreams and schemes
Quirky characters
Heroic characters
Amazing characters
Inspirational characters
Great lines of dialogue
Amazing visual images
Epiphanies
Moments of truth
Comings of age

Moral messages
A great joke
Something that actually happened

All of these are *legitimate components of story* but are not yet story.

Think of a building site where all the materials for the house are neatly stacked: all the wood for the frame, all the glass for the windows, all the pipes, all the electrical fixtures and wiring, the heating units, the bricks for the chimney. Even the screws and nails and dowels. Everything needed to build that house is laid out in neat, organized piles.

But is it yet a house?

The parts have to fit together properly. The floor has to bear weight. The windows need to look outside. The roof mustn't leak. The plumbing ought to work. And it's got to fit onto its designated lot. All of that just to make it a *house.*

And still, after all that work, until the structure becomes a residence to its inhabitants, it is not yet a *home*. The analogous truth exists in constructing your screenplay. All the components can be neatly stacked, the structure can be built according to blueprint, but it is still merely a "house" until that spark of life is ignited. So what *is* that Rumpelstiltskin factor that turns straw into gold, notes and rhythm into melody, character and plot into a story?

The books of Lajos Egri, long read with biblical veneration, stipulate that **theme** is the soul of drama. His premise is that a story's premise contains the theme, which in turn defines the outcome and the direction by which the story reaches its outcome, which is its meaning. In his paradigm, the meaning (jealousy leads to murder, for example) essentially defines the story. The meaning is pre-known to the writer, and the events of the story are tailored to manifest that meaning.

I must take the heretical risk of disagreeing with Mr. Egri. I believe that writing from theme is the writer's enemy. In my classes I write the word THEME inside a large circle, and then draw a diagonal line through it, like a traffic sign forbidding left turns.

This is not to say that a screenplay should not have a theme. But I ascribe to Norman Mailer's ethos when he says, "I discover truth at the point of a pencil." Let the theme, the meaning, be *discovered* through the writing of the story, rather than letting theme be the nucleus around which the story coalesces.

The issue I am addressing here is not about linguistics or terminology. It goes to the heart of the creative process. It is what the story is *about.* Most of the teachers who taught us to read literature were not writers themselves. From the earliest Aesop's Fable to *War and Peace*, they have taught us to look first for the thing that is important to them about literature, the aspect of it that is accessible to them, namely its moral or meaning, its message. What is the author trying to say?

Every writer knows that what the author is trying to say is *each and every word.* Is it fair to reduce *Moby Dick* to "Obsession leads to destruction"? Does it mean anything to say that? Had you not read *Moby Dick*, would that phrase give you any visceral sensation of that specific book?

As we progress further in our educational careers, theme and meaning become the center posts, the expository essays we are compelled to write throughout high school and university. By the time we start thinking about wanting to write ourselves, the notions of story and theme are so hardwired in our brains that we allow theme to become the guiding principle in the creative process.

Here is the inherent problem. An expository essay, whether it is a 150-word opus in junior high school or your 150-chapter Ph.D. dissertation, begins with a topic sentence that states the premise that the essay is asserting. It proceeds through a logically reasoned set of arguments in its defense and then offers a conclusion summarizing the efficacy of the case that has been proven.

This is a perfectly acceptable paradigm for a critical essay. But a critical essay is not a story. Even looking at the difference in the most simplistic way, we don't want the audience to know the ending of the story at the beginning. In a critical essay, the "end" is the beginning. The point is made and proven.

The verbs that define the essence of critical writing are *prove*, *define* and *defend*. A very different set of verbs defines creative writing. E. L. Doctorow makes the analogy between writing a story and driving at night on a winding road where you can see only as far ahead as the headlights illuminate. But, he says, eventually you make the whole journey. The verbs of creative writing are *explore*, *discover*, *surprise* and *delight*.

An essay is meant to be predictable. A story is not. My theme here is: **THEME LEADS TO PREDICTABILITY.**

The *meaning* of a story is not the essence of a story. The theme that it illustrates is like the handle of a suitcase. It is a convenient and efficient way to grasp it and carry it from place to place. But it does not reveal any of its belongings. How would you answer if, after a beautiful night of passion, your lover asked you, "What did you mean by that?" What does a peach tree mean by a peach? What does a cloud mean?

If we write from theme, then consciously or unconsciously, just as each paragraph in the body of a critical essay supports the argument of the topic sentence, so each scene of a theme-driven screenplay will be an illustrative expression of the meaning of the story.

One luxury of being a critic, a theorist, is getting to see a work of art as *a completed work*. The writer never sees it from that vantage point. During the entire process of creation, the writer is spinning the cables and building a bridge across an abyss. In front of and below us is a deep, open chasm. All we see is the unfinished span in front of us. Theme is a safe and convenient handhold to negotiating that chasm, but safety exacts a great price.

Generally the symptom of a theme-driven story is that very soon it becomes predictable. Characters become less dimensional because they are meant to stand for something, for some part of the thematic whole. Scenes become didactic and contrived. And the ending is visible from 20 miles away. A lot of network movies-of-the-week are conceived thematically. Rarely do you see a character with interesting contradictions.

How do you feel about murder? Should people get away with it? Too general a question? Okay, what about a girl who murders her own mother? Should that be an act that is thematically endorsed? Is matricide a good thing or a bad thing? Or, in Egri's terms, is there some act we can thematically posit that *leads* to matricide?

If theme is driving the bus of your story, chances are good that you will end up writing a message, not a movie. Here I'm thinking of *Heavenly Creatures*, that amazing 1994 film from New Zealand written by Frances Walsh and Peter Jackson. It dramatizes the close and powerful friendship between two adolescent girls who want so desperately to keep from being separated by their parents that they bash in one of the mothers' skulls with a brick.

How would you expect a film to leave you feeling about these brutal little murderers? Certainly they must be punished, must they not? Would any punishment be large enough to satisfy our sense of justice? What happens narratively at the end of this film is that the girls are separated. One goes to Canada, the other stays in New Zealand. They will not see each other again for 50 years—until after this very film is made.

But the important thing about this film is how we (the audience) are made to *feel* at the end of the story. If this screenplay had been written from theme, we might very well decide that separation was too lenient a punishment for these horrible miscreants. If the punishment should fit the crime (another thematic statement) shouldn't they be, what, sterilized? Made to suffer amputation? At least incarcerated for many, many years? Shouldn't we be reviled at what they did and hate them for doing it? We certainly should not have sympathy for them, should we? The mother was not abusive in the slightest degree. A bit over her head, perhaps. A bit flummoxed. Certainly frightened at the intensity of the relationship in which her daughter was enmeshed. (There is only the slightest hint at homosexuality. It is beyond sex, closer than sex, more intimate than sex.)

But no. At the end of the film we *do not* hate them. We do not revel in their punishment for the heinous act, nor delight in their despair at being separated. Rather, we feel something more compassionate and profound. As we do for Romeo and Juliet, or Shakespeare and his beloved at the end of *Shakespeare in Love*. We ache. They have sacrificed so much, and we have experienced so deeply and profoundly their desire to be together, that when that desire is unfulfilled, we feel awful.

In *The Last Seduction*, written by Steve Barancik, the protagonist spends the entire film seducing a young man, bedeviling and manipulating him into the ultimate mission of getting him to kill her husband. Thematically, should we not despise this woman? And should we not despise the hired killer in *Day of the Jackal*? Thematically speaking, political assassins have to be bad, right? And yet we are fascinated by both characters. How can that be? How is it we care about Don Corleone, and in that same movie see the FBI guys as antagonists? Is the theme of that movie "Crime pays"? What is the "theme" of *The Godfather*? For the characters *in* the story, it's that the Mob is no worse than the government. For others, maybe it's that the sins of the father are visited on the sons. Or that wealth corrupts. Or that we can't escape our fate. But none of that accounts for our sense of empathy with Don Corleone.

Look at all the characters Alan Ball created in *American Beauty*. We were allowed to experience the gamut of each one's emotional palate. As writers we want our audience to wonder what will happen next, not to know it. We want them involved viscerally, fearing for the safety and rooting for the triumph of our protagonist. We want characters that have dimensions, darks and lights.

This would not have been possible if the story had been written from theme. What is the theme of that film? Coveting thy daughter's 16-year-old friend leads to death? Befriending the abused son of a latent homosexual, abusive father leads to death? Quitting your lousy job and trying to find happiness leads to death?

Writing from theme disables a writer's capacity to create complex, multidimensional characters and correspondingly cripples, maims, amputates and otherwise diminishes the characters themselves. It reduces them to one dimension, to the idea of themselves. If you want to become the writer of sharp, unpredictable, volatile, exciting scenes and stories, I want you to think about one word, and place this word at the center of everything.

And here in class I erase the word THEME from that large circle. In its place I write in large letters the word

DESIRE.

WRITERS GYM EXERCISES

Exercise #1

Sit in a bus or restaurant or mall and watch the people go by. Invent a life for each of them (occupation, family circumstances, sexual preference, favorite food, astrological sign, psychological aberrations, favorite team, favorite food, favorite book, favorite everything, least favorite everything).

That's the easy part. Now, place these characteristics into a living context. What did these people do yesterday? What is their most ardent desire? What would they trade for it? What stands in their way? What inner obstacles? What external obstacles? Invent an exciting, interesting scene in which desire and obstacle lock arms.

[NB: Desire creates volition, which creates action/event. **DESIRE is the spark that converts characteristics into character.**]

Exercise #2

Make a list of your ten favorite movies. Identify what the main character most wants. Can you trace a clear path from beginning to end of the character's footsteps in search of that desire?

Two people are in bed. A siren or alarm is heard. Or the phone rings. Or a doorbell. WRITE THE SCENE.

You will have to ask yourself: Who are these people? Who are they to each other? What are the immediate circumstances? How does the alarm affect them? What do they do? Are they at cross-purposes? How so?

Place ordinary people in extraordinary circumstances or extraordinary people in ordinary circumstances.

CHAPTER 8

What Story Is

Form follows function. What something *is* derives from the function it is meant to perform. A coffee cup, as beautifully painted and sculpted as it might be, must first of all hold hot liquid and be of a shape and mass, weight and size that facilitates coffee drinking.

Does a story have a function? Yes, it does. At the very least, its function is to entertain. Whatever other peripheral functions may be piggy-backed upon it (preach a moral, espouse a personal philosophy, frighten, arouse sexual excitement), if it does not captivate its audience, none of those other purposes will be accomplished.

Let's travel back in time to the era of early man. The most concrete things we know about preliterate civilizations come from cave paintings. For the most part, they depicted scenes of the hunt: the animals brought back as food, their ferocity before they were brought down, and the lithe, athletic, cunning, brave acts of the hunters. These were not sentimental times. Only the strong survived. There were no crosswalks or golden parachutes. Warriors ate. Artist-wimps starved. Unless we could find some way to make ourselves necessary.

We were too unathletic and neurotic to stalk a lion or spear a warthog. But at night we were just as hungry. How could we earn our scraps of meat? Did we have any skill that possessed social value? Yes, we did. Do. The painters, the poets, the storytellers could bring the story of the hunt back to the women, the children, the aged and the infirm who had to remain at home and were not witnesses or participants in the hunt firsthand. We could be their surrogate eyes and ears. We could bring the adventure back to the village. We could transport them to the scene. We could do what their own legs and bodies were not physically capable of doing.

We could put them there. The participants could tell the gist of it: "See. Kill. Eat." But we could do something more. We could make them feel like they were there. Your uncle Mort can throw a couple of trout into the sink that he caught on his fishing trip. Hemingway can write *The Old Man and the Sea.* The ancient storyteller would make the village see the fierce and treacherous, gigantic living beast that this roasting meat had so recently been. He could take them inside the courageous heart of the hunter, make them feel the tide of battle, smell the blood, feel the teeth bite, the claws slash, and taste the ultimate glory of the kill. If he knew the psychology and vanity of one of the hunters, he might make that individual's valor seem ten times more real. He could glorify his exploits, describe the strength of his arm in hurling the stone, his speed in bringing down the deer, his courage in facing the bear or wrestling the lion, his prodigious heart. And if he were convincing enough, someone would tear off a hunk of rib and throw it on the ground close enough so that he could get it before the dogs did.

For screenwriters, not much has changed except for cable rights.

Western culture traces its roots of poetry and theater back to the works of the Greek epic poets and playwrights. What are *The Iliad* and *The Odyssey* if not more sophisticated tales of war and heroism, valor and death, ordeal and survival, the exploits of warriors, gods and kings? And how did the tales of these exploits return? With the poets who went along on the expeditions. Wimps with lyres. The embedded journalists of their day.

Form follows function. It was the poet's job to bring the exploits of battle back to the village, to those who could not be there. To re-create what it looked like, felt like, sounded like to be there. So that wives and children of fallen heroes could hear the songs of their loved ones' deaths. The enemies they took down with them. How they looked in battle. They didn't yet have stylus and tablet. (And you're worried that you don't have the latest 8.9 edition of Perfect Screen Pro with added "Punch Up Dialogue" feature!) The epic poems were in a set rhythm and rhyme so they could be remembered.

Today we have video cameras and satellite uplinks to put us right in the thick of cataclysmic events as they unfold. But from a storyteller's point of view, far more profound societal changes have evolved over the centuries than mere advancements in technology. Gods, kings and warriors were the dramatis personae of early drama. Only their exploits, their battles and their moral struggles were recognized as the terrain of theater. The highest echelon of men involved in the highest pursuits of civilization.

This is no longer true. We are a far more egalitarian civilization. This is not to say societies are not stratified, that there are not economic classes of people, that there are not boundaries and divisions along the lines of skin color, ethnicity and religion. But in today's world, *stories* of any group or of any individual are equally accepted realms of drama.

The story of World War II can be told from General Patton's point of view or from Private Ryan's, from a regiment of Navajo windtalkers or Tuskegee airmen. We are no longer limited to drinking the wine of the gods. We can now also write about *A Raisin in the Sun*.

But with freedom comes responsibility. In stories of men engaged in heroic enterprise, all the glorious values of story are inherently given: whether a character lived or died. The manner in which he faced his moment of truth. Did he die a hero or a coward? Which side of his nature arose? All of this is played against the backdrop of the biggest question of all: Were the armies of one's homeland victorious in battle or were they defeated?

What more can you ask a drama to deliver? Elevated lives in dire situations. Heroic characters with fatal flaws. King against king. Man against the gods. All designed to create catharsis—that release of pity and terror, as Aristotle describes it. The poets who could do this most effectively won the prizes, got the commissions, gained currency and popularity. The "facts" of the battle were equally known to everyone. But some people could tell the story better than others. What distinguished one writer over the others was his ability to interpret those events, to imbue them with his insight into the human heart in a way that evoked deep feelings in the audience. These versions became sought out. These storytellers were made to tell and retell their tales (and thus were fed more consistently).

But where do we find stories today, when the epic battlefields have been downsized to living rooms and bus stations? Where do we find the equivalent passion and scope? How do we find importance in whether the last movie house in a small town in Texas stays open? Or whether Lars's blowup girl is a real girl? Or whether *Juno* finds a couple to adopt her baby. Why do we care what happens in *Manchester by the Sea*? Why had we *Better Call Saul*? What makes Kimmy Schmidt unbreakable? What are the *Big Little Lies*? Or even the Pretty Little ones? What remains so irresistibly compelling about those white middle-class *Ordinary People* in Minneapolis or the young black kid growing up gay and bullied in *Moonlight*?

How do we bring the epic scope down to the level of everyday life? While writing *stories* in the vernacular, how do we find the *emotional eloquence*, the life-and-death urgency that once was the sole province of gods and kings?

Here's the best definition of story that I can come up with:

Footprints in the sand left by a character in quest of his or her heart's desire against impossible odds.

Let's look at each part of that definition.

FOOTPRINTS IN THE SAND

This correctly suggests motion. Volition. And indeed, in the same way that a fireplace is built of bricks, a film story is built of events. Verbs. Action words. Screenwriting is a verb-oriented endeavor.

Recalling our **GOLDEN GUIDING PRINCIPLE OF STORY:**

***Events* are the building blocks of story.**

LEFT BY A CHARACTER

Stories are about people. (We include under the banner of *person* any sentient creature.) I rankle when I hear people say a movie like *The Treasure of Sierra Madre* is about *greed*. It is not about greed. It is about *people* who are greedy. Movies are not about abstractions. Say it again with me in unison: **Movies are about characters.**

IN QUEST OF

Again, quest is a call to verbery. Quest is an active verb. Knowing, realizing, learning are less so. They are more internal. A quest is external, and movies are external. They are composed of elements an audience can see and hear.

HIS OR HER HEART'S DESIRE

This is huge. The heart's desire. It must be the most important thing at that moment of the character's life. That "thing" can be curing Ebola or something about Mary. It can be solving a crime or committing one. It is not the price tag of the thing itself that establishes its narrative value; it is the value afforded it through the currency of what the protagonist *does*, about what is sacrificed and risked in the effort to attain it. Even if all that the character wants is a loaf of bread, getting it should not be a piece of cake. Rather, it must be...

AGAINST IMPOSSIBLE ODDS

What makes even the most ordinary person interesting? When he or she is in extreme circumstances. Sometimes the world thrusts them upon us (a flood, a murder, a lottery win). Sometimes we take them upon ourselves (falling in love, trying to better our circumstances). Sometimes there are combinations. A modern writer's job is to find in the quest of ordinary people the deeds and passions that place that character's life and happiness at the same risk as that of the warriors of Troy.

It is not merely enough for something to have happened. The emotional, narrative, physical and psychological terrain through which the character's "quest" takes us must be interesting. And entertaining. The audience does not owe us its attention. We owe them. Your story, my story, any story has no inherent value merely because it exists. If you had one vacation week per year, you would not choose to take it at a boring, commonplace locale merely because it had a hotel and a bus went there.

When you think about it, even the smallest story is larger than the largest life. How much can really happen in 90 minutes of an actual life? Whereas in a story well told, all the agony and ecstasy of a lifetime can be ours.

The most basic tenet of the way I see story is that it begins not with theme but with **DESIRE**. In the present tense of the story, what is the most important thing for the protagonist? **Our number one job is to make whatever is important to the protagonist important to the audience**. If we do it, many shortcomings of craft will be forgiven. If we do not, all the technique in the world will still leave an audience feeling underfed. The story is art. The telling of it is craft.

Each of the major narrative forms (prose fiction, theater, film) has its own inherent way of telling a story. Form follows function. In Part Two, The Big Picture, we explore the craft of telling a story through film.

WRITERS GYM EXERCISES

Buy a pack of 500 index cards—the six-color kind. Play your favorite film on video or DVD. Write a separate scene card for each significant narrative event. [NB: Opening a window is not a significant narrative event. Jumping out of a window is.] **You will likely end up with 70 to 100 cards. Remember this number when you set out to do your stories.**

We will revisit this pile of scene cards several times in subsequent chapters. For now, find the **first and last** scene in which the protagonist appears. Examine those circumstances.

In *The Godfather,* for instance, Michael Corleone is introduced at his sister's wedding. He is dressed in his ARMY UNIFORM, which sets him apart from the other men in their shiny Italian suits. His girlfriend is also totally an outsider. Michael tells her the story of how Luca Brasi helped Michael's father get Johnny Fontane out of a contract by holding a gun to the man's head and saying that his signature or his brains would end up on the paper. The soul (not sole) purpose of the scene is for Michael to say the line that defines who he is at the beginning of the story: He says, **"That's my family, Kay, it's not me."**

Now, let's leap ahead to the final scene. Michael lies

to Kay after having annihilated all his enemies. The door is closed behind her, and the last thing we see is the ring on his finger being kissed and his being called "Godfather."

Did you ever play with a Slinky, that spiral length of slender, springy metal? (Now plastic, of course.) If you think of the first link in your left hand as the scene where we meet the protagonist, and the last link in your right hand as the final image of the protagonist, then the terrain under the arc that the Slinky describes is the landscape of the story.

The story is about how the protagonist gets from here to there.

1. Check out your favorite film. Stop it after each scene and write down the significant plot event that took place. This is among the most powerful exercises you can do. Repeat it twice weekly.

2. Remember the first story you were told. Write it down with as much detail as you can recall.

3. **Sherlock Holmes and Moriarity**.

   Do this with a writing friend. Each of you separately concoct a perfect crime: circumstances, motive, execution, getaway. Perpetrator. Victim. Write it out in some detail.

   Then exchange papers. Create a character who will solve this crime. How will the hole in the plan be discovered? By what means of detection?

Interlogue

By Scott Kosar

"It's about a guy who hasn't slept in a year…"

That's all I knew about *The Machinist* when I pitched it at UCLA's famed MFA Program in Screenwriting. I knew my character was an insomniac and a loner. I had a vague notion that he passed his evenings haunting junkyards and railroad tracks in search of scrap metal. That's about all I had.

That … and "The Ackerman Scenogram."

It's exactly what I was looking for…

I came to UCLA's screenwriting program to learn *structure*. Thank god I met Hal Ackerman. I took his legendary "434" workshop not once but *three times*, because I couldn't get enough of his passion for the craft of screenwriting. I couldn't get enough of his wisdom. I couldn't get enough of his tough love.

And I couldn't get enough of that fucking *Scenogram*!!!

I knew the good stuff when I saw it. After all, I was a recovering drug addict fresh out of rehab when I started Hal's course in 1998. I also knew about a character that made bad mistakes in his life that he couldn't come to terms with.

I just didn't know how to *write* about him.

So Hal taught me.

He taught me to write screenplays.

He gave me the tools I needed to turn my questionable (and wholly *unmarketable*) ideas into a screenplay I was actually proud of.

He taught me that good characters want something so badly that they'll go to any length to get it. So I had Trevor of *The Machinist* throw himself in front of a moving car in order to acquire the requisite bruises he needed to file a bogus hit-and-run report that would yield him an address he so desperately wanted.

He taught me that a screenplay needs an *inciting event* to disrupt the status quo of a story and set its plot into motion. So I had Trevor cause a machine shop accident that resulted in the loss of a coworker's arm. (By now you can see why I thought my screenplay was unmarketable).

He taught me that a good script needs *unifying devices* that create story cohesion and advance the plot. So I had different characters utter the same off-hand remark to Trevor *("If you were any thinner you wouldn't exist")* as a means of creating some cohesion between Trevor's real and illusory worlds while advancing his oddball criminal investigation.

He taught me how a 1st Act ends with a *Point of No Return* that irrevocably changes the protagonist's life while sending him/her headlong into a spiraling conflict from which there seems to be no escape. For Trevor, that moment comes in his shop foreman's office during a deposition that raises questions about Trevor's sanity that he can no longer ignore. This sends him on an Act 2 quest to prove his sanity (to himself as well as others), and he's not above hurling himself in front of a moving car now and then if it will help him achieve his *objective*.

He taught me how to use index cards (I already knew how to use Post-It notes, right, Hal?) to build plot and shape screenplays that had rising action, clever turning points, and even (God willing) an effective story resolution.

Hal taught me everything I know about writing. I've applied his lessons to every screenplay I ever wrote, including the remakes of *THE TEXAS CHAINSAW MASSACRE* (2003) and *THE AMITYVILLE HORROR* (2005).

Thanks, Hal, for teaching me the Ackerman way to write screenplays that sell.

I love you.

Scott Kosar's credits include THE TEXAS CHAINSAW MASSACRE *(2003),* THE AMITYVILLE HORROR *(2005),* THE CRAZIES *(2008), the A&E series* BATES MOTEL *(2014 - 2016) and the upcoming Netflix series* THE HAUNTING OF HILL HOUSE. *Kosar's script for* THE MACHINIST *(starring Christian Bale and directed by Brad Anderson) was written at UCLA's MFA Screenwriting Program.*

PART TWO

The Big Picture: Story Structure

CHAPTER 9
Act One

As conflict is argument between characters, plot is argument between events.

I had been living in New York, writing Off-Off-Broadway plays and tending bar in the Village when I decided to come west. My well-thought-out plan was to write and sell a screenplay for an obscene amount of money, then return to New York and continue the serious, Barton Finkular business of writing plays.

My plan had one minor flaw. I had never written a screenplay. Well, two flaws. I had never even *seen* a screenplay. But in my divine arrogance I reasoned, how hard could it be? The sum total of my preparation was having seen some bad movies and thinking, I can write one as bad as that!

Stanislavsky would tell students who thought they knew everything, "You are about to enter the next phase of your education." And I was about to enter mine.

The first humbling lesson I learned was that writing even a crappy script is harder than it looks. And indeed, my first few alleged screenplays were really stage plays with camera directions.

But I watched a lot of films and read some screenplays, and I started to get the hang of it. (This was in the early '70s, an era of brilliant individualistic films.) My scripts were becoming more cinematic. More action, less dialogue. I was getting there. I thought.

I gave my newest screenplay to my agent. (*That* was progress! I *had* an agent!) He reacted cautiously. He said he liked the dialogue, the characters and the story premise, but he couldn't tell where the first act ended. I knew he was kidding around with me. I had been to the theater; I knew what act breaks were. The curtain comes down. The audience goes outside for coffee and cigarettes. If there was one thing I knew, it was that movies did not have act breaks. Somebody once defined being absolutely sure as being wrong at the top of your voice.

THE NEED FOR STRUCTURE

Some people like to plan things meticulously, and others need to be completely spontaneous. Each kind of person drives the other crazy. Planning, structure, guidelines—are they safety nets or prisons? Itineraries or cookie cutters? Do they give an artist the freedom to be free, or do they stifle that freedom? Every human trait is like a long guitar string with the opposite ends of that trait at each end (adventurous/cautious). We each have a fret that's our note, our place of comfort. In regard to the need for structure and planning, which kind of person are *you?* Where is *your* note on that guitar string? How does that affect the work you do before you write FADE IN?

Many new writers (and not only new writers) carry with them a suspicious mistrust of adhering to a pre-existing form for fear that it will ultimately stifle their imagination, inhibit their creativity and foster deadly conformity. I was one of those people. It took me a long while to realize how an understanding of screenplay structure can be a powerful ally. And I come to you with the zeal of a convert.

The next time you're among a large group of people, look at them closely. People are usually pretty distinctive. It's rare that we'd mistake one person for another. And the more intimately you know them, even the small, subtle differences of height, weight, facial features, coloring, voice, attitude and body language make a world of difference. And yet, *structurally* we are all built to the same proportions. Our heads are one sixth of our full height. Our bodies have the same ratio of shoulder-to-hip, knee-to-toe. It's true of screenplays as well. A thousand different scripts, though built in the same proportion of pages per act, may be as different and individuated from one another as human beings are. I read at least 50 new scripts every year. Multiply that by 17. I've never read two alike.

So let us embrace structure without fear.

WHAT STRUCTURE IS NOT

Structure is not a mere arbitrary delineation of how many pages constitute a first act, second act and third act. Function defines form. What is interesting and necessary about our heads goes beyond their mathematical proportion to our full height. They have some pretty vital functions as well. So do the thoraxial cavity and the mid-torso and the limbs. In a screenplay, too, function defines form.

It is obvious that if we were architects commissioned to erect a 30-story office tower in midtown Manhattan, we would not run helter-skelter on spontaneous impulse for the placement of walls, floors, windows and support beams. Nor would we dismiss as too boring the consideration of plumbing and wiring. We would not argue for a free-floating parking structure above the roof, cool though the idea might be. The building would have to fit into the prescribed, pre-existing space. We could not have a garden atrium if it intruded into the adjacent building.

The same care and forethought needs to follow the inspiration for a screenplay idea, and precede breaking ground.

STRUCTURAL PRINCIPLE #1: More than any other form of fiction, a screenplay is a work of architecture. The parts of its anatomy are defined by their function. Audiences don't want to wait 20 minutes for the elevator to find out what the story is about. They don't want the floorboards of story logic to creak under their feet. That makes audiences wary. They reclaim their freely given suspension of disbelief, and proceed cautiously. We want them to charge in with confidence and take the whole ride arms up, head thrown back, mouth wide open. Let's build the thing so it does that.

THE THREE-ACT SCREENPLAY STRUCTURE REVEALED

Screenplays are structured in three acts. If you say this is arbitrary and capricious, I agree with you. Why three? Why not four? Broadway dramas are mostly two acts. They used to be three. Musicals were always in two. Now they often have no intermission. Shakespeare's plays were in five acts, Molière's in four. Movies are in three for now. In ten years, after the influence of the Internet has permeated our groundwater, we may see movies as having 10 acts or 56. But for now there are three.

As a way of learning structure myself, I invented a diagram I call the SCENOGRAM. The Scenogram is an X-ray of the internal spine of a story. I originally used it as an instrument for analyzing the structure of existing films. It identifies 11 key "**fence-post**" scenes that occur at approximately 10-page intervals. With the exposition scene (or scenes) and the inciting event, these thirteen scenes form the stepping stones of the narrative.

We will have a more complete discussion on the uses of the Scenogram in story construction in Chapter 11. But in the upcoming discussion of the key structural scenes in each act, I refer to these key scenes alternately as fence-post scenes or Scenogram "box scenes." They are weight-bearing scenes; the equivalent of fence-posts you

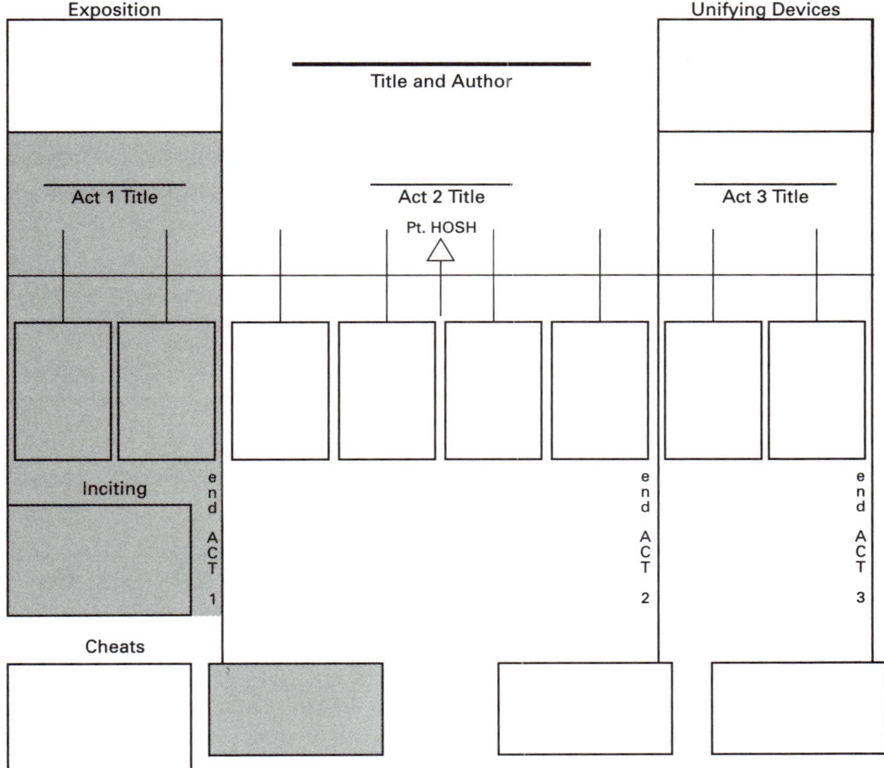

imbed into the ground that clearly define the shape and size and dimensions of the yet-to-be-erected fence.

Act One is usually 25 to 30 pages. Act Two generally ends between page 75 and page 80. The third act is a full act, 25 to 30 pages long (assuming a full script of approximately 110 pages). A nice symmetrical proportion: 30-50-30. But use that only as a template. Some stories have shorter first acts and longer second acts. Some have truncated third acts. The idea is not to impose a strict militaristic precision on it. The exact moment that the sun crosses the equator may be 3:27 p.m. on March 21. But we feel Spring beginning when something in the air does something to our blood. And *usually* that happens around the 21st. Something happens in the blood of a screenplay, too, that defines the end of an act.

Everyone hold hands. We're going to walk through the 13 "stepping stone" fence-post scenes of the internal spine of a screen story. We're going to approach these scenes in terms of their function. If you don't know what the scene must do, how can you possibly make it do it? If you were an inexperienced builder and didn't know that those square shapes on the diagram were meant to be windows, you might not leave room for the glass.

Exposition

Exposition scenes are the "Once Upon a Time" scenes of a movie. They address the journalistic W's: the who, what, where, when and why of a story. Stage comedies dating back to the Greek and Roman eras and all the way up through the 1940s were pretty cavalier about exposition. Typically, a maid and manservant engaged in a pseudo-conversation that began with, "As you know, the master of the house has been away these four months in Verona and during that time his daughter, who was supposed to be safely in the convent, has been meeting secretly with the son of their archenemies." Etc., etc.

Modern conventions call for a more sophisticated immersion into the story. Although, if you think back to some classic TV shows like *Mission: Impossible*, *Hill Street Blues* and *L.A. Law*, the vehicle for exposition was pretty blatant. The self-destructing tape of *Mission: Impossible*, the briefing of *Hill Street Blues*, the staff meeting of *L.A. Law*. Some of the modern shows are so adept at playing with structure, they will play the present tense story as total flashback as Vince Gilligan often does in *Breaking Bad*, where the whole episode will make the opening shot (a flash forward) make sense. He outdoes himself in *Breaking Bad*'s subsequent prequel. *Better Call Saul*, where a couple of seasons' worth of episodes are leading us toward an ending we have been given at the beginning. That approach has been done before, of course. Famously, even among the newest generation's crop of film buffs, is Charles Brackett, Billy Wilder and D.M. Marshman Jr.'s *Sunset Boulevard.* Gilligan does it differently and effectively, and that always feels new.

But for the most part, stories are meant to hit the ground running. We expect the exposition to flow organically from the characters' lives. (In the chapters on scene writing, we explore the tenet of exposition being a by-product of conflict.)

Here are **THREE TASKS YOUR EXPOSITION SCENES OUGHT TO ACCOMPLISH.** But first, one caveat. These opening scenes are called exposition scenes because that is their primary function. They do not need to contain all the exposition that will ever be required. New information can (and should) be laid into subsequent scenes as the story makes it imperative.

ESTABLISH THE UNIVERSE OF THE STORY

The story's "universe" may literally be in another galaxy, as in the seemingly unending saga of *Star Wars*, or it may be within a small and specific subculture of modern society. It may be the contemporary Monterey of *Big Little Lies*, or the tiny room of *The Room*. It might be *Fargo*, or a bus. It might be the nearly recognizable make-believe world of *La La Land*, or the very real world of *Manhattan*; Woody Allen's, or Sam Shaw's series about the Manhattan Project set in the 1940's at Los Alamos.

Our first job is to make that world real and palpable to our audience. How do we do it? What will be the first thing we write after FADE IN? What will make the audience feel and experience something essential to that world? In *The Last Picture Show*, it's a dusty, empty street. In *Barton Fink*, it's the Broadway stage. In *2001: A Space Odyssey*, it's the dawn of man. In *Walkabout*, the first "universe" is an ultramodern, sterile, civilized city. Soon after that, the story shifts to the prehistoric Outback.

But we are still ahead of ourselves. There is a question that precedes

"What is the first thing we write after FADE IN?" It is the more basic question of where does the story start? And that question is preceded by the most basic question of all, which is, **whose story is it**? From that question follows many others: What happens in that story? What makes it a story? Who is the character at the beginning? What are the defining circumstances of his or her life?

I am deliberately omitting from this litany of questions "What is the story *about?*" Because the answer to that question will nearly always be thematic: a coming-of-age story. A story about empowerment. Nature versus nurture. If all you knew about *The Godfather* was that it was a story about the sins of the father being visited on the sons, would that give you even the slightest inkling of that film? Could you write that story given only that theme? You might be able to write the *outcome* of *The Godfather*, but not those complex, contradictory characters you loved and hated and felt intimate with and understood.

But if you say it's the story of the youngest of three brothers—a war hero who has always stayed outside the family business, but who is drawn in when his father is assassinated and ultimately becomes the head of the family and most ruthless and powerful mobster in New York—then you have a sense of *the story*. Not *the meaning* of the story, but the essential movement of story. The two powerful, opposing internal forces. In the same way that conflict in any one scene is the result of two characters exerting opposing forces, in the DNA of a story, there are those same primal tectonic forces pitted against one other.

So where do we start?

Aristotle, in his benevolent clarity, has told us that the beginning is that thing before which there is nothing else. This is one of those great, profound truths that is greatly and profoundly useless. Taken to its Aristotelian logical extreme, this could mean that every story would begin at the first moment of time, because clearly that would be the one thing before which there was nothing. Or if that seems too extreme, if the story is about a specific person, what about starting at the moment of the protagonist's birth? Or conception? Or his or her mother's birth or conception?

Instinctively you know these are bad ideas. But what determines the difference between an idea that is pretty damn good and one that is so much better? How do we decide on our **Point of Entry** into the story? Maybe you're sick of these questions and ready for some answers. But you have to learn to ask them because you can't get a really helpful answer until you've asked the right questions.

Earlier, you were asked to do the Slinky exercise, to identify the first and last scenes in which the protagonist appeared. Let's think now about why those writers made those choices. Since we can never separate plot and character, let's recall some of the important building blocks we have discussed:

> Plot is character in motion.
> Who a character is, is what he or she does. Or does not.
> Driven by desire.
> Diverted by choices.
> Repelled by the nearly equal and opposite force in the core of the spinal cord.

Michael's story in *The Godfather* is how he gets from the Army geek who tells his girlfriend, "That's my family, Kay, it's not me," to the point where his ring is kissed and he is called "Godfather." The story of *Rocky* is getting from the Philadelphia club arena to going the distance with the champ. The story of *Rabbit-Proof Fence* is the girls getting back home from where they are kidnapped.

The concept applies to multiple story lines as well. In *The Hours*, Virginia Woolf's story begins with a suicide attempt and ends with its success. Clarissa's (Meryl Streep) story begins with her sleeping in the same bed but very much apart from her lover, and it ends with their relationship changing to something more alive after the poet's death. Laura Brown begins as a young, suicidally depressed woman and ends as a woman whose son has committed suicide and is forgiven by a young girl she has just met.

In all these stories, profound, life-changing events occur, of course. Our job is to bring the character to that place of possible change. It is that process and that vantage point that affords the clearest look into a character's soul, into the causes and possibilities of that character's life.

As writers, we must know our end before (or at the same time that) we know our beginning. We want to start our character as far away as possible from where he or she will end; or in a point of juxtaposition that will make the journey most interesting. If Rocky had been a leading contender at the beginning, getting the shot to fight the champ would not have had the same impact. On the other extreme, had he been a plumber with no fight experience, a bout with the champ would have been hard to believe.

To briefly review the first task of the exposition scene(s): We must establish the universe of the story, but specifically reveal where our protagonist fits in that universe.

Defining Action For Your Protagonist

Who we are is revealed in everything we do. Introduce your character engaged in the activity that defines for us who that character is. In doing so, you are going beyond merely supplying information to an audience, you are creating an experience of that character. Think about your favorite movies. Recall how the protagonist was introduced.

What *defines* a character? What defines any human being? In Western capitalistic society, often it is our occupation that defines us—the thing we do for money. Many characters are introduced in the contexts of their jobs. But not all. *Fargo* didn't open with Jerry Lundegaard in a used-car lot. Rocky wasn't collecting debts. Don Corleone wasn't gunning down a renegade olive oil importer. There was something the writer felt was *more essential* to those characters, *in this story*.

Here are a few examples of Defining Action.

We meet Rocky in the ring. He is a slow, clumsy, left-handed palooka whose fury is engaged only after he is fouled. He grabs a smoke after the bout, nets about 30 bucks for the fight after trainer's fees and locker fees are deducted, and takes a bus home.

The two look-alike characters in Gary Ross's *Dave* each has a defining act. The president arrives on the White House lawn by helicopter, ditches his "show" dogs as soon as he is out of the camera's view, and peels off from his wife without a word. His doppelgänger (also played by Kevin Kline) is introduced at a silly promotional event, riding a pig.

In Joel and Ethan Coen's *Fargo*, the protagonist is a car salesman. The scene (the defining act for him in the STORY) is Jerry hiring someone to kidnap his wife so he can collect the ransom, which his father-in-law, Jerry hopes, will pay. And though he is towing a car in the opening and has brought it to give to the kidnappers in partial payment, there is not the slightest indication that he's a salesman.

One of my all-time favorite films is *Queen of Hearts*, written by Tony Grisoni and not to be confused with the slightly more popular *King of Hearts*. It's funny, emotional and suspenseful; it is peopled with rich, multidimensional characters; it deals with deep and complex ideas about love and family; and it does so totally through the narrative and psychological truth of the story.

Among the many things I love about the film's opening sequence is that there is practically no dialogue. The few words that are spoken are in Italian (without subtitles). We are in an Italian village (UNIVERSE OF THE STORY) with medieval stone walls. A young man looks lovingly through his window at his beloved in her bedroom across the courtyard. She smiles at him. Moments later, her witch of a grandmother pushes her away from the window and slams the shutters closed. In 30 seconds we know who the protagonists are, what they want, and what the opposition is.

Then the young woman is brought into a parlor where a well-dressed man awaits her. He snaps his fingers and his assistant hands him a beautiful bolt of ornate silk, which he presents to the grandmother; clearly a wedding bribe. She pushes her granddaughter toward the man, but the young woman cannot go through with it and bolts from the room. Before going after her, the old woman *first picks up the gift.*

(Remember the principle of character that who we are is revealed in what we do. **Great movie writing weaves these perfect choices organically into the narrative of the story.)**

The ardent lover gets an idea and cuts down a clothesline. When grandmother and suitor knock, then bang on the girl's locked bedroom door, then break it in, they find her window wide open and the girl gone. She's eloped with her lover and the chase is on. The elopers run through the narrow cobblestone streets. The rich man's men cut off their escape. With all escape routes blocked, they run into an open building and climb the interior stairway.

At the entrance to the building, the rich man demands a knife from his compadre. The lovers reach the top and climb outside onto the narrow roof. The jilted groom, far richer and more physically imposing than the young swain, climbs onto the roof with his knife bared. The lovers are forced closer to the edge. The man takes his beloved's hand. No words are said. They take a lover's leap off the tower to the gasping horror of all the villagers below.

They fall into a passing hay wagon that carries them away safely to their destiny. And now a Voice Over kicks in. It's a child's voice speaking in proper English. "That's the way Mom and Dad got married. It was very romantic. At least the way Dad tells it." We learn so much more in that moment beyond the specific information conveyed by the words. We know that they escaped to England, got married and raised a son, and that the story is told through his point of view.

We come back for a moment to the rich man on the tower. The VO explains, "Mister Barbariccia, the butcher's son, swore an oath of vengeance." And when we see him pull that sharp knife along his open palm and the drops of blood splatter below, we *believe* the oath of vengeance.

This entire sequence most eloquently uses the visual language of cinema to create external events that allow us to experience the internal truths of the characters. We are not merely *told* information, we are made to experience it. And as writers, that is exactly what we want to do for our audience.

Incidentally, not just your protagonist, but EVERY CHARACTER should be introduced through a defining action.

Propitious or Auspicious Occasion

This is the beginning or ending of something. A birthday, anniversary, marriage, divorce, getting a job, losing a job, a first date, a last date, a birth, a death. Moving in or moving out. Graduation. Retirement. It gives the story a sense of moment. I don't consider the propitious occasion a mandatory component, but you'd be surprised how often it is used. Like every other technique, it must derive organically from the circumstances of the story. You'd fire the architect who put a turret on a ranch house.

Juno begins with her discovery that she is pregnant. (The actual moment of sex is thrown in there, too.) *Sea of Love* starts on the protagonist's 20th anniversary on the job. *About Schmidt* (Alexander Payne's film before *Sideways*) opens with the protagonist's last day. Last hour. Last minute. *Barton Fink* opens on a performance of Fink's play. Not night number 34. Opening night.

Ghost World begins with high school graduation. Ditto for *Y tu mamá también*. Marleen Gorris's gorgeous film *Antonia's Line* is told predominately in flashback, but the present moment is the day of her death. And the flashback begins the day she returns to her village at the end of World War II. *The Hours* opens on the day Virginia Woolf kills herself. William Goldman's script for *All the President's Men* starts with Nixon giving the State of the Union address. Woody Allen's *Crimes and Misdemeanors* opens with Martin Landau's character being awarded Man of the Year—and ends with a wedding.

Remember, though, that this is art. Rules need not be arbitrarily applied. There is nothing significant about the day *Rocky* opens. (True, July 4, 1976, is approaching, and the story is based around that bicentennial event.) There is nothing externally noteworthy about the day *Fargo* begins. Or *Shakespeare in Love* or *The Last Seduction*. Having *Sea of Love* begin on Keller's 20th anniversary on the job is not just a statistic. It influences the narrative by offering the character a most profound character choice. He could retire. ("Open up a motel. A polygraph school.") But he does not. And *why* he does not is a vital part of his character.

The opening in *The Godfather* does not merely add spectacle and a convenient forum for introducing the cast of characters. There is a tradition that no Sicilian can turn down a request on his daughter's wedding day. So it provides a clear road into the soul and psyche of Don Corleone.

The opening-night party at Sardi's is used in *Barton Fink* to reveal the pretentious side of Barton's personality. When his agent asks if he's seen the reviews, he says no, though we have just seen them being read to him—and seen his *apparent* disdain for them.

In Diane Thomas's script for *Romancing the Stone*, the cause for celebration upon completing her book reveals the character's lonely existence: airplane bottle of champagne (which she has difficulty opening), no tissues to wipe her tears of joy (she blows her nose in a Post-It on which she has written a reminder to herself to buy tissues), and of course she has no man to celebrate with, just her cat and the romantic poster from one of her many successful books with the shadowy silhouette of a man. *Queen of Hearts* begins on what *should* have been Mr. Barbariccia's wedding day. The emotional engine of the revenge story is directly derived from what happened that day.

Think about the opening sequence of your own screenplay. Are there some vivid visual details that individuate and bring to life its universe? In what activity and circumstance do you want the audience to meet your protagonist? Is there a particular occasion on which your story might effectively begin?

PITFALLS TO AVOID: WHAT EXPOSITION IS NOT

We've talked about what exposition scenes need to do and how to go about doing it. Of equal importance to writers is knowing what exposition is NOT. This can help us mightily in avoiding some of the exposition pitfalls waiting out there to befall us, and also to recognize those we have already made.

The Big Blurt

Have you ever been stuck in a plane or a bar alongside someone who tells you his or her life story when you don't want to know it? It's like a big vomit pail of information. We don't want to inflict that on our audience. And yet we sometimes think that because the scene is called an exposition scene, it is our obligation or our only opportunity to divulge to the audience every knowable fact about our protagonist.

I don't make a habit of holding work up as a negative example, but in full recognition that any opinions I have are merely my own, there is a particular film whose opening sequence is an example of practices I'd urge you to avoid. The film is called *2010*, the sequel to *2001*.

The movie begins with successive screens containing long paragraphs of writing. This goes on for quite some time. When we have read enough of the history of the initial *2001* to bring us up to date, the live action of the film begins. A Russian scientist speaks to an American scientist at an American-satellite tracking installation. Our guy (Roy Scheider) is on a stanchion; the Russian is on the ground below him. Thus they have to shout. Perhaps the raised voices are meant to inject a tone of urgency to the scene. Various other devices—bets and negotiations—are force-fed into the content of the scene. But for quite a long period of time the basic thing they are doing is diverting sluiceloads of information, ostensibly directed at each other, to its true repository, the audience. They are talking *toward*, but not *to* each other.

The writer-director decided that the audience needed to have a huge amount of information, and the purpose of this scene was to deliver it. But is the audience made to *care* about the information? Rent the movie. Form your own opinion.

EXPOSITION PRINCIPLE #1:

It is far more interesting when a character needs to HAVE information than when a character needs to GIVE it.

Think about the Robert Redford character (Bob Woodward) in *All the President's Men.* Every line of dialogue in his opening scene is punctuated with a question mark. His adversary, a country-club lawyer, wants to divulge no information. Whatever tidbits Redford extracts are worth gold. The great chaotic family dinner scene in *Little Miss Sunshine* is centered around young Olive needing to know what happened to her uncle… why he tried to kill himself. Her desire gives all the comedy that swirls around that table its emotional center.

TECHNIQUE: Dole out pieces of information as the characters in the story situations create the need for it. Let each scene have the specific purpose of dramatizing one important piece. *Sea of Love* is a nice illustration. There are four exposition scenes, each of which dramatizes a particular side of the Al Pacino character. After three scenes that show him to be a good cop, smart, tough and compassionate, he returns home drunk and lonely and calls his ex-wife at 2 a.m. to complain about a pain in his appendix. She hangs up without saying a word.

A few scenes later, he is investigating a murder with his partner, and he apologizes for the late-night call. We find out HERE, not in the phone call, that his ex-wife is married to his partner. Did the writer know it when he wrote the earlier scene? Of course. Why didn't he say it? **He saved it for the moment where it would have the greatest impact.**

Same deal in *Fargo*. Jerry alludes to being in some kind of trouble. When the kidnappers ask about it, Jerry hedges and deflects and avoids answering. Did the Coens know what trouble he was in? Yeah, you betcha they did.

Avoid the Census-Taker Technique

The forced vomiting of information is the most common form of abuse writers perpetrate on their characters. Running a close second behind the Big Blurt is the Census Taker—having characters ask very "data"-oriented questions as an information-gathering technique.

Cop to it. We've all done variations of this scene:

```
INT. – COLLEGE DORM-DAY

BILL (19) breezes in and finds his roommate
CHAZZ watching TV. This affable dialogue ensues.

                BILL
    Hey, roomie, how long is it now that we've
    been roommates, about eight months?

                CHAZZ
    No, dude, it's only been seven.
```

As if every time roommates run into each other, they do a review.

Or how about a response to someone asking a question or doing something annoying?

```
                    CHARACTER
        Damn it. That's the fifth time in the last
        six days that you've done that. How
        many times do I have to tell you...
```

A first cousin to the census scene is the READING OF THE DOSSIER.

```
                    SUPERIOR OFFICER
        It says here that you graduated twenty-
        fifth in your class out of a hundred and
        you specialized in (whatever...)
```

And finally there is the inoffensive but innocuous and extremely commonly used CATECHISM approach: Q/A/Q/A/Q/A/Q/A/. Well-phrased questions with coherent answers.

```
        Hey, how are you? Long time no see.
        How's life?

        It's good.

        Still doing that sales job?

        Yeah, it's been three years now.

        And your folks?

        Yeah, still running that fruit stand down-
        town.

        See any movies lately?

        A couple last week.

        How'd you like them?

        Yeah, they were pretty good.
```

You might write this dialogue if your objective was to dramatize a couple of people who were bored and boring and had absolutely nothing interesting to say and no energy between them. But you would not write this scene between people you wanted us to care about based on that information.

What is the golden principle of exposition? All together now... "Information is a by-product of CONFLICT. Conflict comes from opposing desires. That scene right there? Zero intensity. Zero desire. Zero conflict.

Avoid Naked Exposition

In these little scenettes we've exposed the beams of the wall. We've given the audience naked exposition in the guise of conversation. Instead of doing that, let's observe the **GOLDEN PRINCIPLES OF INFORMATION:**

1. Information that is important to the writer **will not** be important to the audience unless the writer creates circumstances that make it important to a character.

2. Information is far more important to an audience when there is a character in the scene who needs to HAVE it rather than one who needs to GIVE it.

MAJOR EXPOSITION AXIOM #1: Information is a by-product of conflict. We will discuss this in greater detail in the chapters on scene writing, but file this axiom away for now.

Once your exposition sequence has set up the status quo of your protagonist, an event occurs that changes it all and propels the story into motion. It doesn't matter what you call that scene as long as it occurs at the right structural point and accomplishes its purpose. I call it the Inciting Event.

THE INCITING EVENT

The function of the Inciting Event is to propel the story into motion. It is the instrument of change, announcing the stake of the story. It aligns the reader's compass to the story's polestar, to the "what-it-is-aboutness" of the story. In the exposition scenes, even though there is conflict, even though there are character objectives, even though there may be two or three exposition scenes and they follow in **sequence,** their function has been to establish the status quo, the situation as it is before it changes. Think of the exposition as showing us a lighted match and a fuse. The Inciting Event is when they touch.

Remember, all our discussions of story rest on the bedrock axiom that **event is the building block of story.** Something that **occurs.** It is always an active, **external verb.** Fear, wonder, decide, contemplate, realize—these are all internal verbs that do not propagate action. Escape. Make love. Leave town. Give chase. Murder. Buy car. Animate robot. Sign deal. These are all active, external verbs.

External events have palpability. Something happens to someone. Some force is exerted that sets something that had been inert into motion, or changes its direction. External events are ruled by real physics, real psychology. Newton's laws of motion applied to dramatic writing. Actions cause reactions. Causes and effects.

The Inciting Event is like a continental divide. Everything before it is subject to one set of rules, everything after it to another. Before the Inciting Event, things happen in an arbitrary sequence. These are the exposition scenes. The sequence in which those scenes occur is dictated by the writer, not by the story. The story has not begun yet.

On the other side of the Inciting Event, the sequence of events stops being arbitrary. The laws of cause and effect take over. Everything that happens causes something else to happen. Before the incident, events occurred merely in a **sequence.** Starting with the incident, events now have ***consequence.***

Think about a table with 10,000 dominoes standing on end. During the exposition scenes, a domino is pushed over, falls, and hits the table. Then another is pushed over and it too falls and hits the table. But when the INCITING DOMINO is pushed, it falls into ANOTHER DOMINO, knocking it into ANOTHER DOMINO. And another and another, serpentining all around the table, sometimes causing two or three tangential columns of dominoes to fall and ripple simultaneously in their own ingeniously wrought patterns. Until at last there are no more dominoes left standing.

In the story analogy, each domino stands for a story EVENT. If there is too big a gap between dominoes, one will hit the table without hitting another domino, and the story dies right there. If the dominoes are lined up in one simple, straight line, we have a theme-driven story with nothing unpredictable.

The direction and shape of the story are determined by the imaginative placement of those dominoes. Just as it wouldn't be as impressive to watch those dominoes fall if the designer had to restart the reaction a few times, it is unsatisfying to an audience if the writer has to (or chooses to) impose his hand to manipulate the story once it has started. If we have to step into our own stories to keep them moving, that should be a pure sign to us that we have not done our primary job.

THE INCITING EVENT ESTABLISHES THE STAKE OF THE STORY, the thing we are meant to root for. In *Romancing the Stone*, Joan Wilder learns her sister is being held for ransom in Colombia. This impels her to go there. Going there leads immediately to her meeting her "hero." The energy, the quest, the force that impels the character out of her status quo also reveals the second and opposing internal force within the story's spine.

Some good examples:

David Mamet's *House of Games* is brilliantly constructed. It's practically an instructional manual of every right thing to do. There are three exposition scenes that establish the protagonist, Dr. Margaret Ford, as a successful practitioner, an author of a best-selling book about compulsive behavior, who is exempt from experience, however, and who lives a spartan existence.

In the Inciting Event, a patient tells her he owes a great deal of money to some gamblers. He puts a gun to his head and threatens to use it. Dr. Ford becomes personally involved at that moment. She says, "Give me the gun and I will help." He does. And as a CONSEQUENCE of that promise, she has to go see a guy named Mike. This becomes the principal relationship of this dark, subversive melodrama.

Similarly, all of the scenes in *The Godfather* that precede Don Corleone spurning the offer by the five families to aid in their heroin plan can and do happen in an arbitrary order, a sequence not driven by narrative force. Think about all the anecdotal moments during the wedding. There are clusters of little storylines: Sonny boffing the bridesmaid, the FBI taking pictures, all the different people requesting favors of Don Corleone. There's Frankie Fontaine. And of course there is the memorable Hollywood sequence with the horse's head winding up in bed with the producer. All of this is great. None of it is the story.

The *story* is Michael Corleone's becoming the new don. The event that sets that story in motion is his father declining to join the other families in selling heroin. That results in the attempt on his father's life. That results in Michael's bonding with his father. (Wheeling him down that empty hospital corridor, those footsteps echoing ominously, Michael assures his father, "I'm with you now, Pop.")

There is no absolute rule dictating the page number on which the Inciting Event should occur. But do it before page 10. A good place to shoot for is around pages 6 to 8. A reader does not want to wait too long for this engagement to occur. In some stories, most often in the action-adventure genre, the Inciting Event occurs very early. In *Star Wars: The Force Awakens*, in the midst of a slam bam action scene where an entire village is being wiped out, the crucial MAP to Luke's whereabouts is hidden in a rolling droid, found by a scavenger who trades it for food. Its beeps and whistles are understood.

In most TV episodes the teaser serves that purpose, setting up the action and hooking the viewer. Think of your favorite TV action shows. See how that works.

Following the exposition and Inciting Event, we now get to the Scenogram Box Scenes.

FENCE-POSTS: SCENOGRAM BOX SCENES 1 & 2

If we think of each act as a complete work, then the Box Scenes are the scenes ending its first, second and third acts. They are the payoffs to the setups. They give shape, substance and direction to the story.

In *The Godfather*, Michael's exposition scene is "That's my family, Kay, it's not me." His Inciting Event is seeing the newspaper headline that his father has been shot. His first Box Scene is the hospital scene we just discussed: "I'm with you now, Pop." His second Box Scene is volunteering to kill Sollazzo and the police captain. In the event that ends the act, he kills them.

END OF ACT ONE

This event is where the entire act has been headed. It must be a substantially larger event than anything that has preceded it. Think of it as the **IRREVOCABLE ACT, THE POINT OF NO RETURN, the event after which the protagonist can never be the person he or she was before the Inciting Event.** It is crucial that you think of the end of the act as **an** ***EVENT***—never a decision, never a thought, never a plan—always an event, after which the protagonist can never go back to being the person he or she was at the beginning of the story.

The organizing principles in the FIRST ACT of *Juno* take us from the act of fertilization to the confirmation of Juno's pregnancy (A SIDE NOTE HERE… As writers, it is a useful technique to give our protagonist a dramatic foil, a character in whom the protagonist willingly or unwillingly confides. This is a most effective and organic way to transmit important narrative or internal truth to our audiences). This generates the important decision Juno makes to terminate the pregnancy. She goes to Women Now, runs into an **opposing force**, a high school friend who is picketing alone in the name of Jesus against abortion. In keeping with the all-important VOICE of Diablo Cody's screenplay, it is not the morality that affects Juno's decision, but the odd weird detail that unborn babies have fingernails. In that waiting room she (with the great help of the director) focuses on everyone in the room having fingernails, and she flees without doing what she came there to do. (SCENOGRAM BOX #1)

ANOTHER IMPORTANT SIDE NOTE HERE… She changes her mind, and in doing so, changes the direction of the story. But it is AN EXTERNAL NARRATIVE EVENT that causes the change, not an internal thought process.

So now what? Again, the voice of the story which plays comedy through serious life events has Juno and her friend Leah looking for prospective adoptive parents in, of all places, the Penny Saver. There, after rejecting several ads, Juno settles on the perfect couple. While broadly comedic, the writer also grounds us in the true values Juno seeks in the people she wants raising her offspring. (Here we also get some darkly comic history of the mother who deserted her.) The selection of the adoptive couple is SCENOGRAM BOX# 2

SCENOGRAM BOX #3… THE ACT ONE CONCLUSION is Juno informing her father and stepmother. Again, the nucleus of emotional reality is surrounded by comedy. The UNIFYING DEVICE OF FINGERNAILS is there, organically. After her dad expresses his disappointment in her, saying he thought she was a girl who knew when to say when, she replies, "I don't know what kind of a girl I am." And THAT becomes the stake of the story.

This story line is woven harmonically around the relationship between Juno and Paulie Bleeker, the baby's father. Paulie is quite NOT the most assertive romantic young lad. He is sweet, naïve, unworldly, and way over his head. When Juno tells him she is pregnant, he can only relate it to what parents and teachers do. She needs him to take an active role in the decision. It is beyond him. She feigns indifference to his inability to step up.

NB: many stories have two interwoven plot lines, especially genre pieces that have the A Story (the murder mystery, say) and the B Story (the love story). It is a most helpful strategy to Scenogram BOTH STORY LINES. Using *Juno* as our model for the Paulie-Juno story: ACT ONE: They begin as friends who have had sex. ACT TWO: Pregnancy pushes them apart, and Juno into an unwise closeness with the adoptive father. ACT THREE: They discover they are in love.

In Anthony Minghella's script and film *Truly Madly Deeply*, the moment occurs at the 30-minute mark. The story is ALL character, so time is well spent developing the character of Nina (played breathtakingly by Juliet Stevenson), establishing the people in her life, and exposing the gaping emotional hole in her soul where lives the pain of the loss of her deceased lover. At the end of the first act, given rebirth by the intensity of her grief of missing him, he returns to her.

Structures Have Principles of Organization

Not always, but sometimes, there are other logistical changes from Act One to Act Two. Change of place, change of time. In Act One of *The Godfather* Michael is in New York. In Act Two he is in Italy, and in Act Three he is back in New York.

A popular film the year I began teaching at UCLA was *Desperately*

Seeking Susan (written by Leora Barish). At the end of Act One, the protagonist is knocked on the head, and when she wakes up she believes she is Susan, the woman she has been obsessed with. At the end of Act Two, she is knocked on the head again, and when she awakens she has returned to her original identity.

There is no absolute hard rule you need to abide by regarding where the first act ends. Most audiences won't even know there are such things as "acts" in the movies they see. But we need to know. It's usually around the 20- to 30-page point. If we keep in touch with the FUNCTION of the act, then our own inner sense of balance will tell us whether that point of no return is most effectively placed at the front or the back end of the 20- to 30-page sector.

Get this moment right, and it will point the way to Act Two. Miss it and you're sailing in the South Pacific without a compass.

WRITERS GYM EXERCISES

Take 10 movies off your video shelf and watch their opening scenes. Observe how the world is evoked—how and what you know about where the story takes place.

Observe the circumstances in which the protagonist is introduced. How are the two strands of DNA—event and emotion—braided together?

What do you know, and what do you feel? Does the scene make you interested in the character?

And if we're talking about defining acts, what could be more memorable than the opening monologue Francis Ford Coppola and Edmund H. North wrote George C. Scott as *Patton*?

Make a list of 10 words that define *you* right now at this phase of your life. Now think of an act, an event, into which you could be placed that would create for an audience the experience granting them that knowledge. Look at the first three you have selected. How do you think an audience would feel about such a character? Have you (the writer) given the audience a road into the inner life of the character? Have you created a climate that generates any strong and specific feeling toward the character?

CHAPTER 10
Acts Two and Three

Second acts are where good stories come to die. They are the Killing Fields, the Donner Passes, the Bermuda Triangles of screenplays. Many a script born in exultation wallows at the end of the first act, loses resolve, staggers in wobbly circles, falls to its knees, throat parched, eyes wild, face distended, blistered by the sun, gasps and expires. Unfortunately, many of these movies get made, but that is a topic for another book.

ACT TWO

Analogy No. 73. If you were climbing Mount Everest, when you left your first base camp at 9000 feet, you'd make damn sure you had filled your knapsack with a warm jacket, a bottle of water, a couple of pitons and various other well-thought-out provisions for the successful ascent to the next base camp. What do you need to have in your screenwriter's knapsack to make it through Act Two?

There is one absolute, single most important commodity you must have. Without it, even with the aid of digital compasses, GPSs, satellite uplinks and climbing shoes from The Sharper Image, you will flounder and become lost. You must have your destination. You

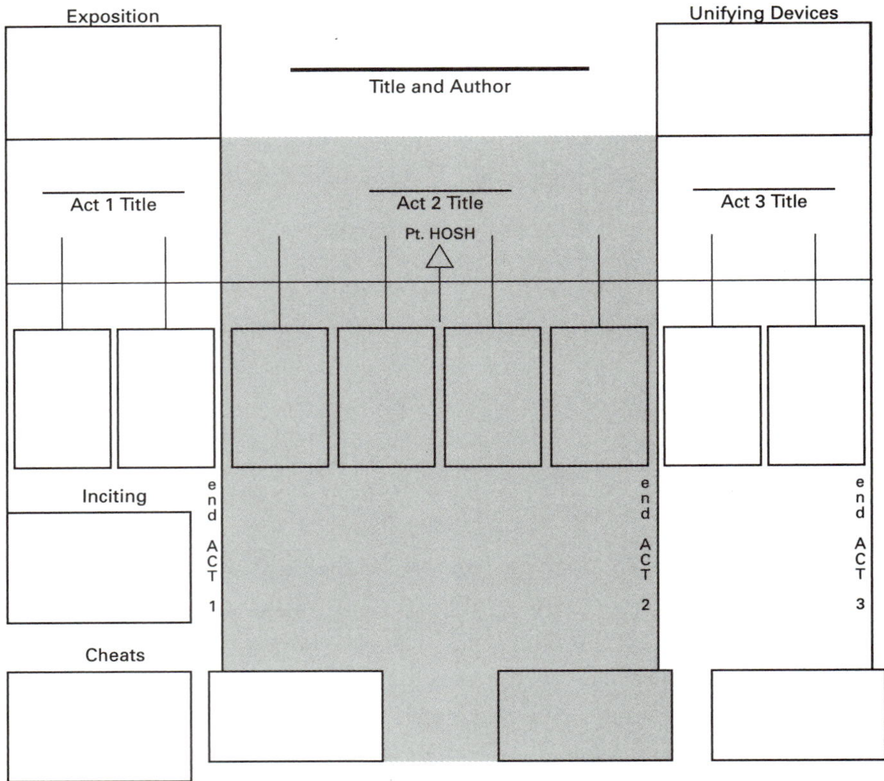

must know the scene that is going to end the act.

THE SINGLE MOST IMPORTANT STRUCTURAL EVENT IN YOUR SCREENPLAY IS THE EVENT THAT ENDS ACT TWO.

It defines the importance of everything that has come before it and propels us toward the climax. It brings to the surface of your story its two most powerful and combating forces. If your story has truth, and if the emotional and narrative wires have been well braided, here they will fuse. What the story means and what is happening in the story will become one thing: the screenwriting equivalent of the perfect wave.

There are several helpful ways of thinking about this moment. One good definition is the worst thing that happens to the protagonist short of death:

- **Michael Corleone's new bride gets blown up in the car.**
- **Rocky's moment of doubt. He can't face the champ.**
- **Madison exposed as a mermaid, and Tom Hanks' character is repulsed by the idea of dating a fish.**
- **The cousin in *Rabbit-Proof Fence* is caught and taken away.**
- **The family in *A Walk on the Moon* is torn apart.**
- **In the three stories in *The Hours*, the poet plunges to his death in front of "Mrs. Dalloway." Virginia Woolf's escape to London is thwarted by her husband. Laura Brown can't get out of the bathroom. (Or Laura Brown leaves her child to go kill herself. As you watch the film, which is the worst tragedy—killing herself or having to live her unbearable life?)**

Richard Walter has described this moment as "The Big Gloom," and I wish I could think of a better way of saying it so I wouldn't have to quote him.

Another way to think of the end of Act Two is: the event after which the protagonist is as far away as possible from achieving his heart's desire:

- **The character in *Splash* wants love in his life, has it and now rejects it.**
- **Rocky wants not to be a loser, and loses his resolve to fight for it.**
- **Michael Corleone has the lightning bolt of love that will change his life and keep him out of the family business. And he loses her.**
- **In *The Bridge on the River Kwai*, the character played by William Holden nearly dies while escaping from the Japanese POW camp.**

- **In *Juno*, the "perfect couple" Juno selects to adopt her**

baby split up and NOT when she is two months pregnant so she can easily find replacements, but when she is nearly due to deliver.

There is a third paradigm that I would describe as the moment where the thing that had been most important is challenged by the thing that had been growing in importance. The character has to make a profound choice and one gets jettisoned. A good example appears in *Sea of Love*, where the most important thing for Detective Frank Keller (Al Pacino) at the beginning of the movie was to solve the murder. By the end of the second act he is consumed in a torrid romance with a woman (Ellen Barkin) who he now strongly suspects IS the killer. Her fingerprints are on a glass. But he DOES NOT TURN THEM IN. He smudges them so he doesn't have to find out. He'd rather die than lose what he has with her. At the frenzied final scene he forces a gun into her hand and tries to make her kill him.

Jack Nicholson, in Richard Condon's *Prizzi's Honor*, expresses the similar paradox in somewhat different terms: "Do I marry her or do I ice her?" In *The Professional*, young Natalie Portman wants to learn to be an assassin from the title character. He wants first to be alone, and then out of necessity he protects her. The end of Act Two is the confluence of those two powerful forces.

In his role in *Splash*, Tom Hanks has the major act thrust upon him. The obsessed mermaid hunter sprays water on Daryl Hannah, revealing her "mermaiditude." Hanks's character in *Big*, though, has the decision to make himself. It's his birthday. His 13-year-old best friend wants to be with him. But he has plans with Susan (Elizabeth Perkins). Best friends/home/getting back to his childhood HAD been the most important drive for him all along. Sex/adult stuff was becoming more important. In having to choose one, the character jettisons the other.

AXIOM #1: Before you write even the first word of your second act, know how the act will end.

Some questions often asked at this moment: How do you know if what you have is good enough? How do you know where to look for something better?

Remember Superman? He had his Achilles' heel, kryptonite (in fact, do you remember Achilles?) Your protagonist needs to have his kryptonite. A weakness. A vulnerability. An exposed metaphoric heel. Superman's kryptonite was completely external. (Although it has psychological depth if you think about the idea of being a hero in a strange place but ordinary in your hometown.) The more depth your character has, the deeper into character that flaw is likely to submerge.

A good example is the movie *Vertigo*. In the script, adapted by Samuel Taylor and Alec Coppel, Jimmy Stewart's character is a cop with a fear of high places, who is dropped from the police force following a botched arrest. The climax of the film rests on his conquering vertigo. Before you watch this movie, see if you can anticipate the kind of scene that will end the second act. Watch for the end of the first act. Think ahead again. What's the worst combination of things that can happen?

Quite often, one particular trait in a character's psyche will contain that character's Achilles' heel. The outer life of the story will connect to the character's inner life as that particular weakness of character is tested. The story must lead inevitably but unpredictably to the circumstance where the mettle of the character is tested.

Structurally, the best place to have the character tested and lose is at the end of Act Two. Think about the protagonist in the screenplay you are currently writing or have just written or are contemplating writing. If you were a dastardly person who also knew your protagonist's hidden weaknesses and fears, and if it was your sworn mission to physically and emotionally destroy this person, to tempt him or her with the possibility of achieving his or her absolute heart's desire, how would you do it? What circumstance would you invent that would expose his or her greatest vulnerability? What would be the worst thing that could possibly happen?

In the script you are writing, *make* it happen. TORTURE YOUR

PROTAGONIST. In the script you recently "finished," did you make it happen? If you did not, you know what you have to do.

This goes against our grain. We writers are mostly nice people. Generous of heart and spirit. When we see a fellow human being in distress, our impulse is to give that person consolation and solace. These are lovely human traits. But as writers we must jettison those annoyingly charitable traits and become brutal, unmoved by our characters' travails. We must not be so quick to reel them in from the cold, nor so compassionate as to protect and nurture them and shield them from pain. Rather, we want to expose them, bring them to the moment of their worst nightmare at the worst possible time. (Uh-oh, did I just describe the relationship you're trying to get out of?)

With the act-ending scene in place, your second act now has a destination. In the next 50 to 60 pages, the story will traverse a dramatic distance beginning with the PONR (Point Of No Return at the end of Act One) and concluding at the low point. I want you to consider a philosophical question. You invest five hundred dollars in the stock market. Its value increases to ten thousand dollars and then plummets to zero. Did you lose ten thousand dollars or five hundred?

Anyone who answered five hundred, get out of show business and find a nice corporate-level management job. Of course you lost ten thousand! It doesn't matter that you never had it. It *feels* like you lost ten thousand.

If it's in our reach, it feels like it's in our hands. So whatever your protagonist has to lose at the beginning of the story must increase exponentially. (Watch *The Maltese Falcon*, and track the increasing value of the bird.)

If your protagonist enters the dangerous, unknown waters of Act Two with an investment value of five hundred dollars, we have to inflate his value to ten thousand during the second act, so that when he plummets to zero, the fall is heavily felt.

Each genre has its own mint of currency. In action films, it is the scope of the quest, the villainy of the antagonist, the affront to the hero. In horror films it is the growing ring of terror, the elimination of the circle, the growing isolation to the last one left standing. In character-driven films it is the accessing of intimacy and depth in the characters' lives: Kenneth Lonnergan's *You Can Count on Me*, David Mamet's astonishingly un-Mametlike adaptation of *The Winslow Boy*, and Dylan Kidd's brilliant *Roger Dodger* are some fine examples.

The important thing to remember is to place the important events on the tips of the structural gear wheels that will allow them to most fully exploit their dramatic weight. Think about Michael Corleone's bride getting blown up in that car. Would it have been as significant dramatically if it had happened the day after he met her? Or before he met her?

So, to summarize our progress in mapping the second act, knowing the final scene gives the act a dimension, a destination, a direction, but not yet a shape, not yet a route. Fortunately there are some engineering tricks that can further our progress.

Of the 13 key structural scenes (Exposition, Inciting Event plus the 11 Scenogram Box Scenes), we looked at the first five in Act One. The next five occur in Act Two.

SCENOGRAM BOX SCENES 6–10:

Just as we did in Act One, we will set our Act Two fence-post scenes deep into the bedrock of the story, at approximately 10-page intervals. (See Scenogram on the following page.) Additionally, somewhere around the midpoint of many organically well structured films, there is a moment when the protagonist tries something new, takes control of his or her own destiny in a way that has not been done before. In *Splash*, the protagonist's dilemma has been his inability to believe love will ever find him, and he at last tells Madison that he loves her. (As this is a comedy, this act will ultimately result in his redemption.) In *The Godfather*, Michael Corleone reveals the secret of his identity to the father of his beloved as an act of faith to win his approval.

On the Scenogram, you will see this moment noted at the top of the line as a little mountain peak triangle. I call this elevation PT. HOSH in honor of my esteemed UCLA colleague Howard Suber, who identifies this turning-point moment in his class on screenplay structure. If you read the letters of PT. HOSH backward, they stand for **H**oward **S**uber's **O**ne-**H**our **T**urning **P**oint.

A traveling circus used to come to Los Angeles and set up not far from where I lived. There'd be this huge expanse of material spread across the parking lot. Elephants would be hitched up to pull several very tall poles into upright position underneath the material. Once all the poles were standing, the once flat, shapeless glob of material TOOK FORM and became a circus tent.

The Scenogram Box Scenes perform the same function as tent poles. They give shape and dimension to the story. A powerful point to bear in mind, though, is that merely because these unconnected points seem to steadily ascend, then peak, then unabatedly descend, the events of the story need not, indeed should not, follow such a predictable and unimaginative pattern. We're engineering a beautiful mountain road with cutbacks and unexpected views of lakes and condors, not a freeway past a lot of malls. (A method for executing this is discussed in Chapter 11 on scene cards.) Once again, though, it is *we* who must do the heavy lifting. We are both the elephants and the elves.

ACT THREE

Act Three is an act. Too often it feels like a mere afterthought, a third child, a whiskbroom sweeping up the broken glasses of Act Two and calling it a day. But it is, or it can be, a full act as long or nearly as long as Act One. Scenogrammically, it has three boxes (11–12), the **final large box being the CLIMAX** of the film.

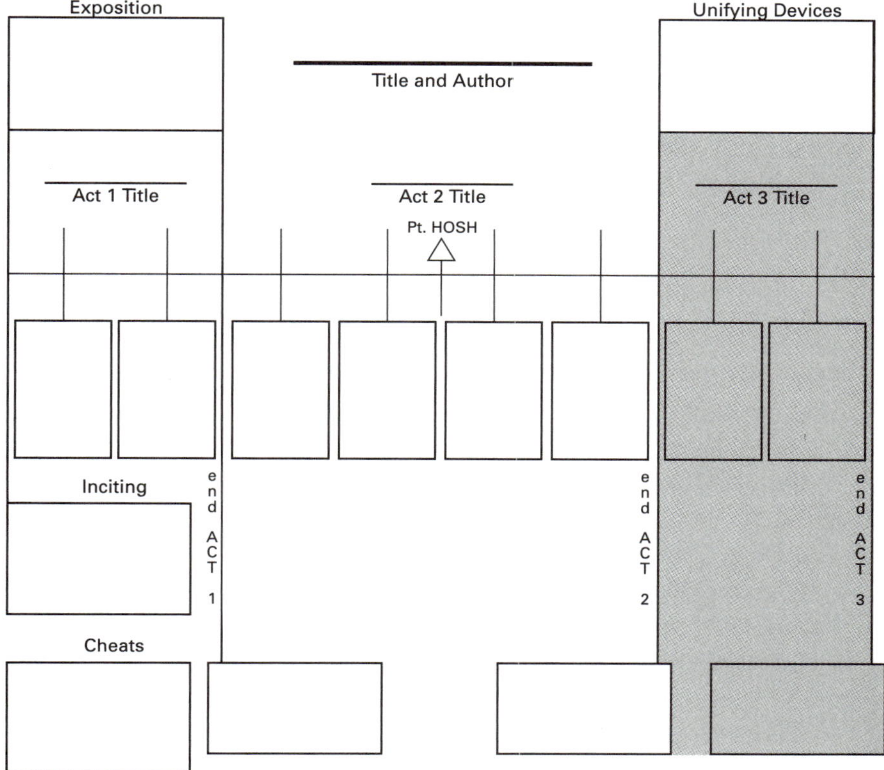

A very generic paradigm will have the protagonist dwelling emotionally with the consequences of the Act Two Big Gloom. (Tom Hanks mooning over rejecting Darryl Hannah because she's a mermaid, for example.) **The FIRST BOX** might be an action taken to alter that course, which comes after the emotion felt causes the character to reorder his or her priorities.

There will be obstacles, more external now, to the successful completion of that new choice. (The mermaid is dying. He decides he's crazy to reject her. He'll take her back. BUT she is under close guard. So there is a caper to effect her escape that is almost successful BUT the Army is alerted and gives chase, leading up to the CLIMAX.) Her time on earth is over, and she leaps into the water and waves goodbye to him. Will he join her? To do so he'll have to abandon his home, his life, everything he knows. He is plagued with indecision. At last, he repeats his childhood moment of falling (jumping in with both feet) and takes the long-delayed leap of faith. And there is almost always a dénouement, something after the climax. Here, it is a lovely underwater ballet between the two of them, with him able to breathe underwater with her.

CLIMAX

From the very first day we thought about our story, we have probably had a fairly good idea of how it was going to end. Even in stories that are conceived thematically, stories of "empowerment" or "coming of age," we have a sense of where the story is going, that it is being drawn toward a magnetic pole. Even if that pole is buried under the earth, it still exerts a force.

But as we approach our story's "geothermal north," that force must manifest in a real event or sequence of events. When we are writing our scripts and reach this point, we are so close to the finish line that we have the impulse to sprint home, and in doing so get rushed and careless and plunge narratively in too straight a line. But the greater danger occurs even before we begin to write the script, in the early stages of story development. Just as in human development, we are susceptible to different diseases at different stages of our lives; so the screenplay is susceptible to different ailments in each of its acts. In writing Act One we talked about the writer imposing too much information, cramming the character's knapsack too full of exposition, rather than letting information present itself as **a by-product of conflict**.

In Act Two there is the danger of bloatage, of losing sight of the pole star, of wandering aimlessly in the trackless desert. The malady that is site specific to Act Three is the **unearned ending**. You may not have applied this specific term to the syndrome, but you've felt it when it happens. **The protagonist is either unduly punished**

or (far more commonly) unduly rewarded. The ending has occurred because the writer ordained it so, rather than coming from the unpredictable but inevitable force of the character following his or her powerful desire. It comes out of theme, not out of story. It is imposed and not organic.

We all have an inner sense of justice tempered by our own level of mercy and sense of humor. A story's ending both derives from and appeals to that intricate harmonic resonance. As an audience, we want the protagonist's **ORDEAL TO EQUAL THE REWARD**.

You pay for what you get. Rocky goes the distance with the champ and gets the girl, BUT at the price of his one vanity—the busted nose that had never been broken. Hanks and the mermaid reunite in love, BUT he can no longer live on earth. In *Big*, he returns home to his childhood, BUT at the cost of losing the woman he fell in love with and all the trappings of adult success he had acquired.

As writers we can exercise gigantic emotional power with the effective use of this knowledge. The simplest and most direct way is by giving a film its earned "happy" ending. We want to be sure that we put the character through enough of an ordeal to earn it. As we said earlier, torture your protagonist. The girls in *Rabbit-Proof Fence* more than earned their arrival home. Rocky earned the girl.

But we can also use this tool indirectly. We can cause a desired emotional response by scrupulously *withholding* a character's well-earned happiness. In *Shakespeare in Love* (written by Tom Stoppard and Marc Norman), Will and Viola go through so much to be together. In the end they are not. They have earned their happiness, but life has withheld it from them. (And they knew it from the beginning. Inevitable but unpredictable.)

An even more extraordinary example is *Heavenly Creatures*. Throughout the story we are kept on an intimate level with the two girls even though they clubbed one of their mothers to death. In the end, that act registers NOT as a horrible, cruel, inhuman, barbaric act for which they should be severely punished, but as part of the ordeal that they went through to be together. Amazingly, when at the end of the story they are separated and will never see each other again, we do not feel they have gotten their just desserts; we feel awful for their lost friendship. Friendship came hard-earned in the multiple Academy Award-winning film *Moonlight*. (Screenplay by Barry Jenkins with story credit to Tarell Alvin McCraney). The film comes neatly structured for us in its three parts: "Little," "Chiron," and "Black," based on the name of the lead character at three ages. Little is bullied and tormented by his peers. In a poignant end to Act One, he leaves the home of JUAN, the one adult male figure who has sheltered him, instructed him and been a surrogate father to him, when Juan admits that he sells drugs and that Little's mother buys them.

In Act Two, now in middle school, Chiron (still called Little by those who torment him) is in worse shape than when he was younger. The male bonding in this act is with Kevin, his lone friend from his earlier childhood, who has taught him 'not to be soft.' They meet by chance at the beach and have a sexual encounter. Later, Kevin is forced into a game of "go down stay down" and under peer pressure, slugs his friend. It's a heart-wrenching scene. We know Kevin doesn't want to do it. Chiron comes into school the following day a changed boy. No longer soft. He breaks a chair over the head of the bully who provoked Kevin and who has long been Chiron's tormentor. For that he is arrested, taken to prison. Worse than that is the loss of his one friend.

This is the ORDEAL, which in ACT THREE resolves and claims its hard-earned REWARD. Ten years later, Little/Chiron/and now Black is out of prison and has become a replica of the one father figure in his life, Juan. Kevin calls him out of the blue. He too has served some time and now is a chef. He invites Black (now living in Atlanta) to visit him in Miami. Their meeting is awkward, fraught with memories that are both painful and persuasive. But their history and closeness prevail.

We can use this device politically. If a group fights for a righteous cause, makes sacrifices, and is still defeated by an indifferent or malevolent corporate or government power, we'll feel empathy for the sufferers. (See *Silkwood, The Insider* and *Mr. Smith Goes to Washington* to observe how different films manipulate this device.)

A common symptom of movies that are theme driven is that in the end, too much is acquired at too soft a price. These are called feel-good movies. And at the risk of sounding like a curmudgeon, these movies do not make me feel good. They make me feel cheated and manipulated, because they lie emotionally. At the end of *Arthur*, after making the difficult choice of the money or the girl, he was given *both*. That bothered me. It was the sacrifice of the one that earned him the other. When he was then given back what he had sacrificed, it felt too easy and reclaimed from me the good, righteous feeling I had had.

When Dr. Ford, at the end of *House of Games*, pilfers the lighter from the purse of the woman sitting next to her, that's a pretty damn subversive act. But we have been with her through *her* ordeal. And as she has learned to forgive herself, that forgiveness rubs off on us and we allow her this trespass and share in her feeling of smug accomplishment.

A film with one of the great, complex endings of all time is *The Bridge on the River Kwai*. It is a perfect illustration of the power of the Ordeal-Reward equation. In the first act, the primal struggle is between the Japanese commander of the POW camp and the captured British ranking officer over the issue of whether officers can be made to do manual labor.

Col. Saito's (Sessue Hayakawa) sadism is pitted against Col. Nicholson's (Alec Guinness) stubborn insistence on upholding the Geneva Convention. He resists threats, punishments, bribery and temptation, and is locked in a metal box and left out in the sun for days. But he endures and survives and prevails. His ordeal has earned the reward. The British take over the building of the bridge and no officers have to work. Nicholson wins Round One.

In Act Two the British take over, and miraculously Saito becomes the underdog. We realize that he is a mere functionary and he MUST have this bridge built to accommodate the railroad being built through the jungle. He is at the mercy of his prisoners, who know more about how to build the bridge. Suicide with honor is the impending choice. We are brought intimately into HIS ordeal.

Meanwhile, Shears (William Holden), a wisecracking, cynical American, escapes from the prison, and we experience the horrors of his near-death ordeal through the trackless jungle of Southeast Asia. When we discover him at a posh officers' club, getting R&R, tanned and healthy, cavorting with a nurse, we are pleased for him. He has earned this reward for the ordeal he endured.

But now comes Act Three. This is a film that decries the insanity of war. It does so through the story's events, not as a verbal polemic. And so, despite his recent ordeal and his deserved deliverance from it, Shears is compelled to accompany a force headed back into the jungle, to that very same locale, with the mission of blowing up the bridge. He fights against it with every fiber of his being but ultimately is forced to "volunteer."

Meanwhile, back at the bridge, an extraordinary thing has occurred. Through their shared ordeal of building a proper bridge, Saito and Nicholson have formed a kind of bond. They both want the bridge to endure. (The bridge is in itself an **objective correlative—an external manifestation of the inner lives of the characters.)**

In the amazing climax of the movie, Nicholson fights against his own allies to keep the bridge from being blown up. Only in the last moment does he understand the enormity of what he has done. From a writer's standpoint, we must look at this. The immediate goal of building the bridge has become so powerful that it overwhelms his longer-range morality and loyalty. Take that as a positive lesson of how to do the job right, of the power of a character's obsession and how it transcends every other cerebral, moral or thematic force.

This principle is behind our emotional involvement with Walter White in *Breaking Bad.* The things he DOES are horrendous, escalating from allowing the custodian at the school who helped him get needed equipment to be fired, to lying and murder and mayhem. He becomes a real Jekyll & Hyde—a devoted family man and a meth-making crazed megalomaniac. But he suffers. In addition to the many physical beatings he endures, the near-death experiences he endures, he has cancer. He lives under a death warrant. But that is far from the worst of it. He loses or has lost all the truly important things in his life. As a young man, he sold his part ownership in a startup business for pennies. That business has become worth billions, based on his contribution. He lost "the girl" to the same man he sold the business to. In the present tense of the story he is humiliated by one of his own high school students bringing his car to the car wash where Walter works to supplement his meager income. But the far more profound loss he endures is the love and respect of his son and his wife.

You have the force. Use it well. From beginning to end, bury your sword to the hilt in your characters' primal desires and keep the story rooted in what they do to fulfill them. Engineer the situations. Then get out of the way. Resist the urge to impose "meaning" on the scene. If the situations and characters have not done it, don't be seduced by the overblown rhetoric that accompanies film trailers. (Such-and-such character "MUST LEARN" whatever it is that must be learned.)

In a predominance of films and screenplays where the writer imposes meaning before desire and thereby injects the "MUST LEARN" moment, I often find it unconvincingly done. What often happens is this: The writer presents the character with an event by which wisdom and awareness might possibly be achieved. And that's it.

That's the easy part. People are faced every day with the possibilities of enlightenment, but they pass unnoticed. Merely presenting one to a character is no guarantee of its having any effect. Think about narcissists. They spend their lives looking at themselves but never see the most obvious thing—the thing that everyone else sees at one glance: that they are narcissists. There is no "MUST" about learning.

To get the full detonation of our third-act climax, we have to do more than present the possibility. We have to open the blocked channel into the character's psyche to let it all the way in. That's the hard part, and that is what an unearned ending skips but hopes to be rewarded for doing. It is what distinguishes sentimentality from true human feeling.

We are a nation that is getting used to the eviscerated taste of processed foods. It's affecting our taste in art and politics. A lot of the studio films inundate us with so much fake emotion, we're in danger of accepting that as the real taste, like the tomatolike substances we find in supermarkets. As writers, let's keep growing the tomatoes in the garden.

WRITERS GYM EXERCISES

Choose a film and watch it several times. Make a scene list of the important plot events. (Maybe there'll be 70.) With a yellow marker, highlight the 10 to 12 most major plot events.

CHAPTER 11

Snowplow, Scene Cards and Scenograms

The gift of natural storytelling, like the gift of natural beauty or athleticism, is unfairly and unevenly distributed. Studying Michael Jordan's moves on the basketball court will not help your game very much unless you also possess a 48-inch vertical leap. Michelle Pfeiffer's makeup tips will not produce the same results on a face not blessed with those cheekbones and that translucent skin.

The discussion that follows is for those of us who have talent but have to work at it. This chapter discusses three valuable tools for your writer's toolbox. We've already looked at the Scenogram, which in a way is almost the finished house. THE SNOWPLOW and creative uses of SCENE CARDS are two powerful means of getting there.

STEP ONE: THE SNOWPLOW, OR SNOWPLOWING

The result of this process will be the metaphorical delivery of all the building materials to the construction site. All the lumber and cement and steel and glass. Only in our case (I know you remember but I'm going to repeat it anyway), the **building blocks of story are EVENTS**. The things that happen.

WHAT YOU NEED:

1. Your favorite writing implements: pen and legal pad, computer, foolscap and quill. Whatever makes you happy.
2. Uninterrupted time. One hour minimum each time. (Usual number of repetitions required, 7 to 10.)
3. Commitment and stamina.
4. A reasonably good sense of your story's protagonist, what he or she wants, the story premise, and a few key moments along the way, including what happens at the very beginning and a pretty good target area of where it ends.

WHAT YOU DO:

Much like the exercise you were given to do in the last chapter (watch a film and write down the events of the plot), you are going to write down the events that happen in YOUR STORY. The significant difference, of course, is that the movie you watched was *already a movie*. People had already done the thing that you are now being asked to do. Which is the thing that you've been dreading, figuring out all the events that actually happen in the story.

You are going to start writing, and you are not going to stop for the next hour. You are going to write down sequentially what happens in your story. Start from what you know. What happens first? What happens right after that? You don't have to write out each scene in minute detail. Do it just like the list of plot events you wrote for your exercise movie. Describe only the basic narrative action defining the scene.

REMEMBER that you are not writing this for anyone else in the universe to see. You don't have to be neat or grammatical. You will not be judged on any aspect of it. Write no more than what you need to know about a scene that you already know. For instance, if the story begins with an elaborately orchestrated bank robbery where the protagonist gets wounded in the escape by an errant rock thrown up from the tire of a passing car, and if you know all of that, all you have to write is WOUNDED IN BANK ROBBERY.

Then keep going. Write what happens next: *Female cop believes she shot him. It's her first minute on the job. Robbers ditch wounded guy during escape.*

Maybe you knew this much and a few more events before you started. But now the momentum you acquired in writing these events down has gotten the mechanism of your creative imagination lubricated and humming. Maybe a thought hits you that you had not considered before: *Lady cop finds him. She can't turn him in. She brings him to her uncle's cabin in the woods.*

Whoa, you wonder. Who IS this "uncle"? He never existed until a nanosecond ago. Does a biography suddenly come to mind? Who is he to her? Don't do an elaborate genealogy now. Keep to what's happening. And **DO NOT JUDGE**. You are a snowplow. A bulldozer. Keep moving forward. If it is complete garbage, you can trash it later. Your reputation will be unscathed. No one will ever know that a trite word or idea escaped your pen. **KEEP WRITING**. *This event occurs. Then that. Then the next.* If you are at a loss, if your mind is blank for a moment, then write that. *Something happens next, but I don't know what. I'm stuck here and I don't know what happens next. I'm a failure. I'm going to give this up. I'm no good at it. Ooops, wait a minute. What if the "uncle" turns out to be the mother's boyfriend? And he's come back into her life now because—*

And you're back into a vein of story ore. Maybe there'll be gold in the vein and maybe not.

WRITE THEM ALL DOWN!

This is not a time to evaluate; this is a time for loading our wagons with huge chunks of ore from the rock pile, confident that later on we will find enough gold nuggets to justify the blisters and strained muscles from all the heavy lifting.

When new scenes occur in this manner, write as much about them as you can. In the earlier scenes that you already know, it is only necessary to make reference to the scene as you snowplow, without writing out a lot of details that will go into the scripted scene. But for the new stuff, write everything. The setting, if there is something striking about it. The surprises that happen in the scene and how you come to them. Snippets of dialogue if it's there for you.

Question: WHAT HAPPENS WHEN YOU POP OFF IN A DIRECTION YOU TRULY NEVER EXPECTED, AND IT FEELS WRONG?

Answer: Follow it. You never know. Make believe you are spelunking a cave. You find an interesting-looking side tunnel. Leave a marker, tie ropes to your waist for safety, leave breadcrumbs, but check it out. You may find something useful, a subplot you had not considered. Or not. Just like a snowplow or a bulldozer rams ahead, cutting a path as it does so, you are clearing a path through the terrain of your story. Continue until your brain is weary. Rest briefly. Have a cup of tea. Listen to some music. Take a short walk. Do some stretching exercises. Come back. See if any new ideas have arrived in that time. Get back into it, but write more slowly. This will be a tapering-off process. If you can, leave your character at an ambiguous crossroads, looking at a choice of two courses of action. If you've reached your time commitment, this would be a good place to end for now.

Snowplow Session 2:

Repeat the process. With these important provisos:

1. Do **not** start where you left off. START AT THE BEGINNING.
2. Do not look back at what you did the previous day.

This time you will be able to whiz through the early scenes for a longer period without encountering resistance. Again, for scenes you know well, just a line is enough to describe the essential action. Scenes that you invented yesterday can just be referenced, although it is likely you will come up with some new ideas about them today.

Write down everything new.

If today's path follows the exact same route as yesterday's, that's fine. Push through to the place you left off the previous day and keep going. You'll be amazed that there are new ideas waiting there for you. More often, though, there will be divergences, changes in sequence, different ideas on existing scenes. And whole new possible directions. And why not? You are a different writer today than you were yesterday. You've slept on it and given your wildly stimulated subconscious a night to foment and ferment.

If the new slant spins you off in a whole new direction, allow yourself to go there. Don't worry if it contradicts a story sequence you wrote previously. Maybe it will be a side tunnel that leads to a dead end. Or maybe it's a more interesting way to get to where you got yesterday. No harm is done in exploring. You may ultimately toss out 99 percent of these side tunnels, but that 1 percent might lead to a valuable gem you'd never otherwise have encountered.

A reminder: Sometime during this process, you might bog down. **DO NOT LET THAT STOP YOU.** Do not let the pen stop moving. You may have to back up to regain momentum. Rewrite the last two or three incidents that happened. Something new will come, I promise you. Keep pushing. Your verb is to move forward. To break all the way through to the end of your story. It's waiting for you if you can just get there. This is admittedly tedious work. You'd much rather be writing witty dialogue and incredibly cool breakthrough camera shots. Stay with it. If you need external stimulus and inspiration, rent another film in your genre. Watch it and make the narrative event list. Now go back to yours.

While your creative lobe has been doing all this work, the other side of your brain has been scanning the field in all directions like radar, looking for the act-ending events. **However many sessions** it takes you to break through the final barricade and get to the end is the exact right number of sessions it should take. When you have done that, do it one more time—beginning to end. And then once more.

You are now temporarily through with STEP ONE.

STEP TWO: SCENE CARDS

I love scene cards. I find them a far more useful and versatile tool than beat sheets or scene outlines. I use lined three-by-five cards. Some people prefer the four-by-sixes. In this case size doesn't matter. But buy the multicolored packs. You'll see why in a minute.

1. Extraction

If, metaphorically speaking, we've mined a few metric tons of ore with our bulldozing or snowplowing, we now have to find the nuggets in this gigantic pile of slag and pick them out. There are many events that presented themselves nearly every time you snowplowed. There are other events that might have happened only once or twice, but you love them and you know they are going to be part of your story.

Make a **separate scene card for every event.** Use the same criteria to define a narrative event as you did when you did your movie scene lists.

Using bold, dark ink, write in CAPS at the top of each card a brief statement of the DEFINING ACTION of that scene.

If we were doing scene cards for the opening of *Barton Fink*, the headings of the first few might be:

OPENING NIGHT STANDING OVATION

SARDI'S W/ PRODUCERS: PRETENTIOUS RESPONSE TO RAVES

REFUSES THEN ACCEPTS AGENT'S MOVIE OFFER

Each card's title captures the essence of the action. We will put more information on these cards very soon. For now, just label them with their Defining Action.

2. Sequence

Now put the cards in their chronological story order, first through last. Maybe you'll have 40, 50, 60 cards. Maybe more. If you have significantly fewer, you may not have enough bricks to build your house. You might want to look again at a film that is in your genre and make a narrative list of its scenes, and thereby get a sense of where your story is thin and where to look again (snowplow again) for more.

Tell your story to yourself. Tell it out loud to someone you really trust. Someone who you know will listen. And someone to whom *you* will listen. Is something missing from your story? The person does not owe you the obligation of a cure as long as the diagnosis is right.

Subplots and Secondary Characters

Look attentively at the structural life of the films in your genre that you have analyzed. Do they perchance have **one or two subplots** that your story does not? Are there secondary characters that play more important roles in those stories than in yours? Have you gotten your character into serious enough trouble? Have you built up character relationships strongly enough before you tear them asunder?

Snowplow through your story again from the point of view of a secondary character. Do it from the point of view of the **ANTAGONIST**.

For new sequences of scenes that arise, add the new scene cards.

Missing Sections

Perhaps you are aware that there's a big chunk of the story missing. Maybe it's a section that you'll have to research that's set in another city or another time period, and you don't know exactly what those scenes will be. But maybe you know they'll all be in one section of the story. Write on one big card **"MISSING SECTION."** Put it in its chronological place in the deck.

Layering

Using a regular pen, in the lined spaces of each card write down any great ideas that have come to you about the scene—**circumstances, lines of dialogue, a great twist that will make the scene pop. Any detail you don't want to forget.** Especially if it's a scene later on in the story that you won't be writing for several weeks. You think you'll never forget it, that it's too great an idea. You'd be amazed at the things you can forget. Write it down.

Very often while doing this, a WHOLE NEW SCENE OR SEQUENCE OF SCENES comes to mind which you realize are necessary to set up the scene you are now carding. MAKE CARDS FOR THEM NOW.

This process may seem like a drudgy, left-brained organizational task, but underneath it your right brain is humming. It's hyper-stimulated. It's working full time without your knowing it.

Count your cards again. Fifty to sixty is an average number. You may have more or less. Do not panic yet. Given all the variables for style and genre, movie scenes seem to average around two to three pages, closer to two than three. Some writing styles are much tauter. (*Eat Drink Man Woman* has nearly a hundred cards. But most of its scenes are very short. *Raise the Red Lantern* has far fewer scene cards. Stylistically, its scenes are longer.)

We are now going to make our first foray into building a structure.

3. Building Scene Card Columns

Clear off a table or a big area of floor. We're going to lay your scene cards out in eleven columns. Take the **card for the first scene** and place it at the top of where the first column will be. Decide now, if you have not already done so, what event is going to **end your first act**; your protagonist's Point Of No Return. Place that card at the bottom of where the third column will be.

You have now set up the starting place and destination of Act One. You have to get from the first card to the last in 20 to 30 pages.

Now lay the rest of your Act One cards out in those three columns. Each column of scene cards will equal (when written) approximately 10 PAGES OF SCREENPLAY (11 columns, 110 pages).

How many scene cards equal 10 script pages? Calculate your answer using this convenient formula: SP = 3x(3G/2) (eR+7)(12N). Just kidding.

Most scenes run two to three pages. So, four to five cards, depending on the length of the scenes, will usually translate into the neighborhood of about 10 pages. But it is not just a page count we're shooting for. The scene at the BOTTOM OF EACH COLUMN is that column's most important scene. It is the event that the others have been leading up to (setup, setup, setup, setup, PAYOFF!) It is a scene that will change the direction of the story, deepen it, take it to a different level.

[NB: THE BOTTOM CARD IN EACH COLUMN WILL BE THE SCENOGRAM BOX SCENE, THE FENCE-POST SCENE DISCUSSED IN THE PREVIOUS CHAPTER.]

Use a different-colored card (I use blue) for the scenes at the bottom of each column. There will be eleven of them, three in Act One (counting the act-ending scene), five in Act Two and three in Act Three. This is where scene cards are worth their weight in gold. How do your first three columns look? How many cards do you have in each column? Are they pretty evenly divided? Do you like the blue card scenes? Do they hold up the weight of the scenes that precede them? Are they narrative fence-posts?

If your answer is yes, then the blue card scenes become the *constants*, meaning that they are at the 10-page points, and the scenes leading up to them become the variables; meaning that if there are too many of them or two few, they will be the scenes to bear the adjustments.

Maybe one of your columns has 15 cards. If you wrote those scenes, even if some were very brief, you're looking at 20 pages or more. Just as an actor has to hit a mark in order to be in focus for the camera, a writer has to hit a mark, too. How do we get 20 potential pages of script into 10 pages? The situation calls for ingenuity and selectivity.

Ask yourself:

1. Does each scene need to be there? What is it accomplishing? Ask yourself the hard questions about every scene. Is it necessary to tell the story? If you can't get a resounding YES, then out it goes. You cannot be indulgent. Some scenes are there for just tone or mood. OUT. Tone and mood are important and certainly ought to be addressed in a scene, but to justify its place in the story, EVERY SCENE MUST ADVANCE PLOT AND CHARACTER. It must be an event. A brick. Evoke tone and mood through event.

2. Do two or more scenes accomplish the same objective? For instance, perhaps you have included two scenes to dramatize that a character is mean or generous. One scene is enough. Pick the better of the two. But don't throw the card away. Keep it in its own separate pile of beloved darlings whose

essences will be digested into other scenes that do get a resounding YES.

3. Can an event occur later or earlier?

4. Is there a more economical way of accomplishing an objective? Can it be dramatized in one vivid moment, rather than in a two-page dialogue scene?

You can also recognize that a column is too short. Two scenes between blue card scenes will not add up to 10 minutes, and the fence-post scene will not bear enough weight to justify its presence.

Is the solution to pad the scenes? To add extraneous dialogue? Gratuitous bits? Extra characters? Dance numbers? Judging by some films, you might presume that the answer to all of these questions is yes. But no.

Can scenes be reordered without sacrificing logic or momentum? Is there a subplot that is organic to the story that can be woven in? Are there scenes you know need to be here, but you don't know what they are yet?

For this kind of hands-on kneading, I find scene cards a perfect medium. The cards are more easily moved, shuffled, eliminated, combined. They are also visual proof of AXIOM No. 1: **EVENT IS THE BUILDING BLOCK OF STORY.**

ADDITIONAL USES OF SCENE CARDS

Placed holders: If you know there is a scene or scenes missing, you can put blank cards there as placeholders to denote the missing scenes.

Color-Coded Subplots

We see these most often in the mystery or thriller genre, when there is a love story set against the crime story. Many spec screenplays

I've read could use a good, interesting subplot to bolster a main story that grows thin. Like everything else, it must be organic to the whole, not merely tacked on like a back porch. They should each have their own three-act structure that plays inside the umbrella of the story's three-act structure. (*Eat Drink Man Woman*, for example, has five different stories running through it.)

In a script that has multiple storylines, I use a different-colored scene card for the events of each story. This gives you a visual picture of how well the subplots are woven into the fabric. If there is a cluster of scenes and then a long drought, you can see that clearly with your scene cards and make adjustments before you start writing.

RED CARD/GREEN CARD

The Scientific Method, if you remember your grade-school science classes, begins with a hypothesis and tries to *disprove* it. We need to put more of that kind of thinking into our story construction and try to wreck the premise so it does not come true too easily. Again, we get seduced by that heroic "Coming Attractions" voice intoning, "Now the hero must rise above himself and do the thing that could never be done."

If there were no defensive team on a football field, there would be no great excitement if a team were able to cross the goal line unopposed. In story construction, we instinctively take on the role of the offensive coach. But as writers, we must also be the defensive coach. We must implant story events that *prevent and deter the hero's success.* Let us NOT construct a trail of small successes leading inevitably to the larger one and call that a plot.

ADRENALINE EXERCISES

Right now, make a separate GREEN CARD for every important thing your protagonist accomplishes. When you have done that, for each of those green card events, create a RED CARD, an event that WILL ABSOLUTELY PREVENT the event on the green card from being accomplished.

Place these RED CARDS into your scene card array. You have created a problem for yourself. How can that green card occur when you have made it difficult or improbable? If you don't know the answer right away, that's good. Neither will your audience.

An excellent example of the effective use of this technique is *Moonlight*, which we have just discussed. All the terribly destructive, drug addled, emotionally violent scenes with Chiron's mother would be RED CARD SCENES. Every single one of them until the end when he visits her in rehab.

There's also a particularly effective illustration of this technique in *The Godfather*. (Every scene in that screenplay is a great illustration of more things than I know.) We're in the middle of Act One. *The writer* knows that Michael will be the character who will ultimately kill Sollazzo and the police captain. But…**Red Card:** When he is first proposed, the idea is ridiculed. **Green Card:** Then, once he is selected, Sonny and his crew want to find out in advance where the meeting will take place so they can stash a gun there for Michael to use. **Red Card:** But their efforts are fruitless. And as the time for Michael to be picked up draws nigh, they still have not discovered where the meeting will take place. **Green Card:** They find out. One of their guys goes to hide a gun there. **Red Card:** Michael is picked up and instead of driving to the Bronx, where that restaurant is, they go over the bridge to Jersey. **Green Card:** They were doing that to avoid being followed and eventually arrive at the right place. **Red Card:** When Michael goes to the bathroom he can't find the gun. **Green Card:** He finds it. **Red Card:** When he comes back to the table, he does not follow the plan that was laid out for him. He was not supposed to say a word but instead he talks with them some more. It's a psychological red card. We're thinking, *Oh God, does he have the nerve to go through with it?* **Green Card:** He pulls the trigger and kills them. Just as the writer knew all along that he would. But until it happens, the audience is in doubt and filled with anxiety.

This is a great lesson in how external events generate emotion. Practically every moment in that script gives us a lesson about good writing. In this particular sequence, we can see demonstrated the absolute essence of great screenwriting, wherein we are given access to the inner life of the character through external events. All these back-and-forth plot gestures generate fear on our part that Michael will be unable to do the deed. If he does not, the circumstances tell us that he will very likely be killed himself. It is two against one. He has never done this sort of thing. He is an untested commodity. We know for damn sure that his adversaries are well tested. As a result, Michael is the underdog. *And we want him to perform cold-blooded murder!*

Consider the enormity of that statement. This moment is a perfect microcosm of what writers can do when we are in control of our craft. We can make an audience root for a character to murder two people.

But let's get back to the big picture: your array of scene cards representing the three-act structure of your screenplay. How close are you to beginning to write scenes? Let's look again at your scene cards. Is your first act fully plotted? Are your blue card scenes in place? Is each blue card scene about the protagonist? It should be. Is each column fairly even? Do you have fewer than three missing scenes? Do you know your exposition scene and inciting incident? Do you absolutely know the end of Act Two? Do you have your PT. HOSH? Do you have all or nearly all of your blue card scenes for Act Two? Do you have at least a few cards in each of your Act Two columns? Do you have a good idea of the climax and how the movie is going to end?

If your choices stand sturdily under scrutiny, if they feel like sturdy floorboards that bear the weight of jumping, then I would give you my blessing to start writing. But of course you've started two weeks ago. And 90 percent of what you have written will have to be rewritten. But so what? I like your enthusiasm.

Once you have written your first act (which we hope has come out to within five to ten pages of the expected page count), this is a perfect time to snowplow your way through Act Two. In writing the first act, perhaps some new scenes came up. Perhaps you found that you could shorthand others into a fragment of the space originally allotted to them. Characters revealed themselves to you in ways that surprised you and that resulted in some slight alterations of scenes.

You have elements of the story now that you did not have when you did your first snowplow. Do it the same way. Get all the way through it several times, reordering or recasting scene cards as necessary. And stop grumbling. If you want to know real drudgery, install carpets or drive a school bus in Michigan.

STEP THREE: USES OF THE SCENOGRAM

Each of the 11 Scenogram Boxes (below the plot line) coincides with the bottom (blue card) scene of each of your 11 columns of index cards.

It's a compression of all the significant information, and it can be easily taped up at your workstation. It allows you to see how each act can be thought of as a full story (with a title!), and how each of the "blue card" scenes is the end of an act within that story. (Some people think of Act Two as two acts, with the dividing line at PT. HOSH.)

Fill in your 13 Scenogram Box Scenes. If every event is about the protagonist (as they should be), then by reading all 13 scenes—the 11 blue card scenes plus the exposition and Inciting Event—you should have the basic story of the plot. It is an excellent litmus test. Do the cards tell the story? If not, it is time to make adjustments.

Notice that each act has a title. Coherent stories have inherent organizing principles of structure. The **UNIFYING DEVICES BOX** is to make note of events, objects and/or phrases that are repeated several times throughout the story with the intent of creating a coherent whole, a woven tapestry. This and the **CHEATS BOX** are remnants of the Scenogram's original use as an analytic tool.

The Cheats Box

Often in films there are plot moves that enrage us, things done for the writer's convenience that a character would surely NEVER do. Why does the young woman go down to the basement wearing only her negligee? How could the detective have guessed at that clue? How could that bullet kill three people? The CHEATS Box is a venue to vent your spleen against lazy writing. (It is the one part of the Scenogram *not* to be emulated in your own work.) But it's a good place to dump ideas for scenes when you know you are being lazy.

Like everything else, cheats are subjective. What one person thinks is a cheat, the rest of the world might adore and think brilliant. For example, I know that not a lot of people were irked, as I was in watching *E.T.*, that these creatures, who have come across the galaxy and have technology so far advanced, are so terrified by some farmers with rakes and pitchforks that they leave one of their own behind.

Unifying Devices

There was a lovely example of the unifying device in the Oscar-winning foreign film *Nowhere in Africa*. The setting is 1938. A mother and daughter from a German-Jewish upper-middle-class family leave Germany to join the husband-father, who has already emigrated to a desolate little farm somewhere outside of Nairobi. In a letter he tells his wife that things are rough, to buy a refrigerator and not to bother bringing any of their fine china. Instead, she arrives with no refrigerator, a trunkful of their elegant table settings and most galling of all, she has spent nearly all their money on a formal gown! The husband is appalled. That dress IS who she is at this moment (a spoiled, narcissistic, blind-to-the-world daughter of privilege). Using an exterior object to represent the interior of a character is something I (borrowing from T. S. Eliot) call an **Objective Correlative**. More on this later.

The dress has a life of its own woven through the story. At this moment, it is a wedge between their souls. And indeed, for a good part of the film there is a fierce, cold wall around the wife, separating them. Most of his love is directed toward his precocious 9-year-old daughter (and teller of the story). The dress is carefully folded and put away.

The story spans several years, and when the daughter, Regine, is a young adolescent, a scene takes place around that dress. Jettel (her mother) tells Regine the story of buying the dress and then eating cheesecake, and that when Regine's father saw it he nearly sent her back to Germany. Regine is fascinated to learn that her mother has never worn the dress. She becomes the first person to wear it. The putting-on of that dress, with all its narrative and metaphorical subtext, means so many things—mythologically, psychologically, metaphorically, sexually. In the emotional language of cinema, it is not a mere decorative costume idea. It contains the essence of the inner life of the story.

Later that night, Regine takes her mother to a secret tribal ritual. From childhood, Regine has befriended the nearby tribal people, has been accepted by them, has learned their language. (In contrast, when the mother first arrived, she insisted that the house servant learn German!) By now, experience has changed the mother. She speaks the language. She now runs the farm she once despised. With her husband away in the Army, she has become a hard-working, independent woman. She goes to the sacrificial ceremony with her daughter. This time she is wearing the dress, which looks much better on her; her daughter has not yet grown into it. She is completely comfortable when a little boy, fascinated by the jewels on the dress, fingers them. That dress tells us who she is now.

And who decided that she would wear it on this occasion? Lower your hand if you guessed the costume designer. It was the writer of the screenplay (based on Stephanie Zweig's book), Caroline Link.

There are several effective unifying devices in Anthony Minghella's *Truly Madly Deeply*. If you are among those who have not seen it, you must remedy that situation immediately. In the film, you will notice the strategically recurrent use of Spanish, of clouds, of rats, of the cello, of hot and cold. You might ask, isn't there "air" in every scene? Why isn't that a unifying device? That is an excellent question.

Unifying is an active verb. Merely because something is there doesn't mean it has any effect. Unifying devices express themselves directly and significantly in the plot and characters. They accrue meaning through repetition, through modulation and reversal, in their presence and in their absence.

In Mamet's *House of Games*, another writing primer, there are several recurring unifying devices. There is **"the tell."** The story is about gamblers and con artists, so it properly uses their argot. A "tell" is a physical gesture that gives away something about what a character is thinking. Three very important tells are used in the story, one in each act. As the story progresses, their narrative and emotional importance builds. Another nice example in the same film: In Act One, Mike the con man has Dr. Ford pretending to be his girlfriend; in Act Two, she's his wife and lover and, finally, his whore. Money is also used to weave a texture. One of Dr. Ford's patients owes money to the Mob. His marker is for $800. That is what draws her into the gamblers' world. In a poker game, while she is gambler Mike's girlfriend, the pot of the hand quite casually turns out to be...$800. By the end of the movie, the con artists have bilked Dr. Ford out of **$80,000.** A hundredfold increase.

I can assure you that the selection of the numbers was no accident. Mamet is constantly aware of numbers. The locker in the airport at the climax of the film where she shoots and kills Mike is No. 187. In the California penal code, 187 is the code for murder. There are other physical objects used this way as well. In an early scene with her mentor, Dr. Ford admires her gold lighter. "It's old and it's heavy. It feels like something someone gave to you." All through the film, she lights her cigarettes with matches. At the very end, after she has forgiven herself for the crimes she has committed during the film and those implied from her early life, she sits alongside a well-dressed woman at an elegant restaurant and steals her lighter. [NB: This gesture is in unity with Mike's advice to her earlier to steal something, to take something from every experience.]

The issue of forgiveness also runs strategically throughout the story. When we think about unifying devices, we want to look for not the mere repetition of things, but how they are USED to create a tapestry. A subtle refrain.

Here are a couple of examples of completed Scenograms.

The Ackerman Scenogram

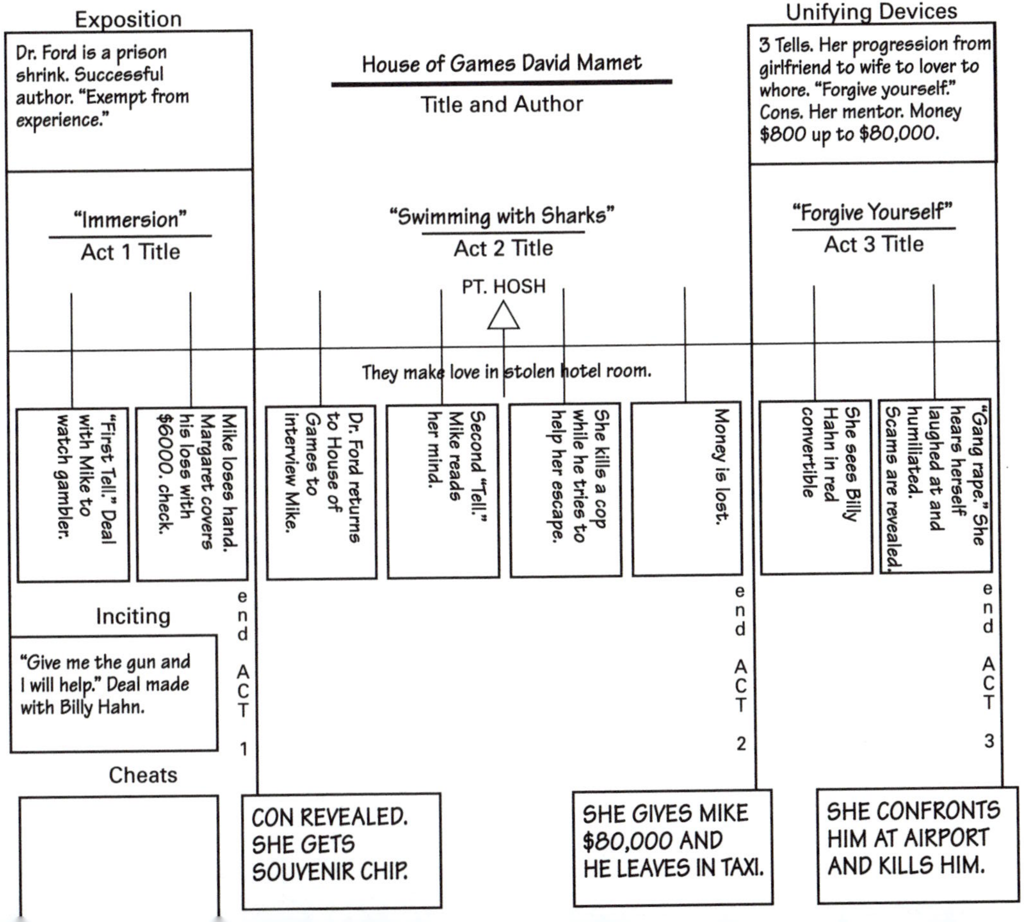

Exposition

Dr. Ford is a prison shrink. Successful author. "Exempt from experience."

House of Games David Mamet

Title and Author

Unifying Devices

3 Tells. Her progression from girlfriend to wife to lover to whore. "Forgive yourself." Cons. Her mentor. Money $800 up to $80,000.

"Immersion"

Act 1 Title

"Swimming with Sharks"

Act 2 Title

"Forgive Yourself"

Act 3 Title

PT. HOSH

They make love in stolen hotel room.

"First Tell." Deal with Mike to watch gambler.

Mike loses hand. Margaret covers his loss with $6000. check.

end ACT 1

Dr. Ford returns to House of Games to interview Mike.

Second "Tell." Mike reads her mind.

She kills a cop while he tries to help her escape.

Money is lost.

end ACT 2

She sees Billy Hahn in red convertible

"Gang rape." She hears herself laughed at and humiliated. Scams are revealed.

end ACT 3

Inciting

"Give me the gun and I will help." Deal made with Billy Hahn.

Cheats

CON REVEALED. SHE GETS SOUVENIR CHIP.

SHE GIVES MIKE $80,000 AND HE LEAVES IN TAXI.

SHE CONFRONTS HIM AT AIRPORT AND KILLS HIM.

The Ackerman Scenogram

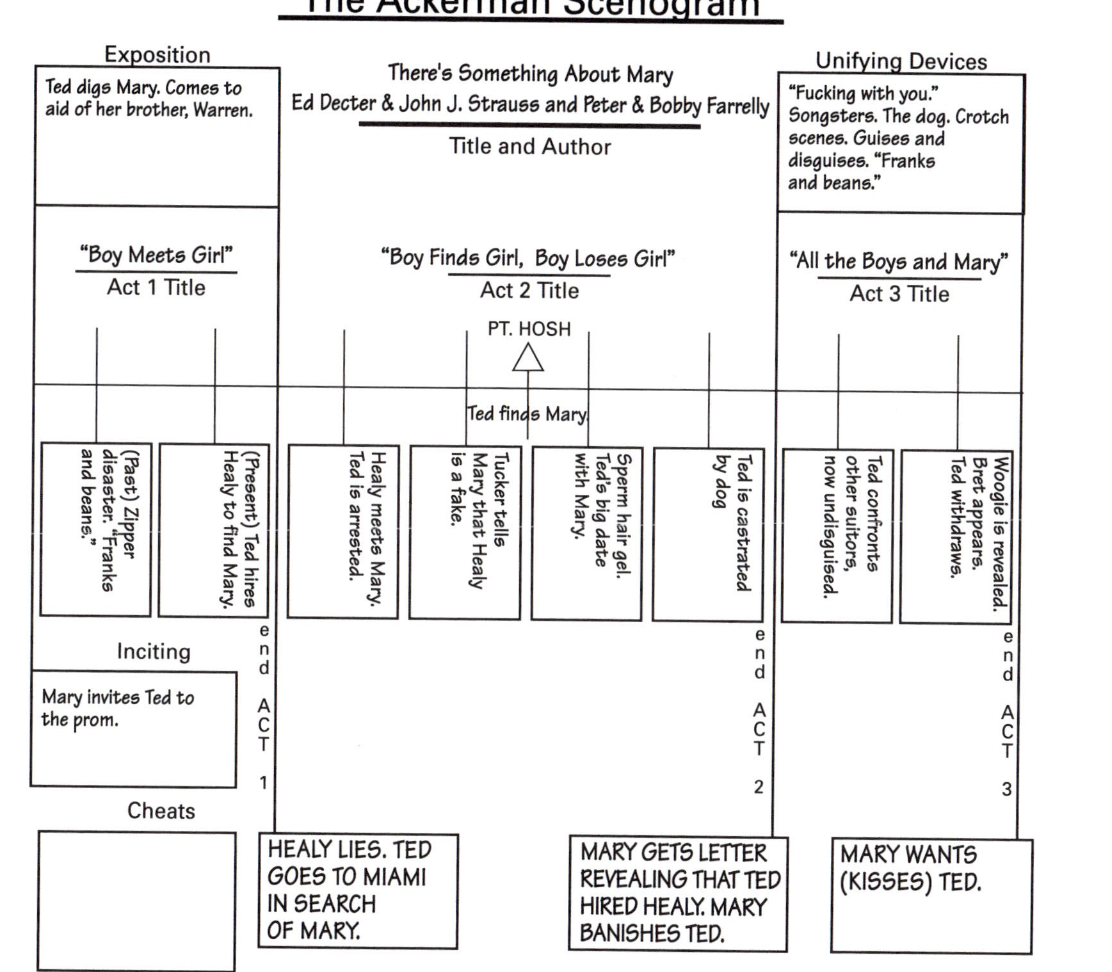

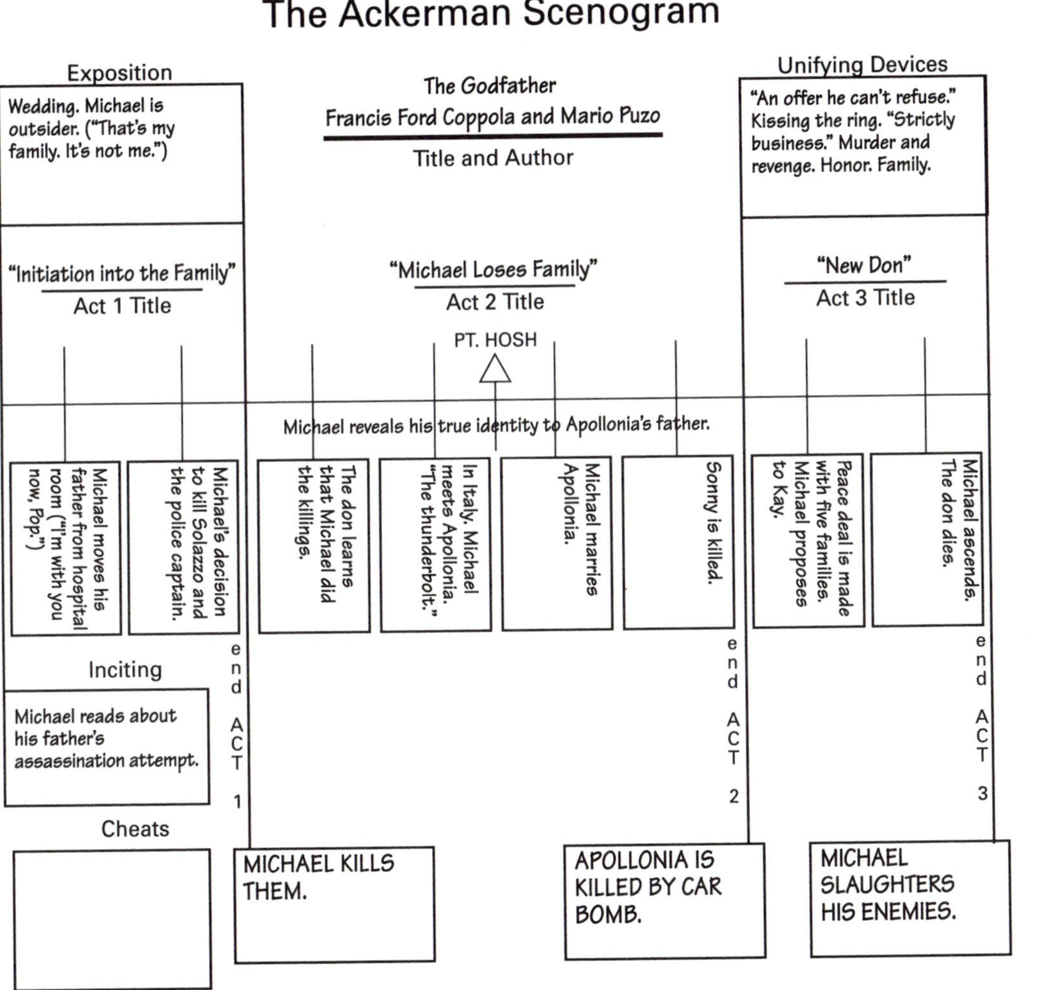
The Ackerman Scenogram
Exposition
Wedding. Michael is outsider. ("That's my family. It's not me.")
The Godfather
Francis Ford Coppola and Mario Puzo
Title and Author
Unifying Devices
"An offer he can't refuse." Kissing the ring. "Strictly business." Murder and revenge. Honor. Family.
"Initiation into the Family"
Act 1 Title
"Michael Loses Family"
Act 2 Title
"New Don"
Act 3 Title
PT. HOSH
Michael reveals his true identity to Apollonia's father.
Michael moves his father from hospital room ("I'm with you now, Pop.")
Michael's decision to kill Solazzo and the police captain.
The don learns that Michael did the killings.
In Italy. Michael meets Apollonia. "The thunderbolt."
Michael marries Apollonia.
Sonny is killed.
Peace deal is made with five families. Michael proposes to Kay.
Michael ascends. The don dies.
Inciting
Michael reads about his father's assassination attempt.
end ACT 1
end ACT 2
end ACT 3
Cheats
MICHAEL KILLS THEM.
APOLLONIA IS KILLED BY CAR BOMB.
MICHAEL SLAUGHTERS HIS ENEMIES.

WRITERS GYM EXERCISES

The five key scenes in Act One of *Heaven Can Wait*: **Exposition**—He's the star quarterback of the Rams rehabbing his injured leg. (It's also his birthday...propitious event.) **Inciting Event**—He's going to start the next game. **Blue Card 1**—He gets hit by a truck and dies. **Blue Card 2**—Heaven made a mistake. He'll be put back. But his body has been cremated. **Act End**—He becomes Leo Farnsworth.

Go back over the films you've analyzed and scene-listed. Break them into acts. Give the acts a title.

The Poster. You've seen them in the display cases at movie theaters. You've seen the full-page ads in your Sunday paper. There is artwork, there is a Madison Avenue ad-line.

Make one for your movie. Take this assignment seriously. It is another way of forcing you to focus on what your story is. What is the central visual image? What makes it appealing to people in a city where you are not yet known or loved? What do you find compelling and magnetic about this story? How will you seduce others into thinking the same?

Interlogue

By Dave Johnson

It's a beautiful day in Los Angeles on March 14th, 2017. I'm driving through Hollywood on my way to meet my longtime professor and good friend, Hal Ackerman. He's picked the location for lunch, the iconic Musso & Frank Grill, Hollywood's oldest restaurant. Walking through the front doors of this 1919 establishment is like time traveling back to the golden age of cinema. This is where Charlie Chaplin challenged John Barrymore to a horse race down Hollywood Blvd. Some say a drunken Douglas Fairbanks was responsible for saddling up their mounts. True story? I don't know, but it's a good tale, and that's what Hollywood is built on. What I do know is, sitting down in one of the wood-paneled booths at Musso & Frank's, and drinking the world's driest martini for lunch, makes you feel like a "made man." Which is fitting, because I see myself as a "made man." That is, if you consider working as a professional screenwriter for the last 15 years something to hang your hat on. I do. I've worked too hard not to. The man I'm about to meet for lunch knows this. He should, because he's the one who "made" me.

Hal has been a guiding voice in my career since the first day I walked into his screenwriting course at UCLA twenty years ago. It's important to note I'm one of those rare intellects with not one college degree in screenwriting, but two. Take that, parents and high school counselors! It should go without saying, I've read a lot of screenwriting books throughout my education and career. Yet, when I look at my bookshelf at this very moment, there's only ONE screenwriting book present, the one in your possession right now. The others took the long, sad ride to Goodwill as I slowly lost the need for them. Not this book. This book stays. I can't let this book go. There's just too damn much to learn from it. Which brings me to a question that I'm often asked.

Can screenwriting really be taught? My short answer is: I have no idea. Here's what I do know. If you solemnly swear that in every screenplay you write, every scene will have woven into its architecture the element of CONFLICT, you'll be on your way to becoming a better writer. Hal asks all of his students to make this pledge, and insists they sign a "Conflict Agreement." He will ask the same of you in his book. I know, that's a lot of pressure! Don't worry, Hal will show you just how it's done. The process is so simple and obvious it's hard as hell. The good news is, if you're willing to honor Hal's agreement, you will be taught screenwriting whether you know it or not. In fact, why are you still wasting your time reading this foreword? Hal's doing one-armed push-ups in the parking lot while eagerly awaiting your arrival. There's room in his Writers Gym for everyone. He's whipped me into shape, and countless more who have not only gone on to tell their stories, but sell their stories. Won't you join?

Dave Johnson has developed and sold feature films to Disney, 20th Century Fox, Paramount Studios, New Regency, Universal Studios, Fox Animation, Sony Animation and Fox 2000. The War with Grandpa *(starring Robert De Niro, Uma Thurman and Christopher Walkin) has just wrapped production.*

PART THREE

The Small Picture:
Scene Writing

CHAPTER 12

Dancing the Wadoogee

I require all my students to sign the legally binding document below and to display it prominently in their workspace. I urge you to do the same. (But display it in your workspace, not theirs.)

CONFLICT AGREEMENT

I solemnly swear that in every screenplay I write, every scene will have woven into its architecture the element of CONFLICT.

____________________________ __________

Screenwriter Date

The directive to have conflict in every scene seems simple and obvious. The operative word here is seems. In practice, this directive disappears like good judgment on a bad weekend. There may be certain circumstances where you may believe conflict is not necessary, and for that eventuality, please refer to the following Waiver of Conflict application:

APPLICATION FOR WAIVER OF CONFLICT

I believe that the scene detailed below does not need conflict, and therefore I am requesting a temporary injunction.

Screenplay TITLE: ______________________________

Scenes from page ______ thru page ______

Reasons that the scene will work better without conflict:
(Use blank paper as needed)

Approved (FIVE SIGNATURES REQUIRED):

Present Instructor ______________________________

Head of Writing Division ______________________________

Department Chair ______________________________

Associate Dean ______________________________

President of Writers Guild ______________________________

The notion that every scene should have conflict is not some arbitrary dictum. It arises from the basic tenet that we want our scenes to come alive. The proposition at work is HOW DO WE MAKE EVERY SCENE WE WRITE COME ALIVE?

Let's begin with the obvious axiom that every scene must have a definite reason for its inclusion in your screenplay. In broad terms, it must move the story forward and expand character. As true as this axiom is, it may not be specific enough to shed a guiding light on a particular scene of yours. If you told a child that to be healthy he had to eat right, he might sincerely wish to follow that good advice but not be equipped with enough understanding of nutrition to do so. Or suppose you were captured by alien beings and, under penalty of death if you failed, commanded to bring one of them sexual pleasure. Would you know where to touch? What would make a Klugfreagel feel good? You'd want to know as much as possible about its physiology and erogenous zones, its architecture and the functions of all of its parts. Dare you pursue writing a scene with any less accurate a roadmap of how to bring it to its climax?

Scenes are the building blocks of story. If a story is a chimney or a brick wall, then scenes are the individual bricks. As such, they must have the structural integrity to support not only their own weight, but also the weight of scenes that are built on them. Most first drafts of scenes crumble under their own weight. They are born bad, with flawed DNA, predestined to be stale or talky, out of focus, overwritten, misshapen, an overnight valise crammed with eight days' worth of underwear, shirtsleeves and pant legs sticking out.

We are going to examine why that is true and apply some remedies and preventions. In order to do that, we must again think about function. From the overview of the story, within the Big Picture, the function of a scene is to move the story forward and expand our appreciation of character. Just as within the context of the human body, the function of the heart is to pump blood. But that statement offers no insight into how the internal mechanism of the heart functions. The following discussion describes how the internal mechanism of a scene works and how you can make it an organ capable of performing its narrative function.

WHAT A SCENE IS NOT

A scene has one purpose, one sole justification for its existence. That purpose is not to create mood, not to establish tone, not to foreshadow, not to lay in symbolism, not to be the writer's pulpit. (Though any and all of these may legitimately occur as incidental or intended side effects of the scene's primary function.)

A scene does not gain entry into the exclusive *CLUB 75* (the number of scenes that make up the entire exclusive membership of your screenplay) merely because it accurately depicts something that happened in life, even in your life. A scene is not a repository for the characters talking about an issue that fascinates the writer or about all the topics that may happen to come up while they're chatting. A scene is not there merely to *tell* or even to *show* something about the character.

Ultimately, even the *content* of a scene ought not to be merely what the writer ordains, though very often we force it to that purpose, bending the characters' will and forcing them into words and deeds that are inconsistent with their psychologies because we "need" things to be done and said. In this practice, we are guilty of the most heinous character abuse.

So what IS a scene? What makes it hale and healthy? Inevitable and unpredictable? Functional and aesthetic? Off the nose and on the money? Original and necessary?

GOLDEN GUIDING SCENE-WRITING PRINCIPLE #1:

Every scene you ever write is an arena for the characters doing

everything in their power to get what they most want in that moment.

If you build the arena effectively and if the combatants within the ropes are well matched, then everything that you want to happen in the scene (Writer's Objective) will evolve organically out of what the CHARACTERS want (Character Objective). That is what you aspire to.

If we were to peer through an electron microscope at the cellular structure of a scene, this is the paradigm we would see:

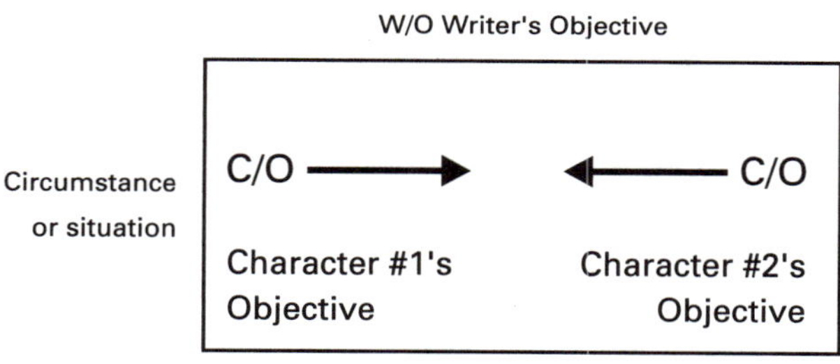

There are three terms that I give to the cellular components of a scene. By examining how each contributes to the life of the scene, we will hone our abilities to create the scene's life force, learn how to recognize the symptoms of its absence, how to diagnosis the cause of its absence, and how to address those causes. The three terms are: **Writer's Objective, Character Objective and Scene Circumstances.**

THE WRITER'S OBJECTIVE

As the term implies, this is why the scene exists; the narrative and emotional tasks that the writer has written (or conceived) the scene to accomplish. I like to represent this objective as two braided strands of DNA.

E1 for EVENT. Something occurs.

E2 for EMOTION. We feel a certain way in response to it.

Let's follow a simple chain of events as an example of this double helix.

1. EVENT: An ardent lover pours his heart out to his beloved and is cruelly rejected. 1A. EMOTION: We feel pathos for him.

2. EVENT: He goes up to the next girl he sees on the street and says the exact same thing to her as he said to the first girl. 2A. EMOTION: The writer has now made us see him as an insincere putz and we're glad Girl #1 rejected him.

3. EVENT: Girl #1 has a change of heart and apologizes for misjudging him. 3A. EMOTION: Hmmm. How *do* we feel about that? Maybe we're happy for him. Maybe we're wary on her behalf. It depends on many variables.

4. EVENT: She sends him on a dangerous mission. 4A. EMOTION: Now how do we feel? Has he become an underdog again? Are we rooting for him? Has the danger outweighed the "crime"?

If you were in the audience, who would you be rooting for or be fearful of? Who would have your sympathy? Do you suspect that Girl #1 is using him? Who's the cat and who's the mouse in your scenario? The answer depends on the sum total of how all the previous scenes were executed. How did the girl win him back in Scene #3? Had she had a change of heart? Or an ulterior motive? Did she see something unexpected in him, or did she reveal a previously hidden aspect of her own character? Is he naïve? Skeptical? Too needy? Does he resist? Whose side are we being manipulated into taking?

If 500 people are reading this page right now and were to write Scene #3, there would be 500 different scenes.

ADRENALINE EXERCISE: WRITE SCENE #3

Invent who the characters are. Embellish the circumstances that lead up to this moment to fit you. Imagine how Scene #1 went down. Be sure in your mind of why she is trying to get him back. Now write it. Really. Close this book. Write the scene.

What was your thought process as you conceived the scene? What idea came to you first? Dialogue? Action? Setting? A punchline? Which character did you want the audience to root for? What did you do in the scene to help effect that rooting interest? Did you do anything at all? Was it something you considered? If you did not think about BOTH strands of DNA (Event/Emotion), go back and write the scene again.

CHARACTER OBJECTIVE

Presuming that we now have a good idea about what we want the scene to accomplish, we now approach the most critical application of screenwriting technique. This is the RUMPELSTILTSKIN moment, where straw gets spun into gold. In scene-writing terms, it is the moment where the WRITER'S OBJECTIVE must be sublimated into CHARACTER OBJECTIVES. But instead, too often we behave like parents who force their kid into medical school because *they* want their kid to be a doctor. In writing terms, we allow our own needs for the scene to be accomplished without regard to character. We see this occurring most blatantly in opening scenes, where the narrative objective of the scene is to convey information to the audience. And a character will projectile-vomit chunks of predigested information, presumably at another character, but really over that character's shoulder and right at the audience.

In the paradigm that follows, the diagram represents exactly what we DON'T want to do. It shows the Writer's Objective skirting the Character Objectives, accomplishing the objective but out of character. It feels like the character is just blurting to the audience.

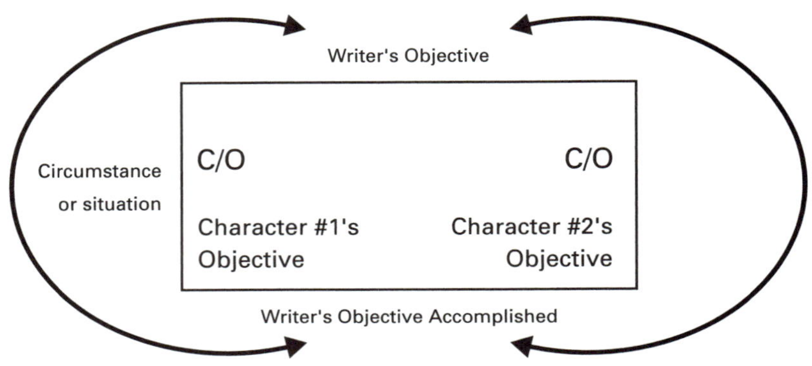

All the genetic material for the EMOTION strand of the scene's DNA resides inside the box. If the scene diverts around the box, the narrative task will be accomplished, but the emotional component will not be engaged and no one will give a damn. Have you ever noticed yourself feeling that way while watching a movie? Now you know why. And more importantly, you know how to avoid doing it.

The more difficult path, but the path that will open for you the possibility of becoming a better writer, is **through the box.**

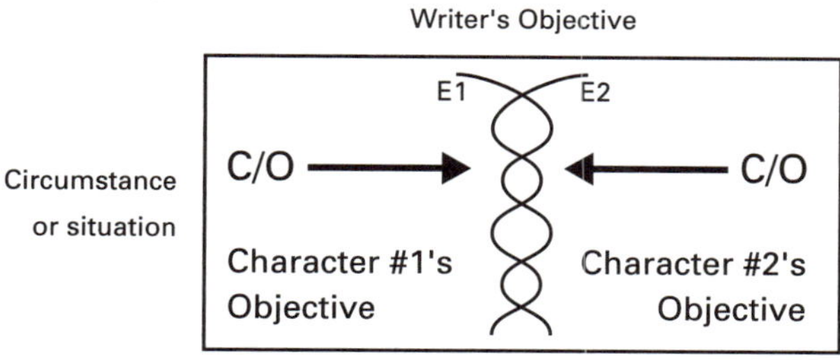

Inside the box are the materials for the one true energy source of every scene. And that single source, like the sun to our solar system, is the sole origin of heat and light. It is DESIRE.

Too often, writers mistakenly place a planet in the center: Theme. Meaning. Information. Mood. Tone. Foreshadow. Like Jupiter, Saturn, Neptune, these are formidable objects. But there is only one sun. In both the Big Picture (story) and the Small Picture (scenes), **DESIRE is the engine.** The term I use to designate the manifestation of desire in each individual scene is Character Objective.

The definition is simple. It is the thing that the character most wants in the present tense moment of the scene. But among the hundreds of gifted writers with whom I have worked over the years, the consistent execution of this principle is by far the most difficult to grasp.

Think of the Character Objective as the point of an arrowhead. The arrowhead is designed that way to afford the deepest penetration. In order to hone a Character Objective into an arrowhead, it must possess certain criteria. **It must be URGENT, IMMEDIATE, NECESSARY and SPECIFIC.** It must be the most important thing in the universe to that character in that moment.

How might a writer convey the importance of an event to a character? One way is that the character might proclaim it to be true. ("This is the most important thing in my life.") But some characters' proclamations may not be true. And even if the words are sincere, talk is easy. A vow, a pledge has no weight until it manifests in deeds. Among the most powerful dramatic gestures that writers possess is giving a character CHOICE. Give a character a choice between two "either/ors" so that a decision has to be made. (His wife says one thing, his mother says something else. Who rules?)

I've dubbed this the "Call Waiting" principle and will talk more about it later on.

SCENE CIRCUMSTANCES

The logistics of a scene play a significant role in conveying a sense of urgency. If a character is hanging from the hands of Big Ben, we get a pretty focused sense of urgency. That moment in *Shanghai Knights* also demonstrates another principle: The difference between immediate character objectives and longer range "pole stars." In that film, the dangling heroes have a long-range mission to catch the bad guys and get the jewel back. But in this absolute present tense of that scene, the objective is to get off those clock hands alive.

Similarly, a character may have the long-range objective of "living a happy life" or "getting the guy or the girl," curing Ebola, going the distance with the champ or finding the end of the rabbit-proof fence. But these are all long-range super-objectives. In an individual scene, the objective might be to parallel park or get a waiter's attention. To purchase a ticket, start a car, stop a flood, mow the lawn, lower the price of a used car. No doubt you notice that these objectives are all expressed as active verbs. Do's or Don'ts. A character objective is about what a character wants, needs and desires enough to ACT on right NOW.

The other tricky differentiation is between the character's actual objective in the scene, *which will remain constant*, and the strategies for accomplishing that objective, which also may be constant but more likely will vary.

If you remember your high school chemistry (as I do, thanks to the one great teacher I ever had, Max Boysen), an atom has a nucleus and rings of electrons in orbit around it. The character objective is the nucleus of every scene. The tactics or strategies—and every succeeding attempt the character makes—are the rings of electrons.

The schematic of that would be:

> CHARACTER WANTS SOMETHING (Objective)
> Tries one tactic…it doesn't work.
> Tries a second tactic…it doesn't work.
> Tries a third tactic…it works. Or it doesn't.
> Scene ends. Or character keeps trying.

A great scene that illustrates this principle is in *Lost in America* (by Albert Brooks and Monica Johnson). The husband and wife, played by Brooks and Julie Hagerty, have cashed in their home and their stocks and bonds, all for a Winnebago and their nest egg. They're going to travel the country and find themselves. The first night in Vegas, she goes mad at the tables and loses everything. Their entire nest egg. In the scene, Brooks's objective is to convince the casino owner (a great performance by Garry Marshall) to give them their money back. Marshall's objective is a little more subtle. It is not simply *not to give the money back*. That would have been a perfectly viable objective, but not too interesting a scene. He wants to maintain good will. So he comps the room. But that's not what Brooks wants. He assumes his ad exec persona and conceives a campaign that will not only get his money back but will enhance the hotel's image.

The scene is built on a gorgeous comedic premise—attempting with absolute obsessive sincerity to accomplish the impossible. And as each foray of an idea is presented and affably rejected, each "orbit" is clearly distinguished. When one is defeated, he jumps to the next. Rent the film and study this scene as an example of "taking Vienna," of taking a scene to its limits and beyond but never at the expense of character. Observe Marshall's objective running concurrently, and each thing that he does to accomplish it. And observe what causes the scene to nearly end…and finally end.

One of the great truths about scene writing is that the protagonist's Character Objective does not have to be fulfilled to accomplish the Writer's Objective. When somebody goes all out and is defeated, even all out on a quixotic, obsessive quest like getting money back from a casino, that Emotion strand of DNA has been pulled and tugged and dragged through the box. The audience has gained INTIMACY with your character through the ordeal, and they feel for the protagonist.

The farther a character goes to get what he wants, the more that is sacrificed, and the closer we come to feeling how important that thing is to the character and thus, to knowing that character. And the more intimately we know a character, the more deeply we will bond with that character no matter how awful the things are that the character does. We'll delve further into this when we talk about character and "anti-heroes."

But for purposes of understanding how to sharpen the arrowhead of Character Objective, recognize the two parts: what the character wants, and the ascending progression of things he or she does to accomplish it.

Three words: **WANT DO GET.**

What does the character **WANT**? What does the character **DO** to **GET** it?

I've put these words together into a acronym: **WADOOGEE.** In every moment: What do your characters **WA**nt? What do they **DOO** to **GE(E)**t it?

Yes, characterS. Not just character. Everything that applies to the objective of Character #1 applies equally to Character #2 and to any other principal character in the scene. Ninety-five percent of scenes that go wrong do so as a result of the **absence in one or both characters of a clearly delineated objective.** In most of these scenes, the lead character usually has a pretty well defined objective. A lot of the trouble comes from Character #2. Very often that character is given no organic objective at all. He or she is there as a vehicle for #1 to talk to, to bounce off. Or to provide information. (The dreaded "**Catechism Scene**." As we've discussed earlier, Question/Answer. Question/Answer.) These scenes are boring at best and lies at worst. Sometimes a writer will ordain that a character yield some information (Writer's Objective) that the character would NEVER reveal to the person asking it.

Seen through your increasingly sophisticated point of view, we can see how the **CENSUS INFORMATION** scene is an expression of Writer's Objective superceding Character Objective.

EXT. – COLLEGE DORM ROOM – NIGHT

BRIAN (19) plays fantasy football on the computer as his roommate, NICK, bops in sipping a brewski.

BRIAN
Hey, dude. How long have we been roommates now, about a year?

NICK
Closer to two. You moved in at the end of sophomore year. Plus we went to the same high school, so we go way back.

BRIAN
That so blows my mind. Who would have thought that with your father being a land developer and my parents being tree huggers that we ever would have been friends this long?

NICK
Well hey, let's hope that being in love with the same girl won't break that friendship up.

Obviously the writer wanted us to know something about the lads' history (Writer's Objective). On one level you might say, "Well done. Mission accomplished." But is it well done, or just done? Let's not overly praise ourselves. Can it be done better? How good, for you, is good enough? The problem is that there are a lot of successful models of lazy writing. Are you a writer willing to get away with the least you can do? Or do you want to see how good you can be?

The craft comes in covering our tracks, in concealing our Writer's Objective. Otherwise the scene is wearing its underwear on the outside. What kind of slice of life could we dramatize that would create for our audience the experience of these lads' friendship; our goal being not merely to transmit factual information, but to elicit an emotional response. Check out, for example, *Y tu mamá también*, *Ghost World*, *Kissing Jessica Stein* and, of course, *Jules and Jim*.

ADRENALINE EXERCISE

Two good friends are seeing the same person. How would you go about telling that story? What are the first thoughts that come to your mind? No good. Throw them away. What do you think of next? Still too easy. Good for you—you've thrown the next idea away before I even told you to. You don't think I can read your thoughts, but I can. You were thinking about that moment when they all accidentally confront one another.

But you haven't asked yourself the important questions yet, have you? Who are these people? How did they meet? Who was with whom first? What is the substance of their relationships? What draws them together? Who do you want *us* to want to be the couple? In THIS moment? In future moments, that can change. And won't that be fun! Where would they go together?

> Would the two different pairs go to different places? What else differentiates them? What would be a perfectly defining scene for each pair? What would that look like and feel like? Where would it be? What would they be doing? How did they get there? Was it easy? Hard? What were the obstacles? Who picked up whom? Did they meet there? Have the arrangements been in place for a while, or was it spontaneous? Does the other friend know? Suspect? Or not? Did the other friend have plans with either of the two that got changed? Blown off? Forgotten?

Unless you build a real emotional and physical set of circumstances in which your characters reside, **an emotional landscape**, as well as a set of **life circumstances** around them, your characters will be general, generic and not especially interesting. We want our scenes to dance the WA**DOO**GEE. Not the WA**talk**EE, not the WA**think**EE. The WA**DOO**GEE. What do the characters DO?

Let's address another common ailment: **THE FALSE OBSTACLE.**

Maybe you are a more sophisticated writer and you know that there needs to be conflict in every scene. But you've never really understood how to create it. So Character #2 says NO to #1, but for no apparent organic reason. He is just there because you've signed your Conflict Agreement, and you know that there has to be an obstacle in the scene. You're halfway there. You're thinking in the right way.

But usually, because there is no real organic reason for the antagonist's opposition, two bad things happen. (1) Your protagonist's stature diminishes to the size that a false obstacle thwarts him. (Because it is the Writer's Objective that he be thwarted at this juncture.) And (2) The opposition relents for no apparent reason.

> You're off the case.
> Ya gotta keep me on it. It's important!
> No!
> I need this case.

No! Absolutely not.
Please!
Oh, okay…

Scientific method.

It's a bad strategy to lower your standards and shrink your characters to fit them. Give your adversaries real motivations.

Having a weak adversary is like the scientist trying to *prove* his theory. Having a strong adversary is trying to *dis*prove it. A formidable adversary brings out the best in your protagonist's character. I am not just talking about the main adversary in the story, but even the smallest events in the story. Even if they take just a moment.

A small moment in *Sea of Love* reveals a writer (Richard Price) who is attentive to conflict and objectives even in the grace notes. A bunch of characters are assembled for a "Meet the Yankees" breakfast. In one of his first roles, a very lean and streety Samuel L. Jackson is held up at the door. The bouncer needs to see his invite and ID. He flashes it with attitude and says, "I'm good."

It turns out that the whole deal is a sting, that the "invites" are warrants, and these guys all get arrested. The cops *wanted* these guys to be in here. So why did that random cop hold Jackson up at the door? The answer is that it was perfectly in character *if it was not a sting* for the doorman to see invites and IDs. It would not be true to the experience of a good cop doing a good sting to just let the guy in.

The beauty of telling the truth is that it creates moments that otherwise would not have existed. If he hadn't been stopped at the door, that defining moment of his would have been lost.

If the opposition is a pushover (too easy) or a clod (a lifeless NO) then there is no energy created to cause the scene to jump orbits, for the writer to be more clever, more desperate, more ingenious, more daring, bold, brave, subtle, inventive. We get no deeper into that character's psyche, and thus the Emotion strand of DNA is inactivated and the audience doesn't care.

Characters don't have to be blood enemies to be in conflict. A loving couple can be in conflict over choosing a restaurant in Paris to celebrate their 50th anniversary. Or who last saw the keys. Or who looks better. Study the second act of Mike Leigh's *Career Girls.* (Watch all of it, of course.) Two women who have not seen each other for 10 years talk about how they saw each other back then. The one's memories are so different from the other's inner experience of the same events. But the disagreements are rapturous because of the levels that the observations reveal. Each character is getting to know the other more intimately, and so are we.

Conflict is the bladed shovel that allows digging more deeply into character. If the word *conflict* has connotations that are too violent, then think of something being *contested.* When Jack Sommersby returns to his plantation after the Civil War, he sees an old friend tilling hostile soil and says it's a nice piece of land that he's got. The farmer says it was once and Jack says that it still is. Is there not conflict, opposition, contestation in that short interchange?

There's another nice example in the early moments of Rocky. He returns to his corner after getting hit hard in the first round. His manager asks if he wants some advice. Rocky tells him no, just to give him his mouthpiece. Like all great scenes, long or short, they are about something specific which reveals something profound and significant about the characters.

It is important that those objectives be SPECIFIC, and for us to become aware of the symptoms of scenes when they are not. Take this as a rule of physics. The fuzzier the objective, the less focused and vague the scene will become.

It's important for us to learn to be our own scene doctors. If you woke up with a headache, fever or sniffles, you'd have an idea of what to do about it. Scenes can have the flu, too. Some telltale symptoms are:

- Big chunks of dialogue.
- Scenes that go on for more than four pages.
- Big long chunks of description.
- The solution to the scenes' issues coming either by one character inexplicably surrendering. ("Oh, all right, fine. I'll do it.") Or through gratuitous violence.

It is important for you to have enough self-knowledge to recognize the difference between a Character Objective and your own Writer's Objective. And to have the discipline and restraint, when there is any doubt, always to **go with the CHARACTER OBJECTIVE**. It is NEVER a Character Objective to give information to the audience, to interpret and transmit thematic material. It is almost never a Character Objective to divulge backstory and character psychology to the audience or to another character. These are Writers' Objectives. Here are some good axioms to remember, especially when you find yourself in the position of forcing a character to give necessary information to the audience:

1. INFORMATION IS A BY-PRODUCT OF CONFLICT.
2. A SCENE IS ALWAYS MORE INTERESTING WHEN A CHARACTER NEEDS TO *HAVE* INFORMATION THAN WHEN A CHARACTER NEEDS TO *GIVE* INFORMATION.

All right, let's take it to the next level. We have imbued our two principal characters with specific, urgent, immediate objectives. Is the scene ready to take life? Nope. There is one more factor. Are those objectives in **direct opposition**? There can be two people in a room with drawn revolvers, but if they are not pointed at each other, there is not necessarily conflict in the scene.

One character's objective might be to eat a sandwich and the other's to check out colleges on the Internet. Conceivably these two objectives can be fulfilled concurrently and painlessly. To quote that famed film critic, Chico Marx, "Atsa no good." The internal architecture of a scene needs two jackals and one bone, a situation where only one character's objective can be fulfilled. Or, where one objective will be fulfilled first. Because conflict leads to intimacy, because intimacy links us to a character's heart and soul, we must be sure that conflict is created, and to do it organically, we must be sure that the characters' objectives are in direct opposition.

As we mentioned in talking about story, we do not always allow our protagonist's objective to be accomplished. It can be an extremely effective strategy to accomplish a Writer's Objective by having a sympathetic character's objective *thwarted.* It makes the audience root more strongly when something that is ardently wished for, and deserved, is withheld.

Revisit *All the President's Men*. Woodward and Bernstein are thwarted constantly. They want information. Information is withheld from them. Because we experience how ardently they want the information and how far they will go to get it, because they are putting it all on the line (ordeal/passion) and getting nothing back (reward withheld), we cannot help but root for them. And remember that that very goal is Job #1.

The skillful and attentive orchestration of SCENE CIRCUMSTANCES is the mechanism through which we lock the two internal forces of the scene into alignment. This is an important and underconsidered aspect of scene conception, but one that can exercise great power. Such questions as WHO is in the scene? WHERE does the scene take place? WHAT has preceded this scene?

Let's look again at a nice short scene from *Sea of Love* that illustrates every point we've been discussing. Following the scene where the twenty-year veteran cop (Al Pacino) has caught 30 at-large criminals, he's outside when a man comes running up the block.

```
                CLARENCE
      Hey man, am I late?

                KELLER (PACINO)
      You got an invite?
```

Commentary: As a result of the previous scene, the audience knows that an "invitation" is actually an arrest warrant. Slap the cuffs on him, right? EXCEPT that the writer has added something to the CIRCUMSTANCES of the scene. **Clarence has a five-year-old kid with him**. This decision is not made by the casting director or the Screen Actors Guild. It was not the actor's kid who happened to be with him. He is there because the writer said so.

KELLER
Who's this?

CLARENCE
That's my son.

KELLER
Invitation is for you only.

CLARENCE
Hey, I can't very well see Dave Winfield
without taking my son.

Keller's partners in the back of the car run the man's name and quietly inform him of the charges.

PARTNER
Grand theft auto. Two counts.

Commentary: The circumstances force Keller to make a CHOICE. Arrest him or let him go. If the charge were petty larceny, of course Keller would let him go. And if it were murder, even though he had his kid with him, he'd be arrested. Grand theft auto could go either way.

Keller makes his decision. Now his objective becomes clear (to us) but not to Clarence, so there is subtext and conflict in the scene. Clarence wants to get in; Keller wants to get him away without embarrassing the kid.

KELLER
Look, we're all booked up.

CLARENCE
Hey man, I got an invite!

Keller surreptitiously shows Clarence his POLICE BADGE.

KELLER
We're all booked.

CLARENCE
Thanks, man.

He backs off and takes his kid the other way. Keller gets into the car.

KELLER
Catch you later.

The sheer power of circumstances.

To review, let's look at all the components working together here. Characters have clear, urgent, specific, immediate objectives. When the first attempt fails, the character goes to the next orbit. And the next and then the next. (Keller says the invitation is just for you. Clarence counters, Keller says we're booked up. Clarence counters, Keller at last shows him the badge. His objective is accomplished.) The action of the scene springs from what the characters want RIGHT NOW. We feel the dread of what will happen to that kid if his dad gets arrested. We feel the inner turmoil in Keller's heart. We feel the father's anger and the unspoken agenda between a black street guy and a white cop. And we feel the father's gratitude. Note that as soon as the Character Objective is accomplished, THE SCENE ENDS.

In this example, the circumstance remained constant through the entire scene. Lots of things conceivably could have happened that would have sent the scene in another direction. He could have been accused of murder or child abuse, in which case they would have taken him in. Or tried to. And a chase resulted. Etc., etc. But the Writer's Objective in this scene was to have us experience Keller making a difficult choice and his humanity winning out. Another cop might have arrested him under the exact same circumstances. But not this cop.

Rapidly changing circumstances can also rapidly change the immediate objectives of a character.

A character's objective may have been to find a perfect spot for a picnic for him and his girlfriend. He then encounters a swarm of bees (whose objective is to sting him). Picnicker's objective quickly changes to getting the hell out of there unhurt. He may have been looking for the perfect picnic spot because he was going to propose marriage. The bees make escape more immediate and necessary. Oops, but what if he realizes he has dropped the engagement ring? Now his objective becomes...what? Is it still to get away? To get away and remember where the ring is? To get the ring, bees be damned?

Each section of this sequence can be called a scene beat. Each is delineated by having a new immediate objective, each being changed by changing circumstances.

ADRENALINE EXERCISE

Write a sequence of five scenes, each in a new locale, so that only by the end do we understand what the character has been after. You may use a TOTAL of 10 words of dialogue in the entire sequence. Have some kind of opposition to the character's desire in each scene. Here's one:

1. A guy in his late 20s dashes down into the subway. A train is coming. He can't wait to buy a token and vaults over the turnstile. A TRANSIT COP yells for him to stop. He makes an apologetic gesture and leaps onto the train.

2. The guy dashes out of the subway stop downtown. He races across the street, nearly getting clipped twice by buses. Horns honk angrily at him but he gets across.

3. He runs up the 60 marble steps to City Hall. Stops and remembers something, and runs all the way back down. He slaps a 20 on the counter and grabs a bouquet of flowers, then dashes off before the vendor can give him his five dollars change.

4. His way is blocked at the entrance. Security screening. Adrenaline is pumping but he tries to control himself. He is scrutinized carefully.

```
                SECURITY GUARD
    The flowers stay with me.

                GUY
    The hell they do.
```

He grabs them and dashes inside.

5. City Hall wedding chapel. Just as the attendant calls a woman's name and a man's. She is alone. Is ready to bite nails. He suddenly appears at her side, casual and cool, and takes her to the Justice of the Peace.

So we have it all now. Writer's Objective. Two Character Objectives. Circumstance. The fully operational scene paradigm works like this:

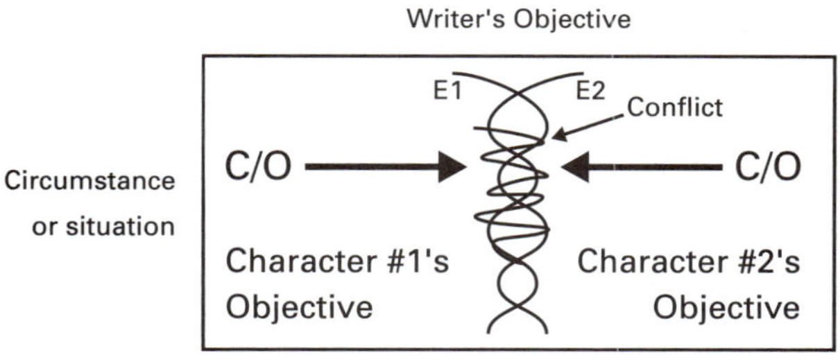

WRITER'S OBJECTIVE sublimated into the box where the CIRCUMSTANCES of the scene place immediate, urgent and specific CHARACTER OBJECTIVES into direct opposition. The electrical storm that is generated between those two powerful and opposing force fields creates CONFLICT, the lifeblood of drama.

The way you TAKE VIENNA is to make sure that all your scenes are dancing the Wadoogee.

WRITERS GYM EXERCISES:

EXERCISE #1

Take out the last screenplay (or partial screenplay) you wrote. Find your favorite scene or scenes. Now go through the script scene by scene and write down the CHARACTER OBJECTIVES for each character in each scene.

Do they yield to examination? Are they there? Are any of them clearly defined? Are there scenes where both characters' objectives are urgent and immediate and specific and directly opposed to each other? What tactics have you given them to be successful? Do they gain power as the scene progresses? Are they dancing the Wadoogee?

Write down your WRITER'S OBJECTIVES for each scene. Both strands of DNA. Who did you want to "win"? How has the narrative advanced? What have you revealed about character that we didn't previously know? Examine the circumstances of each scene. Have you given careful enough thought here? Is there a better locale, a more interesting setting, one that adds drama or comedy? Should some other character be there who is not?

Look again at your favorite scenes. What understanding do you have as to why those scenes were your favorites?

EXERCISE #2

Open the Yellow Pages to two disparate pages. Choose one location from each page. Your job. In five scenes, move your character from Point A to Point B, so that in each scene there is an obstacle he or she has to overcome. It can be physical. It can involve any characters you invent in any situation. The one stipulation is that the character's "mission" is not revealed until the final scene.

EXERCISE #3

Put two ex-lovers in a restaurant, a store, a bus, any public or private locale. Write a scene where they fight over the one major thing that drives one or both of them crazy. Make us side with the character you support in the scene.

Then, using the same circumstances, either continue the scene where you left off or rewrite it, but this time make us empathize more with the other character.

Now, do it one more time. In this version, one character wins the argument but the audience sides with the other.

"TARANTINO EXERCISE"

1. Open the Yellow Pages to two random pages and select two businesses. Move two characters from Point A to Point B by whatever means you invent. Invent a good reason for the journey. Reveal that intent skillfully. If it's huge, understate it. If it's trivial, exaggerate.

2. Then, pick one of the following topics and write a dialogue scene between those two characters, exploring and disputing the topic fully.

   - Standard shift vs. automatic transmission
   - Leaf blowers
   - Teeth
   - Class seating on airplanes
   - Vegetarianism
   - Paying for cable TV
   - Burning CDs
   - Any other mundane topic in the world

   As in every good scene, use the interchange not only to explore the issue, but in doing so, reveal who the characters are, individually and in their relationship to each other.

3. Finally, orchestrate Part 2 into Part 1 and write a sequence of scenes.

CHAPTER 13

Following the Pole Star

All the traits so essential to becoming a writer—imagination, curiosity, dreaminess, fascination, the thrill of discovery, the ability to see all sides, the compulsion to get to the bottom—fueled by an inherent character weakness to procrastinate—all conspire benignly to get a writer lost in his/her story. The Internet has made it easier than it has ever been before. You can Google and Ask in endless loops that encircle infinity. Everything leads to something that leads to something else.

Like the Universe, the Internet is constantly expanding. It has no bottom, no end. There is always something yet to be found. One does not have to be engaged in the specific act of research to be affected. Googling has seeped into our collective groundwater. Just as in a previous generation, one did not have to sit in front of the tube watching MTV to live in a world affected by quick cuts and micro-second attention spans.

So what must we do to stay focused in our stories? How do we not wander endlessly through the universe of story possibility, seduced by each new source of light and gravitation, tugged further from where we began and where we had (light years ago) thought we were headed? If you have read this chapter heading, you probably have a clue to the answer.

Ancient maritime explorers fixed upon one steady point of light in the night time sky and used it as the constant point of reference. As writers, we must employ that same concept of celestial navigation for our characters. THE PROTAGONIST OF OUR STORY MUST HAVE A POLE STAR. In our craft of cinematic storytelling, that pole star is the character's desire. It always comes back to that same basic concept.

WHAT DOES THE CHARACTER MOST URGENTLY WANT?

That is the essential DNA of your story.

Let's look at a few recent films as illustrations. One of my new all-time favorites is *Riding Alone For Thousands of Miles* (English title), co-written by its director Yimou Zhang (*Raise The Red Lantern*) and Jongzhi Zou. It was a completely under-watched film, but loved by those few who saw it (its U.S gross was a paltry $250,000 but it won the San Diego Film Critics Society's award for Best Foreign Language Film and Best Actor for its star, Ken Takakura.

He plays a fisherman living in a remote rugged village in Japan, long estranged from his grown son, when he receives a letter from his daughter-in-law that the boy is terminally ill with cancer. He tries to visit but his son refuses to see him. He is given a videotape of his son's unfinished work and decides that he will complete it.

NB: Relating to discussions in other parts of this book about EXPOSITION—look what has already been done. The father's universe has been established in utter contrast to his son's. His life has been defined through action. And a gigantically significant event has altered the status quo of that life. The entire body of the film is HIS RESPONSE to that stimulus.

It becomes his obsession now to complete his son's work. What is that work? Making a documentary film about a famous Chinese opera singer living in a remote province in China. Everything about the task is even further from this fisherman's sensibilities than it is from yours. That task becomes the emotional pole star for the father and the narrative pole star for the audience,

The forces of the story's universe repel his every effort. Each repulsion seems fatal to the enterprise. Yet he never gives up. Each obstacle repels or deflects his desired intention, and (without giving any of the specifics away because I want you to see this film), while he may have to perform tasks E<F and G in order to get back to B, we never lose sight of the goal because the character never loses sight of the goal because the film makers never lose sight of the goal. Wherever we are, however far off course the character has been thrown, left or right or back, the return path is always there because the ultimate goal is unchanged. The Pole Star.

Because of that, we as an audience are never disconnected from the emotional charge. There is so much craft to be learned from seeing this film—and so much emotional satisfaction and fulfillment.

In a completely different tone, *Little Miss Sunshine* (Academy Award winning original screenplay written by Michael Arndt) is another great example of keeping that pole star in focus. This film is far more of an ensemble piece than *Riding Alone*. In addition to the principal story of Olive's quest to become *Little Miss Sunshine*, three other satellite characters have their own independent story lines:

Richard, her father, is a motivational speaker, desperately trying to reach the agent/producer to market his 7 steps. Frank, Olive's uncle has just attempted suicide, when his rival in love and in Proustian scholarship makes off with the coveted Macarthur award and with Frank's lover. And Dwayne, her Nietzsche reading brother, has taken a vow of silence until he reaches his goal of being admitted to the Air Force.

While we are involved in each of these characters' stories, (effectively done by use of the tools discussed throughout this book—submitting the characters to hardship and obstacles; conflict revealing truth and intimacy), it is Olive's story around which they all coalesce. It is her journey, metaphorical and tangible, that put them all in the van to California for the contest.

Getting there and getting there ON TIME becomes the pole star. All the other characters, each of whom has his own pole star, sacrifices or compromises or deals with his own problems in relation to Olive's. Frank has to confront his rivals (in the most humiliating of circumstances). Richard tries to hide his failures, then takes a long side trip on a ridiculous vehicle to confront his devils, and Dwayne, whose plight at the start seems perhaps trivial, must deal with the crushing reality that his life dream is over. In one of the film's loveliest non-verbal moments, he surrenders to the awkward loving touch of his little sister and resumes life in the family.

As in so many great films, this one builds in emotional depth to the point that it transcends its own narrative premise. After they have come all the great distance, confronting profound physical and emotional traumas, and finally getting Olive into the contest, something larger arises—the possibility of Olive's humiliation. And now, this family that has nearly broken apart to bring her here, (one death, Olive's greatest ally) comes together to keep her out of the show.

It is she who is given the protagonist's responsibility of VOLITION and makes the ultimate choice to go on with it. And now, as she does her rather unexpected act, they come together around her, repelling the taunts and derision of the outside world, celebrating all their neuroses and quirks, snatching their own definition of victory from the world's judgmental teeth, and returning to life in their battered van (surely an Objective Correlative of their lives) to a home life that will be different for the experience.

Among the many lessons in deft application of the art and craft of screenwriting, let us keep focused on our own pole star. With all the side trips and subplots the story takes, Arndt never allows us to lose sight of the story's pole star. Everything is linked to it. We experience all the side events in reference to that unchanging goal.

In some stories the character is unaware of his pole star until some distance in. *The Graduate* is a classic example. Everyone tries to give him advice but he just hides underwater until the story brings his love object to him. Another terrific recent example of that technique is *Hustle and Flow*, written by Craig Brewer. The 2005 film won deserved awards for its music and male star, Terrence Howard (in a sensationally different role than he played in *Crash*).

Djay, the film's protagonist, is a most unlikely choice for a central character, a philosopher/pimp. Credit to their creative courage, neither the actor nor the writer-director succumb to the temptation of sentimentalizing or softening the character or apologizing for who he is. (In one of the most wrenching emotional scenes I've witnessed, he evicts a woman and her baby. Here is the true meaning of "Taking Vienna!")

Like Benjamin at the start of The Graduate, Djay is vaguely dissatisfied with his life but has no clear remedy. In the film's inciting moment, music is reintroduced into his life. The physical object that carries this LARGE, SIGNIFICANT narrative device is small and trivial. Practically a toy. (Keep that notion of contrast filed away close to home.) It is that thing that gets Djay into his FLOW. And that FLOW becomes the story's pole star.

There are so many things we have to retain in our simultaneous awareness chamber. One is that movies are external and we must find external devices to carry internal truths. Skinny Black is coming back to town. He grew up here (the bad side of Memphis) and has become a recording success. Djay's pole star now becomes recording his demo TAPE and getting it into the hands of Skinny Black. This becomes the focus of Djay's every thought and deed. It will be his ticket to be something better.

Again, so many skill sets become manifest that enable this story to grasp us in the gut. Despite his being a lord of his tawdry manor at the start, he is an **underdog**. (No AC in the car). It's a crap subsistence living, pimping and selling dirt weed. The experience of his life feels **authentic**. There is **intimacy**. We don't have to like what he does or even like him. As mentioned earlier, **intimacy trumps morality** and the audience is fascinated. (As with The Godfather or the Devil in Milton's "Paradise Lost.")

Once creating the tape for Skinny becomes the pole star, it unleashes sympathetic sides of him previously unseen...i.e. his creative flow. It also exacerbates the HUSTLER side we've already seen. The ways in which he gets what he wants moment-to-moment do not become sentimentalized. And this leads to scenes of intense conflict and pain. It polarizes the narrative outcome of the two prostitutes he manages. One, who loses faith in him and sees only one side, goes down hard. The other gets to be "in charge." Through his unwavering quest (met with mixed results—but in great stories the journey IS the destination), her desires are discovered and met.

There are beautifully conceived and executed scenes of transformation. Djays and Nola's. There are sequences where hope is raised, dashed, re-raised, redashed, re-re-raised and plunged to the depths. There is never a moment where we have the slightest doubt what the characters WANT. What they do to get it surprises and moves us and astonishes and frightens us. But every moment of the film is driven by that engine of desire. This is a movie that dances the wadoogee.

One moment continues to stand out when I think about this film. After the horrendous confrontation, where he throws the mother and child out of the house, how can the audience ever again be sympathetic to this man? The way in which it is done is an amazing testament to all the principles we've discussed. Watch for this moment when you see the film again. File away in your writer's tool box the understanding or the instinct-to-craft that brought Brewer to this choice. Think about how you might bring your own characters to real depths, which you've been hesitant to do for fear of losing an audience's interest in them.

One of my favorite films of 2006 was *Stranger Than Fiction*, written by Zach Helm. You could not call this a boxoffice triumph (of these four films, only *Little Miss Sunshine* was a clear commercial success... hmmm), but it (or because it) was funny and literate and inventive; and like the other films mentioned here, it has a strong narrative premise, which lesser films fall short of merely executing, and which this one masters and then transcends. How can you not love a character who says his favorite word is "integer"? It's my favorite word in dialogue since Paul Sylbert had Dick Benjamin utter the word "portmanteau" in the 1971 film, *The Steagle*.

Helm tells the story of the story's evolution in a series of three phone calls to Lindsay Doran, the creative executive behind the film—calls that came months apart as the story gestated in his unconscious from "A man hears a voice in his head" (Nice but not a story) to "A man hears a voice narrating his life" (Nicer but not a story) to "The voice predicts his death" (There's your movie)!

There's also the narrative and emotional pole star. Harold Crick is tortured by this incessant voice in his head. Every action of the story grows out of his effort to identify it and purge it. And through that obsessive unwavering desire, the character meets the love of his life (in fittingly inopportune circumstances), and gets to break the chains of the habitual life he has led—one to which death might even have been a pleasant alternative.

Throughout it, and especially at the end, we are graced with wise and humorous and profound observations about the human condition, a delicacy that films rarely try to serve and when they do, the meal is often way overcooked and fatty. Here, it is the sweetest, lightest, most satisfying, bittersweet dessert. (Though I confess I would willingly blindly follow Emma Thompson's voice wherever it led me.)

We've discussed films where the character was connected to the Pole Star from the beginning and where the events of story were designed to forge the connection in front of our eyes. Can it ever be—? I can hear you thinking—that a character's ***pole star changes*** during the story?

Wedding Crashers, written by Steve Faber & Bob Fisher, was one of the huge hits of 2005. (Incidentally the ampersand symbol between the names of two writers signifies they are a writing team. The word "and" between names would indicate a succession of writers and rewriters.) Here is a story where the characters' pole star changes. In the beginning, it is to crash weddings, have fun, get laid. Great joy is celebrated in the elation of making up stories to fit every ethnic occasion, and in reaping the sensual rewards. Those experiences define who they are. And if nothing changed, the film would be only a continuing succession of those events.

BUT

As in all good films, the status quo changes. A CHOICE is presented to the character that carries the imperative of change. One character falls in love. GETTING THE RIGHT GIRL now becomes the character's serious pole star. He is faced with all the usual obstacles—she is engaged, he is an outsider, somewhat below the family's social stratum. But beyond that, the most painful emotional stake is his friendship with his buddy. During all the antics of the opening scenes of the film, the currency of that friendship has been established through the audience's EXPERIENCE of them. (As in the other "broken friendship" stories cited in other chapters—*Kissing Jessica Stein*, *Ghost World*, *Y Tu Mama Tambien*—) the writers make us feel that friendship so we have something at stake watching the possibility of its demise, and we root for it to remain intact.

So, can a pole star be changed? Yes. With these caveats: Do it only once. And make that change become the emotional crux of the story. It would not be effective to have your audience invest in a character whose driving force is to be a manicurist and then simply change career aspirations and want to be a librarian...unless the driving force for that change created, or was the result of, a pivotal change in the character from inside or outside, and there was a strong emotional residue of the previous choice tied into the narrative that became the stake of the story.

That pesky love thing breaks the bond between the crashers. Their friendship ends. Life deteriorates. An offer of reconciliation is refused.

And then, finally...well, you know.

How Does Establishing The Character's Pole Star Help Us Create An Interesting Story?

It maintains the focus on the primary questions we must all ask and answer: Eyes on the prize. Whose story is it? What is the stake of the story? What does the protagonist most want? What will he/she do to get it?

It does NOT imply or impose a direct, straight-line, predictable, unimaginative route to get there. In fact, it allows "veerage." So long as it is never out of sight and everything is in reference to it.

It allows the story to dance the wadoogee without counting the steps out loud.

WRITERS GYM EXERCISE

Make this simple and straightforward. Define the pole star for your protagonist, and if it is an ensemble piece, the pole stars of the significant characters going in.

CHAPTER 14

The Components of Scene Writing

We're among friends here, so we can be honest. A screenwriter does not have to possess great literary skills to be a good, working screenwriter. For writers of prose fiction, theater and poetry, language is virtually everything. For a screenwriter, a certain level of competence is, of course, required. But beyond that, one need not have the loopy prose style of T. C. Boyle nor the grace and elegance and alarmingly perceptive flights of rhetoric we see in the stories of Richard Ford or Lorrie Moore.

Ironically, working too hard to write too beautifully can be at best irrelevant and at worst a detriment. When my UCLA colleague, Richard Walter, encounters a lush passage of narrative prose in a student's screenplay, he acknowledges it with the abbreviation SFN, which means "Save it For your Novel."

What kind of an unjust world is this where a writer is admonished for writing too well? But language *does* have a place in screenwriting. Used effectively, language can be a multipurpose tool. The question, though, is how to use it to its best effect. And here once again, function defines form.

In this chapter we are going to examine the three components of scene writing: DESCRIPTIONS OF CHARACTER AND PLACE, NARRATIVE ACTION and DIALOGUE. By focusing on their function, we also examine the job that each is meant to accomplish, and sharpen our craft and skills so that we are better able to execute them.

WRITING CHARACTER DESCRIPTIONS

We touched on this earlier in the discussion about format, but it bears repeating. The most important and time-saving truth a writer needs to understand about writing character descriptions is that ultimately the character will look exactly like the actor or actress hired to play the role. You may write that the protagonist is five-feet-seven with close-cropped auburn tresses and a series of moles on her face that depict the exact relationship of Cyprus and Sardinia. Even though you may be describing in perfect detail the person upon whom you are modeling the character, harbor no illusion that Kate Hudson will gain or lose height or weight to conform to your specifications.

Age range and body type are usually all we need to supply. Actors are cast as types. There is no shame in guiding the reader's eye to the right folder of résumés. It's hard enough being a writer; let's not try to be a casting director as well. Mid 20s, late 40s. That's enough. The younger the person, the more specific you ought to be about age. The differences between the ages of 6 and 9 are far greater than between 56 and 59. And even between 26 and 29.

Body type. You want to give your reader the feeling of the kind of person the character is, the way in which the person's inner life is reflected in his or her outer life. Find some good impressionistic words. Words that create pictures. You can let yourself be a little colorful here. ("He has a butcher's meaty fingers and bloody apron.") ("When they were handing out good looks, she came back for seconds.")

Casting suggestions are sometimes helpful. They help a reader see and hear the character. It can work against you, though, if your script, whose lead character you describe as "perfect for Brad Pitt," goes to Matt Damon's company.

Have a little fun. It's okay to make your script an enjoyable read. But beware of trying to be too cute. The people reading scripts read hundreds of them. They've seen most gimmicks dozens of times. By the time they see it in yours, some of the novelty just may have eroded for them. So:

- Keep your language fresh and vivid. But don't work overtly hard at it.
- Words create pictures.
- Go LIGHT on the gimmickry.

When a writer becomes so self-conscious about any kind of device that the device starts to show, then it has defeated its purpose. The writer has been distracted out of the story into his or her own beauty contest, and the reader gets pulled out, too. Embellishments are meant to enhance the story and delight the listener, but never to shift the focus from the story to the storyteller.

You never want to leave your reader wanting less.

Here is a sampling of nice character descriptions:

Stallone gives some great impressionistic portraits:

A guy whose hair looks like its been "shaped with hedge clippers."

People at ringside in the thick smoke looking like "specters."

A housewife shouting for someone to cover a two dollar bet.

Notice that these are not long descriptions. They are not self-conscious.

Tarantino has some great impressionistic images, too. He describes a surfer kid having a "Flock of Seagulls" haircut.

Another character is a cross between " a gangster and a king."

Our UCLA writers have learned a lot from emulating the best.

From UCLA writer Marc Arneson's award-winning script, *Commedia del Arte:*

GRAMMA: short, fat old lady with big boobs and a black dress, hangs laundry.

MAMMA: a younger version, steps into the sun next to Gramma.

HERO (25): stands on the platform alone. Duffel bag, dress uniform, gold medal on his chest.

SPATZINO (50s): pushes a two-wheeled garbage can, stops at the door. Tucks in his stained shirt, takes off his hat.

Stock characters are tolerable shortcuts for minor characters when you haven't time and it isn't necessary to individualize them. (Three muggers who leap out of an alley.) But for your primary characters, make them real for yourself. Recognize what it is about them that interests *you*. And find a way to convey it vividly. Remember to give them each a **DEFINING ACT**.

I know several writers who tape up 8x10 glossies of the actors they envision for each role so that they can keep their personalities in mind as they write dialogue. Of course, there are always props and physical deformities. And while, admittedly, some cowboys probably do walk with a limp, and while, yes, some corporate bigwigs probably do smoke cigars, maybe yours don't. Not every runway model is haughty; some are messy and neurotic. The easier, automatic choices you make, the less interesting they are likely to be.

What is wrong with the following character descriptions? (This book is not going to tell you.)

1. JOE WALSH (32) is the first to tee off. He looks like Arnold Palmer in his prime; the youngest vice president that

Paine Webber ever had.

2. MARY VERNON (27), the staff librarian, is the business-attired, mild-mannered sister of the hellion biker we just saw.

3. The FIVE FRIENDS known as the KINK BROTHERS are poised hungrily over the pizza. Marc, 15, is the freckle-faced Yankee fanatic. Pete, 15, is the shy drummer. Eric, 16, acts brave but is scared of girls. Gets all his sex information from books and the Internet. JJ is suburban black. Athlete scholar. Someday he'll have to ask himself what he's doing with these boys. But not today. And Bickford. "Bick." You never know what he's thinking. Not much of it's good.

Okay, I lied. I am going to tell you. But I wanted you to think about them carefully.

In #1. I'd use my own favorite acronym: **HDWK. H**ow **D**o **W**e **K**now? How would an audience know that he's the youngest vice president at Paine Webber? An audience only knows what they hear and see.

In #2. HDWK. How do we know she's a librarian? How do we know she's the sister of the hellion?

#3. A bunch more HDWK. Do you see them all? And the characters are introduced in such a **dense cluster of bland characteristics** that we would have to look back every time one was mentioned later on to remind ourselves who is who.

GIGANTIC GUIDING PRINCIPLE: WHATEVER INFORMATION YOU GIVE THE READER, MAKE SURE YOU DO IT IN A WAY THAT THE VIEWER WILL GET.

How would an audience know that Joe Walsh was a VP at Paine Webber? It might come up in conversation among the foursome. Pretty unlikely, but possible. Maybe there are teams of two, and the opponents whisper about him while he's lining up his shot. There might be a few fairly decent ways of working in that information. But there might not. And the idea of "working it in" has the energy moving in the wrong direction. You don't want to work anything in, you want to create circumstances where it comes out naturally.

Here's the equally important corollary to the Gigantic Guiding Principle:

If there isn't a good, organic way for the information to be revealed to the audience, don't write it to the reader. Save it for another scene.

But here is some excellent news: **The principles that guide effective *character description* retrofit perfectly with the rules we have previously discussed for effective *character creation*.**

Do the terms *Verb of Character*, or *Defining Action* jog any memories from long-ago chapters? And therein lies the key!

If you want us to know that Jacqueline Messier (33) is not only a fantastic soccer mom but also an unflappable hostess, don't TELL us that in your character description. Set a scene at a soccer game. She's in jeans and a sweatshirt. She consoles a kid whose team lost because she muffed a kick. Set another scene at an elegant dinner party. She's in an evening gown flirting with the French ambassador. The same directive applies to introducing many characters in a scene.

Don't make a long list or describe too many in a cluster. Wait until the story finds a moment for them. Introduce them as they enter the story (in an interesting Defining Action). Look at how the characters are introduced in *The Godfather*'s opening sequences. Not as a cast list. But by something they *do*. Sonny shtups the bridesmaid and rousts the FBI and news guys. Luca Brasi talks to himself. Johnny Fontane's entrance is greeted by screams from the teenage girls. Mama sings. Tom Hagen helps execute Don Corleone's directives.

All verbs. Actions.

Who we are is revealed in what we do and how we do it.

DESCRIBING PLACE

The same principles apply to describing place as to describing characters. Impressionistic snapshots. That cabin of your youth that you describe, basking in the dappled morning sunlight, will look exactly like the cabin that the location manager finds or that the set designer creates. Your job is to use whatever physical details you choose to create a feeling around the picture.

To convey the crummy two-bit arena where Rocky has his first bout, instead of describing every detail, Stallone calls it an "unemptied garbage can." This conveys enough for readers to see and feel (and smell) the place.

Every sentence is a picture. The statements are not literal. He does not seek to include the precise dimensions. But you can see this place. And you can feel it and smell it too. The images go to the SENSES, not to the analytic part of the brain.

In Rocky's one room apartment, Stallone gives us some great character details by his choice of a "curling poster of Rocky Marciano" and a mattress with its stuffing falling out nailed to the wall as a punching bag.

Stallone, the writer, is doing everything right. Look at the attention to specific detail and how the images give us the feel of the place and of the person who lives there. How **the outer life illuminates the inner life.** Each action is specific and described without adverbs. And each action tells us something about the character that we didn't know before.

A few other examples:

From Laurie Hutzler's script *Lorraine Loses It,* here's the Lucas family kitchen, 1964.

A bright blue Tupperware lid rolls across slightly askew red and yellow asbestos tile.

In the same house, a baby's room:

The chartreuse bedroom, with a bright orange ducky mobile over the crib, is about the size of a large walk-in closet.

Calling it a ducky mobile and not a duck mobile—just that letter *y*— conveys something of the attitude the writer wants imbued into this setting.

This description of a cityscape at Whitehall Street from *Kissing England* by Sacha Gervasi:

Grey monotone buildings speckled with several generations of bird droppings. A placard which reads 'Ministry of Defense.'

A character (male) in a kitchen "*has a fistful of hazelnuts up a moist goose.*"

The choice of hazelnut and goose tells us something about the kitchen. It would be the kind of place that had hazelnut and goose. Not a college dorm. And he gives us attitude in every description without taking us out of the place, using it to enhance the feeling he wants us to have about the place.

The way I taught him to write was this: He'd write something absolutely amazing. As an ironic joke, I'd tell him to do it better. And he would.

Here's a World War I battlefield scene description from *Commedia del Arte:*

A river of snot-colored GAS hides the mud floor and everything in it.

Beyond the ditch the battlefield is tilled with craters and sown with torn bodies.

An EXPLOSION. Mud and shrapnel.

A SOLDIER dives into the trench, and disappears under the poison phlegm.

ADRENALINE EXERCISES

> In 25 words or less, write a real estate ad to sell or rent the abode in which you currently reside. How do you create the "feel" of the place? What are your snapshots? How does the outer life reveal the inner life?
>
> Write a personal ad describing yourself and the ideal respondee you're looking for. Twenty-five words or less. How do you catch the essence of yourself and another person?

A huge mistake writers often make in describing locale is trying to direct on the page. Resist the temptation to get goofy about camera angles and the order in which we see what. If the scene is in an English garden, do not take us in through the POV of a honeybee. Even though the way you describe the camera shot might be the coolest of all cool ways to shoot the scene, and the film's director, if he has anything near the sensitivity and depth of creative vision that you have, may indeed shoot the scene exactly that way.

Be guided by the idea of the **NARRATIVE IMPERATIVE.** That is to say, choose to write only the details that are **essential to the story.** If the story is about people with moles on their faces arranged in the pattern of large islands, then, yes, mention the moles. If bees figure prominently in the English garden scene, then you might get away with entering with one.

Just as a mass introduction of characters, undifferentiated by what they are **doing**, is hard to absorb, so too is it hard to focus on a litany of objects. Wait to mention them until they enter the story. For instance, you can say we are in a VICTORIAN SITTING ROOM, and give us a detail or two, but you don't have to mention the inlaid writing desk until the character sits at it.

DO be impressionistic. Find the details that create the feel of the place. Strive to be economical in your prose.

All these same principles apply equally to describing clothing and attire. It is hard enough being a writer. We don't also have to be the costume designer.

COSTUMERY: Do not describe the outfits every character wears in every scene. Insofar as decor defines character, you can certainly describe the *manner* in which a character dresses (Armani. Casual. Old enough to be a professor but dresses like a student). But don't dress and accessorize **unless what the character is wearing has a narrative bearing on the scene**.

Here are two terms to remember: **NARRATIVE** and **DECORATIVE**. It is important that you differentiate between them. A decorative choice is made for style and is not imperative to the scene. A narrative choice is part of the storytelling mechanism. Without it, the scene would be completely different. You *need* to specify that Cinderella is dressed in rags and that her stepsisters are elegantly attired for the ball. That's the *story*.

In *American Beauty*, the handle of Carolyn's pruning shears matching her gardening clogs is a statement, a visual metaphor of who she is. But it is observed *not by the writer* in description but *by a character* who knows her.

You don't have to describe every suit that the gang is wearing in *The Godfather*'s wedding scene. But you WOULD say that Michael Corleone is dressed in his army uniform, and you'd say something about Kay's dress. Because they are meant to stand out. The army uniform is a visual way of underlining that Michael is outside the family. It is also organic to Michael's character. He is a decorated war hero.

We are not interior decorators. We are not costume designers. We are not cinematographers. We are not location scouts or landscape artists.

We are not designing the soundtrack. We are storytellers. The screenplay is an instrument for telling a story. **Whatever in your script doesn't move the story forward does not belong in the script.**

How does setting move the story forward, you ask? The setting for any scene you choose should not be a neutral, arbitrary choice. It should be an arena for characters to be placed into conflict. Say only enough about it to allow it to perform its function.

If your elegant prose takes too long to read, if it exists to show off your writing prowess, if it is doing anything other than the function for which it exists, give it a haircut. Shear. Shave. Clip. Prune. Amputate. Undo. Delete. Toss out. Eliminate. Create a separate file, a dog pound for abandoned phrases. Put all your clipped ringlets there for posterity, to show your children and future lovers. Just get them out of your screenplay.

ADRENALINE EXERCISE

Take the last scene you wrote, or an entire screenplay. Use a yellow highlighter pen and mark only the descriptive phrases that create vivid pictures. Be a little brutal with yourself. Pretend you're editing your uncle's slide show of his annual trip to Cincinnati. Which would you want to see? Everything else...let go of.

WRITING NARRATIVE ACTION

Things happen. People interact. Events occur. How do we describe thrilling action? How do we describe an intense, quiet interchange? How do we keep our readers on a clear path so they do not have to be constantly using a machete to hack through the brambles and dense underbrush of our writing?

The TV show *Gunsmoke* began a new genre in the 1950s called the adult Western. Characters had depth and psychology, and the stories did not all end in gunplay (despite the provocative name of the show). These Westerns still run on various oldies stations. Watch a few. Especially in the dramatic scenes, after nearly every line of dialogue there follows a significant pause, wherein we see the reactions of each of the other characters in the scene.

Until they are broken of the habit, many screenwriters tend to write this way, incorporating a great deal of *behavior*, describing with the accuracy of a surveillance camera each character's responses moment to moment. Taking, as it were, the *emotional temperature* of each character in each instant.

It's hard for new writers to hear this as a criticism. It feels like a skill, not a deficit. We are writing the scenes the way we are visualizing them on the screens of our internal cineplexes. But we must realize that we are effectively transcribing the movie, retrowriting the shooting script, and, in doing so, we are drinking that nice tall glass of hydrogen peroxide. Eliminating this underbrush from the scene is difficult because it feels equally useful and necessary. But once again we must be guided by the principles of scene writing that we have spoken about in previous chapters. Remember the golden axiom: The sole purpose for the existence of a scene is as an arena for characters doing everything possible to get what they want in that moment. If we keep that as the focus of our writing objective, if we think of it as the arrow that we are propelling toward its target, then anything that interferes or deflects or impedes or delays that arrow should be seen as vestigial and should be eliminated.

We often overdescribe the completion of simple acts. Exaggerated example:

Mona approaches the car. She reaches with her left hand and grasps the door handle. Her thumb places pressure on the button. It yields slowly to her increasing force. The lock releases. Cocking her elbow and flexing her wrist, she pulls open the driver's side door. Her hips swivel and her weight shifts to her forward knee as she lowers her torso down into the bucket seat. She places the key into the ignition and turns. The engine comes to life. She drives away.

There is nothing in that description that is not true. But unless the point of the scene was that a weight-activated bomb was set in that car, all we really need to say is "She gets in the car and drives away." And even that might be too much. We might get away with "She drives off." Or, "She waves goodbye and gets in." Or, depending on the content of the preceding scene and where the next scene begins, all we might need is to see the car. If we see her in a restaurant later with the car parked outside, we know she got there.

ADRENALINE EXERCISE

Scene A. A cat whines at her empty dish. Harry looks despairingly at the empty cabinet. Outside, the blizzard is still howling. The cat howls louder.

Scene Z. Harry opens a can of the cat's favorite food.

Question: How much do you write to get there? Do you show him plodding outside to the car, driving to the market, tromping through the parking lot? Getting stuck in a snow bank? Getting home? Taking his snow-covered clothes off? Opening the can? What do you show, what do you imply? The answer to such questions is always the same. **It depends on what the story is!**

If this were a story like *After Hours*, which began with a character out to do one simple thing and ended with his accomplishing it, but on the way an adventure of gigantic proportions ensued, then you would, of course, write the things that happened. *But.* If it were a romantic comedy and Harry wanted to prepare a great meal for his new girlfriend and had gone to the market for fresh ingredients but had forgotten the cat food, then all we'd need to know was that he went back for it. We could see him surrender to the cat and walk toward the door. We'd just have to cut to later, when we see the cat eating, to know what had transpired.

The beautiful and frustrating thing is this: In either of those two examples, our inventive minds might come up with some great business to take place along the way, hilarious sight gags, encounters with colorful characters that result in clever dialogue. In one story, that would BE the story, and you'd write it. In another story, the exact same material would derail the story, so you'd (A) keep it in anyway because it's so good, or (B–Z) do the right thing and cut it.

Here's an excellent piece of narration that opens another UCLA award-winning script: *Flesh and Blood*, written by Dave Johnson.

EXT. – TOWN OF MURPHY – DAY – YEAR 1878

RAY MORRIS (40s), races a blood-streaked HORSE past dark corridors of SALOONS and clapboard buildings. He beats his mare for more speed, checking over his shoulders with each kick. Eyes of panic.

A WOMAN clutches her son to her chest as Ray nearly tramples them. He slices quickly through the bustling town.

One image forces Ray to pull the horse's reins. A CROSS.

INT. – MURPHY CHURCH – DAY

The REVEREND BROWN stands before his congregation, the Holy Book in his palms like Jesus himself. He belts out the first verse of "Be Not Afraid." The others leap in.

The church doors SLAM open. Sunlight floods the room. The hymn ends as quickly as it started. All eyes on Ray in the doorway. His sweaty face. His BLOOD-stained shirt.

Ray peels off his hat, hiding a gut wound.

Dave does a lot of things right here. First of all, just look how the scene sits on the page. There is a lot of open space. The writing does not daunt the eye. It looks accessible. Look at that first paragraph. The locale is introduced as the backdrop for some urgent action. The horse is *blood-streaked.* The town has *corridors of saloons.* He *beats* the mare for speed. He nearly *tramples* a mother and her baby. He uses active specific verbs. *Beats. Tramples.* The choice of specific and effective **verbs** obviates the need for a lot of adverbs. Adverbs slow things down. This scene is about speed. We don't want words in this scene to slow the pace. We want our language to enhance the emotional feeling that the words generate intellectually.

Then, *boom.* Something stops him. An external object. A CROSS. Notice that the writer doesn't tell us what his facial expression is at seeing the cross or *tell* us that it's a powerful symbol in his life. He has something happen. A verb. The rider stops. Where a woman with a child is nearly trampled, this stops him. This **gives currency** to the cross.

This warrants a brief digression to the idea of establishing currency and how symbolism works and why it doesn't work. Symbols are not universally interpreted in the same way. **A symbol doesn't stand for what you want it to mean until you *make it mean it*.** A bird could mean peace or it could mean birdshit. In *Rabbit-Proof Fence*, an early scene identified the bird as the girls' spiritual guide. So when it returned in Act Three, we knew it was not a vulture ready to prey on the waifs, but their salvation.

Let's look at a trickier example. HOME. What values does that word connote? A place of nesting, of comfort, familiarity, warmth. All good stuff. Like *The Wizard of Oz:* "There's no place like home." As writers, when we express the idea of home, will it always and automatically stand for those values?

Let's glance at how "home" was used in two very interesting movies from the mid-90s: *Naked* (Mike Leigh) and *What's Eating Gilbert Grape* (no question mark; Peter Hedges). The character in *Naked* is a feral creature, a dark but brilliant man who gets the crap beaten out of him and is nurtured back to health by a former girlfriend (who he has treated like crap.) She paints a traditional picture of "home" for him and offers it as refuge. Home in that movie, though it is rejected by the protagonist, is that place of warmth and refuge. It earns its truth because of the way it is presented in the context of the film, in the specific things the girlfriend says and by the situation in which it is offered. It carries narrative and emotional currency.

For Gilbert Grape, home means something very different. It is the weight around his neck. It is his enslavement. Crushing responsibility. Tied to his father's suicide and being the heir apparent. He is constantly beset with its upkeep. And in the end, as a gigantic visual dramatization of his release from it all, the house goes up in flames. Deliberately. The same word, *home*. Two very different symbolic values in two different films.

So how do we do it? An extremely effective mechanism through which a person, place or thing can attain either real or symbolic value is by giving it currency. How do we impart value to a commodity whose value is unknown? We place it in juxtaposition to something of KNOWN value. For instance, a kid shovels snow for a week and gives up candy bars to earn enough money for a ticket to a concert. So we know how much that concert means to him. Now let's say that a girl he likes needs to buy an outfit for a big audition. Does he give her the money? Which will be more valuable to him?

Let's return to the scene from *Flesh and Blood.* We cut to inside the church. Reverend Brown is introduced through a DEFINING ACT. Look what confidence this writer has in his reader and in himself. He doesn't take extra time to say how he's dressed or whether he has white hair or spectacles. But what a great phrase he uses: "the Holy Book in his palms like Jesus himself." That external detail gives us a powerful sense of the man's interior life. It causes us to see everything we need to see. It allows us access to his inner life through his outer life.

This is a beautiful, fast, unpretentious example of the most ELEMENTAL (and elusive) skill in screenwriting. Writing "visually" means finding **EXTERNAL MEANS** to convey **INTERNAL TRUTHS**. Now, with the congregation singing, the stage is set for Ray's **entrance**. *The hymn ends as quickly as it started.* So the currency of the hymn is trumped by Ray's entrance. We are given a new detail here about Ray. His shirt is blood-stained. He peels off his hat, hiding a gut wound.

This is a **narrative** act, not **decorative**. When character business is the writer's way of indicating how an actor will express an emotion, that is a decorative act. And we must not write them in. On the other hand, when the act has a narrative imperative, like taking off his hat to hide a gut wound, this is definitely what the scene is about. The scene would not be the same without it. So it's in.

Here's another nice axiom to use as a way of making language work for you. Especially if you're describing fast-paced action:

Don't let it take longer to read than it would take to do.

You needn't write in complete, well-parsed sentences. Subject verb. Subject verb. Verb. He whirls, shoots, dives. Lay off the sound effects. The KABOOMS. There are better ways to be exciting. Some tricks: Arbitrarily **drop down two lines** in order to:

- Separate each action to a separate line. It creates the staccato feeling of rapid cutting without using camera direction.
- Differentiate between the actions of different characters.
- Differentiate different areas of the same locale.
- Even when none of these conditions apply, and even if it feels completely arbitrary, double-space after a maximum four to five lines of description. There is no good, organic reason to do this. But do it anyway. It makes the "black stuff" (the flattering term studio executives give to the ink on the page) look less daunting.

Readers look for a balance in screenplays between narrative action and dialogue. You don't have to do a word count or get too anal about it. But if your scenes go on for several pages with all dialogue or with none, I'd re-examine those scenes.

WRITING DIALOGUE

An ear for dialogue, like a sense of humor, like a great singing voice, is an innate gift. In basketball, there is the phenomenon of the "pure shooters." They can pour in shots from every angle, from all over the court. Their shots go cleanly through to the bottom of the net. Larry Bird was one. Other players have other great skills but have to work their butts off to become feared shooters. Magic Johnson was one. And like him, if our work ethic and motivation are strong enough, we can hone and greatly strengthen our dialogue skills.

There is some bad dialogue that everyone can hear. It's clunky. It's off-kilter. It's like singing that is so off-key that even someone who's tone deaf can tell. I hope you're not that bad. But even if you are, there's hope.

Most "bad" dialogue doesn't seem to be bad on the surface. It sounds reasonable enough. It expresses the thoughts that are required to be expressed. It gives necessary information. It asserts certain emotions. Both characters express opposing points of view. A few dabs of back-story and memory subtly worked in. Everything the manuals say. And yet...it's not very exciting. It's there. It functions. Like a drone. Not much fun to hear read aloud. It occasionally catches a rhythm, a little spark, but it doesn't ignite, and then it just kind of isn't there anymore.

We're going to attack these cases of DIALOGUE DOLDRUMS at the source. To understand how to write good dialogue, we have to recognize—and I know you're sick of hearing this word, but here it is again—the FUNCTION of dialogue.

The function of dialogue is **not** merely the accurate reproduction of human conversation. It is also **not** a storytelling device, though it is frequently misused to that end. It is **not** a repository for the writer's psychological diagnoses, though we have heard dialogue that has been forced to labor under that burden and felt it buckle under the weight, like a spiderweb catching coconuts. It **is** a way to capture the essence of an interaction, in words. Not an interaction. The *essence* of an interaction. Writer-director Floyd Mutrux once spoke to a class of mine and said that writing dialogue is like writing *headlines.* He was saying "write just the essence." As Louis Armstrong told some kid, "Put away the notes. Let's play some music."

There are two powerful machines every writer must have in order to write good dialogue, and they must be used constantly. They will not wear out with overuse; in fact, they will become more acute. They are located on either side of your head. No, not your stereo speakers. Yes, your ears. Before we can learn to speak, we've got to learn to listen. And to hear.

Good dialogue tells us about the characters; bad dialogue tells us about the writer. Dialogue is often written "on the nose," meaning that the characters are prosaically saying the obvious truth. Often these are truths that we'd know from the circumstances of the scene and have no need of hearing them put into words. It is like playing the identical notes in unison with the right hand and the left. There is no harmony, no distance between word and action for harmonics to resonate.

Raymond Carver wrote a short story called "What We Talk about When We Talk about Love." The dialogue between a couple whose marriage is breaking up can be a diagnostic dispute about the dynamics of the relationship, or it can be about an unmatched sock, or the car parked crookedly in the garage. One scene is going to be generic, technical, dry and wordy. The other is going to be volatile, unpredictable, specific, funny, poignant. Or at least it will have those possibilities. The other is born barely breathing and is not going to get more interesting.

So now we have a specific focus. How do we keep dialogue off the nose? Let's use what we've already digested to guide us. Every scene has one reason for existence: to be an arena for characters doing everything possible to get what they want in the moment. Hence, dialogue must serve *that* purpose. **Dialogue must function as (a large or small) part of a character's efforts to accomplish his or her immediate objective.**

- It is **never** a character's objective to give information to the audience.
- Characters **ought not to be complicit** with the writer's intentions for them.
- A character's objective is **not** to tell the story or to supply biographical information, backstory, mood, symbolism or psychological diagnosis.
- Characters on page 19 cannot have read ahead to page 63 and act or speak based on that future knowledge.

We talked about the nucleus of the scene being character desire, and the rings in orbit around it as the successive strategies for accomplishing it. If action is the medium, the level of action will have to intensify. If dialogue is the medium, then its intensity will have to increase.

There are so many films with great dialogue throughout: *The Lion in Winter*, *Two for the Road*, *Rocky*, *Ordinary People*, *All the President's Men* and nearly everything by David Mamet, but I especially love *House of Games* and *The Winslow Boy*. The incredible run of Woody Allen films from the 70s and 80s: *Annie Hall*, *Hannah and Her Sisters*, *Interiors*, *Manhattan*, *Crimes and Misdemeanors*. So many of the fast-talking movies of the thirties. Lately: *You Can Count on Me*, *The Hours*, *Ghost World*. There are some fantastic dialogue scenes in *Lost in America* (the scene with his boss where he doesn't get the job, and the "refund scene" with the Vegas casino boss described earlier) and in *Tootsie* (many, many scenes, but the early one in particular, where Sydney Pollack's character tells Dustin Hoffman's character no one will hire him.)

Good dialogue expresses the voices of its characters. Sometimes they may talk a lot, sometimes not. Silence can at times be far more eloquent than spoken words, and often the best dialogue is the dialogue not written.

In the scene I have cited from *Sea of Love*, when Frank Keller (Al Pacino) makes a drunken late-night call to his ex-wife saying he thinks he has appendicitis, the unspoken text is, "Denise, I'm lonely and I miss you and you were the only person I could call for solace." But he could never be so direct with her. The question for dialogue is not "what is the truth?" but "how would this character express that truth in this situation?" His ex-wife, awakened from sleep and with her new husband, *could have said*, "How dare you call me in the middle of the night again? I've told you a dozen times to stop." Ah, but what is her objective in the scene? Her objective is revealed in what she **does**. She hangs up. *Without speaking a word.*

Characters have to tell *their* truth, not *the* truth. And they have to do it in their way.

This illustrates an interesting INVERSE PROPORTION about dialogue. It is almost always true, in a confrontation between two characters, that the one with the *least* dialogue is the stronger. Think of the classic Western hero, the man of few words. It translates.

ADRENALINE EXERCISE

> Write a long peroration for one character and have another character deflate him with a word.

Among the many things you want to avoid in writing dialogue is what I call the "catechism" scene. This is where a series of direct questions yields direct answers, where the answering character is there clearly for the convenience of both writer and protagonist.

The way to avoid that—and here we go back to Character Objectives again—is to give BOTH characters in your scene a reason for being there. Two jackals, one bone. *All the President's Men* is a great object lesson in how to do questions right. In many encounters Woodward and Bernstein make no headway at all. The people they question are not merely generic stone walls. They are very drawn, their circumstances are specific. What the protagonists need from them is clear and urgent, and their ways of avoiding or refusing emerge completely from their character and situation. And in the scenes where they *do* manage to extract some kernel of new information, it comes as the result of great effort, effort that keeps throwing them to the next and next (metaphorical) ring of electrons. In every scene the writer keeps pushing. **How far will a character go to get what he wants?**

Keep each of your characters in his/her own agenda. Characters do not have to answer one another, or to tell the objective truth. The scene we looked at earlier in Dave Johnson's *Flesh and Blood* has a nice dialogue sequence after Ray, with his bloody gut wound, seeks refuge in the church. Dave does a thousand things right here. Remember in the previous scene, Ray tore ass in on a horse, nearly trampling a woman and child. In contrast to this, his adversary will enter not faster and wilder, but slow and cool.

```
The creak of the church door opening. Fear keeps
Ray's head from lifting.

                    REVEREND BROWN
          Join us, stranger. The Lord always makes
          room for one more.

Spurs from shiny black boots approach Ray,
splintering the wood floor.
```

[NB: He doesn't say "CUT TO CLOSE UP." But he gives us the feeling of it.]

```
A MAN sits beside him.

                    STRANGER (OS)
          Hello, Raymond.
```

[Commentary: The little touch of calling him by his full name. Who is in charge here and who is in danger? Ray, with his gut wound and trapped with a powerful adversary, is the underdog. We feel apprehension for his safety...at the very least.]

The stranger is dressed in neatly pressed black vest and pants. His handsome face is smooth and shaven, almost polished.

By the look on Ray's face, this is someone you don't want sitting next to you, not now, not ever. The stranger is SAM BUTLER (50s.)

[Dave may overdescribe just a little bit. But I like it here, because what he is doing subtextually is having Ray stew in his fear next to this guy, and he makes us experience that by making us wait to see what happens next. The key is that he has so successfully engineered the situation that we ARE involved with the character.]

SAM BUTLER
Go on, mista' preacher man.

The Reverend dives back into the holy book.

RAY
This is a holy place, Sam. God's temple.

SAM BUTLER
Beautiful, ain't it?

RAY
Let me be.

[This next line tells me I'm in the hands of a writer with skills and a voice. It's page 2. My confidence in him zooms.]

SAM BUTLER
Not a big churchgoer myself, mind ya. I only gone two times.

RAY
Please, Sam. It was a long time ago. I was

just a foolish young'n.

[What have we just learned? There's a past. Something happened. Something Ray did.]

REVEREND BROWN (OS)
Out of the depths I cry to you, O Lord. Let your ears be attentive to my cry of mercy.

SAM BUTLER
The first time was my wedding day. Can't top that, no sir. You know the other time I sat in the house of the Lord, Raymond?

RAY
I got caught up in it, Sam. We all was stupid.

[**INFORMATION IS A BY-PRODUCT OF CONFLICT**. As Ray's unmet objective tightens the noose of danger around his throat, the growing desperation squeezes more information out. All driven by his objective. And Sam stays right inside his objective, too. He does not respond to Ray's pleas but keeps his own agenda in the driver's seat.]

SAM BUTLER
It was my wife's funeral. Couldn't top that one either. You ever been to a funeral, Raymond?

Ray looks for an escape route. Silhouettes of armed men loom in the stained-glass windows.

[Look how economically he writes that. We see everything, and in doing so, see into the hearts and minds of both men. Where are our sympathies now? We know what *EACH CHARACTER* wants to happen next. Do we know what *will* happen next?]

REVEREND BROWN (OS)
We wait for the Lord. Our soul waits. And in his word we put our hope.

SAM BUTLER
Well, have ya?

Ray bounds up to the Reverend, grabbing him as a shield. The congregation GASPS.

RAY
I ain't gonna die, Sam. God forgave me for what I done. Why can't you?

REVEREND BROWN
(To Sam)
Find forgiveness in your heart, son. We're all God's children.

Sam pulls a ruby-eyed Colt .45 from his vest.

RAY
Not this one.

Sam aims. The Reverend Brown raises his arms, hiding Raymond behind the Bible.

[Is there the slightest doubt what the absolute immediate, urgent, specific objective is of each character in this moment? Look at their Wadoogees! And how far each goes to accomplish it.]

REVEREND BROWN
Oh Lord.

RAY
God damn you, Sam Butler. Damn you to hell. You deserved what you got. You should be the one up here askin' for forgiveness, Not me—

BLAM!

[I don't love "blam." But it's a great example of a strong one-syllable reply to a four-line piece of dialogue.]

Ray goes white. The Reverend drops his arms, looking at a dime-sized hole through the Bible's core. Ray's life escapes his flesh with that bullet.

The writer does so much right here:

- The dialogue stays in the moment.
- It comes from each character's individual emotional landscape.
- It is in each character's individual voice.
- It deepens character.

Character Objectives drive the scene.

Information is a by-product of **conflict**.

Dialogue carries the **emotional thread** of DNA while narrative is carried by event.

Events tell the story so the characters can talk to each other.

We are **not told** about the characters. We **experience** them.

He is cruel to his characters. They are kept in (what I like to call) the **Discomfort Zone**. If characters are sailing too smoothly, we lose interest in them.

Be nice to your friends and mates, be cruel to your characters.

There are **no camera directions**, but the narrative leads our eye.

The only **parenthetical directs a line of dialogue to a specific character**, but does not direct the utterance of the line.

The overall effect of the scene is brilliantly achieved. As viewers we are left with a disquieting sense of **emotional ambiguity**. Should forgiveness have prevailed here, or was revenge justified? That is the very question we will explore in the story. But the way he achieved the ambiguity is a great example of how to do it, of how to Take Vienna in a scene. The character (Ray) traverses the full gamut of emotions, from abject fear all the way to defiance.

A lot of writers, when they wish to depict a character who has ambivalent feelings, keep that character right on the center line, leaning (emotionally) neither right nor left very far. Scenes written this way will have to be flat, because the strategy the writer used in trying to dramatize ambivalence was to keep the character's emotional life shielded. A better way is to let the scene go all the way to one side, then all the way to the other. Think of it as scraping plaque from an artery. You want to scour both walls, not just the center. And finally, the scene LOOKS GOOD ON THE PAGE. He made it look nice for the customers. There is a nice mix of dialogue and action. Not too much of that black stuff. There's air and breathing room.

WRITERS GYM EXERCISES

Exercise #1

Write two versions of the same situation: A guy comes home from the racetrack and his mate is not pleased that he's been there.

In Version #1 his first line is, "I won almost three thousand dollars."

In Version #2 his first line is, "I almost won three thousand dollars."

Exercise #2

Go to a large newsstand and buy an out-of-town newspaper. The smaller the town, the better. Go to the Social Announcements page. Pick out a couple just getting married. Use whatever is written about them to invent their lives. Make them real enough for you so that you can do the following:

Write a scene or sequence of scenes that includes the

one where they are most in love.

Write a scene from their lives five years later. Don't do the obvious, or the next to obvious. Write them until something comes up that really surprises and delights you, something you had not thought of. (I don't mean that an elephant falls from the sky.) Something that brings them to life.

In the same newspaper, find the crime blotter. Outline a series of scenes that would best tell that story. (Which character would you introduce first? The arresting officer? The perpetrator? The victim? The judge? An innocent bystander? What would that character be doing? What are the strengths of that choice? Could you think of something better? More interesting? Why *that* point of entry into the story? Would it start the story too early, too late?

Select a scene that would have dialogue in it, and write it.

How do you know how these people sound? What are you hearing? Do you know the region?)

When you're finished, **read it out loud**. Or have your writing group or actor friends read the parts. What do you think? Believable? Alive? Dead?

If it doesn't work well, you will think it is because you don't know what Creole jargon sounds like or how they talk in Wyoming. And there is definitely truth in that. But remember what I told you earlier. Most scenes that go wrong do so because the characters' objectives are not sharply delineated.

Read the scene again. What are the characters' objectives? Are they absolutely clear? Is the scene completely about the characters' Wadoogees?

Let's digress briefly and speak about **dialect**. There are two ways to think about dialect. Write it or don't. Writing dialect means altering the spelling to approximate the way the words will be pronounced. Most people will tell you NO DIALECT. I'd abide a small bit just for flavoring. But don't try to spell out every word phonetically. A great thing about regional argot is not just the pronunciation but the great local expressions, the rhythms of speech, lyrical or laconic. For example, a fierce little 90-pound, 90-year-old grandmother comes bursting into the kitchen of her Kentucky farm house, where her grandson's new Northern wife is cooking breakfast and demands, "What smells so loud?" In this scene, whether we spell out the word "so" or write it "suh" is **not** the distinguishing characteristic of that line.

Sentence construction. An Irish lover talking about a raging river with his lover on the other side: "And over it I'll build a bridge that never more true love shall sever." A Californian wouldn't say it that way. Or a New Yorker. Or a Norwegian.

Go through a page of your latest screenplay. Just one page. Read your narrative descriptions out loud. Take out all facial expressions and hand gestures. With your yellow highlighter pen, highlight only the narrative action that moves the story. Everything else gets saved for your scrapbook of great unused lines. Have you repeated the same word several times? The same noun? Say it in a different way. More economically. You don't have to say, "He heads for the barn. "INT. – BARN" tells us he's in the barn.

Eavesdropper Journal

You must commit yourselves to becoming active

listeners. When immigrants were told that the streets of America were paved with gold, they were very disillusioned to come here and find that it was not true. For writers, it is true. The streets are cobbled with gold nuggets. So are buses and nightclub restrooms, cafes and restaurants, the lobbies of theaters, your family's dining room table, beauty parlors, radiation waiting rooms, law offices, interior decorators' conventions, team locker rooms, park benches, the beach. Wherever people are, wherever they speak to one another.

KEEP A SMALL NOTEBOOK AND PEN WITH YOU AT ALL TIMES.

You never know what you'll hear, and when you hear a great phrase or an amazing conversation, you've got to write it down. You think you'll remember it, just like you think you'll remember at what age your children passed each of their milestones, but you won't. An overheard conversation can be a gift from God. And when God offers you a peach, you don't say, "No thanks, I've already eaten."

CHAPTER 15

Tricks, Techniques and Stunning Acts of Legerdemain

In this chapter we look at the more frequently used nonlinear storytelling devices such as Voice Over, Flashback and Flash Forward. We also examine some specialized tricks or techniques that are very helpful additions to your writer's toolbox.

FLASHBACK AND VOICE OVER

New writers often ask: "Is it all right to use Flashbacks?" Or, "Is it okay to have a Voice Over?" The questions really being asked are less about the potency of the technique than whether the technique is currently in vogue. And more profoundly, will their script be consigned to the trash bin for committing the unpardonable sin of being blatantly unhip?

These are valid concerns, as they reflect on the mentality of the movie business (no oxymoron jokes, please). There is no group of people more Pavlovian about following successful trends than executives in the entertainment industry. As the studios and their satellite production companies become increasingly corporate, fewer "story people" are promoted into the decision-making positions. With notable brilliant exceptions, people with creative titles know less about the creation of the product they manufacture, and a good deal more about marketing it.

The prevailing group sensibility is defined by conventional wisdom, and there are few people in the infrastructure who are sure of their convictions and courageous enough to risk their great jobs by going out on a limb. Witness that for many years certain genres were out. No one would make a Western or a sports movie. Until one became a surprise hit. Then everyone wanted one. Until the market became saturated with crappy versions of the genre. Then, rather than recognize that they have simply made some crappy movies, the "wisdom" once again became that the (fill in the blank) genre was out. And it will be. Until someone else makes a good one (meaning that it makes money!) and it is in again.

The big open secret is that successes are lucky accidents. Nobody really knows what they did right to make something a hit, or what somebody else did wrong to make it a flop. Within that larger context, with an awareness of the need for incumbents to stay on the cutting edge and of their their subsequent disdain for anything that falls behind it, it is no small wonder that a hopeful entry-level writer is concerned that his or her spec script might be tossed aside if it contains an out-of-favor device.

Here's the healthiest approach I can recommend. Accept as true that you're never going to be as hip as the people on the inside, so don't try to be. Use a different strength. Write your screenplay in as fresh and original a way as you can. Sing in your own voice. If you try to sing in somebody else's voice, you won't be as good at it as they are, and who will be left to sing in yours? Tell the story that you want to tell using the most effective means at your command. If this means using Voice Overs, Flashbacks, Flash Forwards, not moving directly from left to right but in a nonlinear fashion, then do so.

BUT WITH THIS CAVEAT.

Any time you use such a device, you are calling attention to it as a device, and (1) you had better use it effectively, and (2) it had better be the best way of telling the story. If you know sports, here's an analogy. Would you throw a behind-the-back pass in a situation where you didn't have to? Even if no damage was done, you'd be seen as a show-off. And if perchance that pass was errant and jeopardized your team, you'd be booed. And deservedly so. Your operative question ought not to be, "is it okay to use Flashbacks?" but "*what is the best way to tell this story?*"

Obviously, many films have used Flashbacks with great success. *Ordinary People* (Alvin Sargent, from Judith Guest's novel) comes immediately to mind, as well as *Catch-22* (Buck Henry, from Joseph Heller's novel). In both films, fragments of memory (told through Flashback) gradually become more coherent as the character becomes more in touch with them, and ultimately are the narrative devices that break open the story's mystery. There is a *narrative imperative* to the technique. It is organic to the telling of the story. It is not just cool.

Billy Wilder, Charles Brackett and D.M. Marshman Jr.'s *Sunset Boulevard* starts at the end, then flashes back to the beginning, and from there proceeds in a straightforward manner (if you call a Voice Over from a dead man straightforward). Many films have used that concept since. A first cousin to it occurs in the very brilliant *American Beauty*. In that film the protagonist (and source of VO narration) is not dead yet, but quite accurately informs us that he soon will be.

Another beautiful example of total Flashback is in Marleen Gorris's *Antonia's Line*. This film won the Oscar for best foreign film a few years ago, and you must see it. The story opens with the narrative voice telling us that this will be Antonia's last day on earth, and then flashes back to the day she returns to her Dutch farming village at the end of World War II. From there it moves forward through three generations of daughters' lives, to the final day of Antonia's.

The structure of *Memento* (and before that, Harold Pinter's play adapted to film, *Betrayal*) is quite ingenious, starting at the end and moving sequentially toward the beginning. There is a sweet metaphysical overlay to *American Beauty* that makes it stylistically organic for Lester to be talking to us before and after his death. The drama of *Memento* is all about the shifting sands of trust and loyalty. Telling the story in reverse enhances the unfolding of those undulations.

There is a nicely executed VOICE OVER technique Eric Heisserer's screenplay for *Arrival*. Louise Banks (the lead character played by Amy Adams) speaks specifically to another character in the story. (As it is revealed to her by the visiting aliens that TIME is nonlinear), she tells the story of her daughter's life to her daughter who is simultaneously unborn and deceased. Like many techniques, directing the VO to a character has been done before. In this case it folds in to the story's theme as well.

There are so many films that use Voice Over successfully. In addition to those already mentioned, there is Woody Allen's *Manhattan*, Don Roos's *The Opposite of Sex*, and scads of 1940s film noir detective tales. For every example of these techniques used well, there are many more where they are used badly. Not badly as much as ineffectively, arbitrarily. All right, badly.

FLASHBACKITIS

Every action any character ever takes, every thought or event theoretically has an antecedent memory that may serve as a "flashback landing pad." Why take one and not another? Why take any at all? Let's discuss the answer the way financial planners talk. What are the upside benefits? What are the downside risks? And most important, what indicators do you look for to know whether you're in profit or loss? What are the symptoms of acute Flashbackitis? When do we go for treatment? When do we consider a radical flashbackectomy?

A typical topical symptom of **UFBS (Unnecessary Flashback Syndrome)** is a certain dizziness that occurs from the whipping back and forth between time zones. Are you (the writer) starting to *consciously look* for matching moments between the adulthood and youth of your character? For wrinkles in time? This is an example of style leading content. It will lead you into a very cerebral, symbolic, stylized exercise, and usually away from feeling. You will become so focused on giving full realization to the device that you will succeed in giving *full realization to the device.* That is a very different verb and Writer's Objective than *telling the story.*

There is another, more profoundly weakening effect that Flashback can have. Its surface symptoms are less apparent and less easy to spot. I felt that it seriously afflicted a film as well done as *Lone Star.* In simple terms, the Flashback scenes had all the energy. Nearly all of the most vivid scenes, the moments of highest tension and passion, were in the Flashback scenes. I felt very little dramatic urgency in the present tense.

Whether or not you agree with that particular example, look at your own work. Have your Flashbacks taken over like kudzu vines? Are they sapping vital energy out of the present? Are they tiresome? Are they done for mood? Or for effect? Does it feel like you are slogging through a snowdrift, that there is no tensile strength to the present, that each step is going hip deep into the snow until it finds emotional bedrock, that you are expending great amounts of energy but not getting very far?

Have the courage to ask yourself the hard questions. Why are you flashing back? Is the history you are uncovering necessary to the telling of the story? Is going back there to retrieve it necessary? Is there an organic way it can play out in the present? **Let the style be organic to the story.**

VOICE OVER

The examples of films that demonstrate the ineffective use of Voice Over derive from the same principle. The basic question you must ask is always the same. *What is the best way to tell this story?* What would using it accomplish for you? Are you using it as an enhancement or as a crutch?

When a Voice Over is working well, it gives the audience access to the inner thoughts of the character or characters. It provides us with "information" that could come only from that source. Remember that "information" does not mean facts and factoids. VO is used most effectively as a road into the character's psyche.

Audiences can only know what they see and hear, and are thus privy to a character's inner life except solely as it is revealed through the things they do and say. Thus VO can be a valuable tool, especially if what the character is doing or saying does *not* fully reveal the vital inner truth. When best used, VO provides a different perspective to the character and/or the action.

A chillingly effective use of VO is at the beginning of Kasi Lemmons' *Eve's Bayou.* How's this for a provocative line? "I was eight years old the summer I killed my father." Would that get you interested in the story? It sets us up to enter a story where we will find an abused child under the sway of a sadistic parent. But instead, we encounter a girl who adores her father. But she has told us she killed him!

VO should be used as counterpoint, not as a caption.

In its most commonly occurring abuses, Voice Over tells us what we are seeing without adding much perspective. If you have a scene where a kid tries to climb a fence and falls into a mud puddle, you don't need the VO saying "I was a clumsy kid." Have him say "I always had my own sense of grace."

We don't want to become too narratively dependent on the Voice

Over. Like Flashbackitis, when too much of the energy is sapped out of the content of the scenes we are watching, they can become dried up, desiccated, brittle and crumbly as a molted insect shell.

Often there is a **specific person to whom the VO is being directed.** It might be in the form of a letter or a confession to someone in the story. It might be a diary or an unseen friend. Or it might be the audience. You as the writer should know exactly who your speaker is addressing. It will determine the manner in which the character speaks. (A letter to a lover will sound different than a letter to a newspaper.) It will determine the level of truth and reliability, the tone, the sense of humor; in short, the very *voice* of the Voice Over. A film in which (for me) Voice Over did not enhance the story was *Age of Innocence.* While much of the VO was taken directly from Edith Wharton's novel, I could never quite identify the narrative voice with a character in the story.

SUBTEXT

Subtext is an ingredient, like teamwork or grace under fire. Writers know it is a great thing to have but are at a loss to know how to find it. Typically, writers try to write it into amazingly significant facial expressions. ("He smiles, knowing that the world will be a better place and that good will triumph.") That's gotta be one hell of a smile.

Creating Subtext takes an understanding that scenes work in sequences. You need to plant in Scene A the seeds for Subtext in Scene B. Remember the scene we had examined from *Sea of Love* where the guy comes running up with his kid in hopes of seeing the Yankees? The first thing Frank Keller asks is to see his *invitation*.

The tension in that scene derives from the scene that preceded it, where the audience learns that the piece of paper Clarence thinks is an invitation is really an *arrest warrant!* Take away Scene A and Scene B would be forced to convey all of what is now contained in the Subtext with significant looks.

Here are two simplistic scene sequences. Version One: Two glasses of beer sit on a coffee table, a man and a woman on either side. A third man stands by the door. He nods to the woman, and she picks up the glass closest to her. Version Two: Add a previous scene where a poison pill is dropped into one of the glasses of beer. When the man nods to her, we know that he is telling her to drink from the glass without the poison. Or with the poison!

Subtext, like the tango, takes two.

SYMBOLISM

The less you think about Symbolism, the better off you are. Most efforts to be symbolic regrettably succeed. The result is that something in your screenplay is symbolic of something else. And this enhances your work how? (Other than it being something you envision critics raving about or grad students writing about in their dissertations.)

Like Flashbacks and like Voice Overs, self-conscious symbolism and its cousin, Foreshadowing, are devices that we think are necessary because they were taught to us as the essence of literature by people who held only the suitcase handle and never opened it up and sniffed the perfumes and the dirty socks.

Symbolism is derived from the context of the story. Or not at all. The same is true of foreshadowing. It depends on the internal light source and what it is that is casting a shadow. We noted in the previous chapter about the polar opposite meanings of "home" in *What's Eating Gilbert Grape* and *Naked*. In one it symbolizes a return to innocence, refuge, a safe, secure place. In the other it is a yoke, a crushing obligation, an anchor. Did the writer just decide and ordain that these symbolic meanings applied? No, my darlings. It does not work that way. Meaning evolves from the accumulated events of the narrative. You cannot write: *A dove flies into the scene. A symbol of peace.* You CAN write: *A dove flies into the scene.* But you cannot presume that it symbolizes peace.

A symbol does not mean what the writer tells us it means. It means what the story tells us it means.

THE OBJECTIVE CORRELATIVE

I borrow the term *Objective Correlative* from T. S. Eliot and adapt it to mean an external object that represents a character or a state of mind. Rocky's locker is Rocky's manhood. When it is taken from him, it is like a castration. In *Truly Madly Deeply*, the cello is Jamie. In *About Schmidt* (by Louis Begley and Alexander Payne), when he sees his carefully prepared reports in the garbage, it represents the entirety of his life's work.

PLOTS AND PLANS

Michael Corleone sits in the sedan with rival family leader Solazzo and police captain McClosky. The car turns onto the George Washington Bridge heading for New Jersey. Michael's heart drops into his stomach and so does ours. Why?

Michael gets up from the table in the restaurant and goes to the men's room. He searches behind the toilet for a gun and does not immediately find it. Our hearts drop into our stomachs. Why?

Michael returns from the bathroom and sits down with the men again and resumes talking. Our hearts drop into our stomachs. Why?

Because all these occurrences went directly counter to meticulously plotted **Plans**. After an exhaustive and nearly failed attempt to discover in advance where the meeting would take place, the

Corleone family found out it was going to be in a small restaurant in the Bronx. When the car heads for Jersey, Michael is suddenly completely vulnerable.

A gun was to be taped in the bathroom for Michael to use. When it is not there, he is suddenly vulnerable.

He was to come out of the bathroom shooting. With those arrangements carefully driven home, and with Michael's life hanging in the balance, any deviation from that plan causes us great anxiety. The technique works in the same way Subtext works. Set up a plan in Scene A, have it go awry in scenes B, C, D.

There are three ways to handle Plans.

1. Have a plan. Let it go awry.
2. Give the protagonist no plan at all. Everything that occurs is a surprise to the protagonist and the audience. The benefit is that the audience has the same experience as the character—being confronted with circumstances it has to respond to immediately.
3. Have a plan. Let it all work out smoothly. Lovely and nice for the protagonist. Boring for the audience. Remember, we want to keep our character in that **DISCOMFORT ZONE**.

If the story protects the protagonist, the audience won't have to.

HORRIFIC HEROES AND HELLISH HEROINES

The heroine of *The Last Seduction* meticulously and cold-heartedly seduces a young man so he will kill her husband. We root for her to succeed. Do we endorse murder?

We admire and respect and feel ennobled in the presence of Don Corleone. If it was an FBI picture starring Adam Sandler against the Mob, would we root for the Mob?

We are at the very least fascinated by, and perhaps even unconsciously rooting for, the assassin in *The Day of the Jackal* (Kenneth Ross's screenplay based on Frederick Forsyth's novel).

The cable and streaming television shows of the last decade have really run with this idea. *The Sopranos*, if not THE pioneer show, certainly was a spearhead. We are not spared the graphic scenes right in our faces of all the cruel and violent things he does to his enemies, not to mention undermining his own wife. There is *Dexter*, a serial killer, the previously mentioned Walter White of *Breaking Bad*, Jimmy McGill aka Saul Goodman of *Breaking Bad* and *Better Call Saul*. And spates of others. *Girlboss*, *Girls*, *Fargo*, *The Mindy Project*. Where executives once demanded likability in a lead character, now they look for the opposite.

The films noted above are among hundreds of other equally good examples of two powerful dramatic techniques. They are *intimacy* and *innocence by disassociation*.

Intimacy

You can't be reminded too many times of the powerful subtextual effect that Intimacy carries. The more time we spend with a character, the more we become invested in that character. So true is this axiom that the decision is often made never to see or hear a character for fear of the audience overly empathizing with that character. The more deeply we are involved in a person's (or character's) life, the more we love the person and forgive or ignore some of the person's acts.

If we were with the parents in *Heavenly Creatures* for the entire movie, and at the end of it these girls came in and killed the mother, we'd have no sympathy at all for them and mourn the victim. But we are in the hearts and minds of the girls throughout. We are traveling on their **emotional current.**

We are brought into the private wishes of Don Corleone for his son. In light of all we see him do for others (which is all we see him do), and in light of the very human thing he wants, we feel intimate with him.

The destructive behavior of the Charles Bukowski character is self destructive. He inflicts more pain on himself than on anyone else. In that behavior, we come to realize that he feels he is unworthy of anything better. That touches a very deep part of him.

There is also the **ordeal/reward** equation. When we endure a character's pain, we take it as our own and wish for relief. We see this syndrome played out in life so often when a killer shows grief and remorse. A smart lawyer will try to personalize the perpetrator, humanize him. As writers we have to be careful.

In *Splash*, the Tom Hanks character has a conversation with a girl who is moving out on him. We never see her or hear her voice. If she were personalized, we would feel too much of her pain of being with a man who cannot say he loves her. And that would go counter to the writer's objective.

The complete opposite approach is taken in *Queen of Hearts*, where the creators want the audience to feel for the victor and the vanquished. Indeed, that dual empathy is almost what the story *is*, since its emotional source resides in the heart of the woman being claimed by both men.

The concept is powerfully illustrated in the Oscar-nominated documentary, *Winged Migration*. This is an amazing film that takes its audience close up into the flights of migratory birds during their epic migrations over thousands of miles. We feel their ordeal, their desire. We see a few of them die. Some are shot. Some are too weak to make the flight. One with a broken wing is devoured by crabs. We feel awful for this bird. But if the documentary *were about the crabs*, we would have experienced the pain of *their* lives, the uncertainty of *their* procreation and birth, the vulnerability of *their* young to some other predator, and celebrated their finding this meal. And perhaps if we had spent the entire film with a hard-scrapping Louisiana Delta family, experienced their travails, known their souls, we might have felt relief when, with his last shell, the young son felled a duck and fed his family. This is **EMOTIONAL INTIMACY**.

Innocence by Disassociation

Or, if you want to make a bad person seem nice, make everyone else around him or her worse. It sounds like a joke, but truly you will be surprised at how often that technique is used. Some large examples:

Don Corleone says no to the five families. They want to sell heroin and use his connections to abet the cause. There are four against one. But he stands firm to his principles. Moreover, in contrast to their united front, his own ally, Sonny, speaks out of turn and compromises his bargaining position and his effectiveness as a parent. The don has to apologize for Sonny's breach. He is just "a principled old warrior with old-fashioned values and dreams for his family that we fear won't come true."

In *The Last Seduction*, following a coke deal, the protagonist's husband slaps her hard across the face. Everything she does subsequently (stealing his money, seducing the assassin) is in response. And up to the last minute, she is the wronged party and all her acts are emotionally justified. Also, she is made the underdog. She has to hide from him. He is in search of her. She is (let's say it together) vulnerable.

In *The Day of the Jackal*, we first experience the torture of citizens under the brutal authority of the French secret police. So when someone is hired to assassinate French president Charles DeGaulle, we enter the world through the emotional current of the wronged parties. We somehow don't respond morally. Our emotions are engaged, and because of the ordeal/reward principle, we want some abatement to their suffering, and the Jackal is the medium.

Both the Innocence by Disassociation and the Intimacy principles are engaged here. The "enemy" has been made worse, and we are brought into his world. Into his emotional current. At first he is the underdog. Every part of the task that he must successfully perform to get himself and a suitable weapon into place takes great cunning and ingenuity and is played out very intimately. The long-range objective is broken down into many short-range and specific and necessary objectives. We've already discussed the limitless power that focused Character Objectives exert. We're with him.

Furthermore, the head of the French Secret Service, the force charged with finding the assassin, is a pompous, arrogant goat. We'd want him to fail at finding his nostril with his left index finger. And for half the picture, we are rooting for the assassin. He is not sugar-coated. He is cold and calculating, totally professional. He sleeps with a woman in a chateau and kills her the next morning. And yet...

Then something drastic happens. Command is taken away from the Secret Service jerk and given to a fussy little provincial detective. Our rooting interest changes. Now the Jackal has all the advantages and the inspector is the underdog. We stay intimate in both characters' lives. Our loyalties are remarkably divided throughout.

In *The Bridge on the River Kwai*, this happens in *triplicate*. In the beginning Saito is the "pure evil" enemy. But through the middle and by the end we have experienced his vulnerability, felt the weight on his soul. He has lost face, failed his mission and must die. We also experience a small but poignant glimpse into the heart of Alec Guinness's character, Col. Nicholson. His career has been undistinguished. He has been home with his wife for merely two months out of his 30-year career. He'd like this bridge to stand for centuries as his modest legacy. He fights against his own men to save the bridge!

A gorgeous truth of fiction is that audiences can suspend their moral judgments when fascination is strong and compelling enough. This is why some of the great fictional characters are villains. Which man interested you more in *Silence of the Lambs*: Hannibal the Cannibal, or Clarice Starling's sexist and manipulative (but legally delegated) boss?

Innocence by Disassociation is a bit of a trick. Intimacy is the real art.

Pamela Gray does something difficult and rare in *A Walk on the Moon.* That she pulls it off is part of why I love the script. That she thinks to try it is part of why I love her. She has three principal characters in a love triangle: a husband, his wife and her lover. **And none of them are villains**. They are all sympathetic characters. The story is set at the Catskill Mountain summer resort that Jewish families inhabit. This is the summer of Woodstock and the summer of the moonwalk. She involves her heroine in an adulterous affair with the traveling blouse man while her husband is back in New York City working. It would have been so easy and easily accepted by an audience to make the husband dorky or abusive or inattentive—a bad husband, a philanderer, a bad father. But she resists that temptation. Played by Liev Schreiber, Marty is a good man. Conventional, yes. (But so is she.) Devoted, sweet, a good father and husband.

The scene between Marty and his wife, Pearl (beautifully played by Diane Lane in a more deeply written role than the similar character in *Unfaithful* which gained her all the attention and an Oscar nomination), on the night before he goes back to town, could easily have made him out to be a lout, someone any wife would be justified in cuckolding. It would have made the writing of Pearl's seduction by the blouse man much easier. But instead, this is the scene:

[NB: The reference to "doing Chuck" comes from a popular song they hear on the radio in which names are rhymed. Their young son, Danny, is dying to "do Chuck" so he can say the deliciously forbidden word. This is used as a unifying device: At the end of the story he gets to do it. This scene is from the shooting script:]

31. INT. BUNGALOW – MARTY AND PEARL'S BEDROOM – NIGHT

The room is lit only by moonlight, which washes over Pearl, in bra and slip, as she hangs up her dress. The clock RADIO plays Eddie Fisher's "WISH YOU WERE HERE." Pearl shudders from the cold and closes the window. In the b.g., a toilet flushes. Pearl crosses to the dresser, opens her top drawer, and takes out a nightgown. As she places the nightgown on the dresser, Marty enters, comes up behind her and kisses her neck.

PEARL
(Playful)
Is this because of me or Mrs. Dymbort?

MARTY
A little of both.

She turns around and hits him.

MARTY (CONT'D)
I'm kidding. I'm kidding.

He takes her in his arms and they kiss.

MARTY (CONT'D)
You're the only girl for me, Pearlie.

They kiss again, passion mounting. Marty guides Pearl towards the bed.

PAMELA'S NOTE: Filmed scene starts here with them already in bed.

PEARL
(Whispering)
You wanna do Chuck a different way?

He looks at her, startled.

MARTY
What kind of different way?

PEARL
I don't know. We'll experiment.

Marty looks uneasy, then starts to undress.

MARTY
Well...O.K.

PEARL
We don't have to.

MARTY
No, it's just... I thought we were doing it pretty good the old way.

PEARL
We were. I just thought it might be fun.

MARTY
(Uncomfortable)
O.K...What did you have in mind?

There's an awkward pause. Suddenly, Marty leaves the room. Pearl stands there, confused. After a moment we hear Marty off-screen.

MARTY (O.S.) (CONT'D)
(John Wayne)
O.K., pretty lady—there's a posse out lookin' for me so I ain't got much time.

Marty steps into the doorway wearing Daniel's little cowboy hat and holding Daniel's holster around the waist of his boxer shorts. Pearl laughs.

MARTY (CONT'D)
Is this different enough?

The holster drops to the floor as Marty lifts Pearl and heaves her clumsily onto the bed.

Pearl is a good wife and mother. But she is watching her 15-year-old daughter (Anna Paquin) come into womanhood. Pearl never had a childhood. She got pregnant at 17. And there is a battle between mother and daughter as to who gets to be the flower child.

Pearl falls under the gentle sway of the blouse man (Viggo Mortensen), and they have an affair that erupts to a climax where she dances bare-breasted at Woodstock, and is seen by her daughter.

In a series of great scenes, Pamela brings this family conflict to a white heat and tears down the family unit she has so exquisitely built. She does it without denigrating any of the characters, without making any of them moustache-twirling villains, without making them gratuitously evil or stupid, shallow or foolish. She digs deep *into* character, not out of it, and finds those ineffable truths that make us human. And in the end, when the family reunites, we believe these ties have been tested to their limits and have somehow held, welded by the torch of something that feels very much like love.

Here is the final scene between Pearl and Walker (the blouse man). He wants her to come to California. Marty, her husband, knows what has happened. They have met. Walker had come to the rescue of their son after the kid had been stung by wasps. He knew what to do and was there to do it. The cards are stacked against Marty. This is the full scene as written, with Pamela's notes indicating the small piece of the scene that was shot.

(137) EXT. – WALKER'S HOUSE – DAY

It's a sunny morning and Walker's working in a vegetable garden on the side of his house, putting the last of the summer harvest into a basket. Pearl approaches, holding his red t-shirt.

PEARL

Hi.

Walker turns and smiles.

WALKER

Hi. How's Daniel?

PEARL

Better. He's O.K.

WALKER

Good.

He wipes his hands on his pants and starts to move towards her to kiss her. Pearl holds out his shirt.

PAMELA'S NOTE: Viggo Mortensen added his character smoking. It showed the character's pain since when he interacts with Pearl earlier he says he quit.

PEARL

I can't go.

Walker is silent. He takes the shirt.

The following two lines are cut from filmed scene.

PEARL (CONT'D)

My family...I just...

WALKER

I know. I saw.

PAMELA'S NOTE: Filmed dialogue ends with Walker's next line.

WALKER

I'm in love with you, Pearl.

Next lines of dialogue are all cut from scene.

PEARL

I know.

(A beat)

I love Marty. I love my children. I've hurt them...I need to try to make things work. I want to.

They stand there for a moment. She touches his arm.

PEARL (CONT'D)
What will you do?

WALKER
I think I'm gonna go anyway.

He reaches over and gently touches her cheek.

WALKER (CONT'D)
I'd rather sleep under the stars with you, Pearl.

Pearl puts her hand over his, closes her eyes for a beat, then opens them.

PEARL
I have to go.

Pearl moves toward him and they embrace for a long time. Walker looks at her, then kisses her. Pearl lets the kiss happen, then breaks the embrace. She starts to walk away, then turns back around.

PEARL (CONT'D)
Walker, do you think I made a fool of myself?

WALKER
How did you feel?

PEARL
I felt beautiful.

He looks at her, confirming her answer. She smiles and walks off.

PAMELA'S NOTE: He embraces (not kisses) her in filmed scene and Pearl runs away.

COME IN LATE, GET OUT EARLY

These are not only rules governing your hotel stay. You've

heard this before.

1. Enter in deep. The best place for most scenes to start is the closest point to the essence of the action.

2. End the scene as soon as the objective is either accomplished or terminally thwarted. Don't make it an "oh, and while we're talking, there's something else I want to discuss."

CURRENCY AND CALL WAITING

These are two extremely helpful techniques for getting those things that are very clear in your head down onto the page. It is most important for an audience to know what is important to a character. But how do we bring the audience into that state of knowingness? The most obvious way is to have the character announce the information. Stand him on a chair, have him make a solemn pledge that (fill in the blank) is the absolute most important thing in life to him. That ought to do it, right?

If only.

"What are words?" Falstaff asks in his soliloquy on courage. Then he belches. "Air." And it is true. How many times have you heard people swear this is the last drink they'll ever have, the last cigarette they'll ever smoke, the last time they will go back to that relationship? In your experience, have those vows often proved to be reliable indicators of behavior?

Words can be taken back, ignored, never meant, too hard to live up to, equivocated, modified, reinterpreted, forgotten, discounted, denied. Whereas actions have weight. They have **consequence**. Words are air, actions are bricks. When domino #2 falls against domino #3, it knocks #3 into #4 and #4 into #5. When domino #2 says I'm going to fall against you so you may as well knock #3 over, nothing changes.

If you are a character and you pay $300 for that puppy, that rose, that ticket, that pencil, that bag of white powder, that loaf of bread, that kiss, the audience knows exactly what its *cost* is to you. And if we also saw how you came to have that $300, then we would know more. Did you win $10 million in the lottery? Did you work three weeks in a car wash? Did you sell your car for it, or your house? Did you steal it? At what risk and from whom? And at what cost? Then we would know its *value*. Its worth. To you.

Taking this knowledge and working backward into our screenplay, we want our audience to know (translation: *experience*) a truth about our character. An effective means of dramatizing it is to place an object of unknown value alongside something of known value and have the character need to choose one or the other.

A weekend with a lover or studying for the bar exam. What about a planned weekend with a lover or helping a friend? Lover or work? Money or life? (Remember Jack Benny's famous line when he is being held up at gunpoint and the gunman demands, "Your money or your life." After a long, long pause he replies, "I'm thinking.") The entire premise of the film *Indecent Proposal* is built on this device. Would a husband take a million dollars to let another man sleep with his wife?

(A more daring premise might have been Redford offering 10 million if the *husband* would sleep with him, but anyway—)

Who we are is revealed in what we do and in the value we place on the things in our world; what we are willing to give up to attain them. A vital skill in dramatic technique is to bring those qualities to your characters' lives. Never forget the basic rules of scene writing. Create a *situation*, a circumstance where a character has to make a difficult choice. And remember, this does not mean a character has to sit and *deliberate*. A choice can be presented and acted upon in a moment. A chase scene. A baby in the road. Swerve and you go off the road. Go straight and you hit it. Your protagonist hasn't eaten in two days and finds a wallet with 30 dollars in singles. Eat or return it?

This is a specific and practical application of one of the basic Golden Principles: Event is the building block of action. Screenwriting is a verb-dominated craft. Outer life events are designed to reveal the inner life of the character. **This continually moving intersection of plot and character is called the story.**

Call waiting is an effective strategy of establishing currency. You're on the phone. Another call comes in. Who do you stay on with and who do you call back? The choice you make is an irrefutable statement of which call is more important to you at that moment.

The "call waiting" scenes in your screenplay by no means have to be *phone calls.*

- Your character has a date with one guy, but then her real heartthrob calls and says yes. Whom does she go with?
- The job interview and the kid's championship game are at the same time. Which does he attend?
- At a dinner party, two people vie for your attention. Which one gets it? The boss or your kid? Too easy a choice? How about overbearing boss or injured kid? Or understanding boss or spoiled kid?

It's a great device that can be used unobtrusively between and among principal characters, or with a minor character for just a line.

DIRECTION IN DIALOGUE

Instead of writing character behavior into narrative action or parentheticals where we will be scolded for directing on the page, do what Shakespeare did. Have another character in the scene refer to that behavior. "Wow, you eat fast!" Or "Take your arm off my shoulder." Or "Why are you huffing and puffing? We only walked a block." There's a scene in *Tootsie* where Dustin Hoffman is walking Teri Garr home after a party. She says she had a good time but is having an emotional breakdown. He asks, "Why are you crying?"

It's a nice exercise for keeping your characters emotionally rooted in the moment and observant of their surroundings.

WRITERS GYM EXERCISES

Character Autobiography

Write the full name of your character down the left side of a page, one letter on each line. On each line, write a true statement about the character (or from his or her voice), beginning the first word of each line with each letter of the character's name. So, for a character named Holmeyer:

He lives with a rabbit
Open hearted
Loves bridges
Means well
Ebbs when he should flow
Yearns for love
Even tempered
Runs from life

Try it with all your main characters. Try it with your own name, too.

Genres

Two cars, a sports car and an SUV, arrive at the same parking spot. Write the scene or sequence of scenes in

- A romantic comedy
- An action/adventure
- A film noir mystery
- Science fiction

You may change the vehicles and characters, inhabiting them as you please. Now go write your script.

Here is **another great use for scene cards**. You have built them into ten-page columns, the blue card at the bottom being your payoff scene, your fence-post scene, your Scenogram Box Scene. You can write in 10-page blocks. Everything that precedes that event is somehow tied to it, relates to it, builds toward it, is subservient to it. You can write each 10-page block as a story unto itself. Doing so will give you a good hard-edged rhythm. Before you start, make sure that within that 10-page block there is at least one significant red card scene, an event that will prohibit the thing that happens in the Box Scene from happening. This guarantees that you will be ingenious enough to devise a scene that supercedes the effect of that red card scene so that the Box Scene can occur as planned.

PART FOUR

The "Rees": Research and Rewriting

CHAPTER 16
Research

Like sex, research—which is really *pre*search—can be a pleasant and socially acceptable strategy to avoid writing. It appeared many times on the Master List of Procrastinations.

There are, of course, legitimate circumstances that justify or even ordain the necessity of doing research. Sometimes it is just for a few facts. (Was Washington, D.C., the capital in 1789? When did they start giving the polio vaccine orally? What were the hit songs in 1996?) But more often, if any research is needed at all, then a great deal is needed. You may be writing a period piece or contemporary story set within a substratum of society you don't know well, or a story set in an exotic geographic locale. (Exotic is anything you don't know. If you've never been to Hoboken, Hoboken is exotic.)

We have to know enough about the world we are depicting (or creating) to make it believable, to put the audience inside that world. All the applicable laws of physics, psychology and sociology must be in place. This chapter is not intended as a "how-to" on research. It's more a discussion of how *much* to. And usually writers do too much.

Being in a state of "knowingness" is essential to an author. We are admonished, are we not, to write what we know? Plato's guidance is to *know thyself*. Physicians are scolded to *heal thyself*. The question then is, what must a writer "know" to be in a state of knowingness sufficient to create the illusion of truth? Not *truth*. Truth is a surveillance camera. The *appearance* of truth. Verisimilitude.

One of our writing students, defending a scene in response to his classmates' criticism that it didn't feel believable, swore, "But that's exactly the way it happened!" To which my colleague, Professor Lew Hunter, replied, "The truth is no excuse for a scene that doesn't work."

The truth is no excuse.

Understanding this is to understand a basic tenet of art and literature. I had a professor of medieval poetry at Queens College named Sears Jane. He taught that "truth" with a small "t" is *what happens to have happened.* "Truth" with a capital "T" is *what happens.*

Many scripts suffer from a condition called **Researchitis**. The writer has worked so hard, has gleaned so much fascinating information, that the temptation to display it all is overwhelming. Research tells us a lot of "truth," a lot of things that happen to have happened. There are endless facts and factoids we can uncover, discover, learn, be amazed to learn, be astonished and shocked to know about a period or about a character, or about anything! But if a writer in the year 3002 were researching THIS period, how much of all that was possible to know would he need to know in order to render this period believable?

Would his audience have to be educated about day trading and the World Series, Saddam Hussein and curly fries? The number of gallons of jet fuel consumed by a fully loaded 747 flying from New York to Amsterdam? The Academy Award-winning song?

How do we temper our delight of discovery and our desire to show the audience (our surrogate parents/lovers) "Look what I found!" with the restraint of storytelling?

The answer lies not in Aristotle, not in Egri. It is in the pancreas.

Imagine that you are writing a contemporary story. Think about the two-line character description you'd write to introduce your principal characters. Among the many truths you might conceivably know is their blood-sugar level. But in the normal course of events, would you ever think to include that? In all the writing you have done so far, how often have you thought your audience needed to know that information?

And yet, when researching a period, writers find ways to cram similarly irrelevant (but fascinating) nuggets they scooped up in the library, or on the Internet, or interviewing this incredible hairdresser. It's understandable. Everything we discover doing research is brand new to us, and everything new feels equally interesting. We want to pass it on. We want to be the repositories of interesting ideas, discoveries. We want to be vessels.

How do we know what is narrative and what is merely decorative? How do we know what stays and what goes? Which is screenplay and which is award-acceptance speech material? **Apply the litmus test of the pancreas**. Does the story demand it?

Yes, it is a fascinating psychic coincidence that the Gold Rush in America and Marx's *Communist Manifesto* occurred in the same year. But is it relevant to the story I'm telling?

If you were writing a mystery-thriller, where the accused murderer's story hinges on his knowing about the time change from Daylight Savings to Standard, or if the story turned on Denver's being in one time zone and Indianapolis another, or that there was one state that did NOT switch to Daylight Savings Time, then that information would be narratively crucial. And you would use all of your skill to acquire and weave that accurate information into the organic texture of the story in the most interesting way that served the needs of the story. But if your story was set in Denver, and it was about a school library censoring books and had nothing to do with time zones, then time zones would never be mentioned. Empirically, the fact is equally true in both cases. Dramatically, it is relevant in one, not in the other.

The same dynamic occurs in researching an exotic culture or subculture or occupation. It is not necessary for a character who is an orchestra conductor to describe each note in terms of its number of vibrations per second. Nor would it make interesting or believable conversation for a person in India to mention the number of foot/tons of silt carried away by the Indus River annually.

BUT. **If it is important to the story that the facts be supportable by the Truth of the situation, then as a writer you had better get it right**.

Before you have your story turn on George Washington sending a telegram to Congress, you had better check to see if that technology existed back then.

Hollywood production is great at re-creating historical accuracy. There are directors and art directors who are fanatical about it. But no degree of accuracy with props and costumes will ever make up for the writer's not capturing the spirit of the time and weaving that spirit into the texture of the story, both in character psychology and in narrative choices.

In appendix A at the back of the book is a list of Internet sites used for research by some of our UCLA writers.

CHAPTER 17
Rewriting

Let the bells toll. You have written FADE OUT. You have done it. You have come to the end. You can look way back to the other side of that huge, uncrossable chasm you have now crossed. You remember the moment when you got the brilliant idea that this would make a great screenplay. You remember the decision to take it on, the stepping-over that line into the realm of "I will." That day might seem like a long, long time ago.

You have snowplowed and you have scene-carded. You have been to the Writers Gym diligently. You have worked on your weak muscles. You have structured. You have let yourself be inspired and frustrated, elated and despondent, but through it all you have come to work. You have shown up. You have been the elves. You have faced adversity with courage. You have read some of your first pages and nearly barfed. Or maybe you actually did barf. But you have also persevered. You have dug down through the mud to the strongbox that was buried underneath. You have had some of the best days and worst days of your life. Or maybe best minutes and worst days.

But look who won in the end! You have a draft that even a harsh critic would have to admit is not too horrible. You are emotionally exhausted. Maybe you did a 16-hour sprint to the end. You don't even want to look at what your room looks like.

It looks like a place that has been inhabited by a writer, not a human being. You have barely enough energy to spell-check it and print the sucker out.

You want to take a shower. You want a stiff drink. You want to hold the thing in your arms and offer it to heaven like Kunta Kinte. You want to think about the world genuflecting to you. The ads in *Variety*. The new car. Your award acceptance speech.

The last thing, I mean the very last *thought* you are capable of holding in your mind right now, is rewriting. And that's good. Nature is our friend. Because the last thing you are capable of doing right now is rewriting it. This is not to say the script does not need work. But before we talk about that, let's look at what you have done, at what a first draft's (here's that word again) function is in the overall process. Anne Lamott calls it the *down* draft…just get it *down*. I've heard it called the puke draft. I wish I could do my great pantomime for you of a guy trapped inside a rickety house, propping up timbers, stopping leaks, holding in a windowpane.

Completing the first draft means that we can step gingerly out of that house. We won't slam the door too hard, but we can step outside and it will stand without our holding it up. We can walk around it, see where it's solid and where it teeters, where the wind might blow it over, and where it looks stately and grand. But first there is the incredible relief that it's standing!

There are people who don't get this far. People who leap helter-skelter into FADE IN without doing the prep work that you did, and whose stories flame out after 30 pages. There are people who work and work at the first 30 pages, honing them, buffing one section of a hardwood floor to an amazing luster but leaving the house unbuilt. They think they can make it perfect the first time through. They do not understand the primary law of screenwriting physics, which is:

BEFORE YOU CAN WRITE A SECOND DRAFT, YOU

MUST FIRST WRITE THE FIRST DRAFT.

Give in to it. Surrender to a force more powerful than yourself. Accept with serenity that before you write the second, third, fourth and fifth drafts that you have to write the first. *And that it does not have to be perfect.*

That it can *never* be perfect. Even if something *could* possibly be perfect, since you become a better writer every day, you'd constantly have to bring every part of it up to the new level of possible perfection you have achieved, and some part of it would always be a little less perfect than the rest. Does that sentence alone not make you crazy?

So lighten up. Write a damn good, kick-ass first draft, make three copies, give two to extremely trusted reading buddies who love and respect you enough to be honest, and put the third one away. Ask your friends to make written notes. Page notes if they choose, and an overall impression. Once they have done that, put them away with your draft. And let it sit for at least three weeks. It's important that you take enough time away from your script so that when you reread it, you don't remember it too well. Only then can you be distant enough from the process that created it so that your critical faculties engage.

At UCLA we're on a 10-week quarter system. First drafts of ideas pitched in week 1 are due at the end of week 10. Four weeks later the process starts again. I think it's a great idea to write a whole new screenplay before looking back at the first one. You'll be amazed at how much you've learned subliminally that will go into the first draft of the next script. Harbor no illusions: it will be no closer to "completion" than was the first draft of your first one. What will be better about it is that you will have tried to do more. Your understanding of what a screenplay can be will have expanded, and so will your ability to fulfill it. But it will still lag as far behind as it did the first time. You will feel just as frustrated. Just as inadequate. Just as unequal to the task.

And that is how a writer evolves.

When you are ready to read your first draft, take it out of the drawer, but don't read your friends' notes yet. Read the draft yourself first and make your own notes. Some writers are in love with their words, and many more barf when they read them. Try to see the story as though someone else had written it. It'll help you get over the shock of imperfection. You'll start to see chunks of story scaffolding fall away. Chunks of dialogue dropping off and revealing some pretty good exchanges. Gold ingots under the lead molds. You'll see scenes that weigh eight thousand pounds, scenes that exhaust you to read.

Suddenly it will click in your brain. Maybe as you glance idly at that Conflict Agreement you signed and forgot about. And you'll realize these dead scenes have no conflict in them. The words *Character Objectives* will explode into your consciousness. You will examine scenes and discover that what you had thought at the time were clear and sharp Character Objectives were instead cloudy and unspecific. A lightbulb goes on. You think maybe you understand something important.

Now read your friends notes. How do their comments gel with what you have begun to realize?

A serious note about looking for reasons to discredit criticism. The reason people can't listen to criticism (and I'm not talking about malicious, amputating criticism, I mean loving criticism from trusted friends) is that we are afraid the work we did is the best possible work we can ever do. And if the work isn't good enough, then *we ourselves* aren't good enough, and the game is over right then. You can think of criticism as an act of affirmation that the person giving it knows you can take and work with, and that he or she has the ultimate faith in you that you *can* make it better.

Someone doesn't need to supply the right *remedy* for his or her diagnosis about your script's ailment to be correct. If you get a consistent sense from readers that something is missing, even if they cannot satisfy your challenge to tell you what it is, or if their ideas for a remedy are completely off base, you'd still be wise not to dismiss the value of the diagnosis. It isn't their job to solve the problem for you. If they alert you that a floorboard is creaky, that they needed to hold on to the wall for security, it's your job to find out whether the board is warped or if there is merely a screw loose, or whether the whole damn foundation is rotten. Your job.

HOW TO REWRITE

There are two distinct levels of work that a script might need—the equivalent of having a procedure done in the doctor's office or needing hospitalization. The rewrite is the more severe. The superficial treatment would be called a dialogue polish. (The Writer's Guild minimum for a polish is much less than for a rewrite. Employers have been known to contract a writer to do a polish and ultimately have them do a full rewrite.)

But let's not jump too far into the future. You've completed a first draft of your spec script, gotten some notes. Now what do you do? How do you start your second draft? The natural instinct is to hold on tenaciously to as much as possible. I like to take the opposite approach. I think of myself as the prime minister and all the scenes as my cabinet. I ask all of them to submit their resignations. There are several members whose resignations I will not accept and they will remain. But I want to have the creative freedom to start from scratch if I need to.

Revise means to see again. I ask myself the same questions I asked at the start of the process. Whose story is it? What does he want? What will he do to get it? What is the worst thing that happens to him short of death? Will he change or at least come to the possibility of change? Am I interested? Do I care? What is a truly memorable circumstance in which I can introduce him, with surprises and twists? Something that gets the audience sitting up in their seats.

Then I snowplow all over again. Of course the ideas will come to mind now in the context of the script's already having been written. But you will know how certain scenes have to be modified. Those modifications will set up new circumstances that will engender new moves, new scene ideas, some of them merely slight alterations, others more radical. Your starting point might be ten pages later. Or earlier.

In the earliest drafts of *Chinatown*, the whole story was about Jake Gittes's past and his dismissal from the police force in disgrace. Twenty-seven drafts later, that backstory has completely molted into a few lines in a few scenes, though the feeling and the repercussions certainly exist in the present.

Your story may not change to that profound degree. But the more receptive you allow yourself to be to the possibility of change, the more confident you will be that if a scene stays, it really belongs.

Repeat the process of snowplowing just as you did for draft one. Then make new scene cards for new scenes and place them into the pre-existing pack you had made. Remove cards for deleted scenes or for radically altered scenes. They might possibly have new headings.

Reorder the cards in sequence. Lay them out in columns. This is a critical juncture. The new shape of the story begins to be determined now. Take all the time necessary to really **know your act breaks**. Think carefully about the notes you got and your own reaction to reading the first draft. Is it possible that the root cause for some of these problems was structural? Is the scene you have for the end of Act One really a point of no return? Is there an emotional buildup to it? Does the inciting scene happen early enough? Is there a way to strengthen the way it plays against the exposition scenes? What about the end of Act Two? Now that you know the characters better, their desires and weaknesses, is there a better place you can take the act end than you did in the first draft? Maybe even a far better scene? An event you're afraid to use because it is so dire the character could never recover? That's the one to go for!

Give close scrutiny to the last 10 pages of Act Two and all of Act

Three. You may have been so anxious to finish that you sprinted to the end and gave the last act short shrift. In the rewrite, do the third act first, with your best energy.

Does your story need some more red cards? Do things happen too easily? Do not take the character directly from the idea that will be triumphant to its execution. The end of *The Treasure of the Sierra Madre* doesn't have them all riding in together saying "Look at the cool stuff we found." But even if the protagonist succeeds in the end, don't let the audience off the hook too soon.

FINISH STRONG.

Think of all that happened in *The Godfather* after Michael's return. The whole story with Kay plays out. Michael's consolidation of power in his own family. And the incredible bloodbath wherein he wipes out all his enemies including his sister's husband (who she married in the opening scene).

One of the great plot turnarounds occurs as we plunge into Act Three of *The Bridge on the River Kwai*. The Holden character, who barely escaped the Japanese prison camp alive, is commandeered by the British to go back into the jungle to find the prison camp and destroy the bridge. The ordeal is filled with drama and adversity. The climax is an amazing tour de force of screenwriting by Michael Wilson, Carl Foreman and Pierre Boulle. The three gigantic principal characters in the end are pitted against one another in a way you'd never have imagined at the beginning.

Mere knowledge (the "must learn") is not enough. That knowledge must be put to the test. So, at the end of Act Two of *Splash*, when the Tom Hanks character sees that Daryl Hannah is a mermaid and rejects her, he has to wallow in that despair for a while before he changes. Even after he sees the error of his ways, the escape is a "mission impossible." They make it out of the confinement tank. But this is not yet the end of the movie. It only sets up the end of the movie. The bad guys (the entire U.S. Army) give chase through New York. At the climax of the film, it's splash time again. She has jumped in. To have her, he must jump in as well. But it will be at the cost of ever living on earth.

Check out your own ordeal/reward ratio. Does it feel right? Is the ending earned? Are the events telling the story? **LET THE EVENTS TELL THE STORY SO THE CHARACTERS CAN TALK TO EACH OTHER.**

At the end of *The Bridge on the River Kwai*, there is one verbal anti-war statement. The story works three hours to earn that one line. It's actually just one word, repeated: "Madness."

Check your script. Have you used characters to carry your polemics? Look closely at the written scenes. **IS THE CHARACTER ACTING IN A WAY TO GET WHAT HE or SHE WANTS RIGHT NOW?** As soon as that thread is broken, stop and fix it. Wherever the telegraph wire is broken, that's as far as the electricity goes.

Do you feel the direct cause-and-effect relationship leading from one scene to the next? Does what happen in Scene 3 provoke the events of Scene 5 and make them unavoidable?

Write your second draft. Store in a cool, dry place and begin the process on your next script. Again, this is in the case of voluntary rewrites. When your script is bought and you are working at the behest of its purchasers, you are in a very different environment. Here, changes are forced upon you by executives whose vehemence sometimes exceeds their intelligence. Or there may be a group of people you have to please whose ideas are all contradictory. This is a glimpse into why it is called Development Hell. But we are discussing voluntary rewrites.

How many times do you need to go through it? How many drafts until you can send it out? A couple of years after Pamela Gray won the Goldwyn Award for *The Blouse Man* and the script was optioned, I asked her to speak to my writing class and to bring in all the drafts she had done thus far. Stacked on the floor, the pile stood higher than her knee. Three years later, when the film came out (under the title

A Walk on the Moon), I asked her how high the script pile had gotten. She pointed to her chin. And she wasn't exaggerating by much.

They don't get better every time, either. I've seen fourth drafts that were worse than the second and third. We can get so analytical in our approach to a script that we write the life right out of it. We lose that messy, exuberant, uninhibited enthusiasm of the first draft. It's hard to find again once it's lost. It's easy to sharpen it to the inevitable point of dullness. When do you stop flaying a script that won't leap up and dance? When is it time to move on? It would be great if there were a concrete answer that always applied. I believe dogged perseverance is a valuable trait for a writer to possess, but prudence dictates that after three drafts—first draft, rewrite and polish—if the script is getting no better, then maybe it's time to pull the proverbial chain and flush. Or at least leave it alone for a full year.

AND THEN WHAT?

You want to get your screenplay into the food chain. Luckily, your first cousin is a hot agent at William Morris and your dad used to run a studio. Or if not, exploit any personal contacts you have. Do you know anyone? Do you know anyone who knows anyone?

If you have to start cold, you are by no means excluded from the game. But it will take more effort. Some people are more cut out for it than others. *Writing* and *marketing* are two very different verbs.

There are many good sources for contact information on agents and managers, including the *Hollywood Creative Directory*, the Writers Guild and a comprehensive book by K. Callan entitled *The Script is Finished, Now What do I do?* There is a great template for a letter in William Goldman's book *Adventures in the Screen Trade.*

Persevere.

Interlogue

By Sacha Gervasi

I'm writing a movie and it's killing me. I've just passed page 100 in the script and I'm not even at the end of the first act. I have no idea what the story is, and the characters sound—well, I don't really have to tell you if you've ever written a first draft of anything.

In any case, there's absolutely no point in continuing, I decided this morning in the shower, since my story is about as commercial as a black-and-white musical about a sect of mute roller-skating nuns set against the fall of the Ottoman Empire. And to top it all off, two nights ago I played the first full game of soccer I've played in fifteen years. I am now in what my doctor calls a "walking coma." He charges me more than fifty dollars per word for this. So I can't move AND I can't write.

I call my great teacher, Hal Ackerman, to see if he will meet me at a nearby café to commiserate, to see if, somehow, he can ease the pain of all this first-draft madness. And you know what the first thing he does is? He asks me to write a preface for this bloody book! BASTARD. I need drugs, not more writing. But I agree, of course. And the reason I agree is not just that Hal is a brilliant teacher and a brilliant friend, which he is. It is because a few years ago at this very same café, I remember breaking down in front of him because I just couldn't finish the script I was writing in his class. Lots of beginnings.

No endings. That seemed to sum up my life. It was time to book my flight back to London.

Hal waited until I was finished and then gently told me the truth: no matter how terrible it was, I *had* to finish it. He told me screenwriting is hardly ever about being great before it is about being willing to endure an awful amount of pain, the pain of being faced with one's own mediocrity. "If you can allow yourself to be a bad screenwriter first," he said, "then you allow for something magical to happen."

I don't know why, but I listened. A few weeks later I finished the unfinishable script. It was certainly horrible, but I had done it. "Just as you have to finish it now," he reminds me.

I return to work with Hal's words ringing in my ears. If I keep going there is a remote chance the script may not be a complete disaster. And if it isn't a complete disaster, then perhaps one day it could even turn into an actual film, with actual actors saying the lines that I am spewing out in a demented frenzy while splayed nude on my kitchen floor drinking low-fat chocolate milk and listening to the Cocteau Twins' *Heaven or Las Vegas* album very loud indeed. A hope in hell is still a hope, after all.

So to all of you out there hoping to do this for a living: Listen to Hal. He knows what he's talking about. The truth is, being a screenwriter is hard, but it could be the most satisfying thing you'll ever do. And if you're a writer you'll know it. And if you know it, then all you have to do is sit down and begin.

And don't even think about not finishing.

Sacha Gervasi's credits include The Terminal, *starring Tom Hanks and directed by Steven Spielberg*, November Criminals, *and* Henry's Crime. *He has added directing to his resume with* My Dinner with Herve, *starring Jaime Dornan and Peter Dinklage*, Hitchcock, *starring Anthony Hopkins, Helen Mirren and Scarlett Johansson, and* Anvil: The Story of Anvil.

PART FIVE

Afterthoughts and Additions

CHAPTER 18

A Short Chapter on Writing the Short Film

As faculty director of the UCLA Student Film Festival, I have seen more than a thousand short films over ten years—live action and animated, fiction and documentary. Among them have been the thesis films of such gifted artists as Alexander Payne (*About Schmidt, Election, Citizen Ruth*), Brad Silberling (*Moonlight Mile, City of Angels*), Gina Prince-Bythewood (*Love & Basketball*), and many others whose stars are on the horizon.

Each year the hundred or so newly finished films are prescreened over a long weekend. Watching 18 hours of student films in a weekend might sound like the third ring of hell. But it is a fantastic learning experience. It is like a centrifuge: the good, the bad and the mid-range are blatantly delineated, and it is so clear what works and what doesn't work and why.

Obviously, a 10- to 20-minute short is not meant to be a commercial product in the way that a feature film is. But too many students take this declaration of commercial independence as a directive to make their films the polar opposite of Hollywood commercial ventures. It is a classic case of tossing out the baby with the bathwater. For not only are the abuses of commercial filmmaking consciously rejected—the splash and pizzazz, the car chases and SFX—but sometimes so are its strengths. Particularly, story and character.

In their place, expanding into that vacuum far too often, we find the bane of undisciplined art gone awry, self-indulgence. It isn't pretty. Whether a film is long or short, an audience goes to experience the characters, not the author. Too often the camera becomes a soapbox for the writer-director's feelings about gender, race, sexuality, politics, morality, all of which are valid passions for an artist to express. But the mere fact that an artist feels passionately about a subject does not necessarily make the treatment of that subject artistic. Whether it's a quill in our hand or a camera, we must remember that we are storytellers.

And while the criteria for what suffices as a story may be more lenient in a short film, and while we may be supported by our classmates for our ability to capture allegorical imagery and fracture time into pixels, if all of these techniques do not exist in the service of story, the product becomes more of an exercise. For whatever its duration, six seconds or six hours, a film is meant to be evocative and entertaining. This does not mean *mindlessly* entertaining. Entertainment can be mindful.

A short film is almost always about one thing. One moment. One event. One punchline. One revelation. One life-changing or illuminating occurrence.

In constructing your short film idea, imagine that you have only enough film and money to shoot three scenes. Visualize three boxes. In the first box place the one significant event that emotionally dramatizes the protagonist's life circumstances as they are. What would be the most interesting and telling ONE CIRCUMSTANCE that would dramatize who that character is? In Box #2 place the climactic event. In Box #3, the event that defines the character's circumstances in his or her changed world.

That is your basic spine. Those three scenes have to tell the schematic of the story the way someone learning a language constructs sentences of subject, verb, object. Now add sparingly. If you were given resources for two more scenes, where are they most needed to tell the story? Maybe they'd go in Box #1 to set up the emotional life of the character and to move us to root for his or her desire to change. Keep building it this way, from the core out. Sparingly. What is most needed? What will give you the most emotional bang for your buck?

Character Objectives and Writer's Objectives apply just as rigorously in the short as in the feature. Scenes must have conflict. Characters are driven by their Wadoogees. Symbolism, mood, foreshadowing, theme, Flashbacks—all must derive from the story, not from the writer-director.

Once the film is shot, of course it will be too long. In its assembly it will be too long. In its rough cut it will be too long. In its getting-there cut it will be too long. And at last, in its final cut, **it will still be too long**. Shrink those initial three boxes down. As a director, don't blow all those important lessons you've learned as a writer. Verbs. Objectives. In deep, out early. If you have a great nine-minute story living inside of a 14-minute film, it is like having a size three foot in a size nine shoe. I can't remember one film I've ever seen that was too short.

CHAPTER 19

Living Your Writing Life

Yes, it's great to be lying on the sofa on a Sunday afternoon, newspaper over your face, eyes pleasantly closed, and when someone demands "What are you doing?" you answer truthfully, "Working."

There's a series of interviews published by the *Paris Review* called *Writers at Work*, in which writers talk predominantly about their craft, their writing habits. I think the first one I read was Arthur Miller's. He described sitting in his elegant study, looking out his picture windows at his Connecticut wooded meadow, having breakfast, watching the deer, and I thought, *Yes! That is the only way to do it!*

Then the next interview was with a writer who went months without writing a word, then locked herself in her basement, guzzled coffee and Jack Daniel's, smoked incessantly, didn't eat, and didn't emerge until she had a completed manuscript. And I thought, *Yes! That is the only way to do it!*

After every interview I read—and every one was different—I thought, *Yes. That is the only way to do it*. And for each of those people, yes. It was. The question you have to ask is, what is the only way for **you** to do it?

I have found some small, helpful tools that have worked for me, for colleagues and students over the years.

1. DRESS FOR WORK. GO TO WORK.

If you are having trouble staying focused on writing in your home environment, make it feel like work. Carve out one area that is separate from everything else. Make it your work area. Don't use it for anything else. Dress for work. Put yourself into your writing persona. Let people know that you are at work and not free to drive them to the airport.

If your life allows it and your personality supports it, work at regular hours. Your body and internal mechanisms will start to form a cellular pattern just as they would with any other exercise program. We can program ourselves to expect and not quite crave writing, but to feel its absence. Writing becomes the default position rather than not writing.

Rituals sometimes help. Remember the sweet moments in *Shakespeare in Love*? He spit in his hands, twirled the quill to get it hot, spun around and got to work. But even HE needed a muse. Have your special coffee or tea in your special cup. Wear that shirt or scarf. Become the writer—you.

2. MUSIC/READING

Some people like music playing in the background, or have a particular song or kind of song that inspires them. For others it is the same song every time. Some vary the music to create the specific mood that their first scene of the day needs to evoke. Reading a great short story often turns me on—the stunning use of language, the insights into the human condition expressed with brilliant economic ease.

3. CLEARING THE PALATE

Some people need to get certain things done first so their minds can be clear to write. There is great satisfaction in crossing the three of four chores off the list and having the next block of time cleared physically and mentally for writing. Of course, there is the obvious danger that the list can take up the entire day. Beware that *inspiration* and *preparation* don't cross over the line into you-know-what—*procrastination.*

4. WRITING BLOCKS

I hate the proliferation of new "diseases" and "conditions" that have always existed but now are being dubbed with three-initial terms for the sole purpose of marketing drugs to suppress their symptoms. Unhappiness and stress and staccato behavior are built into the internal physics of the human condition, just as blizzards and tornadoes are part of the climate. That doesn't mean we should medicate against rain.

Some writing blockage is a natural part of the terrain. There is burnout, just as there is in anything else. Doctors need vacations. So do firefighters. Even farmland needs a season off every few years to replenish. So do writers.

And even in the day-to-day there are roadblocks. But let's make the analogy of driving your car. Every day you encounter roadblocks, detours, dead ends, traffic jams. You don't abandon the car or just sit there at the dead end waiting for someone to come and pave the road. You turn around, retrace your path, find a detour. We are able to do this because we have achieved a level of familiarity with driving. Familiarity diminishes fear. If we have not yet achieved the familiarity that experience brings in writing, it is easy to feel overwhelmed.

Don't make Writers Block a disease. Don't identify yourself by your ailment. "I can't write, I have writers block" is a self-propelling statement. Once you say you have it, you have it because you say it. Our minds are extremely susceptible to suggestion. A great deal of what we believe is the result of a subtle kind of self-hypnosis.

Just as an unathletic kid may make excuses for not playing rather than be embarrassed, so, many of us say we can't write because we have WBS (writers block syndrome). There's an anthem among guys who have been in prison: "You do the time, don't let the time do you." Do you see how it applies here? To hell with hiding your ineptitude. Revel in it. Dare to be stupid! Ultimately the feeling of missed opportunity hurts longer and deeper than does the derision heaped on you from the outside.

Remedies For Writers Block Syndrome

Exercise. Many of the exercises in this book are designed to get you writing, to prime your physical and emotional pumps. They are nonthreatening. Do as many reps as necessary.

Writing in sequences. Among the collateral benefits of the Scenogram and scene cards is that they give you clear, contained, finite writing sequences. You don't have to hold the entire script in your head (your onboard RAM); you can focus on 10-page sections. They are easy to hold, and there is a great feeling in their accomplishment.

Yogurt Culture. The way you make yogurt is you start with yogurt. A small dollop placed in a warm container of milk will convert it overnight into yogurt. The important thing is not to eat it all but to save a dollop to make tomorrow's portion. A woman from Lebanon once told me that her family had an unbroken yogurt culture dating back several centuries. How does this apply to writing? Save a dollop. Don't write to exhaustion. Leave work with something more in your onboard RAM. Two great things happen. During the night, that tablespoon of "scene yogurt" creates another small container of yogurt. You come to work the next day filled with optimism and enthusiasm, not dread. You KNOW what you are going to write. Once you have written that page or two that you kept in reserve, you will be delighted to find that you have not drained the well, that there is more there. But remember to leave some at the end of the next day, too.

Page quota. John Updike set a goal for himself to write three good pages every day. That doesn't sound like such a huge undertaking, but it adds up to a thousand pages at the end of a year, even with a few days off. Think about that. Even ONE GOOD PAGE every day gives you three completed screenplays at the end of a year.

You've heard this before. The journey of a thousand miles begins with the first step. Every day that you do anything with commitment makes you that much better at it the next day. Not necessarily better than somebody else is. Better than you were the day before. That's all we can do.

Dusting under the dining room table legs. Do not fall prey to perfectionism. There is a myth some writers perpetuate that they can't go forward until everything behind them is perfect. Allow me to offer this medical opinion. Yes, you can. You can spend a week getting one scene right, and at the end of writing the first draft, realize that you don't need that scene in the script at all. Limit the amount of rewriting you do to one pass through the scene you did yesterday, and then move on. If you must rewrite more, then allow yourself to go back beyond that scene only after you have finished each full act.

I find that after scripting a full act it is a good time to snowplow forward. It reconnects you with everything you're about to do, and you might come up with some new material or better ways of plotting what you already have. While you were writing that first act, changes may have occurred to your characters which you had not anticipated. New characters might have appeared who require story room in the next act.

Your Wadoogee. It's not just fictional characters that have Wadoogees. What do you *want* from your writing life, and what are you going to do to get it? The answer is not obvious and it is not the same for everyone. Some people write for money, some for fame, for glory, for notoriety, to change the world, to get laid, because they think they should, because it's easy, because it's hard, because if they didn't they'd feel dead. No reason is a better reason than any other reason. The only relevant question for each one of you is: why do you do it? What do you want from it? Time goes by so fast and so slow. What will you make of it for yourself?

Epilogue

There is no appropriate way to end a book on writing, because the evolution of the writing process doesn't end until the writer ends. So let's keep at it as long and as well as we possibly can. There is no other way to answer the question: how good a writer can I become?

Be brilliant. Take Vienna.

Research. Clean house. Practice the trombone. Surf the Net. Watch TV. Hang out with friends. E-mail. Play video games. See movies. Shop. Make phone calls. Build things. Think about writing. Talk about writing. Network. Give up. Raise children. Read screenplays. Drink. Drive. Draw. Have sex. Chain smoke. Run. Play tennis, handball, racquetball. Work out. Nap. Daydream. Organize closets. Defrost refrigerator. Make lists. Do yoga. Play music. Groom the dog. Fall in love. Fall out of love.

Or...

Your choice.

APPENDIX A
Websites for Research

I asked my writing students to give me their favorite research websites. The following list is in no way meant to be exhaustive. And given the volatility of Internet life, I cannot vouch for their continued existence. But FYI, these sounded pretty interesting.

www.lonelyplanet.com If you click on the "thorn tree" link, you will get a menu of postings for every country/area in the world. Want to know if there's a bus that goes from Mojcar to Almeria? How much Mongolian fermented milk it takes to get drunk? You can ask very specific questions.

www.scriptcity.com For old and new screenplays.

www.nba.com Scores, stories and stats.

www.rotten.com A seriously demented site that contains images and stories about murder and death. Not for the weak of stomach.

www.who2.com Thumbnail profiles and juicy facts about filmmakers, writers, actors, and famous people of all kinds.

www.latimes.com

www.filmradar.com Very helpful listings of events, contests, interviews, links.

www.google.com The Rolls-Royce of Internet search engines.

www.infoplease.com Almanac of dictionaries, encyclopedias, atlases. Covers U.S. and world history, biographies, sports, arts, entertainment, business, society and culture, health and science.

www.biography.com Covers the same people as the cable show on A&E.

www.cia.gov/library/publications/resources/the-world-factbook/index.html Information on every country in the world.

www.adherents.com Any statistic about any religion in the world.

www.lexisnexis.com Not free. Lawyers use this to access periodicals, public records, business information and court records. Find out how much your ex-boyfriend put down on his new house.

www.artchive.com Art history.

www.parkmaps.com As the name implies.

www.bartleby.com Internet publisher of literature, reference and verse.

www.cinema.ucla.edu The UCLA Film and Television Archive.

www.IMDB.com Internet Movie Database.

www.writersstore.com All things writing and writers.

www.wga.org Writers Guild of America. Writers contracts, minimums, links.

www.thesaurus.com

www.moviebytes.com Contests, software.

www.ifp.org Hook up with the indie crowd.

www.thisistrue.com Truth is stranger than fiction.

www.bizarrenews.com

www.hotelsurplus.com Can't afford a desk? Now you can.

www.curezone.com Natural health and wellness.

www.ask.com Ask questions. Get answers.

www.pantheon.org/mythica.html Encyclopedia of folklore, mythology and legends.

www.nytimes.com Requires subscription but no fee.

www.script-o-rama.com Links to dozens of sites that have scripts.

www.refdesk.com Facts. News source. Family friendly.

www.quoteland.com Quotes on every topic by every author.

www.truecrimelibrary.com True crime stories.

www.dictionary.com has a thesaurus link. Best of all, they offer a free *word of the day* subscription.

www.interviewinghollywood.com This is the hottest new site — in depth interviews with Hollywood pros — the best new site for filmmakers of all kinds right now!!! Ask your cinematic heroes any one of twenty to forty questions. It's amazing.

www.film-foundation.org For Filmmakers and film preservation.

www.simplyscripts.com SimplyScripts — links to hundreds of free, downloadable scripts, movie scripts, screenplays, and transcripts of current, classic and maybe a few soon-to-be-released movies, television, anime, unproduced and radio shows. A screenwriter's resource.

www.itvfest.com ITVFest is the festival where innovation, ingenuity and independent television converge.

www.donedealpro.com Focuses on the business and craft of screenwriting.

sfy.ru Best site for free movie scripts and screenplays.

www.shootingpeople.com US and UK Indie Film Community.

www.Scriptology.com The Scriptology Theme Library is an invaluable tool for any FileMaker user, or developer, who desires high-quality layouts.

www.johnaugust.com A ton of useful information about screenwriting from screenwriter John August.

www.IndiePix.net The leader in distribution of truly indie film and download-to-own DVD short and feature films.

www.rsdb.org Database of racial slurs.

www.feedbooks.com ebook retailer.

www.marxists.org Communism.

https://uwdc.library.wisc.edu/collections/AfricaFocus/ African collections.

www.Timesofindia.indiatimes.com India.

www.Quora.com Links to everything.

www.Narrativefirst.com

https://gointothestory.blcklst.com/ Screenwriting blog of THE BLACKLIST. Craft!

www. screenwriting.io A script doctor "on call."

www.storysense.com/index.html The most commonly asked questions about screenwriting in a free 81 page book.

www.screenplayscripts.com Script consultations.

www.moviecliches.com This is a list of the most annoying and common logic flaws and stereotypes found in movies.

www.wikipedia.org is a multilingual, web-based, free content encyclopedia.

www.ilm.com Industrial Light and Magic.

www.kleemanandmike.com/cartoon Simple but cool animation from Kleeman and Mike.

smithmag.net/afterthedeluge/2006/12/31/prologue-1 A graphic novel about the devastating 2005 tsunami from online zine, Smith Mag.

www.99rooms.com 99 Rooms is part interactive photo story and part game. Very addictive.

www.goodmagazine.com A very smart online zine about environmental issues.

makezine.com/blog I can't rave enough about Make Zine blog. If you like making your own fun or useful stuff, from a guitar to a robot to a motherboard, you will like this blog.

www.cynopsis.com Cynthia Turner's Cynopsis is a series of email news blasts for media professionals by a media professional.

APPENDIX B
Eavesdropper Journal Scenes

These are a few sample scenes that resulted from students keeping their Eavesdropper Journals.

INT. – GETTY GIFT MUSEUM – DAY

Two NUNS gaze at the posters on display. ESTHER stares for a long time at a bronze statue of a naked Greek boy.

MARY
I'll buy it for you.

ESTHER
You know I don't have space in my room for that.

MARY
Just loan me the money and I'll buy it for you.

ESTHER
Mary. We're nuns. Why would I want a poster of a naked Greek man?

MARY

The rooms can get pretty lonely. Someone to keep you company at night.

They giggle together.

ESTHER

I can just hear the talk. Come on, you biddy. Let's go find the others.

EXT. – FARMERS MARKET

-I already took it.

-No, you didn't.

-I did. I swear I did, Mom.

-When?

-While you were getting Starbucks.

-I don't believe you.

-You never believe me.

-I don't understand. This stuff has no side effects. You want to go back to Dexedrine? You remember the headaches?

-You don't believe me, do you?

INT. – MANI'S BAKERY – DAY

-Isn't Curtis amazing?

-Oh my God. His use of color is like, amazing.

-So amazing.

-He reminds me of Andy Warhol, but with, like, I don't know.

-I know.

-Has he ever shown? Besides here?

-I don't know, But he should. He will. He is so amazing. I don't even think this is his best work.

-Amazing.

-Totally.

INT. – DOG SHOW

LADY: But Barky got first place at the county fair last year.

JUDGE: I'm sorry but this is not the county Fair.

LADY: I know that. But what's wrong with Barky, huh? How come he didn't make it to first place?

JUDGE: You know it's against the rules for judges to speak with contestants.

LADY: Aw, who cares about rules. I want to know how come Barky didn't win the prize.

JUDGE: Well, if you insist, Madame. He is not first-place material because his uh, parts, uh, were not adequate.

LADY: What parts? What wasn't adequate?

JUDGE: (Whispering) His testicles.

LADY: Are you telling me his BALLS weren't big enough?

JUDGE: Well, yes. And now excuse me. I must go to the next judging round.

The lady follows him to the next pavilion.

LADY: Barky does not have small balls. Hey, I'm telling you, Barky is no under-sized wimp.

The Lady picks up her small dog and turns it belly up.

LADY: Look at these balls! You aren't gonna find bigger balls on a dog. Any dog.

The judge ignores her.

LADY: Stop. Look at them. LOOK AT THESE BIG BALLS!

SECURITY stops her from following the judge into the arena.

LADY: Don't worry, Barky. Don't you listen to that mean old judge. Mama says you've got the best and biggest balls in town.

INT. – AIRPORT

TWO FLIGHT ATTENDANTS prepare for their shift.

#1: You know that outfit you wore to the mixer last weekend?

#2: Yeah?

#1: I heard Karen say to someone that it made you look fat.

#2: She said that about me?

#1: She sure did.

#2: That's really rude. It was a loose-fitting dress but I don't think it made me look fat. God, I can't stand people who talk behind other people's backs.

They ride in silence along the people mover.

#2: Karen can be a real fucking bitch, you know? If anyone looks fat it's her. Shit, she even looks fat next to Glen. Now he's a fat slob and a half...

INT. – A TRENDY BAR – NIGHT

Two smashing-looking women (20).

#1: My first time really hurt. He was really big.

#2: Mine, too. He really bounced a lot.

#1: You could hear me moaning around the block.

#2: I ached for a week. Wanna see a picture?

She pulls out a picture of herself on a HORSE in full riding gear.

INT. – PIZZA HUT – NIGHT

Two friends at a long table laden with pitchers of beer and plates of pepperoni pizza. DAN is a large bearded man in his 20s, smoking Marlboros as if they were going out of fashion. DAVE, (20s) lean non-smoker.

DAN: Well, I'm back in the raptor mode. I'm on the prowl.

DAVE: What happened to Amy?

DAN: Put it this way. It's over. She said she'd love to be with me but the timing wasn't right.

DAVE: Sounds like she blew you off.

DAN: Dude, that's what I thought. I asked her, "Tell me you don't love me." But she said she thought I was a bright, intelligent guy and we would make a great couple. But she says it has to do with timing.

DAVE: What does she mean by timing?

DAN: I don't know. But I'm going to play the field again. No girl will turn down a guy like me. The raptor is back!

He puts his third Marlboro out in the crust of a slice.

DAVE: Yep, who would deny you?

APPENDIX C

Ages of Writers When They Won Their Academy Awards

Hollywood is often accused of ageism and sexism. Here is a list that I hope will inspire you to realize that you are not too young OR TOO OLD to take your best shot.

1927–28: (Adaptation) Benjamin Glazer, 41—*7th Heaven*

(Original Story) Ben Hecht, 36—*Underworld*

(Title Writing) Joseph Farnham, 44

1928–29: Hans Kraly, 43—*The Patriot*

1929–30: Frances Marion, 42—*The Big House*

1930–31: (Adaptation) Howard Estabrook, 47—*Cimarron*

(Original Story) John Monk Saunders, 36—*The Dawn Patrol*

1931–32: (Adaptation) Edwin Burke, 43—*Bad Girl*

(Original Story) Frances Marion, 42—*The Champ*

1932–33: (Adaptation) Victor Heerman, 40, Sarah Y. Mason, 37—*Little Women*

(Original Story) Robert Lord, 33—*One Way Passage*

1934: (Original Story) Arthur Caesar, 42—*Manhattan Melodrama*

(Adaptation) Robert Riskin, 37—*It Happened One Night*

1935: (Original Story) Ben Hecht, 41; Charles MacArthur, 40—*The Scroundrel*

(Screenplay) Dudley Nichols, 40—*The Informer*

1936: (Original Story) Pierre Collings, 34; Sheridan Gibney, 33—*The Story of Louis Pasteur*

1937: (Original Story) William A. Wellman, 41; Robert Carson, 28—*A Star is Born*

(Screenplay) Norman Reilly Raine, 43; Heinz Herald, 47; Geza Herczeg, 49—*The Life of Emile Zola*

1938: (Original Story) Dore Schary, 33; Eleanore Griffin, 34—*Boys Town*

(Screenplay) George Bernard Shaw, 52; W. P. Lipscomb, 51; Cecil Lewis, 40; Ian Dalrymple, 35—*Pygmalion*

1939: (Original Story) Lewis R. Foster, 41—*Mr. Smith Goes to Washington*

(Screenplay) Sidney Howard, 41—*Gone with the Wind*

1940: (Original Screenplay) Preston Sturges, 42—*The Great McGinty*

(Original Story) Benjamin Glazer, 53—*Arise, My Love*

(Screenplay) Donald Ogden Stewart, 46—*The Philadelphia Story*

1941: (Original Screenplay) Herman J. Mankiewicz, 44; Orson Welles, 26—*Citizen Kane*

(Original Story) Harry Segall, 49—*Here Comes Mr. Jordan*

(Screenplay) Sidney Buchman, 39; Seton I. Miller, 39—*Here Comes Mr. Jordan*

1942: (Original Motion Picture Story) Emeric Pressburger, 39—*The Invaders*

(Original Screenplay) Ring Lardner, Jr., 27; Michael Kanin, 39—*Woman of the Year*

(Screenplay) Arthur Wimperis, 68; George Froeschel, 51; James Hilton, 42; Claudine West, 52—*Mrs. Miniver*

1943: (Original Motion Picture Story) William Saroyan, 35—*The Human Comedy*

(Original Screenplay) Norman Krasna, 34—*Princess O'Rourke*

(Screenplay) Julius J. Epstein, 33, Phillip G. Epstein, 33, Howard Koch, 40—*Casablanca*

1944: (Original Motion Picture Story) Leo McCarey, 46—*Going My Way*

(Original Screenplay) Lamar Trotti, 44—*Wilson*

(Screenplay) Frank Butler, 54, Frank Cavett, 36—*Going My Way*

1945: (Original Motion Picture Story) Charles G. Booth, 49—*The House on 92nd Street*

(Original Screenplay) Richard Schweizer, 46—*Marie-Louise*

(Screenplay) Charles Brackett, 52; Billy Wilder, 39—*The Lost Weekend*

1946: (Original Motion Picture Story) Clemence Dane, 58—*Vacation from Marriage*

(Original Screenplay) Muriel Box, 41; Sydney Box, 39—*The Seventh Veil*

(Screenplay) Robert E. Sherwood, 49—*The Best Years of Our Lives*

1947: (Motion Picture Story) Valentine Davies, 42—*Miracle on 34th Street*

(Original Screenplay) Sidney Sheldon, 30—*The Bachelor and the Bobby-Soxer*

(Screenplay) George Seaton, 35—*Miracle on 34th Street*

1948: (Motion Picture Story) Richard Schweizer, 49—*The Search*

(Screenplay) John Huston, 42—*The Treasure of the Sierra Madre*

1949: (Motion Picture Story) Douglas Morrow, 36—*The Stratton Story*

(Screenplay) Joseph L. Mankiewicz, 40—*A Letter to Three Wives*

(Story and Screenplay) Robert Pirosh, 39—*Battleground*

1950: (Motion Picture Story) Edna Anhalt, 36; Edward Anhalt, 36—*Panic in the Streets*

(Screenplay) Joseph L. Mankiewicz, 41—*All About Eve*

(Story and Screenplay) Charles Brackett, 58; Billy Wilder, 44, D. M. Marshman, Jr.,28—*Sunset Boulevard*

1951: (Screenplay) Michael Wilson, 37; Harry Brown, 34—*A Place in the Sun*

(Motion Picture Story) Paul Dehn, 38; James Bernard, 26—*Seven Days to Noon*

(Story and Screenplay) Alan Jay Lerner, 31—*An American In Paris*

1952: (Screenplay) Charles Schnee, 38—*The Bad and the Beautiful*

(Story and Screenplay) – T. E. B. Clarke, 43—*The Lavender Hill Mob*

(Motion Picture Story) Frederic M. Frank, 41; Theodore St. John, 45; Frank Cavett, 45—*The Greatest Show on Earth*

1953: (Screenplay) Daniel Taradash, 40—*From Hear to Eternity*

(Motion Picture Story) Dalton Trumbo, 48—*Roman Holiday*

(Story and Screenplay) Charles Brackett, 61; Walter Reisch, 50; Richard Breen, 35—*Titanic*

1954: (Screenplay) George Seaton, 43—*The Country Girl*

(Motion Picture Story) Philip Yordan, 40—*Broken Lance*

(Story and Screenplay) Budd Schulberg, 40—*On the Waterfront*

1955: (Story and Screenplay) William Ludwig, 43; Sonya Levien, 67—*Interrupted Melody*

(Motion Picture Story) Daniel Fuchs, 45—*Love Me or Leave Me*

(Screenplay) Paddy Chayefsky, 32—*Marty*

1956: (Best Screenplay—Original) Albert Lamorisse, 34—*The Red Balloon*

(Adapted) James Poe, 35; John Farrow, 51; S. J. Perelman, 51—*Around the World in 80 Days*

(Motion Picture Story) Dalton Trumbo, 51—*The Brave One*

1957: (Original) George Wells, 48—*Designing Woman*

(Adapted) Pierre Boulle, 45; Michael Wilson, 43; Carl Foreman, 43—*The Bridge on the River Kwai*

1958: (Original) Nedrick Young, 44; Harold Jacob Smith, 46—*The Defiant Ones*

(Adapted) Alan Jay Lerner, 40—*Gigi*

1959: (Original) Russell Rouse, 46; Clarence Greene, 46; Stanley Shapiro, 24; Maurice Richlin, 39—*Pillow Talk*

(Adapted) Neil Patterson, 39—*Room at the Top*

1960: (Original) Billy Wilder, 54; I. A. L. Diamond, 40—*The Apartment*

(Adapted) Richard Brooks, 48—*Elmer Gantry*

1961: (Original) William Inge, 48—*Splendor in the Grass*

(Adapted) Abby Mann, 34—*Judgment at Nuremberg*

1962: (Original) Ennio de Concini, 39; Alfredo Giannetti, 38; Pietro Germi, 48—*Divorce Italian Style*

(Adapted) Horton Foote, 46—*To Kill a Mockingbird*

1963: (Original) James R. Webb, 53—*How the West Was Won*

(Adapted) John Osbourne, 34—*Tom Jones*

1964: (Original) S. H. Barnett, 56; Peter Stone, 34; Frank Tarloff, 54—*Father Goose*

(Adapted) Edward Anhalt, 50—*Becket*

1965: (Original) Frederic Raphael, 34—*Darling*

(Adapted) Robert Bolt, 41—*Doctor Zhivago*

1966: (Original) Claude Lelouch, 29—*A Man and a Woman*

(Adapted) Robert Bolt, 42—*A Man for All Seasons*

1967: (Original) William Rose, 49—*Guess Who's Coming to Dinner*

(Adapted) Stirling Silliphant, 49—*In the Heat of the Night*

1968: (Original) Mel Brooks, 42—*The Producers*

(Adapted) James Goldman, 41—*The Lion in Winter*

1969: (Original) William Goldman, 42—*Butch Cassidy and the Sundance Kid*

(Adapted) Waldo Salt, 55—*Midnight Cowboy*

1970: (Original) Francis Ford Coppola, 31; Edmund H. North, 59—*Patton*

(Adapted) – Ring Lardner, Jr., 55—*M*A*S*H*

1971: (Original) Paddy Chayefsky, 48—*The Hospital*

(Adapted) Ernest Tidyman, 43—*The French Connection*

1972: (Original) Jeremy Larner, 42—*The Candidate*

(Adapted) Mario Puzo, 52; Francis Ford Coppola, 33—*The Godfather*

1973: (Original) David S. Ward, 38—*The Sting*

(Adapted) William Peter Blatty, 45—*The Exorcist*

1974: (Original) Robert Towne, 40—*Chinatown*

(Adapted) Francis Ford Coppola, 35; Mario Puzo, 54—*The Godfather Part II*

1975: (Original) Frank Pierson, 50—*Dog Day Afternoon*

(Adapted) Lawrence Hauben, 44; Bo Goldman, 43—*One Flew Over the Cuckoo's Nest*

1976: (Original) Paddy Chayefsky, 52—*Network*

(Adapted) William Goldman, 45—*All the President's Men*

1977: (Original) Woody Allen, 42; Marshall Brickman, 36—*Annie Hall*

(Adapted) Alvin Sargent, 50—*Julia*

1978: (Original) Nancy Dowd, 33; Waldo Salt, 64—*Coming Home*

(Adapted) Oliver Stone 32—*Midnight Express*

1979: (Original) Steve Tesich, 37—*Breaking Away*

(Adapted) Robert Benton, 47—*Kramer vs. Kramer*

1980: (Original) Bo Goldman, 48—*Melvin and Howard*

(Adapted) Alvin Sargent, 53—*Ordinary People*

1981: (Original) Colin Welland, 47—*Chariots of Fire*

(Adapted) Ernest Thompson, 31—*On Golden Pond*

1982: (Original) John Briley, 57—*Gandhi*

(Adapted) Costa-Gavras, 49; Donald Stewart, 52—*Missing*

1983: (Original) Horton Foote, 67—*Tender Mercies*

(Adapted) James L. Brooks, 43—*Terms of Endearment*

1984: (Original) Robert Benton, 52—*Places in the Heart*

(Adapted) Peter Shaffer, 58—*Amadeus*

1985: (Original) Earl W. Wallace, 42; William Kelley, 56; Pamela Wallace, 35—*Witness*

(Adapted) Kurt Luedtke, 47—*Out of Africa*

1986: (Original) Woody Allen, 51—*Hannah and Her Sisters*

(Adaped) Ruth Prawer Jhabvala, 59—*A Room with a View*

1987: (Original) John Patrick Shanley, 37—*Moonstruck*

(Adapted) Bernardo Bertolucci, 46—*The Last Emperor*

1988: (Original) Ronald Bass, 45—*Rain Man*

(Adapted) Christopher Hampton, 42—*Dangerous Liaisons*

1989: (Original) Tom Schulman, 38—*Dead Poets Society*

(Adapted) Alfred Uhry, 53—*Driving Miss Daisy*

1990: (Original) Bruce Joel Rubin, 47—*Ghost*

(Adapted) Michael Blake, 45—*Dances with Wolves*

1991: (Original) Callie Khouri, 34—*Thelma and Louise*

(Adapted) Ted Tally, 39—*The Silence of the Lambs*

1992: (Original) Neil Jordan, 42—*The Crying Game*

(Adapted) Ruth Prawer Jhabvala, 65—*Howard's End*

1993: (Original) Jane Campion, 39—*The Piano*

(Adapted) Steven Zaillian, 40—*Schindler's List*

1994: (Original) Quentin Tarantino, 31; Roger Avary, 29—*Pulp Fiction*

(Adapted) Eric Roth, 74—*Forrest Gump*

1995: (Original) Christopher McQuarrie, 29—*The Usual Suspects*

(Adapted) Emma Thompson, 36—*Sense and Sensibility*

1996: (Original) Ethan Coen, 39; Joel Coen, 42—*Fargo*

(Adapted) Billy Bob Thornton, 39—*Sling Blade*

1997: (Original) Ben Affleck, 25; Matt Damon, 27—*Good Will Hunting*

(Adapted) Brian Helgeland, 36; Curtis Hanson, 42—*L.A. Confidential*

1998: (Original) Marc Norman, 54; Tom Stoppard, 61—*Shakespeare in Love*

(Adapted) Bill Condon, 43—*Gods and Monsters*

1999: (Original) Alan Ball, 42—*American Beauty*

(Adapted) John Irving, 57—*The Cider House Rules*

2000: Cameron Crowe, 43—*Almost Famous*

(Adapted) Steve Gaghan, 35—*Traffic*

2001: (Original) Julian Fellowes, 51—*Gosford Park*

(Adapted) Akiva Goldsman, 38—*A Beautiful Mind*

2002: (Original) Pedro Almódovar, 52—*Talk to Her*

(Adapted) Ronald Harwood, 69—*The Pianist*

2003: (Original) Sofia Coppola, 31—*Lost in Translation*

(Adapted) Fran Walsh, 45; Philippa Boyens, 41; Peter Jackson, 42—*The Lord of the Rings: The Return of the King*

2004: (Original) Charlie Kaufman, 46; Michael Gondry, 41; Pierre Bismuth, 42—*Eternal Sunshine of the Spotless Mind*

(Adapted) Alexander Payne, 44; Jim Taylor, 42—*Sideways*

2005: (Original) Paul Haggis, 52; Bobby Moresco, 54—*Crash*

(Adapted) Larry McMurtry, 69; Diana Ossana, 56—*Brokeback Mountain*

2006: (Original) Michael Arndt, 41—*Little Miss Sunshine*

(Adapted) William Monahan, 46—*The Departed*

2007: (Original) Diablo Cody, 29—*Juno*

(Adapted) Joel Coen, 53, Ethan Coen, 50—*No Country for Old Men*

2008: (Original) Dustin Lance Black, 34—*Milk*

(Adapted) Simon Beaufoy, 40—*Slumdog Millionaire*

2009: (Original) Mark Boak, 37—*The Hurt Locker*

(Adapted) Geoffrey Flethcer, 39—*Precious*

2010: (Original) David Seidler, 74—*The King's Speech*

(Adapted) Aaron Sorkin, 49 —*The Social Network*

2011: (Original) Woody Allen, 76—*Midnight in Paris*

(Adapted) Alexander Payne, 51; Nat Faxon, 36; Jim Rash, 41—*The Descendants*

2012: (Original) Quentin Tarantino, 49—*Django Unchained*

(Adapted) Chris Terrio, 36—*Argo*

2013: (Original) Spike Jonze, 44—*Her*

(Adapted) John Ridley, 48—*12 Years A Slave*

2014: (Original) Alejandro González Iñárritu, 51; Nicholás Giacobone, 39; Alexander Dinelaris, Jr., 46; Armando Bo, 35—*Birdman*

(Adapted) Graham Moore, 33—*The Imitation Game*

2015: (Original) Josh Singer, 43; Tom McCarthy, 49—*Spotlight*

(Adapted) Charles Randolph, 52; Adam McKay, 47—*The Big Short*

2016: (Original) Kenneth Lonergan, 55—*Manchester by the Sea*

(Adapted) Barry Jenkins, 37—*Moonlight*

Credits

Kissing England by Sacha Gervasi - Registered 1997

A Walk On The Moon - aka *The Blouse Man* by Pamela Gray - © Copyright 1999

Lorraine Loses It by Laurie Hutzler - Registered 1993

Commedia Del Arte by Marc Arneson - Registered 2002

Flesh and Blood by Dave Johnson - Registered 2002

Sea of Love by Richard Price Copyright 2003 by Universal Studios. Courtesy of Universal Studios Publishing Rights, a division of Universal Studios Licensing LLLP. All Rights Reserved.

Notes

Notes

Notes

About the Author

Hal Ackerman is co-chair emeritus of the UCLA Screenwriting Program.

He has sold material to all the broadcast networks and major studios. His play, *Testosterone: How Prostate Cancer Made a Man of Me*, was the recipient of the William Saroyan Centennial Prize for Drama. Under its new title, *Prick*, it won Best Script at the 2011 United Solo Festival.

He has had numerous short stories published in literary journals, among them *North Dakota Review*, *New Millennium Writing*, *The Pinch*, *Southeast Review* and *Passages* and most recently in the 2016 *Idaho Review and Fiction International* (in the company of many stalwarts). *Sweet Day* was read by Academy Award-nominee Robert Forster and is available at the Harper Collins Publishers Digital Media Cafe. *The Dancer Horse* was nominated for a Pushcart Prize and is available on Audible, read by Adrian Pasdar. *Roof Garden* won the Warren Adler 2008 award for fiction and is published by Kindle; *Alfalfa* was included in the anthology *I Wanna Be Sedated...30 Writers on Parenting Teenagers*. *Belle and Melinda* was selected by Robert Olen Butler as the winner of the World's Best Short Short Story contest.

He has published two successful novels in a detective series about an aging counterculture P.I. *Stein, Stoned* won the Lovey award for best first novel in 2010 and was followed in 2011 by *Stein, Stung*.

His short story collection, *The Boy Who Had A Peach Tree Growing Out Of His Head... (And Other Natural Phenomena)* has just been published by Hadassa Word Press.

EATING *for* ENDURANCE

FOURTH EDITION

ELLEN COLEMAN, RD, MA, MPH

Bull Publishing Company
P.O. Box 1377
Boulder, CO 80306
(800) 676-2855
www.bullpub.com
ISBN 0-923521-75-5

Manufactured in the United States of America.

Distributed to the trade by:
Publisher's Group West
1700 Fourth Street
Berkeley, CA 94710

Publisher: James Bull
Project Manager and Manuscript Editor: Erin Mulligan
Cover Design: Lightbourne
Interior Design and Composition: Publication Services, Inc.
Photo Credits: Adam Pretty / Getty Images–p. 2
Nick Wilson / Getty Images–p. 18
Mike Powell / Getty Images–pp. 32, 58, 84, 126, 154
Jake Martin / Getty Images–pp. 46, 94, 112, 142
David Leah / Getty Images–p. 68
Markus Boesch / Getty Images–p. 102

Library of Congress Cataloging-in-Publication Data

Coleman, Ellen.
Eating for endurance / by Ellen Coleman.— 4th ed.
p. cm.
Includes index.
ISBN 0-923521-75-5
1. Athletes—Nutrition. I. Title.
TX361.A8 C558 2003
613.2'024'796—dc21 2002154328

10 9 8 7 6 5 4 3 2 1

Dedication

In memory of my father, James W. Coleman II, DDS

With love to my family

And thanks to Thomas M. Mirich III, MD

Contents

List of Tables/Figures

List of Tables

List of Figures

Introduction

Eventually almost all athletes will experience poor performance due to haphazard or irregular eating habits. Nutrition-related difficulties are usually due to inadequate fluid or carbohydrate intake and may result in reduced speed, impaired endurance, and difficulty concentrating. Unwanted weight loss or weight gain may also be the result of disorganized food choices. Proper planning can help to prevent these problems and promote optimum performance.

Choosing the proper food is as important to your athletic success as having the most appropriate training program. Although a balanced diet won't guarantee you athletic success, an unbalanced diet may undermine your training.

Most athletes do very well with structure. My philosophy is that you should plan your food intake as carefully as you plan your training. Not planning is what gets people into trouble.

There are sound dietary strategies that you can use to perform closer to your potential. *Eating for Endurance* provides the most current information on nutrition for peak athletic performance. It presents sensible nutrition advice that you can put into practice immediately.

Miles of smiles,
Ellen

1

Recommended Training Diet

Eating for Performance and Health

A friend of mine was training for a 200-mile bicycle ride. A week before the event, he headed out for a hilly 100-mile workout. He noticed that his legs felt stiff and heavy but thought he would loosen up on the ride. He struggled to complete the first climb, standing up in his lowest gear on a grade he could normally surmount with ease. At the top of the hill, he gave up and headed home.

When we met over dinner that evening, he was about to give up on his 200-mile attempt. I told him to rest a day and eat a high-carbohydrate diet while tapering his training for the remainder of the week. He finished the 200-mile ride in his best time ever.

My friend had succumbed to training glycogen depletion.

MUSCLE GLYCOGEN IS THE PREFERRED FUEL for most types of exercise. Replenishing and maintaining muscle glycogen stores during intensive training requires a carbohydrate-rich diet. Depending on the intensity and duration of your activity, you should be consuming 6 to 10 grams of carbohydrate per kilogram of body weight daily. Adequate muscle glycogen stores allow you to exercise harder and longer with less fatigue. A carbohydrate-rich, lowfat diet is also recommended to prevent heart disease, certain cancers, diabetes, stroke, and osteoporosis. The dietary guidelines developed to promote health establish a good foundation for athletes who desire peak performance.

Glycogen Stores and Training

Have you ever had days of training where you felt that you had lost endurance, speed, and precision? Low levels of glycogen in your muscles can cause these bad days.

Glycogen depletion can occur gradually over repeated days of heavy training when muscle glycogen breakdown exceeds its replacement. When this happens, your glycogen stores drop lower with each successive day, and your workouts become more difficult and less enjoyable. The deterioration in performance and feeling of sluggishness associated with glycogen depletion is often referred to as "staleness" and blamed on overtraining.

Glycogen depletion is often accompanied by a sudden weight loss of several pounds (due to glycogen and water loss) and an inability to maintain your usual training intensity. When you don't consume enough carbohydrates or calories and/or don't take days off to rest, you are a prime candidate for glycogen depletion. Most Americans consume 5 grams of carbohydrate per kilogram of body weight—about half of their calories.

Carbohydrate Recommendations for Training

You can prevent glycogen depletion by consuming a carbohydrate-rich diet (6 to 10 grams of carbohydrate per kilogram daily) and taking periodic rest days to give your muscles time to rebuild their stores. You should consume 6 grams of carbohydrate per kilogram daily if you're training hard for an hour each day. Take in 8 grams of carbohydrate per kilogram if you're training hard for 2 hours each day. A diet providing 10 grams of carbohydrate per kilogram is recommended when you're training hard for 3 hours or more each day.

A high-carbohydrate diet is even more critical for recovery from prolonged, heavy exercise. Cyclists in the grueling Tour de France consume about 12 grams of carbohydrate per kilogram and 6,000 calories each day. By keeping your carbohydrate intake high, you can minimize chronic fatigue due to muscle glycogen depletion.

The recommendations for carbohydrates are given in grams per kilogram because this is an easy way to determine how much you need. One kilogram equals 2.2 pounds. For example, a 154-pound person (70 kg) who trains strenuously for an hour needs 420 grams of carbohydrates daily. You can determine the carbohydrate content of different foods by reading food labels. Table 1-1 gives some examples of high-carbohydrate foods. You can also refer to food exchange lists to develop a high-carbohydrate diet.

Table 1-1.
High-Carbohydrate Foods

Food Group	Calories	Carbohydrates (Grams)
Milk		
Lowfat (2%) milk (1 cup)	121	12
Skim milk (1 cup)	86	12
Chocolate milk (1 cup)	208	26
Pudding, any flavor (½ cup)	161	30
Frozen yogurt, lowfat (1 cup)	220	34
Fruit-flavored lowfat yogurt (1 cup)	225	42

TABLE 1-1.
HIGH-CARBOHYDRATE FOODS (CONTINUED)

FOOD GROUP	CALORIES	CARBOHYDRATES (GRAMS)
Beans		
Blackeye peas (½ cup)	134	22
Pinto beans (1 cup)	235	44
Navy beans (1 cup)	259	48
Refried beans (½ cup)	142	26
Garbanzo beans (chickpeas) (1 cup)	269	45
White beans (1 cup)	249	45
Fruits		
Apple (1 medium)	81	21
Apple juice (1 cup)	111	28
Applesauce (1 cup)	232	60
Banana (1)	105	27
Canteloupe (1 cup)	57	14
Dates, dried (10)	228	61
Fruit Roll-Ups (1 roll)	50	12
Grapes (1 cup)	114	28
Grape juice (1 cup)	96	23
Orange (1)	65	16
Orange juice (1 cup)	112	26
Pear (1)	98	25
Pineapple (1 cup)	77	19
Prunes, dried (10)	201	53
Raisins (⅔ cup)	302	79
Raspberries (1 cup)	61	14
Strawberries (1 cup)	45	11
Watermelon (1 cup)	50	12
Vegetables		
Three-bean salad (½ cup)	90	20
Carrots (1 medium)	31	8
Corn (½ cup)	89	21
Lima beans (½cup)	108	20
Peas, green (½ cup)	63	12
Potato (l large)	220	50
Sweet Potato (1 large)	118	28
Grains		
Bagel (1)	165	31
Biscuit (1)	103	13
White bread (1 slice)	61	12
Whole-wheat bread (1 slice)	55	11
Breadsticks (2 sticks)	77	15

TABLE 1-1.
HIGH-CARBOHYDRATE FOODS (CONTINUED)

FOOD GROUP	CALORIES	CARBOHYDRATES (GRAMS)
Grains		
Cornbread (1 square)	178	28
Cereal, ready-to-eat (1 cup)	110	24
Oatmeal (½ cup)	66	12
Cream of Rice (¾ cup)	95	21
Cream of Wheat (¾ cup)	96	20
Flavored oatmeal, Quaker instant (1 packet)	110	25
Graham crackers (2 squares)	60	11
Saltines (5 crackers)	60	10
Triscuit crackers (3 crackers)	60	10
Pancake (4-inch diameter)	61	9
Waffles (2, 3.5" x 5.5")	130	17
Rice (1 cup)	223	50
Rice, brown (1 cup)	232	50
Hamburger bun (1)	119	21
Hotdog bun (1)	119	21
Noodles, spaghetti (1 cup)	159	34
Flour tortilla (1)	85	15
Oatmeal raisin cookie	62	9
Pizza (cheese, 1 slice)	290	39
Popcorn, plain (1 cup, popped)	26	6
English muffin	130	25
Fig bar (1)	50	10
Granola bar (honey and oats, 1 oz)	125	19
Pretzels (1 oz)	106	21

A Healthy Diet Emphasizes Carbohydrates

The Dietary Guidelines are designed to help Americans choose diets that will promote health, reduce the risk of disease, support physical activity, and provide required nutrients. The Food Guide Pyramid is based on these recommendations.

The Food Guide Pyramid (Figure 1-1) shows the foods that should be included in a healthful diet and in what amounts. The grain group forms the base of the pyramid, the fruit and vegetable groups are on the second tier, and the meat and dairy groups are on the third tier. Since fats and sweets should be consumed in limited amounts, these items are grouped in a small section at the top of the pyramid. Alcoholic beverages are also part of this group. Fats, sweets, and alcohol are often called "empty calories" because they are high in calories but low in most nutrients.

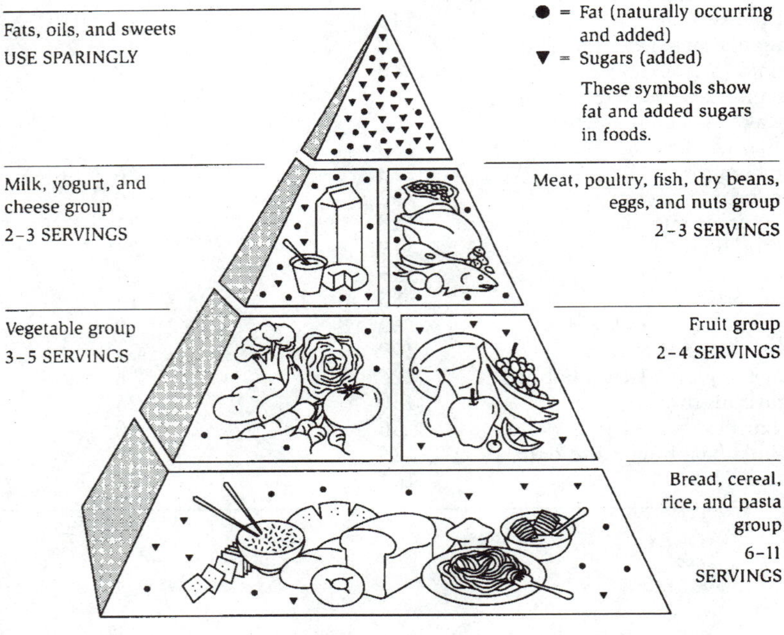

Figure 1-1. The daily food guide visualized with most portions coming from grains and the least from fats and sweets.

All Americans, and particularly athletes, should be eating heartily from the grain, vegetable, and fruit groups since these groups have the highest recommended number of servings and are nutrient-rich sources of carbohydrates. Table 1-2 indicates what counts as a serving from each group.

TABLE 1-2.
WHAT COUNTS AS ONE SERVING?

BREAD, CEREAL, RICE, AND PASTA GROUP
1 slice bread
½ cup cooked rice or pasta
½ cup cooked cereal
1 oz ready-to-eat cereal

VEGETABLE GROUP
½ cup chopped raw or cooked vegetables
1 cup leafy raw vegetables
1/2 cup tomato or vegetable juice

FRUIT GROUP
1 piece fruit or melon wedge
¾ cup juice
½ cup canned fruit
¼ cup dried fruit

MILK, YOGURT, AND CHEESE GROUP
1 cup milk or yogurt
1½ oz natural cheese
2 oz processed cheese

MEAT, POULTRY, FISH, DRY BEANS, EGGS, AND NUTS GROUP
2½–3 oz cooked lean meat, poultry, or fish
½ cup cooked beans, or 1 egg, or 2 tbsp. peanut butter same as 1 oz lean meat

FATS, OILS, AND SWEETS
Use sparingly, especially if you need to lose weight.

The amount you eat may be more than one serving. For example, a dinner portion of spaghetti would count as 2 or 3 servings.

The number of calories that the Food Guide Pyramid provides varies, depending on the foods you choose within the groups and the number of servings you eat (see Table 1-3). The minimum number of servings from the Food Guide Pyramid provides about 1,600 calories if you choose lowfat, lean foods from the 5 groups and eat items from the fats and sweets group sparingly. Eating the minimum number of servings from the pyramid will promote body fat loss for most people while providing adequate nutrients. High-calorie items such as fats, sweets, and alcohol should be limited when body fat reduction is desired. Effective strategies for weight control are discussed in Chapter 9.

TABLE 1-3.
HOW MANY SERVINGS DO YOU NEED EACH DAY?

CALORIE LEVEL*	WOMEN AND SOME OLDER ADULTS	CHILDREN, TEEN GIRLS, ACTIVE WOMEN, MOST MEN	TEEN BOYS AND ACTIVE MEN
	About 1,600	**About 2,200**	**About 2,800**
Bread Group	6	9	11
Vegetable Group	3	4	5
Fruit Group	2	3	4
Milk Group	2–3**	2–3**	2–3**
Meat Group	2 for a total of 5 ounces	2 for a total of 6 ounces	3 for a total of 7 ounces

* These are the calorie levels if you choose lowfat, lean foods from the 5 major food groups and use foods from the fats, oils, and sweets group sparingly.

** Women who are pregnant or breast-feeding, teenagers, and young adults to age 24 need 3 servings.

Source: U.S. Department of Agriculture and the U.S. Department of Health and Human Services.

Consuming the maximum number of servings (with limited intake of fats and sweets) provides about 2,800 calories. Athletes who have higher caloric needs for weight maintenance or weight gain can eat a greater number of servings from the food groups by eating between-meal snacks. Emphasis should be placed on the grain, fruit, and vegetable groups since they generally provide more carbohydrates and less fat than the meat and dairy groups.

Developing a High-Carbohydrate Diet

You can use the Food Exchange System to create a high-carbohydrate diet. The exchange lists are the basis of a meal planning system developed by the American Dietetic Association and the American Diabetes Association.

TABLE 1-4.
FOOD GROUP EXCHANGES

MEAT & MEAT SUBSTITUTES (55–100 KCAL)		
0 gm carbohydrate	**7 gm protein**	**3–8 gm fat**
1 oz poultry, fish, beef, pork, lamb, etc.	1 egg	
¼ cup tuna, salmon, cottage cheese	1 oz cheese	
2 tbsp peanut butter	tofu (2½" × 2¾" × 1")	

STARCH/CARBOHYDRATE (80 KCAL)		
15 gm carbohydrate	**3 gm protein**	**0 gm fat**
½ cup pasta, barley, cooked cereal	1 slice bread, 6" tortilla	
⅓ cup rice or dried cooked peas/beans	½ bagel, english muffin, pita	
½ cup corn, peas, winter squash	¾ cup dry flaked cereal	
1 small (3 oz) baked potato	3 cups popcorn, no oil or butter	
4–6 crackers	¾ oz pretzels	

CARBOHYDRATE VEGETABLES (25 KCAL)	CARBOHYDRATE MILK (90–150 KCAL)
5 gm carbohydrate 2 gm protein, 0 gm fat	**12 gm carbohydrate 8 gm protein, 0–5 gm fat**
½ cup cooked vegtables	1 cup milk: nonfat, lowfat, 1%, whole
1 cup raw vegtables	1 cup yogurt: nonfat lowfat, 1%, whole
½ cup tomato juice	

CARBOHYDRATE FRUIT (60 KCAL)	FAT (45 KCAL)
15 gm carbohydrate 0 gm protein, 0 gm fat	**0 gm carbohydrate 0 gm protein, 5 gm fat**
1 medium fresh fruit	1 tsp margarine, oil, butter, mayonnaise
1 cup berries or melon	2 tsp diet margarine, diet mayonnaise
½ cup canned fruit	1 tbsp salad dressing, cream cheese, cream, nuts
½ cup fruit juice	2 tbsp diet salad dressing, sour cream
¼ cup dried fruit	1 slice bacon

There are three exchange lists: carbohydrates, meat and meat substitutes, and fat. The carbohydrate group is further divided into starch, fruit, vegetables, milk, and other carbohydrates. Each lists foods that have about the same number of carbohydrates, protein, fat, and calories. Any food on a list can be exchanged or traded for any other food on the same list.

TABLE 1-5.
TRAINING DIET MEAL PLANS

FOOD GROUP	NUMBER OF EXCHANGES PER CALORIE LEVEL					
	1,500	**2,000**	**2,500**	**3,000**	**3,500**	**4,000**
Milk	3	3	4	4	4	4
Meat	5	5	5	5	6	6
Fruit	5	6	7	9	10	12
Vegetable	3	3	3	5	6	7
Grain	7	11	16	18	20	24
Fat	2	3	5	6	8	10

These food exchange lists can be used to plan diets from 1,500 to 4,000 calories a day. As a general guide, starchy foods and fruit provide the highest amount of carbohydrates (15 grams) per serving. A serving of starch consists of one slice of bread or small tortilla, 1/2 cup pasta or cooked cereal, 1/3 cup cooked rice or beans, or 1 small potato. A serving of fruit is one medium-sized fruit, 1 cup berries or melon, 1/2 cup juice, or 1/4 cup dried fruit.

Milk is the next highest source of carbohydrates, providing 12 grams of carbohydrate for 1 cup of milk or yogurt (choose nonfat or 1% fat products to limit your fat intake). Vegetables provide 5 grams of carbohydrate per 1/2 cup cooked vegetables, 1 cup raw vegetables, or 1/2 cup tomato or vegetable juice.

Sugary foods such as cookies, cake, pie, soft drinks, and candy can supply additional carbohydrates but are low in most other nutrients. While there's no harm in eating some high-carbohydrate empty calories once you've met your nutrient needs, you can't go wrong adding extra servings of nutrient-dense carbohydrates.

Sugar and Sugar Myths

Sugary foods can help increase your carbohydrate and calorie intake during training. However, these foods should be eaten in addition to, not in place of, nutrient-dense carbohydrate foods. When sugar replaces nutrient-dense or complex carbohydrates in your diet, your intake of vitamins, minerals, and fiber will be reduced. Many sugary baked goods and candy are also high in fat.

Despite claims in the popular press, brown sugar, date sugar, honey, and molasses are not nutritionally superior to table sugar. Although they do contain trace amounts of some vitamins and minerals, consuming these so-called natural sugars will not add significant nutritional value to your diet.

Some athletes think that fructose is a better energy source than other sugars because fructose causes a lower insulin response than glucose. However, consuming fructose does not improve endurance and has even been shown to harm performance. You store twice as much muscle glycogen after eating glucose or sucrose compared to eating fructose. Also, fructose is far more likely to cause gastrointestinal distress, even in small amounts. For this reason, glucose, maltodextrins (glucose polymers), and sucrose are the major carbohydrate sources in sports drinks. Maltodextrins are created by breaking down cornstarch into small glucose chains (polymers).

Consuming sugar before anaerobic exercise such as sprinting or weight lifting will not improve performance, because your body relies on stored ATP, CP, and muscle glycogen for these tasks. Sugar won't provide you with a sudden burst of quick energy, allowing you to exercise harder or longer. In fact, eating too much sugar immediately before or during exercise can increase the risk of gastrointestinal problems (cramps, nausea, diarrhea, and bloating).

Nutrient-Dense Carbohydrates

Your primary carbohydrate sources should be the whole grain products, vegetables, and fruits found at the bottom of the Food Guide Pyramid. These foods promote good health and athletic performance.

The dietary fiber found in these whole grain products, vegetables, and fruits may help reduce your risk of heart disease and certain cancers. The soluble fiber found in beans, oats, dried peas, and legumes can help to lower the cholesterol level in your blood. Since high blood cholesterol is a major risk factors for heart disease (see Chapter 4), consuming more soluble fiber may help reduce your risk for heart disease.

The insoluble fiber found in wheat bran, whole grain products, and vegetables speeds up the movement of food through the gastrointestinal tract. Insoluble fiber may reduce your risk for bowel disorders such as diverticulitis and constipation. Fruits, barley, and vegetables are sources of both soluble and insoluble fiber. Appendix 1 lists the fiber content of selected foods.

In addition to fiber, minimally processed plant foods such as whole grain products, vegetables, and fruits supply vitamins, minerals, and phytochemicals (plant chemicals) that have positive health effects. These foods are "nutrient-dense"—they supply a significant amount of nutrients for their calories. Appendix 2 provides tips for choosing nutrient-dense foods.

Compare a small baked potato with a third of a candy bar. Both contain about 100 calories. The potato provides ample vitamin C, with a small amount of protein, B vitamins, about a half dozen minerals, and fiber. The third of the candy bar provides the same amount of energy (calories), about 3 times as much fat, and little or no fiber, vitamins, or minerals.

Contrary to popular belief, starches such as whole grain breads and cereals, potatoes, corn, beans, rice, and pasta contribute significantly fewer calories for a given amount than foods with high fat or sugar contents. The "diet lunch" of a hamburger patty and a scoop of cottage cheese provides excessive fat calories.

Replacing fats and sugary foods in the diet with nutrient-dense carbohydrates actually facilitates weight loss because the carbohydrates contain fewer calories. Also, the naturally occurring sugars in fruit make them ideal sweet, low-calorie treats.

Carbohydrate Supplements

Some athletes train so heavily that they have difficulty eating enough food to meet their carbohydrate needs. This can happen for several reasons. The stress of hard training can decrease your appetite so that you don't consume enough calories and carbohydrates. Eating a large volume of food can give you gastrointestinal discomfort and interfere with your training. You may even be spending so much time training that you don't have enough rest time available to eat properly.

If you have problems consuming enough carbohydrates, you can use a commercial high-carbohydrate supplement. These products don't replace your regular food but do help supply additional calories and carbohydrates when needed.

Table 1-6.
High-Carbohydrate Beverages

Beverage	Flavors	Carbohydrate Ingredient	Carbohydrate % (Concentration) 12-oz. Serving	Carbohydrate	Sodium
Gatorade® Energy Drink Gatorade	Orange, grape, wildberry	Maltodextrin, high-fructose corn syrup	22	78	200
Endurex R4 Pacific Health Laboratories	Fruit punch, orange, lemon-lime	Maltodextrin, glucose, fructose	15	35	180
Carboplex® Unipro, Inc.	Plain	Maltodextrin, high-fructose corn syrup	24	82	0

Table 1-6.
High-Carbohydrate Beverages (continued)

Beverage	Flavors	Carbo-hydrate Ingredient	Carbohydrate % (Concentration) 12-oz. Serving	Carbo-hydrate	Sodium
Carbo Power® Nature's Best	Fruit punch, orange, grape	Maltodextrin, high-fructose corn syrup	21	75	71
Ultra Fuel® Twinlab Corp.	Lemon, lime, grape, fruit punch, orange	Maltodextrin, glucose, fructose	21	75	0
Carbo Fire® Weider Nutrition International	Tropical punch, orange	Glucose, polymers, fructose	24	83	60

You can use high-carbohydrate supplements before or after exercise, either with or between meals. Though some endurance athletes may also use them during exercise to obtain energy, they are too concentrated in carbohydrate (18 to 24%) to be used as fluid replacement drinks. Your fluid replacement beverage should not exceed 8% carbohydrate (see Chapter 2).

2

Hydration

Don't Forget to Drink

I was the second person to get into lunch at the 100-mile mark of a 200-mile ride. It was 100 degrees F. and I was tired.

I started the second 100 miles with 2 full water bottles. No shade. Hilly steep pitches. I was going very slowly and still felt terrible, riding in my lowest gear. Ten miles out I had gone through both water bottles.

There was no escape from the heat. Cycling produced more heat. Raging thirst. I searched for water but the hills were parched. I felt they would find my bleached bones on the side of the road.

I became disoriented and was on the verge of crying. Not thinking clearly, I went on for 30 more miles. Rounding a corner I thought I saw a bicyclist in need of help and stopped. There was no one there. I was hallucinating. I quit the race.

Other experienced riders felt the same thing—throbbing heads, hot/cold flashes, and sudden weakness. Only 20 percent of those who started the race finished. The environment was so harsh that we couldn't drink enough fluids to replace the fluid we lost.

WATER IS THE MOST ESSENTIAL of all nutrients. Your body requires it constantly. All of the body's important chemical reactions, such as energy production, are carried out in water. Without water, most people could not survive for more than a few days.

Although water has a number of important functions, the most critical function for athletes is the regulation of body temperature. Dehydration—the loss of body water—reduces endurance and increases the risk of heat injury. Consuming cool fluids at regular intervals during exercise optimizes athletic performance and protects your health.

Temperature Regulation during Exercise

Water acts as a coolant to keep the body from overheating during physical activity. During exercise, heat is generated as a by-product of the working muscles. When heat builds up, the body temperature rises. This heat must be removed to maintain a normal body temperature.

During exercise in warm weather, sweat is your main way to eliminate excess heat. When sweat evaporates from your skin, you cool down. Large sweat losses, however, reduce your body's water content. The loss of water in sweat harms your athletic performance and hinders your ability to control body temperature.

During exercise in the heat, blood that was transferring oxygen to the muscles is diverted to skin to help eliminate heat. The competition for blood between the muscles and skin places a greater demand on your cardiovascular system. At the same time, your blood volume is decreasing due to sweat losses. As you become dehydrated, your heart rate, perceived level of effort, and body temperature all increase.

Your body is programmed to protect cardiovascular function at the expense of body temperature regulation. Consequently, skin blood flow and sweat rate will decrease in an effort to conserve body fluid. As a result, your body temperature rises, leading to fatigue and increased risk of heat injury.

In practical terms, when you're dehydrated you can't exercise as hard or as long. During prolonged exercise in the heat, sweat losses constituting as little as 2% of your body weight impair athletic performance and temperature regulation. Inadequate fluid replacement speeds up dehydration, and can ultimately cause a life-threatening heat illness.

Fluid Replacement Guidelines

At rest, you need at least 2 quarts or liters of fluid daily. Exercise greatly increases your fluid requirements. Consuming fluids prior to exercise can reduce or delay the detrimental effects of dehydration. Drink 14 to 22 ounces (400 to 600 milliliters) of fluid about 2 hours prior to exercise. This promotes adequate hydration and allows time for the excretion of excess fluid.

Drinking during exercise is essential to prevent the detrimental effects of dehydration on your body temperature and exercise performance. Drink 6 to 12 ounces (150 to 350 milliliters) of fluid every 15 to 20 minutes during exercise to replace sweat losses. The actual amount you consume will vary based on your individual rate of sweat loss during training and simulated competitive conditions.

A loss of 1 pound of body weight is equivalent to 16 ounces (480 milliliters) of fluid. Follow a fluid replacement schedule that is based on the hourly amount of fluid that you lose during exercise. For example, if you lose 2 pounds per hour, then drink 8 ounces (240 ml) or half of a 16-ounce water bottle every 15 minutes while you are exercising.

There is no safe level of dehydration that you can tolerate before your cardiovascular function and temperature regulation are impaired. You'll perform at your best when your fluid intake closely matches your fluid loss from sweating.

Table 2-1.
Hydration Guidelines

Hydration Guidelines
Drink 14 to 22 ounces of fluid about 2 hours prior to exercise.
Drink 6 to 12 ounces of fluid every 15 to 20 minutes during exercise.
Drink 24 ounces of fluid for every pound of body weight lost after exercise.

Thirst is not an adequate guide to fluid replacement. Most people only replace 50% of their fluid losses during exercise. You need to regulate your fluid intake by drinking according to a time schedule rather than in response to thirst.

Get in the habit of regular drinking during training. Some athletes only pay attention to their fluid intake during competition and become dehydrated in workouts. Adequate fluid intake during training protects against heat illness and enables you to get the most out of your workouts. It also gives you the chance to practice proper hydration techniques.

Weigh yourself before and after exercise (nude is best) to determine how much fluid you're losing. After exercise drink 24 ounces of fluid (about 750 milliliters) for every pound of body weight lost. If you notice a gradual loss of weight during warm weather training, this may be due to chronic dehydration rather than body fat loss. You can also monitor the volume, color, and odor of your urine. Urine that is of small volume, dark yellow in color, and has a strong odor suggests that you are dehydrated.

Fluid Replacement Beverages

Consume sports drinks when you train hard for periods longer than 45 to 50 minutes. Both sports drinks and water replace water losses. However, unlike water, sports drinks improve performance by providing carbohydrate for the working muscles. The sodium in sports drinks aids fluid absorption.

For optimal absorption and performance, a sports drink should contain 4 to 8% carbohydrate (10 to 18 grams of carbohydrate or 38 to 77 calories per 8 ounces). Beverages such as fruit juice and soda that exceed 10% carbohydrate (over 24 grams or 96 calories per 8 ounces) take longer to be absorbed, as do drinks high in fructose. They can cause abdominal cramps, nausea, bloating, and diarrhea. Most sports drinks contain 5 to 8% carbohydrate. Try several different sports drinks during training to find the one that works the best for you.

Electrolytes

Electrolytes such as sodium, chloride, and potassium are necessary for the maintenance of body fluid levels, muscle contractions, and nerve impulse transmission.

Sweating results in electrolyte losses (particularly sodium and chloride) as well as water losses. A sodium deficit may occur under several conditions—when acclimating to a hot environment, following repeated workouts in hot weather, and during endurance events such as 50-mile runs, 100-mile bike rides, and long triathlons

Heat-related muscle cramps (heat cramps) can occur during a triathlon or cycling race, especially in the latter stages of the event. To completely restore body fluids, the salt must be replaced along with the water. Athletes who are susceptible to heat cramps sweat extensively, lose a considerable amount of sodium and chloride through sweating, and have a relatively low daily dietary salt intake

Prolonged exercise in the heat may also increase the risk of hyponatremia (low blood sodium). Heavy sweating and/or

TABLE 2-2.
POPULAR SPORTS DRINKS

INGREDIENTS PER 8 OZ.	CARBO-HYDRATE CONTENT (%)	CARBO-HYDRATE (GRAMS)	CARBO-HYDRATE TYPE	CALORIES	SODIUM (MG)	POTASSIUM (MG)	CARBONATION	CAFFEINE
Gatorade Thirst Quencher GATORADE COMPANY	6%	14	Sucrose, Glucose, Fructose	50	110	30	No	No
CeraSport CERA PRODUCTS, LLC	7%	16	Maltodextrin	76	102	37	No	No
Cytomax CYTOSPORT, INC.	6%	15	High Fructose Corn Syrup, Maltodextrin, Lactate	80	70	77	No	No
Powerade COCA-COLA COMPANY	8%	19	High Fructose Corn Syrup, Glucose Polymers	72	53	33	No	No
PowerBar Perform POWERBAR, INC.	7%	16	Glucose, Fructose, Maltodextrin	60	110	35	No	No
Accelerade PACIFIC HEALTH LABORATORIS, INC.	7.75%	8.5	Sucrose, Fructose, Maltodextrin	93	130	43	No	No
GUO_2 GU SPORTS	5.7%	13	Fructose, Maltodextrin	50	73	20	No	No

TABLE 2-2.
POPULAR SPORTS DRINKS (CONTINUED)

INGREDIENTS PER 8 OZ.	CARBO-HYDRATE CONTENT (%)	CARBO-HYDRATE (GRAMS)	CARBO-HYDRATE TYPE	CALORIES	SODIUM (MG)	POTASSIUM (MG)	CARBONATION	CAFFEINE
Revenge EXTREME SPORTS NUTRITION, INC.	4%	10	Maltodextrin, Fructose, Glucose	50	48	80	No	Yes
NONSPORTS DRINKS								
Coca-Cola COCA-COLA COMPANY	11%	27	High Fructose Corn Syrup, Sucrose	100	35	0	Yes	Yes
Mountain Dew PEPSICO, INC.	13%	31	High Fructose Corn Syrup	110	50	0	Yes	Yes
Orange Juice	11%	27	Sucrose, Fructose, Glucose	112	7	446	No	No
Pedialyte ABBOTT LABORATORIES	2.5%	6	Glucose, Fructose	24	248	187	No	No
Rehydralyte ABBOTT LABORATORIES	2.5%	6	Glucose	24	407	183	No	No
Water	0%	0	None	0	0	0	No	No

repeatedly ingesting low-sodium or sodium-free beverages (e.g. water) for several hours or more increases the risk of hyponatremia. Sweat sodium losses during prolonged exercise in the heat can be considerable, and consuming excessive amounts of water or low-sodium beverages dilutes the amount of sodium left in the blood.

The symptoms of hyponatremia start with confusion and headache and progress to unconsciousness and coma. Although other heat illnesses are more common, hyponatremia is dangerous and its incidence should not be underestimated. To prevent hyponatremia, drink an appropriate amount of fluid (only enough to maintain normal body hydration) and consume adequate salt before, during, and after exercise in the heat.

Adding salt to the diet or eating high-salt foods can help to prevent a sodium deficit and maintain your hydration when you exercise in hot conditions or expect to sweat extensively; 1/2 teaspoon of salt supplies 1 gram of sodium and should replace the amount of sodium lost in about 2 pounds of sweat.

Some endurance athletes benefit from taking low dose sodium tablets during exercise. Or, you can add additional salt to your sports drink used during exercise—1/4 to 1/2 teaspoon of salt to 32 ounces of sports drink.

You lose far more sodium than potassium during exercise. Orange juice, bananas, and potatoes are all excellent sources of potassium. A large glass of orange juice will replace the potassium lost in about 4 pounds of sweat. Potassium supplements aren't necessary and can cause an excessively high level of potassium in the blood, resulting in an abnormal heart rhythm.

Sports drinks containing sodium can also promote rehydration following exercise. The sodium helps to maintain your thirst and keeps you drinking while it delays urine production. This promotes rapid rehydration and enhances your recovery. Drinking plain water eliminates your thirst so that you stop drinking and urine production is stimulated. This can delay rehydration and hinder your recovery.

Weather Concerns

You may be unaware of the substantial sweat losses that can occur during hot, dry weather. Large amounts of fluid evaporate very quickly in these conditions. Since you don't feel sweaty, you may not recognize how much water you've lost.

In addition to temperature, relative humidity is also important. As the moisture in the air increases, the effectiveness of evaporation through sweating decreases. If the air is saturated with water, less evaporation will occur even at cooler temperatures and body heat can build up. When sweat drips off your skin, you're not getting the cooling benefit of sweat. Be aware of intense physical exertion on warm, humid days as well as hot, dry days (see Table 2-3).

Heat Illnesses

Athletes who exercise in hot or humid weather can experience heat cramps, heat exhaustion, or heat stroke. Three factors contribute to the development of these heat injuries: increased core temperature, loss of body fluids, and loss of electrolytes.

Heat cramps, or involuntary muscle spasms, occur during prolonged exercise when there has been profuse and repeated sweating. Heat cramps are probably caused by an imbalance of the body's fluid and electrolyte concentrations. Muscles spasms can occur if the salt lost in sweat isn't replaced. Treatment: Rest, drink fluids containing electrolytes such as sport drinks, and add salt to foods.

Heat exhaustion is probably caused by a reduced blood volume due to excessive sweating. Blood pools in the extremities and the person may faint or feel dizzy. The symptoms of heat exhaustion also include nausea and fatigue. Although sweating may be reduced, the rectal temperature is not elevated to dangerous levels—less than 104 degrees F. Treatment: Rest in a cool

Table 2-3.
Heat Index

TEMPERATURE	**70°**	**75°**	**80°**	**85°**	**90°**	**95°**	**100°**	**105°**	**110°**	**115°**	**120°**
Relative Humidity					**Apparent Temperature***						
0%	64°	69°	73°	78°	83°	87°	91°	95°	99°	103°	107°
10%	65°	70°	75°	80°	85°	90°	95°	100°	105°	111°	116°
20%	66°	72°	77°	82°	87°	93°	99°	105°	112°	120°	130°
30%	67°	73°	78°	84°	90°	96°	104°	113°	123°	135°	148°
40%	68°	74°	79°	86°	93°	101°	110°	123°	137°	151°	
50%	69°	75°	81°	88°	96°	107°	120°	135°	150°		
60%	70°	76°	82°	90°	100°	114°	132°	149°			
70%	70°	77°	85°	93°	106°	124°	144°				
80%	71°	78°	86°	97°	113°	136°					
90%	71°	79°	88°	102°	122°						
100%	72°	80°	91°	108°							

HOW TO USE HEAT INDEX:

1. Across top locate Temperature
2. Down left side locate Relative Humidity
3. Follow across and down to find Apparent Temperature
4. Determine Heat Stress Risk on chart below

Apparent Temperature	**Heat Stress Risk with Physical Activity and/or Prolonged Exposure**
90°–105°	*Heat cramps or heat exhaustion* possible
105°–130°	*Heat cramps or heat exhaustion* likely *Heatstroke* possible
130° and up	*Heatstroke* highly likely

✔ **Note:** *Combined index of heat and humidity. . . what it feels like to the body.

✔ **Note:** This heat index chart is designed to provide general guidelines for assessing the potential severity of heat stress. Individual reactions to heat will vary. In addition, studies indicate that susceptibility to heat disorders tends to increase with age. Exposure to full sunshine can increase Heat Index values by up to 15°F.

■ **Source:** National Oceanic and Atmospheric Administration.

place and drink fluids containing electrolytes. Medical attention may be required.

Heat stroke is a medical emergency requiring immediate action. The body's temperature-regulating processes simply stop functioning. Sweating usually stops and the skin becomes dry and hot. The rectal temperature is excessively high—over 105.8 degrees F. Other symptoms include disorientation, vomiting, headache, and loss of consciousness. If untreated, death occurs due to circulatory collapse and central nervous system damage. Treatment: Aggressive steps must be taken to immediately lower the elevated body temperature. Until medical help arrives, the person can be covered with ice-packs, immersed in cold water, or rubbed with alcohol.

Be aware of the symptoms of impending heat illness. These include weakness, chills, goose pimples on the chest and upper arms, nausea, headache, faintness, disorientation, muscle cramping, and cessation of sweating. Continuing to exercise when experiencing any of these symptoms can lead to a heat injury.

Alcohol

Consuming alcohol before or during exercise won't give you an energy boost. Alcohol is a poor energy source because it doesn't contribute to the formation of muscle glycogen—the preferred fuel for most sports. One 12-ounce beer or 5-ounce glass of wine supplies only 50 calories of carbohydrates—enough to run 1/2 mile.

Since alcohol is a diuretic, don't use it to replace fluid losses immediately after exercise. The best post-exercise drink is one that contains carbohydrates and sodium to replace both glycogen and water.

Drinking alcohol immediately prior to or during exercise can harm performance. Alcohol is a central nervous system depressant that impairs judgment, reaction time, fine motor coordination (speech) and gross motor coordination (walking and balance). Alcohol decreases the output of glucose by the liver, which may cause low blood glucose levels and early fatigue during endurance exercise. Alcohol may also contribute to hypothermia (dangerously low body temperature) during workouts in cold weather.

Drinking excessively the night before exercise can also hurt performance. Aside from the obvious adverse effects of the hangover (headache and nausea) heavy drinking causes dehydration. The diuretic effect of alcohol may increase your risk of developing a heat illness during exercise in warm weather.

Your liver can only get rid of about 1/2 ounce of pure alcohol per hour—the amount found in 1 drink. A drink is equal to 12 ounces of beer, 5 ounces of wine, or 1 1/2 ounces of 80-proof liquor. Moderate drinking (1 to 2 drinks per day for women and 1 to 3 drinks per day for men) the night before or after exercise isn't likely to harm performance or health as long as you are properly hydrated. The upper limit depends on the individual, since sensitivity to alcohol varies considerably. Pregnant women should not drink since consumption of alcohol may cause birth defects or other problems during pregnancy.

Excessive drinking (over 3 drinks daily) is harmful to health. Excess alcohol consumption can increase the risk for automobile and other accidents, high blood pressure, stroke, violence, suicide, birth defects, and certain cancers. Too much alcohol may also cause social and psychological problems, cirrhosis of the liver, inflammation of the pancreas, and damage to the brain and heart.

Alcoholic beverages are also high in calories and low in nutrients—a source of "empty calories"; 12 ounces of beer supply about 150 calories, while 5 ounces of wine or 1 1/2 ounces of 80-proof liquor supply about 100 calories.

TABLE 2-4.
ALCOHOLIC BEVERAGES

BEVERAGE (% ALCOHOL BY VOLUME)	SERVING SIZE (OZ)	CALORIES
Wine (11.5%)	5	105
Sherry (19%)	3	125
Beer (4.5%)	12	150
Stout or porter on tap (about 3%)	12	200
Gin, vodka, rum, whiskey (rye, Scotch), 80 proof (40%)	1.5	100–110
Cordials, liqueurs, 25–100 proof (12.5–50%)	1	50–100
Martini (38%, ¾ oz. alcohol)	2.5	156
Manhattan (37%)	2	128
Bloody Mary (12%)	5	116
Tom Collins (9%)	7.5	121
Daiquiri (28%)	2	111
Gin and tonic (9%)	7.5	171
Piña colada (12%)	4.5	262
Screwdriver (8%)	7	174
Tequila sunrise (14%)	5.5	189
Whiskey sour prepared from bottled mix (17%)	3.5	160

3

Fueling Your Sport

Eating before, during, and after Exercise

It was the last rest stop, the 170-mile mark of a 200-mile cycling race. We had been riding for 10 hours—4 of those hours in 90-degree F. heat.

I was sunburned, breathing hard, hurting. Lying on the ground I ate about 5 chocolate chip cookies, wondering if I could ride another 30 miles. My chief adversary rode up and my heart sank—she looked great.

We had been riding neck-and-neck and she definitely seemed to be the stronger of the two of us. I knew that she hadn't taken a rest or eaten since the 150-mile mark. "C'mon," she said to a friend, "Let's go in and pick up my trophy."

I dragged myself back onto my bike and gave chase. It was sheer determination and concentration on my part that kept my legs moving. My competitor was talking and making jokes, looking like she was one with her cycle.

About 10 miles later she began to fade as I perked up. "What's the matter?" I asked her.

"I don't know," she said. "I feel weak and shaky. "

Slowly our roles reversed. I felt strong. She faded off to the back of the pace line. I pulled the pace line into the finish for the last 15 miles—finishing strong and feeling great.

Later, I learned that my competitor had stopped about ten miles from the finish line. She ordered a shake at a fast food restaurant and fainted. It had been 2 1/2 to 3 hours since she had last eaten.

ADEQUATE CARBOHYDRATE STORES (muscle and liver glycogen and blood glucose) are critical to optimum athletic performance. Eating prior to endurance exercise can help performance by "topping off" muscle and liver glycogen stores. Refueling during endurance exercise can improve performance by maintaining blood glucose levels. Eating properly following exercise is necessary to replenish muscle and liver glycogen after training or competition.

Consuming adequate carbohydrates during training enables you to maintain a desirable training intensity. Also, testing specific foods and fluids before, during, and after training allows you to practice effective fueling strategies for competition.

Eating before Exercise

Many athletes train and compete in the morning without eating breakfast. Continuing your overnight fast lowers your liver glycogen stores—the body's main source of blood glucose. Eating a high-carbohydrate meal before morning exercise helps maintain your blood glucose levels and provides energy for the working muscles so that you can perform at your best. The pre-exercise meal can also keep you from feeling hungry and tired, which can harm your performance.

Consume your carbohydrate-rich meal 1 to 4 hours before training or competition. This allows adequate time for food to empty from the stomach. Exercising with a nearly full stomach can cause indigestion, nausea, and vomiting as blood is diverted from the stomach to the muscles, interfering with your digestion.

The amount to consume depends on the timing of the meal. To avoid potential gastrointestinal distress, the carbohydrate and calorie content of the meal should be reduced the closer to exercise the meal is consumed. For example, a small meal of 4 calories per kilogram is appropriate 1 hour before exercise, whereas a large meal of 16 calories per kilogram can be consumed 4 hours before exercise.

Good examples of high-carbohydrate foods for pre-exercise meals include bread products such as toast, bagels, pancakes, or muffins (adding jam or jelly increases the carbohydrate content), cooked or dry cereal, fruit, sports bars, nonfat or 1% fat yogurt, and liquid meals. Fruit juices, nonfat or 1% fat milk, and sports drinks are good high-carbohydrate beverages. Table 3-1 provides examples of recommended pre-exercise meals.

Limit fatty foods because fat slows stomach-emptying time and may make you feel sluggish. Many popular high-protein breakfast foods (bacon, sausage, and cheese) are high in fat. In contrast, carbohydrates provide the quickest and most efficient source of energy, and unlike fats, are rapidly digested.

You may need to limit the fiber content (especially bran) in your pre-exercise meal to avoid abdominal cramping and a bathroom break during exercise. This is merely annoying during training, but can be disastrous during competition. It's also a good idea to minimize gas-inducing foods such as beans and onions. Extremely salty foods (bacon and sausage) can cause fluid retention and a bloated feeling. Above, all you should choose palatable, familiar, and well-tolerated foods. Drinking fluids with your pre-exercise meal and before exercise helps to ensure that you're properly hydrated.

Experimenting with a variety of pre-exercise meals in training helps you determine what foods you are most likely to handle well before competition. Many people are tense before competing; tension can slow digestion. Even familiar, well-tolerated foods may take longer to digest. Never try an untested food or fluid right before competition. The result may be severe indigestion and impaired performance.

TABLE 3-1.
EXAMPLES OF PRE-EVENT MEALS

BREAKFAST

Orange juice
Blueberry pancakes with syrup
Bagel
Lowfat yogurt
Banana

Cranberry juice
Cornflakes
Lowfat milk
Apple muffin

LUNCH/DINNER

Chicken sandwich on whole-wheat roll
Fruit cup
Fig bar
Frozen lowfat yogurt

Lowfat milk
Pasta with tomato sauce
Salad with tomato, carrots, cucumbers, and mushrooms
Italian bread
Fresh fruit
Lowfat milk
Sherbet

Baked potato with low-fat cheese
Cornmeal muffin
Lowfat vanilla milk shake

Thick crust cheese and mushroom pizza
Lowfat milk
Fresh fruit
Bread sticks

Consuming a high-carbohydrate pre-exercise meal adds to the benefit you get from consuming carbohydrates during exercise. Although the improvement in performance that results from the pre-exercise meal is less than when smaller quantities of carbohydrates are consumed during exercise, it is still very important.

Liquid Meals

A number of commercially formulated liquid meals are available, as shown in Table 3-2. Their fluid and carbohydrate content make them a desirable meal choice either before competition or during day-long competitions such as long triathlons, 200-mile bike rides, or 50-mile runs. You can also use liquid meals for nutritional supplementation during heavy training when you need a lot of calories.

Liquid meals have several advantages over conventional meals. They leave the stomach more rapidly than regular meals, thereby helping to prevent nausea before competition. Liquid meals also produce a low stool residue, decreasing the risk of a bathroom break during exercise. Liquid meals satisfy hunger and supply energy without giving an uncomfortable feeling of fullness. Many athletes value a feeling of "lightness," especially as they enter competition.

You can concoct homemade liquid meals by mixing 1% fat milk, fruit, and nonfat dry milk powder in a blender. For variety, add cereal, yogurt, and flavoring (vanilla and chocolate). You can also use sugar and honey for additional sweetness and carbohydrates. There are several brands of "instant breakfast" powders that can be mixed with milk.

Refueling during Exercise

Taking in carbohydrate-rich foods and fluids during endurance events lasting 1 hour or longer can improve your performance. Consuming carbohydrates provides glucose for your muscles when they're running low on glycogen. In practical terms, this means you can maintain your pace longer and/or sprint harder at the end of exercise.

TABLE 3-2.
NUTRITION BEVERAGES

BEVERAGE	FLAVORS	CALORIES PER 8-OZ. SERVING	CARBO-HYDRATE (GRAMS)	PROTEIN (GRAMS)	FAT (GRAMS)
Gatorade Nutrition Shake GATORADE	Chocolate, vanilla	370	62	18	6
Endura Optimizer® UNIPRO, INC.	Chocolate vanilla, orange	260	57	11	less than 1
Metabolol II® EXTREME SPORTS NUTRITION, INC.	Chocolate, plain, orange smoothie	200	40	18	3
Ensure ABBOTT LABORATORIES	Chocolate, strawberry, vanilla	254	35	9	9
Nutrament® MEAD JOHNSON NUTRITIONALS	Chocolate, banana, vanilla, strawberry, coconut	240	34	6.5	11
Sustacal® MEAD JOHNSON NUTRITIONALS	Chocolate, vanilla, strawberry, eggnog	240	33	5.5	14.5
Go! SCIENCE IN SPORT	Vanilla, chocolate, strawberry, banana, orange cream	235	40	14	3

The breakdown of liver glycogen supplies glucose to maintain your blood glucose level. As your muscles run out of glycogen, they take up more blood glucose, placing a drain on the liver glycogen stores. The longer you exercise, the greater the utilization of blood glucose for energy. When the liver glycogen is depleted, your blood glucose drops. While a few people may experience symptoms of low blood sugar (hypoglycemia) such as dizziness, most simply have to reduce their exercise intensity because of muscle fatigue.

Eating carbohydrates helps to maintain blood glucose levels when your muscle glycogen stores are diminished. Thus, carbohydrate utilization (and therefore energy production) can continue at a high rate and your performance is enhanced.

Consume 30 to 60 grams of carbohydrate (120 to 240 calories) every hour you exercise. You can obtain this amount from either carbohydrate-rich foods (such as sports bars, gels, fig bars, fruit, and cookies) and/or sports drinks.

Each carbohydrate form (liquid versus solid) has its own advantages and drawbacks. High-carbohydrate foods can be easily carried and provide a feeling of satiety that you won't get from drinking fluids. Sports bars, fig bars, and cookies have a very low water content and so are more compact. By comparison, high-carbohydrate foods that have a high water content, such as fruit, take up more room. For example, to get the amount of carbohydrates supplied by one Power Bar (47 grams), you'd have to eat 1 1/2 bananas (45 grams).

However, the low water content of some high-carbohydrate solid foods also has a downside. You need to drink plenty of water when you eat solid food, especially a sports bar. Otherwise the food can settle poorly and you may feel like there's a rock in your gut. In addition to aiding your digestion, drinking water while eating solid foods helps you to hydrate adequately. Drink at least 8 ounces of water for a sports bar and 4 ounces for a gel.

Eating 1 banana (30 grams of carbohydrate), 1 PowerBar (47 grams of carbohydrate), 2 gels (about 50 grams of carbohydrate), 4 small fig bars (42 grams of carbohydrate) or 2 large graham crackers (42 grams of carbohydrate) every hour supplies an adequate amount of carbohydrates.

Sports drinks are a practical source of carbohydrates because they also replace your fluid losses. They provide the right proportion of water to carbohydrate to provide energy quickly and replace fluid losses. Drinking 24 to 48 ounces of a properly formulated sports drink (4 to 8% carbohydrate) each hour also provides the proper amount of carbohydrates. For example, drinking 24 ounces of Gatorade every hour provides 42 grams of carbohydrate.

Try to eat and drink *before* you feel hungry or tired, usually within 30 minutes after starting to exercise. Consuming small amounts at frequent intervals (every 15 to 20 minutes) helps to promote hydration, maintain blood glucose levels, and prevent gastrointestinal upset. Your foods and fluids should be easily digestible, familiar (tested in training), and enjoyable (to encourage eating and drinking). As with the pre-exercise meal, never try a new food or fluid during a race.

Ultraendurance Events and Relay Races

The importance of proper refueling and rehydrating during ultraendurance events (those lasting over 4 hours) cannot be overemphasized. Adequate nutrition can mean the difference between successfully completing the event or dropping out of it. The food and fluid you consume during an ultraendurance event are more important than what you consumed in the days before the event. Your two primary nutrition goals during ultraendurance events are to maintain adequate hydration and normal blood glucose levels.

Proper hydration is the most important nutritional concern during prolonged exercise. You can have adequate muscle glycogen stores and blood glucose and still collapse from heat exhaustion or stroke.

During ultraendurance events and relay races, you want to optimize carbohydrate absorption during exercise periods and glycogen repletion during rest periods. When your gut blood flow is low (as during intense cycling or running) stick with sports drinks and gels to promote rapid gastric emptying and carbohydrate absorption. When your gut blood flow is moderate (as during moderate cycling or slow jogging) eat easily digestible carbohydrate-rich foods such as fruit, grain products (fig bars, bagels, graham crackers), lowfat yogurt, sports bars, and liquid meals in addition to drinking fluids. When your gut blood flow is normal (as during rest) consume high-carbohydrate meals in addition to drinking fluids. See Table 3-3 for the nutritional content of common sports bars and gels.

TABLE 3-3.
SPORTS BARS AND GELS

SPORST BAR OR GEL	CALORIES	CARBO-HYDRATES	PROTEIN	FAT	FIBER
Gatorade energy bar GATORADE	260	46	8	5	2
PowerBar POWERBAR, INC.	230	45	10	2.5	3
Harvest Bar POWERBAR, INC.	250	45	7	5	2
Clif Bar CLIF BAR, INC	240	39	12	5	5
Luna Bar CLIF BAR, INC	180	24	10	4.5	2
PR* Bar PR* NUTRITION, INC.	190	19	14	6	0
Balance Bar BALANCE BAR COMPANY	200	22	14	6	2
Gu Gel GU SPORTS	100	25	0	0	
Power Gel POWERBAR, INC.	110	28	0	0	
Clif Shot CILF BAR, INC.	100	23–24	0	0	

Recovering from Exercise

Replacing your muscle glycogen stores following strenuous training is important to minimize chronic fatigue. Based on the time you spend training, consume 6 to 10 grams of carbohydrate per kilogram per day.

It's also important to take in carbohydrates immediately (within 30 minutes) after hard workouts that last several hours. Consuming high-carbohydrate fluids and foods right after prolonged training and competitions increases your glycogen storage and may help you recover faster. Replenishing muscle glycogen stores after exercise is particularly beneficial if you train hard several times a day. This enables you to get the most out of your second workout.

Many people aren't hungry after heavy training. If you are not, consume a high-carbohydrate drink such as fruit juice or a high-carbohydrate supplement. This will also promote rehydration.

After hard workouts, consume 1 1/2 grams of carbohydrate per kilogram within 30 minutes of exercise, followed by an additional 1 1/2 grams per kilogram 2 hours later. The first carbohydrate feeding can be a high-carbohydrate beverage and the second feeding can be a high-carbohydrate meal.

For example, a 70-kilogram man should consume 105 grams of carbohydrate within 30 minutes of exercise and the same amount 2 hours later. For the first feeding, he drinks 18 ounces of Gatorade Energy Drink. His second meal 2 hours later is a meal that provides 100 grams of carbohydrate—2 cups of spaghetti with 1 cup of tomato sauce and 2 pieces of French bread.

The next nutritional strategy necessary for an adequate recovery is proper fluid replacement. It is essential that you completely replace your fluid losses between workouts. Weigh yourself after exercising and drink 24 ounces of fluid for each pound lost. Consuming sports drinks following exercise promotes rehydration, thereby enhancing your recovery.

Carbohydrate Loading

You can improve your performance when you exercise for longer than 90 minutes by maximizing your muscle glycogen stores prior to the event. During endurance exercise that exceeds 90 to 120 minutes, your muscle glycogen stores become progressively lower. When they drop to critically low levels (the point of glycogen depletion), you cannot maintain high-intensity exercise. In practical terms, you've "hit the wall" and must drastically reduce your pace.

Carbohydrate loading can increase you muscle glycogen stores by 50 to 100%. The greater your pre-exercise muscle glycogen content, the greater your endurance potential. You can carbohydrate load using a 6-day, a 3-day, or 1-day regimen.

Table 3-4 gives an overview of the 6-day diet and training regimen used for carbohydrate loading. On the 6th day before the event, you exercise hard (about 70% of VO_{2max}) for 90 minutes. On the 5th and 4th days before the event, decrease your training to 40 minutes. During the first 3 days, you consume a normal diet providing about 5 grams of carbohydrate per kilogram per day. On the 3rd and 2nd day before the event, you reduce your training to 20 minutes. On the day before the event, you rest. During the last 3 days, you eat a high-carbohydrate diet providing 10 grams of carbohydrate per kilogram per day.

For the 3-day regimen, you exercise hard (about 70% of VO_{2max}) for 90 minutes 3 days before the event. You rest and eat a high-carbohydrate diet (10 grams of carbohydrate per kilogram per day) until the event.

A 1-day carbohydrate loading regimen has been proposed to minimize disruptions to your training and competition preparation. On the morning of the day before the event, skip breakfast and warm up for 5 minutes. Next, exercise at the highest intensity that you can maintain for 2 1/2 minutes followed by a 30 second all-out sprint. For the next 24 hours, rest and consume 10 grams of carbohydrate per kilogram. Start taking in carbohydrates within 20 minutes of completing the exercise.

TABLE 3-4.
TRAINING AND DIET REGIMEN FOR GLYCOGEN LOADING

	TRAINING	EATING
DAY 1	90 min • 70–75% $\dot{V}O_{2max}$	50% Carbohydrate 5 gm/kg
DAY 2	40 min • 70–75% $\dot{V}O_{2max}$	50% Carbohydrate 5 gm/kg
DAY 3	40 min • 70–75% $\dot{V}O_{2\,max}$	50% Carbohydrate 5 gm/kg
DAY 4	20 min • 70–75% $\dot{V}O_{2max}$	70% Carbohydrate 10 gm/kg
DAY 5	20 min • 70–75% $\dot{V}O_{2max}$	70% Carbohydrate 10 gm/kg
DAY 6	Rest	70% Carbohydrate 10 gm/kg
DAY 7	EVENT	EVENT

You must be endurance-trained or carbohydrate loading won't work. Also, the exercise to lower glycogen stores must be the same as your competitive event because glycogen stores are specific to the muscle groups used. For example, a runner needs to decrease glycogen by running rather than cycling.

It's essential that you decrease your training the 3 days prior to competition. Too much exercise during this period will use too much of your stored glycogen and defeat the purpose of the whole process. The final 3 days, when you taper and eat a high-carbohydrate diet, is the real loading phase of the regimen.

If you have difficulty consuming enough carbohydrate from food, you can use a high-carbohydrate supplement. If you have heart disease, diabetes and/or high blood triglycerides, you may have problems if you carbohydrate load. If you are in doubt, check with your doctor before attempting this regimen.

For each gram of glycogen stored, additional water is stored. Some people note a feeling of stiffness and heaviness associated with the increased glycogen storage. Once you start exercising, however, these sensations will work out.

Carbohydrate loading will help only for continuous endurance exercise lasting more than 90 minutes. Greater than usual muscle glycogen stores won't enable you to exercise harder during exercise of a shorter duration. In fact, the stiffness and heaviness due to increased glycogen stores can hurt your performance during shorter competitions such as 10-kilometer runs.

Carbohydrate loading enables you to maintain high-intensity exercise longer, but will not affect your pace for the first hour of exercise. You won't be able to go out faster, but you will be able to maintain your pace longer.

4

Fat

Friend or Foe?

One Wednesday night I visited a friend who planned to run a marathon on the following Saturday. He was cooking dinner, which consisted of steak, a baked potato with sour cream, vegetables smothered in butter, a salad with lots of dressing and bread. For dessert he planned to eat cake. While he was cooking, he ate a half a bag of corn chips. "What are you getting ready for?" I asked him. He replied, "I'm carbohydrate loading." "No you're not," I said. "You're fat loading."

MOST AMERICANS, whether active or sedentary, eat about 34% of their calories as fat. Reducing dietary fat can help to decrease your risk of heart disease (our nation's number one killer), stroke, and certain cancers.

Limiting fat intake is also beneficial for weight control. Fat is the most concentrated source of calories in the diet, supplying twice as many calories by weight as carbohydrates or protein. Dietary fat is also more readily converted to body fat than dietary carbohydrates.

Fat as an Exercise Fuel

Whereas the total glycogen stores in your muscle and liver amount to only about 2,000 calories, every pound of fat supplies 3,500 calories. Fat is a major fuel for low- to moderate-intensity exercise.

Even though fat makes significant energy contributions during prolonged endurance exercise, you shouldn't eat a high-fat diet. Most athletes store more body fat than they'll ever need and excess body fat impairs athletic performance. Also, if you eat more fat you'll take in less carbohydrates. Your muscle glycogen stores cannot be adequately maintained on a high-fat diet.

Endurance training itself causes several major adaptations that significantly increase fat utilization. Endurance training increases the number of capillaries in the trained muscles, so that the muscles receive more blood and oxygen. Also, endurance training increases the activity of the specific muscle enzymes that are responsible for burning fat.

When your body uses fat for energy, it spares muscle glycogen. Since muscle glycogen stores are limited and fat stores are abundant, slowing the rate of glycogen usage improves endurance.

Your VO_{2max} and lactate threshold also have a positive effect on the contribution of fat during endurance exercise. In general, the higher your VO_{2max} and lactate threshold, the greater your ability to use fat.

Proper pacing is also important to maximize fat utilization in endurance events. You'll use less fat and more glycogen by going out too fast and by continuing at a pace that is too fast. Your optimal long-term pace is the speed that allows you to burn more fat and conserve glycogen. High-intensity workouts (e.g., interval training), are done to increase speed, not to improve fat utilization.

Fat and Health

Most U.S. health agencies recommend limiting fat intake to about 30% of total calories. Because saturated fat significantly increases the cholesterol level in the blood, it should provide less than 10% of your total calories. Dietary cholesterol should be limited to less than 300 milligrams per day. An elevated blood cholesterol level is a major risk factor for heart disease, as are diabetes, high blood pressure, inactivity, smoking, and obesity.

The National Cholesterol Education Program defines a desirable blood cholesterol level as below 200 milligrams/dL. A blood cholesterol level of 240 milligrams/dL or more is considered high; 200 to 239 milligrams/dL is considered borderline high. These levels are important, as a person with a cholesterol level of 240 milligrams/dL is at double the risk for heart disease as a person with a cholesterol level of 200 milligrams/dL. Please see Table 4-1 for more details on blood cholesterol levels.

TABLE 4-1.
BLOOD CHOLESTEROL LEVELS

BLOOD CHOLESTEROL LEVELS	
LDL cholesterol	
Below 100	Optimal
100–129	Near or above optimal
130–159	Borderline high
160–189	High
Over 190	Very high

TABLE 4-1.
BLOOD CHOLESTEROL LEVELS (CONTINUED)

BLOOD CHOLESTEROL LEVELS	
Total cholesterol	
Below 200	Desirable
200–239	Borderline high
Over 240	High
HDL cholesterol	
Below 40	Low
60 or above	High

The way in which cholesterol is transported in the blood also affects your risk of developing heart disease. Cholesterol is transported in the blood attached to protein as a substance called a lipoprotein. Low-density lipoprotein or LDL, is the main component of the total cholesterol level. LDL deposits cholesterol in the artery wall and increases the risk of heart disease. High-density lipoprotein or HDL, on the other hand, removes cholesterol from the artery wall and actually decreases the risk of heart disease.

A LDL cholesterol level below 100 milligrams/dL is considered optimal and a level below 130 is "near or above optimal," as shown in Table 4-1. A level of 130 to 159 milligrams/dL is considered borderline high and a level of 160 milligrams/dL is considered high.

A high level of HDL cholesterol is protective against heart disease and levels of 60 milligrams/dL or above significantly decreases heart disease risk. A low level of HDL cholesterol (less than 40 milligrams/dL) significantly increases your risk of developing heart disease.

In general, decreasing your intake of saturated fat and cholesterol lowers your LDL cholesterol and total cholesterol levels. Endurance exercise and weight loss raise HDL cholesterol levels. See Table 4-2 for more information on how to reduce fat and cholesterol in your diet.

Cutting Down on Fat Intake

You can eat a high-carbohydrate, lowfat diet by following the training diet guidelines outlined in Chapter 1. The following are further recommendations to cut down on fat intake.

You can lower your fat intake by cutting down on both "hidden" and "visible" sources of fat. Fat is hidden in dairy products, meat, eggs, nuts, and fried foods. Be aware of the hidden fat in favorite foods such as ice cream, cheese, French fries, chips, granola, cold cuts, bacon, nuts, hamburger, and baked goods (cookies, pies, cakes, and pastries). Visible dietary sources of fat include margarine, butter, cream, mayonnaise, oil, salad dressing, gravy, sauce, sour cream, and cream cheese.

You can reduce your intake of total fat, saturated fat, and cholesterol by choosing lean meat, poultry, and fish. Try to eat less high-fat processed meat such as bologna, bacon, salami, and hot dogs. Removing the skin from poultry and trimming visible fat from meat also cuts down on fat. The Dietary Guidelines recommend consuming 5 to 7 ounces of meat, poultry, or fish per day.

The butterfat found in butter, cheese, chocolate, ice cream, and whole milk can also be limited to reduce your intake of total fat, saturated fat, and cholesterol. Substitute nonfat and lowfat dairy products such as 1% fat milk and yogurt, ice milk, and lowfat cheese for high-fat dairy products. The Dietary Guidelines recommend consuming 2 to 3 servings of dairy products each day.

Oils with high percentages of unsaturated fat (canola, corn, olive, and soy oil and their derivative margarines) should be substituted for saturated fats such as butter, lard, shortening, and bacon grease. When oil and margarine are substituted for butter, remember that they are still high in fat and calories and should be used sparingly. Reduced fat substitutes for salad dressing and sour cream can replace the regular higher fat versions.

TABLE 4-2.
HOW TO REDUCE DIETARY FAT AND CHOLESTEROL

	CHOOSE	DECREASE
Fish, Chicken, Turkey, and Lean Meats	Fish, poultry without skin, lean cuts of beef, lamb, pork, or veal, shellfish	Fatty cuts of beef, lamb, pork; spare ribs, organ meats regular cold cuts, sausage, hot dogs, bacon, sardines, roe
Skim and Lowfat Milk, Cheese, Yogurt, and Dairy Substitutes	Skim or 1% fat milk (liquid, powdered, evaporated), buttermilk	Whole milk (4% fat); regular, evaporated, condensed; cream, half and half, 2% milk, imitation milk products, most nondairy creamers, whipped toppings
	Nonfat (0% fat) or lowfat yogurt Nonfat or lowfat cottage cheese (1% or 2% fat)	Whole-milk yogurt Whole-milk cottage cheese (4% fat)
	Nonfat, lowfat cheeses (0–6 gm fat/ounce)	All natural cheeses (e.g., blue, roquefort, camembert, cheddar, swiss)
	Nonfat, lowfat, or “light” cream cheese, nonfat, lowfat, or “light” sour cream	Cream cheeses, sour cream
	Nonfat, lowfat ice cream Sherbet Sorbet Nonfat, lowfat frozen yogurt	Regular ice cream
Eggs	Egg whites (2 whites = 1 whole egg in recipes), cholesterol-free egg substitutes	Egg yolks

TABLE 4-2.
HOW TO REDUCE DIETARY FAT AND CHOLESTEROL (CONTINUED)

	CHOOSE	DECREASE
Fruits and Vegetables	Fresh, frozen, canned, or dried fruits and vegetables	Vegetables prepared in butter, cheese, cream, or other creamy sauces
Breads and Cereals	Homemade baked goods using unsaturated oils sparingly, angel food cake, nonfat or lowfat crackers, nonfat or lowfat cookies	Commercial baked goods: pies, cakes, donuts, pastries, croissants, muffins, biscuits, high-fat crackers, high-fat cookies
	Rice, pasta	Egg noodles
	Whole-grain breads and cereals (oatmeal, whole wheat, rye, bran, multigrain, etc.)	Breads in which eggs are major ingredient
Fats and Oils	Baking cocoa	Chocolate
	Unsaturated vegetable oils; corn, olive, rapeseed (canola oil), safflower, sesame, soybean, sunflower	Saturated oils: butter, coconut, palm, palm kernel, lard, bacon fat
	Liquid, tub margarine or shortening made from one of the unsaturated oils listed above	Stick margarine
	Diet margarine	
	Lowfat or nonfat mayonnaise, salad dressings made with unsaturated oils listed above	Dressings made with egg yolk
	Nonfat or lowfat dressings	Regular dressings
	Seeds and nuts	Coconut

Choose cooking methods that require little or no fat. These include steaming, baking, broiling, grilling, poaching, or stir-frying in small amounts of unsaturated vegetable oil. Foods can be microwaved or cooked in pans that have been sprayed with non-stick products to reduce added fat. Try to limit fried foods, especially when saturated fat is used in their preparation.

Although nonfat and lowfat bakery goods and frozen dairy products contain little or no fat, they do contain calories. Remember to check the food label—fat-free does not mean calorie-free. These products can be loaded with extra sugar (calories) and sodium to improve taste.

High-Fat Diets and Performance

Adaptation to a high-fat diet or "fat loading" is one strategy utilized by endurance athletes to promote fat burning, decrease glycogen use, and enhance performance. Compared to a high-carbohydrate diet, "fat loading" (60–70% energy from fat) increases fat breakdown and spares muscle glycogen during low- to moderate-intensity exercise.

A study done 20 years ago found that cyclists who ate a high-fat diet (85% of calories) for one month used 3 times less muscle glycogen and 4 times less blood glucose during exercise at 63% of VO_{2max}. The utilization of fat rose to make up the difference. Although fat loading improved fat burning, it did not improve performance compared to a diet containing 50% carbohydrates.

Several recent studies tested the effects of 5- and 6-day fat loading periods followed by 1 day of a high-carbohydrate diet on fuel usage and performance during 2 hours and 4 hours of cycling. This short time frame represented a more manageable period for such an extreme diet and minimized the potential health and training disadvantages caused by longer periods of fat loading.

The fat loading diets provided about 4 grams of fat per kilogram and 2.4 grams of carbohydrate per kilogram. The cyclists continued their regular training during the 5- and 6-day periods of fat loading. They rested for 1 day and consumed a high-carbohydrate diet (10 grams of carbohydrate per kilogram) to replenish their glycogen stores.

During both 2 hours and 4 hours of cycling, the fat loading groups burned significantly more fat and less glycogen than cyclists who consumed a diet providing 10–11 grams of carbohydrate per kilogram. The time trial performances and average power outputs were better for the fat loading groups than for the regular groups, but these differences were not statistically significant. Fat loading failed to improve performance compared to a high-carbohydrate diet even with significant increases in fat metabolism.

However, the cyclists were able to maintain noticeably higher power outputs during the time trials that may translate into improved performance on the road. This suggests that fat loading may provide worthwhile and meaningful performance benefits for some ultraendurance athletes.

If you decide to try fat loading, test out a 5-day period of the regimen in training. A high-fat diet takes longer to digest, which is one of the reasons fat should be limited in the pre-exercise meal. Examples of "fat loading" meals include cheese, marbled or ground beef, eggs, butter, and tuna mixed with mayonnaise.

After fat loading for 5 days, you need to rest a day and consume 10 grams of carbohydrate per kilogram to replenish your muscle glycogen stores before doing your long workout. The morning before your long workout, eat a carbohydrate-rich pre-exercise meal. During your workout, consume 30 to 60 grams of carbohydrate per hour.

Fat loading for periods longer than 5 to 6 days has numerous drawbacks. Such high-fat diets have been associated with sudden death and heart rhythm disturbances due to protein and potassium losses. The diet isn't palatable and lacks the variety of nutrients you need for optimum performance.

Your blood cholesterol level can rise on a high-fat diet despite heavy training. Since exercise by itself doesn't prevent heart disease, eating a high-fat diet for a long period of time may increase your risk of developing heart disease.

Training for longer than 5 to 6 days while on a high-fat diet will also be difficult and unpleasant due to the resulting low muscle glycogen stores.

Fat loading will not improve your performance during competitions when you're exercising at a high intensity—above 70% of VO_{2max}. Carbohydrate, not fat, is the preferred fuel during the high exercise intensities at which most endurance athletes train and compete.

Exercise and Body Fat Loss

Some people think they need to exercise at a lower intensity to lose body fat since fat contributes more to the metabolic mixture. However, this assumption misses the point. Regular exercise is beneficial for weight loss because it helps to create a caloric deficit.

The fuel being burned to create this calorie deficit (fat or carbohydrates) is not important—the calorie deficit is important. Although a greater percentage of fat may be burned with low-intensity exercise, the total amount of fat burned is actually greater with moderate-intensity exercise because the total calorie expenditure is higher.

Low-intensity exercise uses a greater percentage of fat than high-intensity exercise, but the fat calories (and carbohydrate calories) are being burned at a relatively slow rate—4 to 5 calories per minute. High-intensity exercise uses a smaller percentage of fat, but this smaller percentage (along with carbohydrate) is burned at a much higher rate—10 to 13 calories per minute. So, the total amount of fat burned is greater during moderate-intensity exercise compared to the same duration of low-intensity exercise.

Many people have confused the proportion (or percentage) of fat used as fuel with the more important rate (or total amount) of fuel utilization, which is a key concept in exercise-induced body fat loss. When the goal of an exercise program is weight loss, the exercise should create a caloric deficit. To lose a pound of body fat, an individual must expend 3500 calories, whether those calories come from fat or carbohydrates.

The person's fitness level must be considered when exercise is recommended as part of a weight loss program. Low- to moderate-intensity exercise is recommended for overweight people who are just starting to exercise. High-intensity exercise is associated with an increased risk of orthopedic injuries. Also, unfit people who engage in high-intensity exercise usually find it unpleasant and may stop exercising altogether.

The only drawback of low-intensity exercise is that the person must exercise longer to achieve a significant calorie deficit. Otherwise, a low-intensity workout that expends 300 calories in 1 hour is just as beneficial for body fat loss as a high-intensity workout that expends 300 calories in 30 minutes.

5

Protein

No Longer Just for Strength Athletes

A cyclist came to see me who was trying to lose weight to improve his performance. While on his diet, he complained that he was constantly hungry and had difficulty training. He also couldn't understand why he wasn't losing weight. I asked him to record his food intake for a week.

He did not eat breakfast prior to his hard 2-hour training ride. For lunch, he ate pasta with broccoli, a little oil, and garlic, and a sports bar. By mid-afternoon, he was starving and would load up on lowfat foods such as bread, fat-free cookies, and sports bars. At dinner, he ate more pasta.

The cyclist couldn't lose weight because he was starving himself earlier in the day and then overeating later in the day. He also was not consuming enough protein.

I recommended that he eat a carbohydrate-rich breakfast containing a modest amount of protein (poached egg on whole wheat toast with fruit) prior to his training ride. Following his ride, he had a mid-morning carbohydrate-rich snack (a sports bar) to help replenish his carbohydrate stores. For lunch, he added several ounces of chicken to his pasta and included a glass of lowfat milk. He had a mid-afternoon snack containing a modest amount of protein (pretzels and string cheese). For dinner, he ate a carbohydrate-rich meal (stir-fry over brown rice) that also provided several ounces of meat, fowl, or fish.

When he added protein to his meals and increased the frequency of his meals, he wasn't hungry and felt more satisfied on less calories. He gradually lost weight and felt better on his training rides.

THE RECOMMENDED DIETARY ALLOWANCE (RDA) for protein is 0.8 grams per kilogram per day for sedentary adults. Endurance athletes need more protein. The factors that influence your protein requirements include your sport (endurance versus strength), exercise intensity, the carbohydrate content of your diet, level of training, and calorie intake.

Exercise and Protein Requirements

During endurance exercise, your body breaks down some branched chain amino acids (leucine, isoleucine, and valine) for energy. This breakdown is proportional to your exercise intensity. The hormonal changes that occur during endurance exercise—an increase in epinephrine (adrenaline) and norepinephrine and a decrease in insulin—promote increased protein breakdown. Following endurance exercise, however, your protein synthesis rises to minimize and repair muscle damage. Endurance athletes require about 1.2 to 1.4 grams of protein per kilogram per day.

When your muscle glycogen stores are low, due to prolonged exercise or a low-carbohydrate diet, as much as 15% of your energy during exercise may come from protein. When your glycogen stores are high, your use of protein drops to about 5%. Consuming a high-carbohydrate diet during repeated days of heavy training helps to both maintain your glycogen stores and reduce your protein breakdown.

Carbohydrate is your major fuel source during strength exercise such as weight lifting. The anaerobic nature of strength exercise prevents your muscles from burning amino acids for fuel. However, you do need more protein during strength training to support a higher rate of muscle synthesis. Strength athletes need about 1.6 to 1.7 grams of protein per kilogram per day.

You need more protein during the beginning of training than later in your training program. Endurance athletes need this extra protein to make aerobic enzymes (proteins) in the muscle, red blood cells, and myoglobin (an oxygen carrier in the muscle similar to hemoglobin). Strength athletes need the added protein to develop their muscle mass as their existing muscle fibers become larger (hypertrophy).

You may be able to boost the anabolic stimulus of strength training by consuming a small amount of protein (7 grams) with carbohydrate immediately after exercise. The increased insulin release in response to the combined carbohydrate and protein feeding increases your muscles' amino acid uptake and protein synthesis.

Consuming carbohydrates following endurance exercise increases muscle glycogen restoration, which is essential for recovery. However, adding a small amount of protein (7 grams) to the carbohydrate feeding may also promote your recovery by minimizing and repairing muscle damage.

You obtain 1.2 to 1.7 grams of protein per kilogram/day when 12–15% of your calories come from protein. These guidelines assume that you are consuming sufficient calories (energy). There is an inverse relationship between your calorie intake and the amount of protein that you need. If you consume enough calories and have a reasonable diet, you'll generally meet or exceed your protein requirements. When you don't get enough calories, your protein requirements increase.

Some athletes don't eat adequate calories due to heavy training or calorie restriction for endurance sports, wrestling, gymnastics, figure skating, or ballet. When you don't eat enough calories, your protein requirement goes up because you're using the protein for energy rather than muscle growth and repair. This happens more often with female athletes than male athletes.

Your total calorie intake is more important than your protein intake when you want to increase your muscle mass. Many athletes mistakenly emphasize protein intake over calorie intake when trying to "bulk up." If you can't gain weight, you probably aren't eating enough calories.

You can get enough protein from your diet. The average American man consumes about 92 grams of protein per day, the average woman about 64. Most comes from animal sources that contain all of the essential amino acids.

You consume more protein when your calorie intake increases due to training. For example, a 70 kilogram man gradually increases his intake from 2,500 to 3,500 calories during training. His protein intake would rise from 94 to 131 grams per day if 15% of his calories came from protein. Relative to body weight, the man's daily intake would increase from 1.3 grams to 1.8 grams/kilogram, which is more than adequate.

Good sources of complete proteins are meat, poultry, fish, dairy products, and eggs. An ounce of meat, poultry, cheese, or 1 egg supplies about 7 grams of protein containing all of the essential amino acids. Milk and yogurt are also excellent protein sources, with 8 ounces supplying about 8 grams of protein. To reduce dietary fat, choose chicken or turkey without the skin, lean meat, fish, and nonfat or 1% fat dairy products.

A list of the protein content of some foods is provided in Table 5-1.

A well-balanced vegetarian diet easily supplies enough protein, as long as you consume a variety of plant foods (beans, grains, vegetables, fruits, nuts, and seeds) and eat enough calories. Since the body utilizes amino acids from foods eaten at different meals, vegetarians don't need to combine specific foods within a meal to achieve complete proteins. Well-balanced vegetarian diets may even decrease the risk of heart disease and cancer, because they are lower in fat and higher in nutrient-dense carbohydrates than the average American diet. Guidelines for vegetarians are provided in Figure 5-1 and Table 5-2.

Table 5-1.
Protein Content in Some Common Foods

Food	Amount	Protein Content (Grams)
Meat, Fish, Poultry		
Lean beef	1 oz	8
Chicken	1 oz	8
Turkey breast	1 oz.	8
Fish	1 oz.	7
Eggs	1	6
Beans, Nuts		
Kidney Beans	½ cup	9
Navy beans	½ cup	7
Garbanzo beans (chick peas)	½ cup	6
Tofu	2 oz.	5
Peanut butter	1 tbsp	4
Dairy		
Lowfat cottage cheese	½ cup	13
Milk, whole, skim	1 cup	8
Yogurt	1 cup	8
Cheddar cheese	1 oz	7
Ice cream	½ cup	4
Frozen yogurt	½ cup	4
American cheese	1 oz.	3
Breads, Cereals, Grains		
Macaroni and cheese	½ cup	9
Spaghetti	1 cup cooked	8
Bagel	2 oz.	6
Raisin Bran	1 oz (⅔ cup)	3
Rice	1 cup cooked	3
Bread	1 slice	2
Vegetables		
Baked potato	1 large	4
Peas, green	½ cup	4
Corn	½ cup	2
Lettuce	¼ head	1
Carrot	1 large	1
Fruits		
Banana, orange	1 medium	1
Apple	1 medium	1

Figure 5-1.
Food Guide Pyramid for Vegetarian Meal Plannning

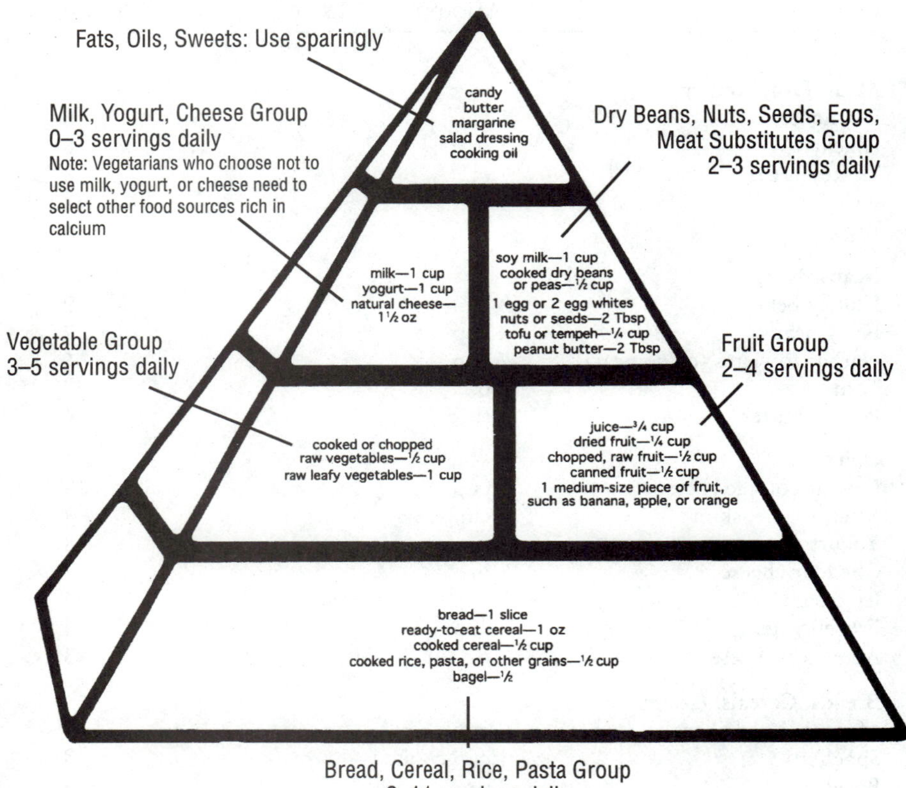

Source: National Center for Nutrition and Dietetics

The American Dietetic Association; Based on the USDA Food Guide Pyramid

Table 5-2.
Vegetarian Meal Planning

The American Dietetic Association provides the following guidelines to help vegetarians plan healthful diets:

- Choose a wide variety of foods, including whole grains, vegetables, fruits, legumes, nuts, seeds, and (if desired) dairy products and eggs.
- Choose whole, unrefined foods often and minimize intake of highly sweetened, fatty, and heavily refined foods.

TABLE 5-2.
VEGETARIAN MEAL PLANNING (CONTINUED)

- Choose a variety of fruits and vegetables
- If animal products such as dairy products and eggs are used, choose lower fat versions of these foods. Cheeses and other high-fat dairy foods and eggs should be limited in the diet because of their saturated fat content and because their frequent use displaces plant foods in some vegetarian diets.
- Vegans should include a regular source of vitamin B12 in their diet along with a source of vitamin D if sun exposure is limited.
- For older children and adolescents, include some foods higher in unsaturated fat (e.g., nuts, seeds, nut and seed butters, avocado, and vegetable oil) to help meet nutrient and energy needs.

Supplements

Supplements containing protein or amino acids are popular among body builders and weight lifters. Proponents of these products claim that they are more rapidly digested and absorbed than protein from food. They may also claim that certain amino acids increase muscle mass and decrease body fat.

These claims are not valid. You may hear that only a small percentage of the amino acids in foods are digested and absorbed. The truth is that about 95 to 99% of the protein from animal sources and about 90% of the protein from vegetable sources is digested and utilized by the body.

Another claim is that these supplements do not need to be digested before absorption and so they replenish your body's protein pool faster. There is no evidence that this happens. It takes hours, not minutes, to rebuild muscle proteins damaged during intense exercise.

A further claim is that the supplements are less taxing to the digestive system than food. Actually, your body quite readily produces digestive enzymes that systematically break down food protein to amino acids before absorption. Thus, chicken or beans or any other food source of protein can be called "timed release" sources of amino acids.

Amino acid supplements usually contain 500 milligrams per capsule, while 1 ounce of beef, chicken or fish supplies 7 grams of protein—7,000 milligrams of amino acids! Compare 1 cup of a lowfat fruited yogurt that contains 10 grams of high quality protein, 18 different amino acids (including 300 mg of arginine), carbohydrates, calcium, magnesium, and potassium to one tasteless 500 milligram arginine supplement.

Arginine and ornithine are popular ingredients in "fat burner" or "weight gainer" supplements. They supposedly stimulate the secretion of growth hormone—resulting in increased muscle mass and decreased body fat. Although injecting large amounts of arginine and ornithine may cause a temporary rise in growth hormone levels, there is no evidence that consuming small amounts of these amino acids has any effect on your growth hormone levels or body composition. Endurance training and weight lifting both raise your growth hormone level far more than injecting arginine or ornithine. Combining the supplements with exercise does not increase growth hormone levels any further.

High-Protein Intakes

Consuming 2 grams of protein per kilogram per day is more than adequate to increase or maintain your muscle mass. Eating more than this amount increases the oxidation (burning) of amino acids. This means that the extra dietary protein will be burned for energy rather than being built into new muscle protein. Using protein for energy is expensive and wasteful. Carbohydrates provide energy more efficiently and at less cost.

A high-protein intake increases the production of urea, which may increase your risk of becoming dehydrated. The kidneys require more water to eliminate the extra nitrogen load imposed by the excess protein. If you're on a high-protein diet, monitor your body weight daily and drink sufficient fluids to match your losses.

People who have impaired kidney function should not consume large amounts of protein because the added nitrogen excretion increases the kidneys' workload. However, there's no evidence that a high-protein diet is harmful for athletes with healthy kidneys.

If your diet provides the recommended amount of protein (1.2 to 1.7 grams per kilogram per day), you probably won't consume an amount of fat that is harmful for your cardiovascular health. To increase your protein intake without increasing your fat intake, choose high-protein foods that are low in saturated fat (nonfat dry milk powder, tuna canned in water, and whey and soy protein powder).

Several best-selling diet books claim that a high-protein, low-carbohydrate diet improves athletic performance and promotes weight loss (see Chapter 10). Consuming a high-protein, low-carbohydrate diet after strenuous exercise slows down muscle glycogen replacement and impairs performance. A high-protein diet also takes longer to digest. By comparison, a carbohydrate-rich diet promotes rapid repletion of muscle glycogen and is easier to digest.

Numerous "high tech" protein supplements may be a convenient way to help you gain weight because they provide additional calories and protein. Although some products contain a variety of ingredients purported to boost weight gain (taurine, whey protein, enzymes), these products are not superior to protein-rich foods.

Dry milk powder (casein) is a high quality, inexpensive protein supplement (1/4 cup provides 11 grams of protein) that provides all of the necessary amino acids at less than half the cost of those heavily advertised "high tech" protein supplements.

Due to the popularity of dietary supplements, it is possible to obtain and consume large amounts of single amino acids. This is not possible with protein-rich foods or protein supplements, since these contain a variety of amino acids. With the exception of the eosinophilia-myalgia syndrome (attributed to contaminated batches of the amino acid tryptophan), there haven't been significant problems reported with the ingestion of single amino acids. However, large intakes of some single amino acids may cause metabolic imbalances, altered neurotransmitter activity, and toxicity. Avoid a large intake of any single amino acid until its safety is determined.

6

Vitamins and Minerals

Is More Better?

I was working with an athlete who was taking loads of vitamins. "Is it all right to take all these vitamins?" he asked me.

I told him about the possible hazards of taking high doses, then asked: "Do you notice any difference?"

The only thing he'd noticed was that his urine was very yellow.

"What about your performance? Are you doing any better?" I asked him.

"I hope so," he said. "I've spent so much money on vitamins that I'd like to think they're doing something."

After we talked, he switched to a simple multivitamin and mineral supplement. When I saw him again, he said his performance was fine and that he felt much better not having to swallow all those pills.

MANY ENDURANCE ATHLETES TAKE vitamin and mineral supplements for "nutritional insurance." They take them to compensate for less-than-adequate diets or lifestyles, to meet the unusual demands imposed by heavy exercise, or to improve performance.

Dietary Reference Intakes

The Dietary Reference Intakes (DRIs) are nutrient-based reference values for use in planning and evaluating diets for healthy people. They expand and replace the Recommended Dietary Allowances (RDAs) published since 1941 by the Food and Nutrition Board of the National Academy of Sciences. See Appendix 3 and Appendix 4 for Dietary Reference Intakes for Vitamins and Minerals.

The DRIs represent a shift in emphasis from preventing nutritional deficiency to decreasing the risk of chronic disease. When adequate scientific evidence exists, the DRIs include levels that may help to prevent diet-related diseases such as heart disease, stroke, certain cancers, and osteoporosis.

The DRIs still include RDAs as goals for daily intake by individuals but also present 3 new categories of reference values.

Estimated average requirement (EAR)—the intake that meets the estimated nutrient need of 50% of the individuals in a specific age and gender group. This figure is used to help develop the RDA and may also be used to evaluate the adequacy of nutrient intakes for population groups.

Recommended Dietary Allowance (RDA)—the intake that meets the estimated nutrient need of nearly all (97 to 98%) healthy individuals in a specific age and gender group. The RDA value will help guide individuals to achieve adequate nutrient intake.

Adequate Intake (AI)—used when sufficient scientific evidence is not available to calculate an estimated average requirement. The AI value is used as a goal for individual dietary intake when an RDA cannot be determined.

Tolerable Upper Intake Level (UL)—the maximum intake that is unlikely to pose risks of adverse health effects in nearly all individuals in a specific age and gender group. As intake increases above the UL, the risk of adverse effects increases. The UL is not intended to be a recommended level of intake. For some nutrients, there may be insufficient data to develop a UL. This doesn't mean that the nutrient isn't potentially harmful at high levels of intake.

Vitamin/Mineral Needs of Athletes

In small amounts, vitamins function as catalysts—substances that increase the speed of a reaction without being used up by the reaction. The fact that vitamins aren't used up explains why they are only needed in small amounts.

Vitamins do not provide energy, although the B vitamins are important for the release of energy from carbohydrates, fats, and proteins (see Figure 6-1). Only carbohydrate, fat, and protein provide energy (calories). This means that in general the vitamin requirements of an active person are not significantly higher than those of a sedentary person.

The B vitamins thiamin, riboflavin, and niacin are required in proportion to calories consumed, and endurance athletes need more calories. However, a balanced diet provides ample amounts of these vitamins. They are supplied by carbohydrate-rich foods such as bread and the whole grain or enriched grain products that are recommended for athletes.

The DRIs take into account the varying nutritional needs of different people. In general, the nutrient needs for the average person are only about 2/3 of the RDA or AI. This means that as long as you consume at least 67% of the RDA or AI for a given nutrient, you are probably protected from a nutritional deficiency.

FIGURE 6-1.
THE B VITAMINS

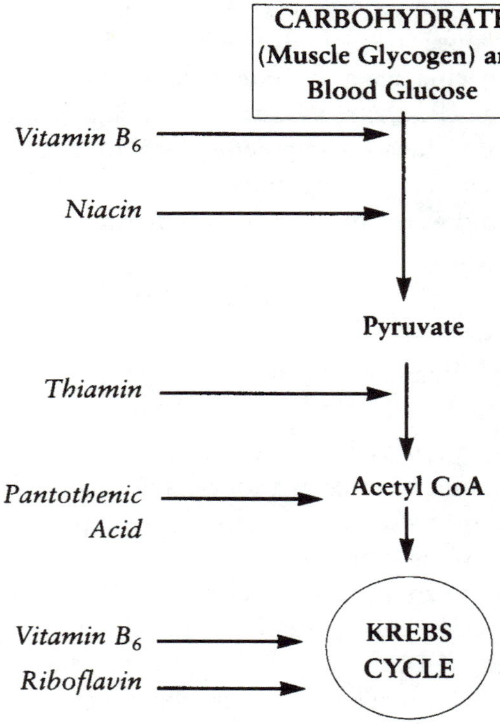

The B vitamins are important for the release of energy from carbohydrate in the muscle cell.

Supplementation at levels exceeding the RDA or AI does not improve the performance of well-nourished athletes. Although vitamin and mineral deficiencies can impair performance, it is very unusual for athletes to have such deficiencies.

There is a close relationship between calorie intake and vitamin intake—the more food you eat, the greater your vitamin intake. Athletes generally eat more than sedentary people and so tend to obtain more vitamins and minerals in relation to their needs. Also, the carbohydrate-rich diet recommended for endurance athletes contains foods with high nutrient density.

Athletes who limit their caloric intake are at risk for nutritional deficiencies. These athletes usually compete in sports that emphasize leanness for enhanced performance (distance runners, wrestlers, lightweight crew) or for appearance (gymnasts, dancers, figure skaters, divers). Weight-conscious active people may also be at risk. A vitamin and mineral supplement supplying 100% of the RDA or AI may be appropriate for these individuals.

Some athletes feel that "staleness" or "flatness" is due to a vitamin or mineral deficiency. When there is a nutritional reason for fatigue, it is usually an inadequate intake of calories or carbohydrates. If you're always tired, you may be training too hard or eating too little carbohydrates or calories. When someone feels better after taking vitamin/mineral supplements, it's probably due to the strength of the belief that the supplements helped—the "placebo effect."

Appendices 3 and 4 list food sources and functions of the major vitamins and minerals.

Iron

Iron is an essential trace element required for the formation of hemoglobin and myoglobin—the oxygen-carrying components of red blood cells and muscle cells. Two-thirds of the total amount of iron in the body is in hemoglobin. When the total hemoglobin concentration drops, the muscles do not receive as much oxygen.

Iron deserves particular attention in this discussion due to the prevalence of iron deficiency anemia—the nation's most common nutritional deficiency. Women are much more likely to suffer from iron deficiency anemia due to menstrual blood losses and inadequate iron intake.

Iron deficiency occurs in three stages. Low levels of hemoglobin (below 12 grams/dL for women and 13 grams/dL for men) are diagnostic indicators for iron deficiency anemia, the third stage of iron deficiency. Since most of the oxygen transported in the blood is bound to the iron in hemoglobin, it is not surprising that iron deficiency anemia reduces both maximum aerobic capacity and endurance.

Exercise may increase iron excretion and so increase the risk of developing iron deficiency in both men and women. Excessive iron losses during exercise are most likely to occur through gastrointestinal bleeding and sweating. Some female athletes (distance runners) also consume foods with low iron bioavailability and are at increased risk of depleting their iron stores.

The low-normal hemoglobin levels found in endurance athletes may be due to the blood plasma volume expansion that often occurs with endurance training. Since there is no decrease in red blood cell mass, your blood's oxygen-carrying capacity is not impaired when hemoglobin levels are low. The moderate increase in your plasma volume may actually reduce blood viscosity and increase cardiac output, thereby enhancing your endurance.

Consume the recommended amount of iron to promote optimal hemoglobin levels. The Recommended Dietary Allowance (RDA) for iron is 18 milligrams for women and 8 milligrams for men. Iron intake averages 6 milligrams of iron per 1,000 calories. Whereas male athletes usually consume more iron than the RDA, female athletes tend to consume less iron than the RDA. This is especially true in sports when the female athlete restricts calories to maintain a lower body weight.

Athletes at risk for iron deficiency, particularly menstruating women, should have routine checks of their iron status. Plasma ferritin (storage iron) and transferrin (transport iron) saturation should be measured in addition to hemoglobin. Although more expensive, these tests are valuable because they can detect iron deficiency early. A low plasma ferritin level and decreased transferrin saturation mean that the athlete is at greater risk of developing iron deficiency anemia. The athlete's iron stores can be increased through diet and/or iron supplementation to prevent the negative consequences of iron deficiency anemia.

While iron deficiency anemia impairs performance, iron depletion without anemia does not. Iron supplements won't improve the health or performance of an athlete with normal hemoglobin levels. If iron supplements are used, they shouldn't exceed the RDA (18 milligrams for women and 8 milligrams for men) unless medically indicated and prescribed by a physician. The Tolerable Upper Intake Level (UL) for iron is 45 milligrams.

Obtaining Adequate Iron

The iron from animal iron sources (heme iron) is more easily absorbed than the iron from vegetable iron sources (non-heme iron). Red meat is an excellent iron source, containing about 1 milligram of iron per ounce. Combining animal and vegetable products (e.g., a meat and bean burrito) increases the iron absorbed from the vegetable product. Vitamin C also enhances non-heme iron absorption, so food high in vitamin C (e.g., orange juice) should be consumed with foods containing non-heme iron (e.g., iron-fortified cereals) for optimum absorption.

Iron-enriched or fortified cereal/grain products can contribute significantly to the iron content of the diet. Beans, peas, split peas, and some dark green leafy vegetables are good vegetable iron sources. Cooking with cast iron cookware also increases the iron content of foods. The more acidic and the longer the food is cooked in cast iron (e.g., spaghetti sauce), the higher the residual iron content of the food. Table 6-1 lists good sources of iron and the milligrams of iron each provides.

Calcium

Calcium, the most abundant mineral in the body, is critical for the conduction of nerve impulses, heart function, muscle contraction, and the operation of certain enzymes. The bones and teeth contain

TABLE 6-1.
PROGRESSION OF IRON DEFICIENCY TO ANEMIA

PROGRESSION	METHOD OF DETECTION	HEMATOLOGIC PROFILE
Iron depletion	Serum ferritin	Depletion of iron stores in liver, bone marrow, and spleen
Iron-deficiency erythropoiesis	Serum iron, total iron-binding capacity, transferrin saturation	Depleted iron stores, decreased levels of plasma iron, increased hepatic formation of transferrin
		Increase of total iron-binding capacity to 400–500 mcg/dL
		Fall of percent transferrin saturation from mean of 30% to about 15–18%
Iron-deficiency anemia	HGB, RBC count hematocrit, mean cell hemoglobin concentration	Fall of hemoglobin concentration to below 12 gm/dL

Source: Adapted from *Physician Sportsmed.*, 1984.

99% of the body's calcium; the remaining 1% circulates in the bloodstream. When the supply of calcium in the blood is too low, the body withdraws calcium from the bones.

Maintaining an adequate intake of calcium is an important nutritional strategy in the prevention of osteoporosis, an age-related disorder in which bone mass decreases and the susceptibility to fractures increases. Osteoporosis is called the "silent disease" because it usually progress painlessly until a fracture occurs, typically in the hip, wrist, or spine.

Osteoporosis cannot be cured—it can only be prevented or its progression delayed. A well-balanced, calcium-rich diet and regular exercise help to decrease the risk of osteoporosis. Dual x-ray absorptiometry is an accurate way to measure bone mineral mass and detect osteoporosis early, with minimal radiation exposure.

Women are more susceptible to osteoporosis because of their lower bone mineral density and total bone mass. Also, after menopause women produce less estrogen, which further accelerates bone loss.

Dietary calcium exerts its greatest effect on bone mineral density from preadolescence to young adulthood. Until peak bone mass is attained at approximately 30 years of age, bone formation exceeds the rate of bone resorption. The amount of bone mass an individual has by age 30 will strongly influence susceptibility to fractures in later years.

Consume the recommended amount of calcium to promote optimal bone health. The Adequate Intake (AI) for calcium is 1,300 milligrams for youths ages 9 to 18, 1,000 milligrams for adults ages 19 to 50, and 1,200 milligrams for adults over 50. Women, in particular, fall short of these recommendations. Female adolescents who have a poor calcium intake and amenorrheic athletes should be doubly aware of their calcium needs because they may be setting themselves up for an increased risk of osteoporosis later in life.

Obtaining Adequate Calcium

Dairy products are the best sources of calcium. An 8-ounce glass of milk or 1/3 cup of nonfat powdered milk each contains about 300 milligrams of calcium. Nonfat or lowfat versions of milk, yogurt, cottage cheese, or cheese often provide the same amount of calcium as the higher fat versions of these foods, but contain less fat and calories.

Other good sources of calcium are sardines (because of the bones) and oysters. Broccoli and greens (kale, collard, turnip, and mustard) are good sources of calcium that contain no fat. Tofu that has been processed with calcium sulfate can also be a good source of calcium. Table 6-2 lists good sources of calcium and the milligrams of calcium each provides.

Many other nutrients influence calcium absorption and bone formation. Vitamin D is important for bone health because its active form stimulates the absorption of calcium from the intestine. On the other hand, high intakes of protein, sodium, and caffeine interfere with calcium retention by increasing the amount of calcium excreted in the urine. Excessive alcohol intake also has detrimental effects on bone mass.

A registered dietitian can advise you on obtaining the appropriate amount of calcium from food and supplements. Calcium carbonate (Tums™ or a generic equivalent) is an inexpensive and acceptable calcium source. Calcium carbonate is 40% calcium, so a 500 milligram tablet actually provides 200 milligrams of elemental calcium. Antacids that contain calcium are essentially the same as dietary supplements. The primary difference between the two is in the marketing—when calcium carbonate is marketed as a calcium supplement, it costs more.

Too much calcium can be harmful. In susceptible people, excessive calcium intake increases the risk of kidney stones. Excessive calcium from diet or supplements may also interfere with the absorption of iron. The UL for calcium is 2.5 grams per day.

Antioxidants

Many people take antioxidant supplements such as vitamins C and E to protect against heart disease, cancer, and other chronic diseases associated with aging. Some endurance athletes also use antioxidants to reduce the amount of muscle damage and soreness caused by heavy exercise.

Free radicals, substances that can cause damage to muscle cells and cell membranes, are released by the body's own normal

TABLE 6-2.
FOOD SOURCES FOR CALCIUM

FOOD	SERVING SIZE	MICROGRAMS OF CALCIUM
Milk and Dairy Products:		
Milk, LactAid Calcium Fortified Nonfat	1 cup	500
Yogurt, nonfat, plain	1 cup	452
Yogurt, lowfat, plain	1 cup	415
Milk, skim, protein-fortified	1 cup	352
Milk, skim, regular	1 cup	302
*Swiss cheese	1 oz.	272
*Mozzarella, part skim	1 oz.	207
*Cheddar cheese	1 oz.	204
*Ricotta cheese, part skim	1 oz.	169
Ice cream or ice milk	1 cup	164
*Cottage cheese, 2% lowfat	1 cup	154
Tofu	3 oz.	150
*Parmesan cheese, grated	1 tbsp.	69
Bread and Grain Products:		
Wonder Calcium-Enriched Bread	2 slices	580
Total cereal	¾ cup	250
Bread, white or whole wheat	2 slices	47
Fruits and Juices:		
Tropicana Season's Best Orange Juice Plus Calcium	1 cup	333
Minute Maid Calcium-Enriched Orange Juice	1 cup	293
Orange	1 medium	52
Fish:		
*Sardines, canned in water, drained	2 oz.	185
*Salmon, canned, drained	3 oz.	167
Vegetables:		
Collards, frozen	½ cup, cooked	179
Turnip greens, chopped	½ cup, cooked	99
Kale, frozen	½ cup, cooked	90
Bok choy	½ cup, cooked	79
Swiss chard, chopped	½ cup, cooked	49
Broccoli, chopped	½ cup, cooked	36
Sweet potato, baked	1 medium	32

TABLE 6-2.
FOOD SOURCES FOR CALCIUM (CONTINUED)

FOOD	SERVING SIZE	MICROGRAMS OF CALCIUM
Nuts and Legumes:		
Almonds	½ cup	150
Soybeans	½ cup, cooked	88
Pinto beans	½ cup, cooked	41

* = High in sodium

Sources: *USDA Handbook 8* and Bowes and Church, *Food Values of Portions Commonly Used.*

process of producing energy. Exercise causes a number of physiological changes that increase the production of free radicals. These include an elevated metabolic rate, increased body temperature, and higher epinephrine levels. The production of free radicals can also be increased by exposure to various environmental pollutants such as smog, cigarette smoke, radiation, and certain pesticides.

Fortunately, your body possesses its own antioxidant defense in the form of enzymes (catalase, superoxide dismutase, and glutathione peroxidase) and obtains the antioxidant vitamins E and C through diet. Each of these antioxidants works at different sites within the body and in a unique way. Their overall goal, however, is to stop the production and spread of harmful free-radical chain reactions.

Vitamin E helps to protect structures that contain lipids (such as cell membranes) from free-radical attack. Vitamin C works to stop free-radical damage in the water compartments found within and between the cells. In addition to being an antioxidant nutrient by itself, vitamin C has the ability to regenerate vitamin E.

Regular physical training itself provides a partially protective effect. Consistent workouts increase the activity of the enzymes that clean up the free radicals, thereby helping to minimize muscle damage.

While antioxidant supplements may protect against muscle damage, they won't help the performance of adequately nourished athletes. For example, vitamin E deficiency does impair endurance capacity and this is associated with greater free-radical damage. However, additional vitamin E supplementation doesn't improve aerobic capacity for endurance athletes who regularly consume enough vitamin E.

Vitamin E supplementation may reduce free-radical production and lessen muscle damage following heavy, prolonged exercise such as running a marathon or cycling 100 miles. Taking vitamin C may alleviate muscle soreness and enhance the return of muscle function following such exercise.

Your age may also determine whether antioxidant supplements are beneficial. Vitamin E was found to stimulate the rate of muscle repair after exercise-induced muscle damage in older, but not younger, individuals.

Populations who eat adequate amounts of fruit and vegetables have a lower incidence of coronary heart disease, certain cancers, and cataracts. While fruits and vegetables are rich in antioxidants, they also provide other nutrients, fiber, and phytochemicals (plant chemicals) that are beneficial for health. Regardless of what supplements you take, you will benefit from consuming the recommended amount of vegetables (3 to 4 servings) and fruit (2 to 4 servings) a day.

Avoid taking large doses of the minerals that work with the free radical-suppressing enzymes—zinc, copper, and selenium. Excess zinc consumption may reduce HDL cholesterol levels, impair immune function, and inhibit copper absorption from foods, possibly leading to anemia. The RDA for zinc is 11 milligrams per day for men and 8 milligrams per day for women; the UL is 40 milligrams per day.

Copper supplements aren't recommended since athletes don't appear to be deficient and there's no evidence to suggest that copper will enhance performance. The RDA for copper is 900 micrograms per day; the UL is 10 milligrams per day.

Selenium is a particular supplement favorite, since it works together with vitamin E to protect cell membranes against free-radical damage. However, research suggests that vitamin E, rather than selenium, is crucial for protection against free-radical damage. There is no reason to take selenium supplements, as most people get enough selenium and an excess intake may be harmful. The RDA for selenium is 55 micrograms per day; the UL is 400 micrograms per day.

7

Being Supplement Savvy

Supplement Recommendations

A runner came up to me after we finished a 10-kilometer race. He was flushed bright red and complaining of severe itching. I asked if he had taken any supplements or medications prior to the run. He told me that he had taken a large dose of niacin prior to the race. His girlfriend worked at a health food store and told him the supplement would dilate his blood vessels and improve his performance. In addition to his unpleasant symptoms, he finished with one of his worst times ever.

THE COMMITTEE ON DIET AND HEALTH (Food and Nutrition Board, National Research Council) recommends that people avoid taking vitamin or mineral supplements that exceed 100% of the RDA or AI. Most people can obtain these essential nutrients from a variety of foods.

The Committee noted possible exceptions in the cases of women who are pregnant or breast-feeding, women with excess monthly bleeding, people on very low-calorie diets, some vegetarians, and people with malabsorption problems. However, these individuals should be evaluated on a case-by-case basis rather than automatically taking vitamin and mineral supplements.

For athletes who do not fit into any of these categories, most health authorities agree that there is no harm in taking a simple vitamin/mineral supplement, provided that it does not exceed 100% of the RDA or AI for nutrients. There is, however, no evidence to prove that such supplementation is beneficial. Just as an adequate diet isn't improved by supplements, an inadequate diet isn't "fixed" by supplements.

Although supplements are suggested when food intake is not adequate to meet specific needs, a balanced diet remains the ideal source of nutrients. In addition to having a variety of nutrients, foods contain bioactive compounds such as phytochemicals (indoles, flavonoids, and isoflavones) and dietary fiber that have health benefits. Supplements don't contain these compounds in the same chemical form or proportion as found in food. By taking a vitamin C pill, an athlete misses out on the dietary fiber, limonene (an anticancer phytochemical), potassium, and energy he or she would obtain from eating an orange.

Nutrients in food are also often "packaged" more effectively than they are in supplements. For example, milk contains both calcium and lactose. Lactose increases the absorption of calcium. Most calcium supplements do not contain lactose.

Nutrition is a relatively young science. Foods may contain nutritional substances that have not yet been identified. Eating a balanced diet, not taking supplements, is the preferred way to achieve nutritional adequacy. Relying on vitamin/mineral supplements as an alternative to making responsible food choices may have a negative effect on performance because the composition of diet (carbohydrate, protein, fat, and calories) is not addressed. You also get more nutritional bang for your buck with foods than you do with supplements.

Consuming a variety of foods from the Food Guide Pyramid each day reduces the need for vitamin/mineral supplementation. If you want "nutritional insurance," eat more nutrient-dense grain products, fruits, vegetables, and legumes and fewer empty calories such as sugar, fat, and alcohol.

Excess Vitamins and Minerals

Consuming doses of vitamins and minerals above the Tolerable Upper Intake Level (UL) can be dangerous. Consuming large amounts of vitamins and minerals can produce serious side effects and upset the delicate balance of these nutrients.

Taking a greater amount of vitamins A and D than your body needs over a period of time can produce severe toxic effects. Prolonged high intake of vitamin A can cause loss of appetite, headaches, irritability, liver damage, bone pain, and neurological problems, including brain damage. The RDA for vitamin A is 700 micrograms for women and 900 micrograms for men; the UL is 3 milligrams per day.

Prolonged high intake of vitamin D can cause weight loss, vomiting, irritability, destructive deposits of excess calcium in soft tissues (like the kidneys and lungs), and potentially fatal kidney failure. The AI for vitamin D is 5 micrograms per day; the UL is 50 micrograms per day.

When you consume more water-soluble vitamins than you need, the excess is eliminated in the urine. Although this increases the vitamin content of the urine, it doesn't help performance.

Large doses of water-soluble vitamins can also cause side effects. Some body builders take large doses of niacin (a B vitamin) to make their blood vessels dilate and stand out. However, large amounts of niacin can cause severe flushing, skin disorders, liver damage, ulcers, and blood sugar disorders. High doses of niacin also interfere with fat metabolism and speed up glycogen depletion.

Niacin may be useful in the treatment of elevated blood cholesterol and triglycerides. However, it should never be used for this purpose without medical supervision. The AI for niacin is 16 milligrams for men and 14 milligrams for women; the UL is 35 milligrams.

Large doses of vitamin C have been associated with diarrhea, kidney stone formation, and impaired copper absorption. Vitamin C can also increase the risk of iron-overload disease in susceptible people by increasing iron absorption from food. The RDA for vitamin C is 75 milligrams for women and 90 milligrams for men; the UL is 2,000 milligrams.

High doses of vitamin E can counteract vitamin K and result in increased bleeding time. Vitamin E supplementation may be contraindicated when an individual is on anticoagulants (e.g. Coumadin) or dietary supplements (e.g. Ginkgo biloba or Omega-3 fatty acids) that increase the clotting time of the blood. The RDA for vitamin E is 15 milligrams per day (about 22 IU of natural vitamin E) and the UL is 1,000 milligrams (about 1,500 IU of natural vitamin E).

Vitamin B6 (pyridoxine) toxicity has been documented in women who have taken supplements to alleviate premenstrual symptoms. Excess vitamin B6 can cause neurological symptoms similar to multiple sclerosis, including numbness and tingling of the hands, impaired motor function, and electric shocks shooting down the spine. Toxicity has been reported in people taking as little as 200 milligrams. The RDA for vitamin B6 is about 1.3 milligrams; the UL is 100 milligrams.

Like fat-soluble vitamins, excess amounts of minerals are stored in the body and can gradually build up to toxic levels. An excess of one mineral can also interfere with the functioning of others. A high iron intake, for example, can produce an iron overload (hemochromatosis) in genetically predisposed people and cause deficiencies of other trace minerals (zinc and copper). If untreated, iron overload can damage the liver, pancreas, and heart. Although iron deficiency affects far more people than iron overload, iron supplements should only be used for diagnosed iron deficiency.

Evaluating Supplements

Many dietary supplements including vitamins, minerals, amino acids, herbs, and other botanicals are marketed to improve performance and health. Some dietary supplements may be safe and provide health or performance benefits, while others may be ineffective, dangerous, or contain ingredients banned by athletic organizations.

Unlike prescription and over-the-counter medications, dietary supplements do not have to be approved by the Food and Drug Administration for safety or effectiveness before they are sold. Dietary supplements are also not standardized, so there is no assurance of product potency (strength) or purity. Due to poor quality control, the amount of the active ingredient may be higher or lower than the amount listed on the product label. A supplement may also contain contaminants or dangerous levels of active ingredients that may cause injury or death.

Some dietary supplements may contain ingredients such as androstenedione in "anabolic/weight gainer" products and ephedrine in "fat burning/energy enhancing" products that can produce positive drug test results for banned substances. Athletes may not realize that a product contains ephedrine or other banned ingredients because an unfamiliar name for the ingredient is used or the ingredient is not listed on the supplement label. At the very least, the unwitting use of banned products may result in a doping suspension.

Considering the plentiful and confusing information that is available regarding dietary supplements, it is a challenge to sort out trustworthy information from questionable information. The following information can be helpful for evaluating dietary supplements and making knowledgeable decisions when choosing supplements.

First, consider your total diet. By definition, a supplement is a substance to augment the diet. Supplements are not meant to replace eating a wide variety of healthful food. Information on vitamin and mineral functions, potential benefits, and upper safe limits of intake is available at the National Academy of Sciences Web site at:

http://www.iom.edu/iom/iomhome.nsf/Pages/FNB+Reports

Check with a doctor or other healthcare provider before using a supplement. Just because a product contains "natural" ingredients does not mean that it is safe. Some products may interact with prescription and over-the-counter medications (as well as other supplements) and cause serious adverse effects. Certain supplements such as herbs can have unwanted effects during surgery. Read the product label, follow all directions, and heed any warnings. Harmful effects from the use of dietary supplements should be reported to the FDA MedWatch Hotline at 800-332-1088.

The following tips may be helpful when choosing a supplement:

- The USP (United States Pharmacopeia) designation on the label of a vitamin/mineral supplement indicates that the product passes tests for dissolution (how well a supplement dissolves), disintegration, potency (strength), and purity.
- Nationally known food and drug manufacturers generally make supplements under the strict quality control procedures they already have in place. The manufacturer should be able to demonstrate that the product passes tests for content potency, purity, and uniformity. If a company does not answer questions or address complaints, do not use its product.
- The supplement label should provide accurate and appropriate information. If statements are unclear or the label makes preposterous claims, it is unlikely that the company follows good quality control procedures. Be wary if the claims for the product sound too good to be true. No dietary supplement will guarantee optimum performance and health.
- Consumer Lab (http://www.consumerlab.com) provides independent test results and information to help consumers and healthcare professionals evaluate and select dietary supplements. Products that pass Consumer Lab's testing are eligible to bear the CL Seal of Approval.
- Supplement Watch (http://www.supplementwatch.com) is dedicated to educating consumers about the potential benefits

and risks of dietary supplements. They provide an independent and scientific evaluation of supplements.

The Food and Drug Administration Center for Food Safety and Applied Nutrition (http://www.cfsan.fda.gov/~dms/ds-savvy.html) provides the following tips for evaluating the supplement information you can find on the Internet:

- Who operates the site? Look for Web sites operated by the government, a university, or a reputable medical or health-related association.
- Is the purpose of the site to educate or sell a product? Most nonprofit and government sites do not advertise and usually provide free access to the site and educational materials.
- Is the information provided supported by research findings? The study should be current, published in a reputable peer-reviewed journal, and cited in the National Library of Medicine database (PubMed at http://www.ncbi.nlm.nih.gov/PubMed).
- Think twice about chasing the latest headline. Science does not advance by dramatic discoveries, but by taking many small steps and slowly building towards a consensus.

8

Body Composition

Debunking the Myth of Bathroom Scales

I worked with a muscular, well-built man about 5'7", 150 pounds, who decided that if he were thinner he could run faster. He had looked at a height/weight table and decided that he should weigh 135 pounds.

He cut his food intake, but kept his mileage the same. Not only did he have a difficult time losing weight — his running form deteriorated. He lost his power and speed. He also became irritable and hungry. He began to fantasize about banana cream pie!

Before he tried to lose weight, I had evaluated his body composition and found that he had 7% body fat at 150 pounds. After his weight loss attempt, I told him to throw his bathroom scale out the window and go back to his old diet. His running form soon returned to normal.

IN OUR SOCIETY, the bathroom scale has a following worthy of a political party or a religion. An unbelievable number of weight loss gimmicks have been spawned by our obsession with weight loss. In the rush to shed pounds, a very important question is often overlooked: "How fat am I?"

The scale cannot differentiate between fat pounds and muscle pounds. The scale does not indicate how fat a person is because fat and muscle, as well as bone and water, contribute to our total weight.

The term "overweight" only refers to body weight in excess of the average for a specific height. The term "underweight" only refers to the body weight below the average weight for height. The scale is biased against stocky, muscular people; it favors thin, slightly built people.

A more accurate indicator of fitness is body composition, which divides weight into two categories. One is the fat-free mass, of which muscle is a major component. The other category is fat and is expressed as percent body fat.

The person who suffers the most when evaluated by weight alone is the stocky, muscular man or woman. Because these athletes may have little fat, they weigh more than average because of a large fat-free mass. To lose weight, they may lose muscle and experience deterioration in their performance and health. This is just one reason why you should have your body composition assessed before you attempt to lose weight.

You are somewhat restricted by your genetic inheritance. Body shape and size are largely determined by skeleton size, since a certain amount of muscle and tissue usually accompany a certain amount of bone. Beyond heredity, your total amount and distribution of muscle mass will depend on the type of training you do. For example, weight training increases muscle mass more than distance running.

Body type is important in most sports, and each sport seems to require a certain body type. A large, muscular person will never be an elite marathoner, just as an elite marathoner would not survive as an interior lineman on the football field.

While body size and shape can be altered only slightly, substantial changes can occur in body composition. These changes can significantly affect your performance.

In power sports, performance can be improved by extra muscle gained from weight lifting. It is also obvious that excess body fat can harm distance running.

An athlete who trains for a specific sport is likely to have the muscle mass that is appropriate for that sport. If, because of genetics, his muscle mass is greater than desired, he will only hurt his performance and health by trying to starve himself thinner.

Body Fat Standards

A healthy level of body fat for men is around 15%. A healthy level of body fat for women is around 25%. The average range of body fat for young adults is 15 to 18% for men and 22 to 25% for women.

Three percent of the total body fat in men is considered "essential fat." It appears that a man cannot reduce his body fat below this limit without impairing his physiological function and capacity for exercise.

The percentage of body fat considered "essential" for women is 12%. This higher level of fat is related to childbearing functions and takes into account sex-specific fat in the breasts, hips, and other tissues.

Many studies have assessed the body composition of athletes. The results suggest that body fat values differ widely both between sports and within sports. Thus, an ideal body fat for a particular sport is difficult to establish. Trying to achieve a percent body fat within a range that is typical for the sport (5 to 8% body fat for a male marathon runner) is more appropriate than trying to achieve a specific percent body fat (5% body fat).

Before you attempt to achieve a certain percent body fat, there are several things to keep in mind. Your success in a sport depends on a variety of factors such as VO_{2max}, blood lactate threshold, anaerobic power, and muscular strength and endurance. Having a low body fat does not, in itself, ensure you will be a superior athlete.

As an upper limit, try to be close to the healthy levels of 15% for men and 25% for women. Beyond this, your ideal percent body fat is where you perform the best.

Your weight and percent body fat should be monitored by a health professional and kept in a range that promotes your health and performance.

Body Composition Assessment

The hydrostatic (underwater) weighing procedure involves weighing a person on land and then determining the weight of the person submerged under water. Since muscle is denser than fat (1 pound of muscle takes up the room of 1/3 pound of fat), people with more muscle and less fat weigh more under water. In other words, they have a higher body density and lower percent body fat.

Even though there are certain technical limitations to this procedure, hydrostatic weighing is referred to as the "gold standard" because it is the most accurate technique currently available to assess body composition. The standard error of measurement for hydrostatic weighing is about 2%. This means that an athlete with a "true" percent body fat of 15% may be measured as having 13% body fat or 17% body fat.

Skinfold measurements are the most practical way to assess body composition. Skinfolds represent the thickness of a double layer of skin and the underlying subcutaneous fat, as determined by metal (not plastic) calipers. The rationale behind skinfolds is that roughly 50% of the total body fat is stored just under the skin as subcutaneous fat. Although less accurate than hydrostatic weighing, skinfold measurements are useful for determining regional distribution of subcutaneous fat in addition to estimating percent body fat. The standard error of measurement for skinfold measurements is about 3 to 4%. This means that an athlete whose body fat is estimated to be 15% could actually have a body fat percentage as low as 11% or as high as 19%.

To ensure accuracy, trained personnel must perform hydrostatic weighing and skinfold measurements. Because of the inherent error in the tests themselves, it is best to have a range of desirable body fat values. Many sports medicine facilities and universities offer body composition evaluation in addition to VO_{2max} testing.

Bioelectrical impedance analysis (BIA) involves passing a small electrical current throughout the body and measuring the resistance encountered. Lean tissue is a good conductor of electricity due to its high water content, while fat tissue is not. The resistance encountered is inversely related to the amount of lean tissue. Early research with impedance revealed large standard errors of measurement (about 7%), while newer techniques provide lower standard errors (3 to 4%) that are comparable to skinfold measurements.

BIA is popular because it's an easy, quick, and non-invasive technique. Unfortunately, BIA tends to overestimate the body fat of a lean person and underestimate the body fat of an obese person. A person must be completely hydrated when the measure is taken if accurate results are to be obtained.

Infrared interactance uses near-infrared spectroscopy to provide information about the chemical content of the body. A fiberoptic probe is pressed on top of the biceps muscle on the upper arm. A light beam is emitted that penetrates the subcutaneous fat and muscle. The beam is then reflected off the bone to a silicon detector in the probe. The accuracy of this procedure is questionable.

Going Too Low

Attempting to reach an unrealistic percent body fat can be as harmful as attempting to reach an unrealistic weight. When your body weight or body fat drops below a certain level, both your performance and health will suffer. Extreme weight loss can disrupt physiological function, nutritional status, hormone levels, bone mineral density, and psychological function.

Chronic fatigue often accompanies major weight loss. While the causes of this fatigue have not been established, both the central nervous system and endocrine system appear to be involved. Depleted fuel stores also probably play a role. When you train hard and consume a diet that is inadequate in total calories or carbohydrates, your muscle and liver glycogen stores become depleted. This causes weakness, fatigue, and impaired performance.

Fatigue may also result from the significant losses of muscle protein that occur when your body is forced to use protein for energy. Athletes who focus on maintaining abnormally low body weight/fat during training often have inadequate intakes of vitamins and minerals as well.

Body Composition Changes with Exercise

Body weight may change little, if any, in the beginning of an exercise program. This is because lean weight initially increases at about the same rate that fat weight is being lost. Individuals can become discouraged when the scales show no change even though body composition (fat versus lean) is changing dramatically. During this time, people should pay more attention to how their clothes fit than what the scale says.

It is even possible to gain weight while losing fat (particularly when resistance training is part of the exercise regime) because of correspondingly greater muscle gain. For example, a person can gain 4 pounds of muscle but lose 2 pounds of fat. This may happen to sedentary women who begin a resistance training program. They may drop a clothing size but gain 2 pounds. Some may even quit exercising when this happens because they're conditioned to judge their progress by scale weight.

It's a good idea to have body composition evaluated before trying to lose or gain weight, and again periodically to measure any muscle gain and fat loss from exercise. Your scale weight isn't an accurate indicator of your body composition. And, it can't give you the real picture of the changes that occur from regular exercise.

9

Losing Fat, Gaining Muscle

Effective Strategies

A muscular runner wanted to lose the weight (over 50 pounds) he had gained following a severe Achilles tendon injury. I asked him to keep a record of his food intake and workouts. After a 30-minute run, he ate breakfast about 6 AM and then grabbed whatever he could find for lunch at school. Hanging out in the teachers' lounge didn't help—it always contained high calorie tempting items such as cakes, cookies, and candy bars. His most difficult time fighting hunger was in the late afternoon when he came home from his teaching job. He would start snacking and continue until he ate dinner with his family.

I helped him plan the meals that he would take to eat at work. Since he ate breakfast so early, he started carrying a mid-morning snack. For lunch, he took a homemade sandwich, fruit, baked chips, and low-fat milk. He avoided going into the teachers' lounge when he was hungry. When he came home from work, he would have a mid-afternoon snack and then hop on his bike for a 1-hour ride. The cycling helped him expend additional calories without aggravating his Achilles tendon injury. He ate reasonably sized portions for dinner and passed on seconds. Occasionally, he'd join his colleagues for a treat in the teachers' lounge or eat dessert after dinner.

When I saw the man about 6 months later, I walked right by him. He had lost so much body fat that I didn't even recognize him. He has maintained his weight loss and stayed in a healthy weight range for the past 5 years.

THE ENERGY THAT YOU OBTAIN from food, as well as your body's energy expenditure, is measured in units of heat called kilocalories, referred to as kilocalories or calories for short. Carbohydrates and protein supply 4 calories per gram, fat supplies 9 calories per gram, and alcohol supplies 7 calories per gram.

Your total daily calorie expenditure consists of your resting energy expenditure or resting metabolic rate (60 to 75%), the thermic effect of food (5 to 10%), and the thermic effect of exercise (15 to 30%).

Energy Balance

Weight loss, weight maintenance, or weight gain is a matter of energy balance. Your body weight will stay the same when your calorie intake equals your calorie expenditure. To lose weight, energy expenditure must be greater than energy intake. To gain weight, energy intake must be greater than energy expenditure. If you want to lose weight, you must eat less, exercise more, or both.

Each person has a specific requirement for calories, determined by age, gender, body weight, and physical activity. Table 9-1 provides a simple method for estimating your resting energy expenditure (REE).

The calorie expenditure of your sport depends on the frequency, intensity, and duration of your activity. The more intense the exercise and the longer you do it, the greater your calorie expenditure.

You'll perform at your best if you achieve your competitive weight (while adequately hydrated) either during the off-season or early in the season. Allowing for an increase in lean tissue and decrease in body fat during training, try to maintain that weight throughout the season.

TABLE 9-1.
ESTIMATION OF THE DAILY RESTING ENERGY EXPENDITURE (REE)

AGE (YEARS)	EQUATION
Males	
3–9	(22.7 × body weight*) + 495
10–17	(17.5 × body weight) + 651
18–29	(15.3 × body weight) + 679
30–60	(11.6 × body weight) + 879
> 60	(13.5 × body weight) + 487
Example	
154-lb male, age 20	
154 lbs/2.2 = 70 kg	
(15.3 × 70) + 679 = 1,750 kcal	
Females	
3–9	(22.5 × body weight*) + 499
10–17	(12.2 × body weight) + 746
18–29	(14.7 × body weight) + 496
30–60	(8.7 × body weight) + 829
> 60	(10.5 × body weight) + 596
Example	
121-lb female, age 20	
121 lbs/2.2 = 55 kg	
(14.7 × 55) + 496 = 1,304 kcal	

*Body weight is expressed in kilograms (kg).

Losing Fat through Diet

The American College of Sports Medicine (ACSM) and National Heart, Lung, and Blood Institute (NHLBI) have provided guidelines for promoting healthy weight loss. The most successful strategies for weight loss are reducing calorie intake, increasing physical activity, and changing behavior to improve eating and activity habits.

Your diet should be individually planned—based on your body weight—to create a daily calorie deficit of 500 to 1,000 calories. This level of calorie restriction produces a reasonable weight loss of 1 to 2 pounds per week (1 pound of fat equals 3,500 calories). A faster rate of weight loss or a larger initial weight loss does not improve weight loss over the long term compared with a more moderate rate of weight loss.

The ACSM and NHLBI recommend a maximum weight loss of 2 pounds per week. Many athletes do better with a smaller calorie deficit of 250 to 500 calories a day and a weight loss of 1/2 to 1 pound of body fat per week.

It helps to keep a diet diary to monitor your food intake. This gives you a good idea of how much and what you're eating to maintain your weight. After identifying where your calories come from, you can decide how to go about decreasing your intake. Individuals that keep a diet diary are more successful at weight loss.

Develop an eating plan that includes your food preferences. If the changes aren't realistic and you don't like what you're eating, you won't stick with it. Plan your food intake 1 week ahead of time just as you plan your training. If you don't plan your meals and snacks, you're more likely to grab high-calorie convenience and fast foods.

The meal frequency of your diet is also important. Most athletes benefit from eating 5 to 6 times per day—3 meals and 2 to 3 snacks. This properly fuels you throughout the day and helps to prevent overeating later in the day.

For example, assume you don't eat enough earlier in the day. Later in the day, you're starving. You'll grab the first thing you see (often a high calorie fast-food meal) and overcompensate by eating too much. This "back-loading" of calories works against losing weight and maintaining even energy levels throughout the day for training.

You can cut calories by eating smaller portions, avoiding second helpings, and eating fewer "empty calories"—foods high in sugar, fat, and alcohol. Choose foods that don't provide a lot of calories in relation to the large volume of food you eat, such as vegetables and fruits.

Portion-controlled diets (structured meal plans and prepackaged meals) help to promote weight loss by providing specific guidance and minimizing choice.

Reducing the intake of dietary fat (to no more than 30% of total calories) facilitates weight loss by also reducing total energy intake. However, reducing dietary fat only produces weight loss when there is an associated decrease in total calorie intake. Continuing to maintain a low fat intake helps to maintain weight loss long-term. A diet low in saturated fat also has a beneficial effect on the serum cholesterol level.

People are much more likely to overeat and gain body fat when given unlimited access to a high-fat diet. Fat is energy-dense, possessing twice the amount of energy found in the same weight of carbohydrates or protein. High-fat foods also tend to be palatable and desirable, which encourages overeating. Lastly, the thermic effect of food (the calorie cost of digestion and absorption) is lower for dietary fat than for dietary carbohydrates and protein.

Your total calorie intake has the greatest influence on weight loss. Some people think they can eat as much food as desired, as long as the food is fat-free. Consequently, they eat too many calories in the form of extra-large portions of starches and fat-free sweets. If you cut back on fat calories but add them back in the form of carbohydrate calories, you're not going to lose weight. It's a simple matter of energy balance that holds true whether you're an athlete or couch potato.

Don't get carried away. If you cut your calorie intake too much, it will adversely affect your training and performance. You won't be able to train as long or intensely. You may also lose muscle mass in addition to fat. Extreme calorie restriction suppresses the immune system and increases your chance of getting sick. It also increases your chance of getting injured—you aren't recruiting muscles normally due to fuel (glycogen) depletion.

Losing Fat through Exercise

Exercise alone does not produce the amount of body fat loss that you can achieve with calorie restriction. It is easier to create a large calorie deficit (500 to 1,000 calorie/day) with dieting. The combination of calorie restriction and exercise is the most successful approach for weight loss. Exercise provides significant health benefits in addition to promoting weight loss. Also, people who continue to exercise are proven to be more successful at maintaining weight loss over time.

Aerobic exercise is usually recommended for weight loss because you burn more calories during this type of activity. However, you should also include resistance training to improve your muscular strength and endurance. An effective weight loss program incorporates both aerobic exercise (5 days a week) and resistance training (at least 2 times a week).

The US Surgeon General's recommendation for physical activity is to participate in at least 30 minutes of moderate-intensity exercise on most days of the week. This represents at least 150 minutes of physical activity per week (5 days, at 30 minutes per day) and is designed to reduce the risk of heart disease and other health problems.

However, the Institute of Medicine's Food and Nutrition Board recommends that regardless of weight, individuals spend 1 hour per day in moderately intense physical activity to maintain cardiovascular health. This is double the daily minimum goal set by the Surgeon General's report.

The new exercise goal of 1 hour per day is based on studies of how much energy is expended on average each day by individuals who maintain a healthy weight. These studies suggest that expending over 2,000 calories per week (200 to 300 minutes of exercise) is necessary to promote long-term weight loss.

You can burn off 2,000 calories each week by exercising 5 days per week and expending 400 calories per session. Appendix 5 lists energy expenditures for various activities.

Overweight and Obesity

The American College of Sports Medicine (ACSM) and National Heart, Lung, and Blood Institute (NHLBI) both define overweight as a Body Mass Index (BMI) of 25 to 29.9 and obesity as a BMI of 30 and above. The higher the BMI, the greater the risk of illness and/or death due to heart disease, stroke, diabetes, cancer, high blood pressure, arthritis, and breathing problems. BMI describes body weight relative to height and relates strongly with total body fat content in adults. Approximately 55 to 60% of American adults are overweight or obese.

The formula for calculating BMI is: BMI = Body weight in kilograms divided by height in meters squared. (To convert pounds to kilograms, divide by 2.2; to convert inches to meters, divide by 39.37.) Appendix 6 is a table of BMI values.

Regional fat distribution is an independent predictor of disease risk. Android obesity (excess fat located primarily in the abdomen or upper body) places an individual at greater risk for health problems than gynoid obesity (excess fat located primarily in the lower extremities or hips). Weight loss is recommended when the waist circumference exceeds 40 inches (≥ 102 cm) in men and 35 inches (≥ 88 cm) in women.

Gaining Muscle

Increasing your muscle mass improves your overall strength and power. Some endurance athletes gain weight for aesthetic purposes. You want to gain muscle rather than fat to help your performance. An effective program to gain weight combines progressive resistance training (weight lifting) at least 3 times a week with an increased calorie intake.

You can generally gain about 1/2 to 1 pound of muscle each week. Since 1 pound of muscle contains about 3,500 calories, you must increase your calorie intake by about 500 calories per day to gain 1 pound in a week. You also have to add in the calorie cost of weight training (about 200 calories per hour workout). These calories are above and beyond the amount you normally require to maintain your body weight.

For example, let's assume that you normally require 2,500 calories per day and you want to gain weight. You need an additional 500 calories per day to gain 1 pound of muscle per week. Add in your 200 calories per session of weight training (3 times per week) for a total of 600 calories per week. When you figure in the extra calories for muscle gain and increased training, you require an additional 4,100 calories per week, or about 585 extra calories per day. This raises your calorie requirement from 2,500 to 3,085 calories per day.

Since muscle is composed of about 70% water and 22% protein, 1 pound (454 grams) of muscle contains only about 100 grams of protein. To gain 1 pound of muscle a week you will need to eat an additional 14 grams of protein a day. This is easily obtained from 1 cup of nonfat milk and 1 ounce of chicken (15 grams of protein total).

Start by keeping a diet diary. This gives a good idea of how much and what you're eating to maintain your weight and how much more you need to eat to gain weight.

Increase your calorie intake by eating larger servings of the foods you're currently eating (just the opposite of what is recommended for weight loss). Take in more calories during the day by adding ample mid-morning, mid-afternoon, and bedtime snacks. Drink commercial or homemade liquid meals with regular meals or as a snack between meals. The following suggestions may also help:

- Consume 1% or 2% fat milk instead of nonfat milk. Add lowfat cheeses to sandwiches or snacks. Eat flavored yogurt.
- Increase your intake of lean meat, poultry, and fish. Legumes are high in protein and low in fat. Eat nuts, seeds, and small amounts of peanut butter for snacks.
- Eat more whole grain products, such as breakfast cereals. Pasta and rice are nutritious side dishes. Quick breads and muffins can be supplemented with nuts and fruit.
- Add fruit to snacks and meals and drink more fruit juice. Dried fruits such as apricots, dates, and raisins make excellent snacks.

- Eat fresh vegetables such as broccoli and cauliflower with melted lowfat cheese or lowfat sour cream dip. Increase your intake of starchy vegetables such as potatoes and corn.
- Fats have a high caloric density and so help to increase caloric intake. Use monounsaturated and polyunsaturated fats and minimize intake of saturated fat.

10

Weight Loss in the Twilight Zone

Wacky Weight Loss Gimmicks

A fit female cyclist decided to follow the Zone diet to lose body fat and improve her endurance. She rode with a group of cyclists to the observatory on Mt. Palomar, which is about 1-mile high. She struggled up the long, steady climb in her lowest gear but eventually made it to the observatory. On the way back down, there was a short climb prior to the beautiful, winding descent. In spite of words of encouragement from another female cyclist at the observatory ("It's just a little hill!"), she felt so bad that she hopped in the sag wagon for the ride down.

AN UNBELIEVABLE NUMBER of weight loss gimmicks have been spawned by the American obsession with losing weight. While some weight loss frauds merely slim down our wallets (instead of our bodies), others may endanger our performance and our health. And, of course, almost all fail to produce permanent weight loss.

An effective weight reduction program includes a nutritionally adequate, reduced calorie intake as well as an increase in physical activity.

Low-Carbohydrate Diets

Many popular weight loss books (*Enter the Zone, Dr. Atkins' New Diet Revolution, Protein Power, Carbohydrate Addict's Lifespan Program,* and *Sugar Busters*) recommend a low-carbohydrate diet. Carbohydrates are blamed for increasing the body's production of insulin and promoting body fat storage.

Zone diet proponents also claim that to "burn body fat" and "reach optimum athletic performance," athletes must eat the "perfect ratio" of 40% carbohydrate, 30% protein, and 30% fat at each meal and snack.

What counts in weight loss is not carbohydrates or insulin, but calories. Body weight depends on calorie balance—how many calories are consumed compared to how many are expended. Eating a carbohydrate-rich diet does not promote fat storage. Fat storage occurs when a person eats too many calories relative to energy needs.

There's nothing magical about these low-carbohydrate regimens—they are just low-calorie diets. People lose weight because of the calorie restriction—not because of what is supposedly happening to their insulin levels. Although Enter the Zone states, "don't focus on calories," the Zone diet provides only about 1,200 calories a day for women and 1,700 calories a day for men.

The loss of body fat is proportional to the calorie deficit—no specific distribution of dietary protein, carbohydrate, and fat speeds up weight loss. When calorie expenditure exceeds calorie intake, weight loss occurs regardless of dietary composition.

Endurance exercise is the best way to crank up fat metabolism. As for gradual loss of body fat, that comes from burning more calories than are consumed, not from some special dietary ratio.

Nutrition Reality Check

Weight loss eating plans should meet the Dietary Guidelines criteria for a "healthy diet." The low-carbohydrate diets advocated by these books fail because they don't supply adequate carbohydrate, vitamins, minerals, and fiber. Some, such as the Atkins' diet, are too high in total fat and saturated fat. Such diets also go against the scientific evidence that consuming a diet rich in nutrient-dense plant foods (whole grains, fruits, vegetables, and beans) helps to prevent health problems such as heart disease and cancer.

Endurance athletes need adequate carbohydrate and fluid to perform at their best. Low-carbohydrate diets harm performance by reducing muscle and liver glycogen stores and blood glucose.

Low-carbohydrate diets are also faulty from a behavioral standpoint, because they tend to reinforce bad habits. Once the person is off the diet the usual eating habits are resumed. These diets distract people from the truth that real long-term weight control requires fundamental changes in lifestyle.

These diets don't encourage people to learn about the composition, planning, and preparation of foods or to make well-educated food selections. Rather, low-carbohydrate diets establish rigid rules and limitations that can realistically be followed only for a short time. Typically, the person abandons the diet and the weight is regained.

Low-carbohydrate diets appeal to the emotions and therefore perpetuate the myth that weight loss can be achieved quickly and easily. Rarely do they address the true need to make basic changes in what are life-long ways of looking at and dealing with food.

Evaluating Weight Loss Programs

"Miraculous" diets tend to produce only miraculous profits for their promoters. They are all based on the dream that a "magic" combination of foods and/or supplements can cause weight loss no matter how many calories are consumed. Believers are more likely to lose dollars than pounds.

When evaluating a weight loss program or product, consider the following points:

1. Does the diet include a variety of foods from the Food Guide Pyramid to ensure nutritional adequacy? Or, does it suggest that one or more foods or nutrients is either the "key" to weight loss or the primary "villain" that keeps people overweight? Be wary of diets that eliminate certain foods entirely or promote eating them in "special fat-burning combinations."
2. Does the program or product make sensational claims such as: "quick and easy," "burns fat and builds muscle," "metabolically proven," "eat all you want and still lose weight," and "energizing"?
3. Is the diet's effectiveness well documented by research published in credible scientific journals (consult a registered dietitian) and not based on testimonials by famous athletes or self-proclaimed experts?

4. Does the diet call for behavior and lifestyle changes? Does it incorporate exercise?
5. Does the diet avoid the use of diuretics and/or appetite suppressants?
6. Does the diet consider the special sports-specific needs of athletes (fluids, calories, carbohydrates, protein, etc.)?

Weight Loss Products

Nonprescription diet aids sold in pharmacies, health food stores, through the mail, over the Internet, and by multilevel marketers are extremely popular. At best, these products are ineffective; at worst they are potentially harmful.

• **Ephedrine**-containing herbs (ma huang, Chinese ephedra, and Sida cordifolia) are sold to enhance weight loss and improve athletic performance. Ephedrine is a central nervous system stimulant that is structurally similar to amphetamines and increases heart rate and blood pressure.

Many weight loss supplements contain caffeine and aspirin along with ephedrine. The combination of these ingredients (the ECA stack) raises the metabolic rate so that more calories are converted to heat (thermogenesis). The ECA stack typically contains 30 milligrams of ephedrine, 200 milligrams of caffeine, and 300 milligrams of aspirin.

Weight loss pills containing ephedrine can cause serious adverse effects such as heart attack, stroke, seizure, psychosis and death. The onset of symptoms such as dizziness, headache, gastrointestinal distress, irregular heartbeat, and heart palpitations following ephedrine ingestion indicate the potential for more serious adverse effects. Combining caffeine (from coffee, guarana, mate, or kola nut) with ephedrine-containing products greatly increases the adverse effects.

Side effects from ephedrine intake can vary and don't always depend on the dose consumed. Serious adverse effects can occur in susceptible persons with low doses. There are also questions about potency and quality control, as the amount of ephedrine in the product may be higher or lower than the amount listed on the product label.

Due to the risk of side effects, indiscriminate use of ephedrine is not advised. Individuals who have heart disease, high blood pressure, diabetes, thyroid or kidney problems, history of seizure, or take antidepressant medications should not take ephedrine. Women who are pregnant or nursing should also avoid using ephedrine-containing products.

Athletes may not realize that ephedrine is in some herbal weight loss products because an unfamiliar herbal name for the stimulant is used. The unintentional use of such products may result in a doping suspension, since the National Collegiate Athletic Association and International Olympic Committee ban ephedrine.

- **Synephrine** is a central nervous system stimulant extracted from citrus aurantium. Synephrine appears to have less negative cardiovascular and central nervous system side effects than ephedrine. Several weight loss supplements include synephrine with ephedrine and caffeine or synephrine in place of ephedrine. There is no scientific evidence that synephrine promotes body fat loss. Synephrine does, however, raise blood pressure in animals. More research is needed on the safety and effectiveness of citrus aurantium as a weight loss supplement.
- **"Herbal fen-phen"** products are marketed as "natural" alternatives to the prescription drugs phentermine and fenfluramine (commonly referred to as "fen-phen").

The main ingredient of most herbal fen-phen products is ephedra, commonly known as ma huang. Ephedra contains ephedrine—the powerful cardiovascular and nervous system stimulant.

Many herbal fen-phen products also contain Hypericum perforatum, an herb commonly known as St. John's Wort and sometimes referred to as "herbal Prozac." There is no evidence that

St. John's Wort promotes weight loss and the herb has not been studied in combination with ephedra. Other herbal fen-phen products contain 5-hydroxytryptophan (5-HTP), a compound closely related to L-tryptophan. Used as a sleep aid, L-tryptophan was pulled from the market after it was linked to eosinophilia-myalgia syndrome. Some 5-HTP products contain the impurity "peak X." Similar impurities were also found in L-tryptophan products that were associated with the epidemic of eosinophilia-myalgia syndrome.

• **Diuretics** promote weight loss by causing the body to shed water. The effect is temporary and the weight returns when the dieter stops taking the pills. Diuretics can also have bad side effects for athletes such as dehydration and electrolyte depletion. Many popular nonprescription weight loss pills contain herbal diuretics such as stinging nettle, uva ursi, and sarsasparilla.

• **Herbal weight loss teas** often contain potent plant-derived laxatives (senna, cascara, aloe, buckthorn), diuretics, and other drugs which can cause abdominal cramps, nausea, fainting, breathing difficulties, fluctuation in body temperature, diarrhea, and even death. The most severe effects have been observed in women who drank the diet tea in excess amounts or over a period of time, and were also restricting food. Many herbal diet teas are on the market and are not regulated or standardized as to ingredients or potency.

• **Green tea extract** may have a mild thermogenic effect due to an interaction between its high content of catechin-polyphenols (epigallocatechin gallate or EGCG) and caffeine. Catechin-polyphenols raise serum norepinephrine levels by interfering with the enzyme that breaks down norepinephrine. One study found that green tea extract containing 50 milligrams of caffeine and 90 milligrams of EGCG significantly increased daily energy expenditure by 4% and also increased fat utilization compared to 50 milligrams of caffeine and a placebo. The excretion of norepinephrine in the urine was also 40% higher during treatment with green tea extract compared to placebo. Treatment with caffeine in an amount equivalent to that in the green tea extract (50 milligrams) had no effect on energy expenditure or fat oxidation. This suggests that the thermogenic property of green tea is due to compounds other than caffeine. More research on green tea extract is warranted.

• **Chitosan** is derived from chitin, an indigestible compound obtained from shellfish such as shrimp, lobster and crabs. Promoters claim that chitosan produces rapid weight loss by binding fats in the stomach and preventing them from being digested and absorbed. Chitosan products are heavily advertised with seductive names like "Fat Magnet," "Fat Blocker," "Fat Trapper," and "Fat Absorb" in television infomercials, magazines, newspapers and Web sites.

In reality, such promotional claims only offer false hope to desperate, overweight people. Research indicates that chitosan doesn't work as a fat magnet. The Federal Trade Commission has won judgments against companies claiming that chitosan promotes weight loss without dieting or exercise.

There is no guarantee that chitosan products are free of impurities or contaminants, since the composition of the product may vary depending on the seawater, the time of year, and the specific shellfish utilized. Individuals who are allergic to seafood should be advised to avoid chitosan products.

• **Chromium** is the active component of the glucose tolerance factor that facilitates the actions of insulin. The supplement chromium picolinate is promoted to decrease body fat increase and muscle mass. Independent research by two United States Department of Agriculture Human Nutrition Research Centers found that the consumption of 200 micrograms of chromium picolinate daily combined with weight training for 8 to 12 weeks did not decrease body fat or increase strength or muscle mass. The Federal Trade Commission ordered the cessation of unsubstantiated weight loss and health claims for chromium picolinate.

• **Pyruvate** is a three-carbon sugar produced at the end stages of the anaerobic energy system from the breakdown of glucose. It supposedly enhances fat loss and increases endurance. Obese, sedentary women who took 22 to 28 grams of pyruvate daily and ate only 500 to 1,000 calories for three weeks lost 37% more body weight (3.5 pounds) and 48% more fat (2.9 pounds) than the placebo group. The deceptively large percentage differences in weight loss amounts to only a couple of pounds. Weight loss supplements usually only contain 500 milligrams to 1 gram of pyruvate.

• **Kelp** (dried seaweed) tablets are sold as a weight reduction aid, an energy booster, and as a natural "cure" for goiter. Kelp is a rich source of iodine, a mineral needed to prevent goiter, but iodized salt provides enough iodine at a fraction of kelp's cost. Excess iodine can be injurious to health.

• **Lecithin** (phosphatidylcholine) is claimed to aid weight reduction and lower serum cholesterol. Lecithin is a phospholipid manufactured by the liver and present in many foods, including soybeans, whole grains, and egg yolks. Phospholipids are powerful emulsifying agents and are essential for the digestion and absorption of fat. Although lecithin helps digest dietary fat, it has no effect on body fat. The body produces an ample amount of lecithin.

• **Growth hormone releasers** usually contain one or more of the amino acids arginine, ornithine, or lysine. They supposedly increase the body's production of growth hormone, thereby promoting weight loss. Growth hormone levels can be raised temporarily by injecting large amounts of arginine, not by swallowing amino acids. Furthermore, elevated levels of growth hormone can cause acromegaly, a disease in which hands, feet, and face become abnormally enlarged.

• **Calorad, Body Solutions,** and their clones are expensive protein supplements that are advertised to help you "lose weight while you sleep." These products usually contain collagen hydrolysate (a degraded protein found in the body), aloe vera (which has a laxative effect and can cause gastrointestinal upset when ingested orally), and conjugated linoleic acids (isomers of the essential fatty acid linoleic acid).

A slice of turkey or a can of tuna provides cheaper and higher quality protein than collagen. The frequent trips to the bathroom produced by aloe vera could theoretically cause weight loss. While some preliminary research suggests that conjugated linoleic acids may promote body fat loss, the consumption of linoleic acids is not an antidote for eating high-fat and high-calorie food.

The purported weight loss associated with these products stems from the fact that the person is instructed to not eat anything for 3 hours before going to bed. Then, right before going to sleep, the consumer takes the product (a whopping 12 to 14 calories) on an empty stomach. The weight loss occurs because the people are eating very little food in the evenings.

These products have not undergone scientific research. The personal testimonials that sales people consider to be proof of effectiveness are completely unscientific and have no merit except to those selling the product.

• **Conjugated Linoleic Acids** (CLA) are isomers of the essential fatty acid linoleic acid that purportedly decrease fat mass and increase lean mass. Animal research suggests that CLA may reduce fat storage, increase fat breakdown, and enhance fat burning. A Norwegian study indicated that CLA supplementation promoted small, but significant weight loss equivalent to a 160-pound person losing 2 to 3 pounds over 12 weeks. An American study, however, concluded that 64 days of CLA supplementation at 3 grams per day had no significant effect on body composition or energy expenditure. While preliminary research suggests that CLA may promote body fat loss, further research is warranted.

• **Hydroxycitrate** (or hydroxycitric acid) is present in high amounts in the plant Garcinia cambogia and supposedly promotes fat loss. In animals, hydroxycitrate inhibits the enzyme that is required for the synthesis of fatty acids and reduces weight gain.

Twelve weeks of supplementation with Garcinia cambogia failed to produce significant weight loss and fat mass loss beyond that observed with a placebo. The compound may be shown to promote weight loss, but this hasn't yet been convincingly demonstrated.

The Cellulite Myth

Many companies have marketed programs and products claimed to remove "cellulite." Cellulite is alleged to be a special type of fat gone wrong—a combination of fat, water, and "toxic wastes" that the body has failed to eliminate.

Cellulite is not a medical term; cellulite is just ordinary fat tissue. Strands of fibrous tissue connect the skin to deeper tissue layers and also separate compartments that contain cells. When fat cells get larger, these compartments bulge and produce a waffled or "orange peel" appearance of the skin.

Women tend to deposit fat in the hips, buttocks, thighs, and breasts, so many women have these "orange peel" bumps, even women with healthy levels of body fat. Anti-cellulite products that don't work include "loofah" sponges, horsehair mitts, cactus fiber washcloths, and "dissolving" creams.

The Spot-Reduction Fallacy

No exercise, dietary, or other nonsurgical treatment can produce spot-reduction. While the amount of body fat is determined to a large extent by eating and exercise habits, the distribution of body fat is determined by heredity. Reduction of a particular part can only be accomplished as part of an overall weight reduction program.

Exercise, even when localized, draws from all body fat stores, not from just local fat deposits. Tennis players, for example, have the same triceps skinfold on both arms, even though their dominant arm is exercised more.

Exercising a specific area does increase muscle tone and may make a person look thinner. For example, localized exercise such as sit-ups can cause substantial reductions in abdominal girth. This is not due to fat loss. Rather, the abdominal muscles are strengthened and are better able to hold in the abdomen.

Exercise does appear to preferentially reduce fat stored in the upper body and abdominal regions (android obesity) compared to fat stored in the buttocks and thigh regions (gynoid obesity). Since android obesity places an individual at greater risk for health problems, exercise confers significant health benefits. Although gynoid obesity is more frustratingly resistant to the effects of exercise than android obesity, it also does not confer as great a health risk.

Gimmicks such as body wraps, vibrating belts, and electric muscle stimulators cannot "melt away" fat. They may appear to work by causing temporary water loss or tissue compression. Although the person using these gimmicks may look thinner for a short time, only the wallet experiences permanent shrinkage.

Wearing rubber, plastic, or sweat suits during exercise in an effort to "melt away" fat is dangerous and ineffective. Weight loss is from fluid loss, not fat loss. The suit prevents the evaporation of sweat, which is necessary to reduce body temperature during exercise. This practice can cause dehydration, heat exhaustion, and even heat stroke. Lounging in a sauna also can cause you to lose weight due to sweating. Of course, your weight will return to normal when the sweat-induced water loss is replaced.

11

Popular Sports Supplements

The Search for the Magic Bullet

A male marathon runner decided to try a "natural" herbal supplement before a long training run. He thought that since the product was "natural," it must be safe, and the product label claimed it would improve his performance. He felt a little jittery during the run but did not run any faster than usual. He developed a headache that afternoon and had difficulty sleeping that night. The following morning, he read the ingredient panel of the supplement and found that it contained ephedrine from ma huang and caffeine from guarana. The runner threw the bottle in the trash and vowed to diligently read the ingredient panel on supplements in the future.

"NEW PERFORMANCE BREAKTHROUGH! Make more energy available to your muscles. Increase your endurance without additional training. Our unique supplement is an energy-releasing substance extracted from natural foods by a secret process. Send $49.95 for your starter capsules now!"

Keep your hand on your wallet. If you're looking too hard for the magic bullet, you may think you have found it in places it doesn't exist.

If you read a typical fitness magazine, you know that there are no shortage of nutrition supplements that supposedly enhance endurance, speed up recovery, improve muscle mass or reduce body fat. Some advertisements even claim their wonder products do all of the above.

All of us seek that "secret ingredient" to enhance our workout and give us the edge over our competitors. In many events the difference between winning and losing is in fractions of seconds, so it is not surprising that we are vulnerable to miraculous claims of these supplements.

The placebo effect by itself is powerful enough to produce beneficial results. When you are convinced that a supplement improves your performance, this belief may enable you to perform better, even though there is nothing inherently useful in the product as such. Just because a friend may ride the placebo effect to better performance doesn't mean that you will.

Evaluating Claims

Be skeptical about the nutrition information you read and hear. Magazines, books, and the media overflow with health advice—some reliable and some inaccurate. Here are some guidelines you can use to evaluate product claims:

Do the claims for the product sound too good to be true? Product marketing plays on emotions and misinformation. Athletes want to believe there are novel ways to improve performance that bypass the rigors of training and diet. Product literature should not promise to dramatically enhance your performance or guarantee fast weight loss. Beware of claims stating that using a supplement is the only way to ensure nutritional adequacy or that ordinary foods can't meet your nutritional requirements.

What are the qualifications of the person recommending the product? A reputable person such as a registered dietitian (RD) has a background or affiliation with an accredited university offering programs in the field of nutrition. Beware the title "nutritionist." It can be used by anyone, regardless of education or training.

Credible physicians and registered dietitians may occasionally recommend supplements, such as specific vitamins or minerals, for certain health problems. However, health professionals shouldn't sell the supplements, as this represents a conflict of interest and exploits the health professional/client relationship.

Practitioners who sell supplements out of their office often recommend them inappropriately. Often these supplements tend to be much more expensive than similar products sold in drug stores.

What evidence is supplied for any claims that are made? Claims should be supported with references to the scientific journals that published the original research. Advertisements may use the picture or testimonial of a famous athlete to promote the product. However, testimonial evidence is by definition biased and uncertain. Controlled experiments that can be confirmed by repeating the study are the best way to document the truth of the information.

Sports Supplements

Many sports supplements have little scientific evidence to back up their claims. Often, studies that are quoted to prove the product works haven't been published in respected journals or the findings of a study are misrepresented. Supportive research may also be poorly designed or use animals or human populations different from the populations buying the products.

Currently popular sports supplements (other than protein, amino acids, vitamins and minerals) include:

• **Androstenedione** or andro is an adrenal hormone (anabolic steroid) that functions as a metabolic precursor to testosterone. Andro supposedly increases testosterone levels, thereby increasing muscle mass and strength. Research indicates that andro does not have an effect on serum testosterone, muscle size and strength, or body composition compared to placebo. Andro does, however, significantly increase serum estrogen levels and decrease HDL cholesterol, which may have adverse health consequences during long term supplementation. The National Collegiate Athletic Association, International Olympic Committee, and National Football League ban andro.

Side-effects of anabolic steroids include: liver problems, unfavorable changes in blood lipids (decreased HDL and increased LDL), uncontrolled aggressive behavior ("roid rage"), increased acne, increased body hair, reduction of testicle size and breast growth in men, and increased size of the clitoris and lowering of the voice in women. Anabolic steroids can also shut off bone growth in adolescents, stunting height.

• **Boron** is a trace element that influences calcium and magnesium metabolism. Boron allegedly raises serum testosterone levels to increase muscle growth and strength. These claims were based on a study showing that boron supplementation increased estrogen and testosterone levels in post-menopausal women! The level of normal male testosterone is approximately 10 times that observed in the study subjects. At present, there is no evidence that boron increases testosterone levels, lean body mass, or strength.

• **Bovine Colostrum** is the "pre-milk" that cows secrete the first few days after calving that contains insulin-like growth factor I (IGF-I) in addition to nutrients and other biologically active components. In theory, consuming a bovine colostrum supplement could increase the IGF-I concentration and have a favorable anabolic effect during strenuous training. Preliminary research suggests that bovine colostrum may have an anabolic effect by increasing serum IGF-I, but the claim that colostrum enhances performance has yet to be convincingly demonstrated.

• **Branched Chain Amino Acids** or BCAA (leucine, isoleucine, and valine) are the primary amino acids broken down for energy during endurance exercise. The central fatigue hypothesis suggests that increased amounts of brain serotonin cause fatigue during prolonged endurance exercise. In theory, consuming BCAA during exercise keeps brain serotonin from increasing, thereby helping to prevent fatigue and enhance endurance. Consuming large amounts of BCAA may increase serum ammonia (which may be toxic), slow water absorption, and cause gut distress. BCAA supplements aren't recommended because they haven't been shown to improve performance, they may not be safe, and it's easy to obtain sufficient quantities from food.

• **Caffeine** is a stimulant found in coffee and the herbs guarana, mate, and kola nut that increases serum levels of epinephrine. Caffeine is a socially acceptable drug that is an integral part of many athletes' diets. Research suggests that consuming 3 to 6 milligrams of caffeine per kilogram one hour before improves performance during prolonged endurance exercise and short-term intense aerobic exercise but has no effect upon sprint exercise lasting less than 90 seconds. This amount does not raise urinary caffeine levels above the International Olympic Committee doping threshold of 12 micrograms per milliliter. Thus, caffeine has the potential to be a "legal" performance aid for endurance athletes.

Side effects of high caffeine consumption include anxiety, jitters, insomnia, irritability, gastrointestinal distress, and irregular heartbeat. Adverse effects of caffeine are more likely at high doses but can vary considerably between individuals. Athletes who are sensitive to caffeine can experience these symptoms at low doses. Although caffeine is a mild diuretic, there is no indication that caffeine increases the risk of dehydration.

Caffeine may enhance performance in 3 different ways. Caffeine is a stimulant and increases alertness and decreases the perception of fatigue. Caffeine may reduce the perception of effort by making it easier to recruit the muscles for exercise. Caffeine may also increase the force of muscle contractions. Lastly, caffeine may increase fat utilization and decrease carbohydrate utilization. Since caffeine affects both the central nervous system and skeletal muscle, it isn't possible to separate out caffeine's effects on the central nervous system from caffeine effects on the muscle.

- **Carnitine** is a compound synthesized in the body from the amino acids lysine and methionine that supposedly increases fat metabolism and decreases body fat. Carnitine facilitates the transfer of fatty acids into the mitochondria (the energy powerhouses of the cell) where they are burned for fuel in the aerobic energy system. There is no evidence that carnitine supplementation increases the use of fatty acids during exercise or decreases body fat. There is no dietary requirement for carnitine.
- **Choline** is a precursor of the neurotransmitter acetylcholine and for lecithin, a substance involved in fat transport. Choline allegedly increases strength by increasing acetylcholine and decreases body fat by increasing lecithin. There is no dietary requirement for choline—the body can manufacture it from methionine, an essential amino acid. There is no evidence that choline increases strength or decreases body fat.

• **Coenzyme Q10** is a catalyst in the aerobic energy system that supposedly optimizes ATP production to increase energy and stamina. There is no dietary requirement for coenzyme Q10. Supplementation with coenzyme Q10 does not improve endurance performance or maximum aerobic capacity.

• **Creatine** combines with phosphate to form creatine phosphate or CP, a high- energy compound stored in muscle. Research suggests that consuming 20 to 25 grams of creatine per day (5 grams consumed 4 to 5 times daily) for 5 to 7 days increases CP stores in athletes by 20%, delays fatigue during explosive sprint performance, and facilitates ATP resynthesis following sprint-type exercise. Long-term creatine supplementation (the loading dose followed by 3 to 5 grams per day for several months) increases strength and repetitive sprint performance by about 5 to 15% and body weight by about 3 to 7 pounds.

Not all studies have found that creatine improves strength, sprint performance, or body weight. Creatine may not improve all high power activities, since nearly all the studies have evaluated activities such as sprints done while running, swimming, rowing, and cycling sprints, and weight-lifting.

• **DHEA (dehydroepiandrosterone)** is an adrenal hormone that functions as a metabolic precursor for the production of testosterone, estrogen, and other hormones. DHEA supposedly increases testosterone levels, serves as a legal alternative to anabolic steroids, and acts as an anti-aging hormone. DHEA is called the "steroid of youth" since levels decrease with age. There is no evidence that DHEA produces anabolic effects (e.g. increased muscle mass or strength) or decreased body fat in healthy, young adults. Side effects include oily skin, acne, increased body hair, liver enlargement, and aggressiveness. The hormone's long-term safety has not been established and, as with other hormones, adverse effects may not be apparent for years. Individuals who have a family history of breast or prostate cancer should not take DHEA. Mexican yam contains a plant sterol ring called diosgenin, which is a precursor for the semisynthetic production of

DHEA and other steroid hormones, but this conversion only takes place in the laboratory and will not take place in the human body.

• **Ephedrine** is a stimulant promoted to improve athletic performance and enhance weight loss. Although some research suggests that the combination of ephedrine and caffeine may improve anaerobic and high-intensity aerobic performance, there are safety, potency, and doping concerns. Ephedrine raises heat production and body temperature and increases the risk of developing a heat injury during exercise in warm weather. At the very least, the unwitting use of ephedrine-containing products may result in a doping suspension, since the International Olympic Committee and National Collegiate Athletic Association bans ephedrine.

• **Gamma-Oryzanol** is a plant sterol derived from rice bran oil that supposedly increases serum testosterone and growth hormone levels, thereby increasing muscle growth. The structural similarity of oryzanol and its plant sterols to cholesterol have led to numerous claims that these plant sterols, like cholesterol, can be converted to testosterone. Gamma oryzanol isn't anabolic because it can't be converted to testosterone by the human body.

• **Ginseng** (extract of ginseng root) is marketed as an adaptogen (enhances immune system to increase resistance to stress and disease), a performance enhancer, and "cure-all." No single drug has all the healthful properties that are attributed to ginseng. The existence of a genuine "cure-all" is unlikely and ginseng has no proven medicinal value. Ginseng does not improve aerobic capacity or performance. Since ginseng root is expensive, the commercial preparations may contain little or no ginseng. The side effects of ginseng are insomnia, and to a lesser degree, diarrhea and skin eruption. The prolonged use of ginseng by adults seems to be relatively safe.

• **Glucosamine** is a naturally occurring aminosugar found in the building blocks of cartilage promoted to retard cartilage breakdown and stimulate cartilage growth. Glucosamine

(1.5 grams per day in divided doses) may stimulate cartilage cells to synthesize cartilage building blocks. Glucosamine may also inhibit the enzymes that contribute to cartilage breakdown. The supplement appears to be most effective for early arthritis and less effective for late arthritis. Additional research on the effectiveness of glucosamine is required.

• **Glutamine** is a non-essential amino acid that is a major energy source for gut enterocytes, lymphocytes, and macrophages. Since glutamine is critical for optimal functioning of the immune system, glutamine supplementation may enhance immune function and decrease the risk of infection.

Plasma glutamine concentration may fall after periods of intense training and muscle glycogen depletion. However, an adequate daily intake of carbohydrates and calories may help to prevent muscle glycogen depletion and overtraining as well as help to maintain normal glutamine status. While some preliminary research suggests that glutamine supplementation (10 grams per day) may reduce the incidence of respiratory infections in athletes, further research is required.

• **Glycerol** is an alcohol that combines with fatty acids to form triglyceride. Glycerol hyperhydration (1.2 grams of glycerol per kilogram along with 26 milliliters of water per kilogram consumed prior to exercise) may increase plasma volume and sweat rate, thereby reducing body temperature and improving performance during prolonged endurance exercise in warm weather. Further research on glycerol's safety and effectiveness is required.

• **HMB** (beta-hydroxy beta-methylbutyrate) is a downstream metabolite of the essential amino acid leucine promoted to increase muscle mass and strength and decrease muscle breakdown after exercise. Preliminary research suggested that taking 1.5 to 3.0 grams of HMB daily during resistance training increased muscle mass and strength, protected against muscle damage, and/or improved muscle repair. However, more recent research has not shown HMB to have these effects.

• **Inosine** is a nucleoside involved in the formation of purines marketed to increase ATP production, increase strength, and enhance recovery. There are no research studies to support these claims for strength performance. Inosine may actually impair endurance performance.

• **Medium chain triglycerides** or MCT are fats that are water-soluble and readily absorbed. MCT supposedly enhance performance by sparing muscle glycogen during endurance exercise. While one study suggests that consuming MCT along with carbohydrates improves endurance performance lasting over 2 hours, most research does not show a performance-enhancing effect. Consuming large amounts of MCT can cause gastrointestinal upset and diarrhea.

• **Omega-3 fatty acids** are polyunsaturated fatty acids found mostly in fish oils that supposedly stimulate the release of growth hormone. Omega-3 fatty acids may be converted to prostagladins (hormone like-substances) in the body and a specific prostaglandin called PGE 1 may stimulate growth hormone release. However, there is no proof that Omega-3 fatty acids improve endurance or strength.

• **Phosphates** are part of adenosine triphosphate (ATP) and creatine phosphate (CP). Phosphate loading may increase intracellular phosphate levels and thereby increase aerobic metabolism. Phosphate loading may increase maximum aerobic capacity, blood lactate threshold, and endurance. The usual dose is 1 gram of sodium phosphate, taken 4 times a day for 3 days. More current research on phosphate loading is needed.

• **Pyruvate** is a three-carbon sugar produced at the end stages of the anaerobic energy system from the breakdown of glucose. It supposedly increases endurance and enhances fat loss. Consuming 25 grams of pyruvate and 75 grams of dihydroxyacetone or DHA (another three-carbon sugar produced in the breakdown of glucose) for 7 days improved both arm endurance and leg endurance in untrained men by 20%. Other researchers in other labs have not reproduced these results and the subjects were untrained men, so the results cannot be applied to women or athletes. The subjects experienced side effects in the form of intestinal gas, flatus, and diarrhea. Commercial pyruvate preparations only contain 500 milligrams to 1 gram of pyruvate and may not contain DHA.

- **Ribose** is a five-carbon sugar formed from glucose. Ribose is a necessary substrate for the synthesis of nucleotides—adenosine, ATP, and inosine. Ribose is also essential for pathways that recover adenosine to regenerate stores of ATP. Ribose supplementation may improve cardiac function and stimulate ATP synthesis in individuals with heart disease. However, the purported performance effects of ribose in healthy athletes have yet to be convincingly demonstrated.
- **Smilax** is a genus of desert plants containing several species of sarsaparilla that supposedly is a legal alternative to anabolic steroids and naturally increases serum testosterone levels. While Smilax does contain substances called saponins that can serve as precursors for the synthetic production of certain steroids, this conversion takes place only in the laboratory, not in the human body. There is no evidence that Smilax is anabolic or functions as a legal replacement for anabolic steroids. The saponins in Smilax stimulate urination, bowel evacuation, sweating, and coughing.
- **Sodium bicarbonate** is a base that buffers lactic acid in the blood. It may augment the body's buffer reserve, counteract the build up of lactic acid in the blood, and improve anaerobic performance. Several studies have supported improved anaerobic performance (400- and 800-meter runs) with bicarbonate administration. Taking 0.3 grams per kilogram of sodium bicarbonate with water over a 2 to 3 hour period may improve 800-meter run time by several seconds. However, athletes who use sodium bicarbonate may experience diarrhea one hour after the soda loading is completed. The effects of repeated ingestion is unknown and caution is advised.
- **Succinate** is a metabolite in the aerobic energy system and marketed as a metabolic enhancer to reduce lactic acid and main-

tain ATP production. Although succinate is an intermediary in the aerobic pathway, extra amounts will not "speed up" the process of aerobic metabolism or ATP production as this is controlled by rate-limiting enzymes within the pathway.

• **Vanadyl Sulfate** is a trace mineral with no dietary requirement promoted to have anabolic effects similar to those of insulin. Vanadyl sulfate has been shown to mimic the action of insulin in individuals with non-insulin dependent diabetes. A dose of 0.5 milligrams per kilogram daily for 12 weeks did not increase strength or muscle mass during a weight training program. Mild gastrointestinal symptoms and other side effects have been reported with vanadium supplementation

• **Vitamin B_{12}** is essential for DNA synthesis and marketed to increase muscle growth and enhance strength. Since vitamin B_{12} is essential for DNA synthesis, the theory is that vitamin B_{12} or dibencobal (a coenzyme form of B_{12}) will stimulate muscle growth by enhancing DNA synthesis. However, there is no evidence that supplemental dibencobal or vitamin B_{12} promotes muscle growth or enhances strength

• **Whey protein** (20% of the total protein found in milk) is marketed as having the ability to enhance immune function and to increase muscle mass more aggressively than other proteins. Compared to the casein protein in milk, whey contains substantial amounts of the amino acid cysteine, which is necessary for the synthesis of glutathione. Glutathione is necessary for lymphocyte production in the development of the immune response. One study found that whey protein supplementation enhanced muscular performance, possibly by reducing oxidative stress and subsequent muscular fatigue. Although the whey protein may have enhanced immune function by increasing glutathione levels, it did not increase muscle mass.

• **Yohimbine** is a stimulant extracted from yohimbe bark that increases serum levels of norepinephrine. Yohimbine supposedly increases serum testosterone levels, muscle growth, and strength, and decreases body fat. There is no proof that yohimbine is anabolic. Tyramine-containing foods (red wine, liver, cheese) should be rigorously avoided when yohimbine is used to prevent a sudden and dangerous increase in blood pressure. People who have diabetes, or cardiovascular, liver, or kidney disease should not take yohimbine.

Supplements and Doping

Using dietary supplements to improve performance may increase the risk of testing positive for banned substances. The supplement may list the banned substance on the ingredient panel using an unfamiliar name for the ingredient. A consumer may not recognize that the herb guarana has a high caffeine content, or that the herb ma huang contains ephedrine.

The supplement may also contain banned substances that are not declared as ingredients. Such ingredients may be added deliberately and not declared, or added inadvertently as by-products of other ingredients or contaminants of the production process. Examples include "mental enhancer" products that contain but do not list ephedrine and "anabolic" pro-hormone products that contain but do not list banned anabolic steroids.

Athletes have a responsibility to be aware of banned substances and to know what they are ingesting. Most athletic organizations have a "Zero Tolerance" policy and do not accept ignorance as an excuse for failing a doping test. When in doubt about the supplement's legality, protect the eligibility to compete and shun the product.

The Bottom Line

New sports supplements are constantly emerging. When evaluating a product, remember that dietary supplements do not have to be approved by the Food and Drug Administration for safety, effectiveness, purity, or potency.

Supplements alone won't enable you to reach your goals. Rather, supplements must be used as part of a sound nutrition and training program. The best way to safeguard your performance, health, and eligibility when using supplements is to be an informed consumer. If you have questions about a particular supplement, contact a registered dietitian specializing in sports nutrition.

12

Fuel Basics

VO_{2max}

The harder you exercise, the more oxygen you require. The amount of oxygen that your body uses is directly related to the intensity of the exercise. There is a point beyond which your use of oxygen will not increase, even when the intensity of the exercise continues to increase. The value at which your oxygen consumption plateaus is called your maximal oxygen consumption (abbreviated VO_{2max}). VO_{2max} is a scientific measurement of your aerobic capacity and is regarded as the best criterion of endurance capacity and physical fitness. A person with a high VO_{2max} can exercise harder and longer than a person with a low VO_{2max}.

To account for individual differences in size, VO_{2max} values take into account differences in body weight. A person's maximal oxygen usage (measured in liters per minute) is divided by his or her weight (measured in kilograms—1 kilogram is equal to 2.2 pounds). VO2max values are expressed in milliliters of oxygen used per kilogram of body weight per minute (abbreviated ml/kg/min).

The delivery of blood by the heart and extraction of oxygen from the blood by the muscles determine your VO_{2max}. Your ultimate VO_{2max} seems to be genetically determined, but whether or not you reach your full potential depends on training.

Values for sedentary college age males and females are in the mid-40s and 30s ml/kg/min, respectively. Male endurance athletes (runners, cyclists, triathletes, swimmers) generally have VO_{2max} values in the 60s, and elite male endurance athletes have values in the 70s to 80s ml/kg/min. Female endurance athletes are usually in the 50s and elite female endurance athletes are in the 60s to 70s ml/kg/min.

Women, non-athletes and athletes alike, have lower VO_{2max} values than men. Women carry a greater percentage of their body weight as fat compared to men. This sex-specific essential body fat is the major reason that women have lower VO_{2max} values. Women also have less total hemoglobin and as a result the oxygen content of the blood delivered to their muscles is lower.

Elite athletes can exercise at their VO_{2max} for only about 8–10 minutes. This means that most of the time athletes are exercising at a percentage of their VO_{2max} (e.g., 95% in a 5–K, 60–80% in a marathon).

Lactate Threshold

The lactate threshold is the point during exercise of increasing intensity at which lactic acid begins to accumulate in your blood. It is usually expressed as a percentage of VO_{2max}.

Your lactate threshold is a better predictor of endurance performance lasting 30 minutes to 4 hours than your VO_{2max}. In fact, the running speed at which the lactate threshold occurs predicts marathon performance better than VO_{2max}.

Untrained people have lactate thresholds at about 50% of their VO_{2max}. Trained people have lactate thresholds at about 70% of their VO_{2max}. This higher level for lactic acid accumulation means that trained people can exercise at a higher percentage of their VO_{2max}.

Energy Systems for Exercise

Most people can explain, at least generally, how power is supplied to the engine of their car. They know that the motor needs oxygen to burn fuel. They know that the engine needs more fuel and more oxygen as the speed of the car increases. And, they know that if they do not supply the car with fuel and oxygen, it simply will not operate.

Similarly, your body must be continuously supplied with energy to perform its many complex functions. When you exercise, your body requires more energy. There must be a way to provide this additional energy or you would stop moving. There are two interrelated systems that supply energy for the body—one is dependent on oxygen and the other is able to function without oxygen.

ATP—The Energy Currency

The energy-rich chemical compound adenosine triphosphate (ATP) is used for all energy-requiring processes within the cell. The energy released from the breakdown of ATP is used to power every body function, such as muscle contraction. So ATP is considered the "energy currency" of the cell. Another energy-rich compound called creatine phosphate (CP) provides a small reserve of quick energy. The energy released from the breakdown of ATP and CP stores can sustain all-out exercise (such as sprinting a 100 meters) for about 6 to 8 seconds (see Figure 12-1).

ATP must be continuously produced to provide a steady supply of energy. The muscle cells produce and maintain ongoing stores of ATP, utilizing glucose from carbohydrates, fatty acids from fats, and to a small extent, amino acids from proteins. The body extracts the energy from dietary or body stores of carbohydrate, fat, and protein to rebuild the energy-rich ATP.

Energy Production

Chains of chemical reactions use food, oxygen, and water to supply energy to our bodies at rest and during exercise. This is referred to as metabolism. ATP is produced continuously within muscle cells through two important energy systems. One of these pathways functions without oxygen and is called anaerobic; the other pathway requires oxygen and is called aerobic.

For a limited period of time (about 1 minute) our body can rely on the anaerobic energy system. The anaerobic system

ATP AND CP

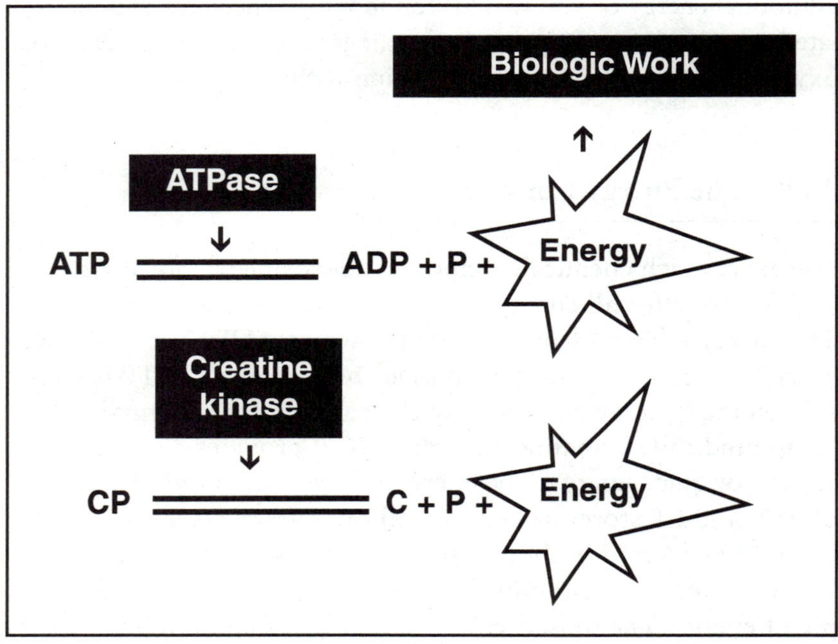

Figure 12-1. ATP and CP are nonaerobic sources of phosphate-bond energy. The energy liberated from the hydrolysis (splitting) of CP is used to rebond ADP and P to form ATP.

supplies most of the energy for an all-out 400-meter sprint. It allows you to briefly exercise at a level that exceeds your ability to provide oxygen to your muscles.

When you exercise beyond a few minutes, such as when you are running a mile, your body needs a continuous supply of oxygen. The aerobic energy system provides almost all of your energy during exercise that lasts 4 minutes or longer.

Anaerobic System

Glucose is the only fuel that can be used when oxygen is not available. Glucose is stored in the muscles and liver as glycogen. Glycogen is actually a long chain of glucose molecules hooked together. In the anaerobic energy system, glucose (from glycogen) is broken down to a substance called pyruvate. When oxygen is not available, pyruvate is converted into lactic acid, forming 2 molecules of ATP.

While the anaerobic system is rapidly providing energy, lactic acid is beginning to accumulate. This impairs muscle function (due to increased acidity) and contributes to fatigue. When oxygen becomes available, lactic acid is converted back into pyruvate, or burned directly by the muscles for energy. Lactic acid can also go to the liver and be converted back into glucose.

The anaerobic system provides you with energy for all-out effort lasting up to 60 seconds, such as sprinting and weight lifting, and when you first start to exercise. It also provides energy for bursts that are common in sports such as soccer, basketball, football, and tennis.

Aerobic System

When oxygen is available, glucose can be broken down more efficiently, without being converted to lactic acid. As shown in Figure 12-2, when glucose is broken down in the aerobic energy system, 36 ATP molecules are produced. This is 18 times more energy than when glucose is converted to lactic acid in the anaerobic system.

Fatty acids (from fat in the diet and body) and amino acids (from protein in the diet and body) can also go through the aerobic system to release energy as ATP. However, protein and fat cannot provide energy without the presence of oxygen. This means that when oxygen is limited, glucose (from carbohydrates) is the only fuel available for ATP production.

The Aerobic-Anaerobic Combination

At the beginning of exercise, it takes time for the heart and blood vessels to get oxygen-rich blood to the muscles. During this lag time, anaerobic ATP production supplies most of the energy for exercise.

THE ANAEROBIC AND AEROBIC REACTION SYSTEMS WORKING TOGETHER

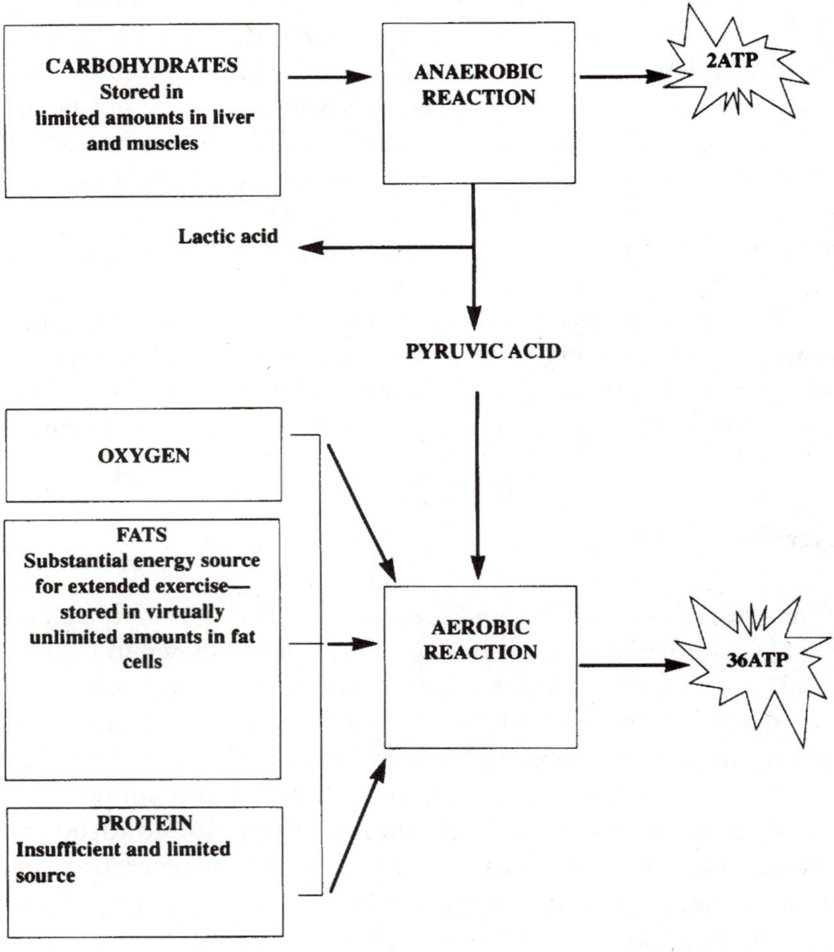

Figure 12-2. When enough oxygen is present in the muscle, the more efficient aerobic reaction system operates to provide the energy (ATP) used for muscle contractions. The aerobic system is very efficient and can produce up to 18 times the amount of ATP produced by the anaerobic system.

After several minutes, oxygen becomes available and aerobic ATP production provides most of the energy needed to sustain exercise. However, when the exercise becomes too intense for enough energy to be produced aerobically (as when running up a hill or sprinting in a marathon), the body relies on the anaerobic system for more energy. This additional ATP is generated at the cost of increasing the lactic acid level in the blood.

In an event lasting several minutes, such as an 800-meter run, the contributions of aerobic and anaerobic ATP are about equal. As the distance (or time) increases, the contribution of aerobically produced energy increases (see Figure 12-3).

Although anaerobic energy production determines performance during sprint-type activities, the capacity to produce ATP aerobically determines endurance performance. Thus, the availability of oxygen in large part determines the potential for aerobic exercise.

Your capacity for exercise intensity and duration are inversely related. That is, as the distance (or time) increases, you have to reduce your intensity, or pace. For example, a runner can't run a marathon (26.2 miles) as fast as a 10-kilometer race (6.2 miles). You can only perform at a certain percentage of your VO_{2max} for any given distance or time.

The aerobic energy system cannot tolerate the same level of intensity as the duration increases. A trained distance runner can run 1,500 meters or a mile at 100% of his VO_{2max}. In a 5-kilometer race (3.1 miles) he can use about 95% of his VO_{2max}. In a 10-kilometer race, he can average about 90% of his VO_{2max}.

During prolonged endurance exercise, there is an additional reason why you can't perform close to your aerobic capacity for the entire distance. During endurance exercise that exceeds 90-120 minutes, your muscle glycogen stores become progressively lowered. When this happens, you must reduce your exercise intensity.

Determinants of Exercise Fuel Usage

A variety of factors determine which type of fuel your muscles will use during exercise. These include exercise intensity, exercise duration, and your training level.

THE ANAEROBIC AND AEROBIC CONTINUUM

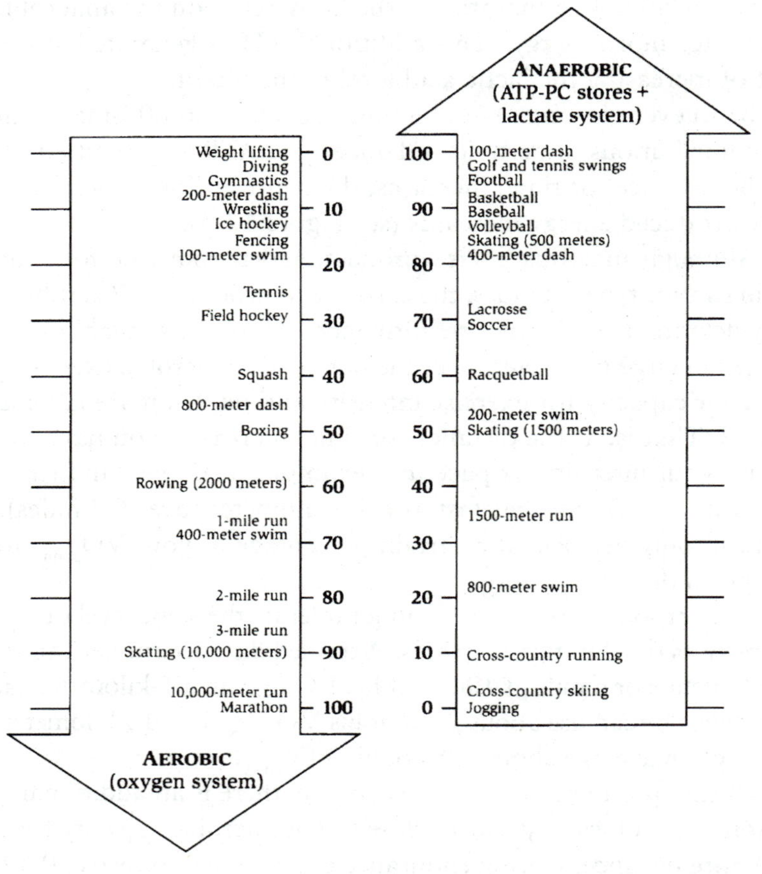

Figure 12-3. Whereas the 100-meter dash is considered a pure anaerobic event and the marathon a pure aerobic event, most other activities use ATP from both systems. Athletes should train both systems in accordance with the demands of their sport.

Muscle glycogen represents the major source of carbohydrate in the body (300 to 400 grams or 1,200 to 1,600 calories), followed by liver glycogen (75 to 100 grams or 300 to 400 calories) and, lastly, blood glucose (25 grams or 100 calories).

Intensity

The intensity of exercise is particularly important in determining your muscles' energy source. High-intensity, short-duration exercise (such as sprinting) relies on the anaerobic system for energy production. Only glucose, derived primarily from the breakdown of muscle glycogen, can be used as fuel.

When glucose is broken down anaerobically, muscle glycogen is used 18 times faster than when glucose is broken down aerobically. A more rapid rate of muscle glycogen breakdown will also occur during high-intensity exercise (over 70% of VO_{2max}) when the anaerobic system is pulled in to assist the aerobic system in ATP production.

Extended mixed anaerobic-aerobic intermittent exercise like football drills, soccer, basketball, and running or swimming intervals also causes a greater breakdown of muscle glycogen.

Muscle glycogen and blood glucose supply half of the energy for aerobic exercise during a moderate workout (at or below 60% of VO_{2max}) and supply nearly all the energy during a hard workout (over 80% of VO_{2max}).

Exercise of low to moderate intensity (up to 60% of VO_{2max}) can be fueled almost entirely aerobically. The hormonal changes that occur with exercise—increased epinephrine (adrenaline) and decreased insulin levels—prompt your muscle and fat (adipose) tissue to breakdown fat into fatty acids. Fatty acids derived from intramuscular fat and adipose tissue supply about half of the energy for low- to moderate-intensity exercise. Muscle glycogen and blood glucose supply the rest.

There are several reasons that fat cannot be used as fuel during high-intensity exercise (above 70% of VO_{2max}). First, the breakdown of fat to ATP is a slow process and cannot supply ATP fast enough to provide energy for high-intensity exercise.

Also, glucose provides more calories per liter of oxygen than does fat. Glucose delivers 5.10 calories per liter of oxygen and fat delivers 4.62 calories per liter of oxygen. When less oxygen becomes available, as during high-intensity exercise, using glucose gives the muscles a distinct advantage because less oxygen is needed to produce energy.

The shift in fuel from fat to glycogen as the exercise intensity increases is also partly due to the accumulation of lactic acid. During high-intensity exercise, lactic acid hinders the use of fat by the muscles. Thus, the muscles must rely more on glycogen for energy production.

Duration

The duration of exercise also defines whether the fuel used will be mostly muscle glycogen or fat. The longer you exercise, the greater the contribution of fat as fuel. Fat can supply as much as 60 to 70% of the energy needs for moderate-intensity exercise lasting 4 to 6 hours.

As the duration of exercise increases, the intensity must decrease, since there is a limited supply of stored glycogen. When muscle glycogen stores are low, fat breakdown supplies most of the energy needed for exercise. However, fat is limited as fuel above 60% of VO_{2max}. Also, a certain level of carbohydrate breakdown is necessary for fat to be burned for energy. To this extent, "fat burns in a carbohydrate flame."

As a result of the relationship between exercise intensity and duration, muscle glycogen is the predominant fuel for most types of exercise. It takes at least 20 minutes for fat to be available to the muscles as fuel in the form of free fatty acids. Most people don't train long enough to burn significant amounts of fat during the exercise session itself. Also, most people train and compete at an exercise intensity of 70% of VO_{2max} or above, which limits the use of fat as fuel.

This does not mean that you have to work out for a long time to lose body fat. When your workout creates a caloric deficit, the body will pull from its fat stores at a later time to make up that caloric deficit.

Training Level

Your training level will also determine what fuel your muscles use during exercise. Endurance (aerobic) training increases your VO_{2max}. This translates into greater fat utilization because a higher VO_{2max} increases your ability to perform more aerobically at the same absolute level of exercise.

Endurance training also increases the threshold at which lactic acid starts to accumulate in the blood. Lactic acid speeds up the rate of muscle glycogen breakdown by interfering with the use of fat as fuel. A higher lactate threshold enables you to use more fat and less glycogen at the same absolute level of exercise.

Endurance training also causes several major adaptations in the muscles that promote greater fat utilization. When you burn more fat, you use less glycogen. This "glycogen sparing" effect is beneficial because muscle glycogen stores are limited and fat stores are abundant.

Lastly, endurance training increases the capacity of the muscles to store glycogen. Thus, endurance training confers a dual performance advantage—your muscle glycogen stores are higher at the onset of exercise and you use them up at a slower rate.

13

Nutrient Basics

The 6 Classes of Nutrients

food satisfies 3 basic needs—it supplies energy, it supports new tissue growth and tissue repair, and it helps to regulate metabolism. These 3 requirements are met by components of food called nutrients. There are 6 classes of nutrients and each class has unique chemical characteristics suited to meet specific body needs. The 6 classes are carbohydrate, fat, protein, vitamins, minerals and water.

Carbohydrates

Carbohydrates such as starch and sugar are the most readily available source of food energy. During digestion and metabolism, all carbohydrates are broken down to the simple sugar **glucose** and used as the body's principal energy source. Glucose is stored in the liver and muscle tissue as **glycogen**. A carbohydrate-rich diet is necessary to maintain muscle glycogen, the primary fuel for most sports.

Sugar and complex carbohydrates (starch) are grouped together because they have a chemical similarity. All carbohydrates are made up of one or more simple sugars, the most common being glucose, fructose, and galactose. The simple sugar glucose connects to the simple sugar fructose to form sucrose, or table sugar. Starches or complex carbohydrates contain anywhere from 300 to 1,000 glucose units hooked together.

Although our bodies use both sugars and starches for energy, a high-performance diet emphasizes **nutrient-dense** carbohydrates. Nutrient-dense carbohydrates, such as whole grain breads and cereals, rice, beans, pasta, and vegetables also supply other nutrients such as vitamins and minerals and dietary fiber and phytochemicals. Sweet foods that are high in sugar (candy bars, cookies, and donuts) supply carbohydrates, but they also contain high amounts of fat and insignificant amounts of vitamins and minerals.

Fruit contains the sweetest of all simple sugars—fructose. Since fruit is mostly water, its sugar and calorie content are relatively low. Like starchy foods, most fruits are rich in nutrients and virtually fat-free.

Fats

Fats, or lipids, are the most concentrated source of food energy. One gram of fat supplies about 9 calories, compared to the 4 calories per gram supplied by carbohydrates and protein. Fats are the body's only source of the essential fatty acids, linoleic and linolenic acid. These essential fatty acids are necessary for growth and healthy skin and hair. Fat insulates and protects the body's organs against trauma and exposure to cold. Fats are also involved in the absorption and transport of the fat-soluble vitamins.

Fatty acids are divided into 2 categories: saturated and unsaturated (including monounsaturated and polyunsaturated fatty acids). These fatty acids differ from each other chemically based on the nature of the bond between their carbon and hydrogen atoms.

As a general rule, saturated fat (butter and lard) is solid at room temperature and is derived mainly from animal sources. Unsaturated fat (safflower, canola, and corn oil) is liquid at room temperature and is derived mainly from plants. Palm and coconut oils are exceptions—they are highly saturated vegetables fats. Monounsaturated and polyunsaturated fats should be emphasized in a healthy diet, since they tend to lower the blood cholesterol level. Saturated fats tend to raise the level of blood cholesterol. A high blood cholesterol level is a major risk factor for coronary heart disease.

Protein

Protein is a major structural component of all body tissue and is required for tissue growth and repair. Proteins are also necessary components of hormones, enzymes, and blood-plasma transport systems. Protein is not a significant energy source during rest or exercise. However, your body will use protein for energy if you're not eating enough calories or carbohydrates (during starvation or a low-carbohydrate diet).

The proteins in both plant and animal sources are composed of the structural units called amino acids. Of the more than 20 amino acids that have been identified, 9 must be provided by our diet; these are called the essential amino acids. Meat, fish, and poultry contain all 9 essential amino acids and are called complete proteins.

Vegetable proteins, such as beans and grains, are called incomplete proteins because they do not supply all of the essential amino acids.

The body can make complete proteins if a variety of plant foods—beans, grains, vegetables, nuts, and seeds—and sufficient calories are eaten during the day. Since the body utilizes amino acids from foods eaten at different meals, vegetarians don't need to combine specific foods within a single meal to achieve complete protein consumption. Well-balanced vegetarian diets may even decrease the risk of heart disease and cancer, because they are lower in fat and higher in nutrient-dense carbohydrates than the average American diet.

Vitamins

Vitamins are organic compounds (they contain carbon) that the body requires in minute amounts but cannot manufacture. Vitamins provide no calories and cannot be used as fuel. Instead, they function as metabolic regulators that govern the processes of energy production, growth, maintenance, and repair. Thirteen vitamins have been identified. Each has a special function in the body and also works in complicated ways with other nutrients. The function and sources of most of the vitamins are shown in Appendix 3.

Vitamins are divided into 2 groups: water-soluble and fat-soluble. Fat-soluble vitamins include A, D, E, and K. These are stored in body fat, principally in the liver. Taking a greater amount of fat-soluble vitamins than the body needs over a significant period can produce serious toxic effects.

While vitamin A is found only in animals, dark orange-yellow and green leafy plants contain substances called carotenes that the body can convert to vitamin A. Unlike vitamin A, dietary carotenes are fairly safe when consumed in large quantities. The body stores excesses of carotenes (which can make the skin look yellow-orange) rather than converting them to vitamin A.

Vitamin C and the B complex vitamins are soluble in water and must be replaced on a regular basis. When you consume more water-soluble vitamins than you need, the excess is eliminated in the urine. However, excessive consumption of such water-soluble vitamins as niacin, B6, and C can also produce serious side effects. Please see Chapter 6 for more information on vitamins and minerals.

Minerals

Minerals are inorganic compounds (they don't contain carbon) that serve a variety of functions in the body. Some, such as calcium and phosphorus, are used to build bones and teeth. Others are important components of hormones, such as iodine in thyroxin. Iron is essential for the formation of hemoglobin, the oxygen carrier within red blood cells. The function and sources of most of the minerals are shown in Appendix 4.

Certain minerals called electrolytes help regulate muscle contraction, conduction of nerve impulses, and regulation of normal heart rhythm.

Minerals are classified into 2 groups, based on the body's need. Major minerals are needed in amounts greater than 100 milligrams per day. Calcium, phosphorus, potassium, magnesium, sodium, and chloride fall into this category. Minor minerals, or trace elements, are needed in amounts less than 100 milligrams per day. Iron, zinc, selenium, copper, and iodine are minor minerals.

Water

Water is the most essential of all nutrients for athletes. An adequate supply of water is necessary for the control of body temperature (especially during exercise), energy production, and the elimination of waste products from metabolism.

Dehydration—the loss of body water—impairs athletic performance and increases the risk of heat illnesses (heat exhaustion and heat stroke). Water is probably the nutrient most neglected by athletes. It's easy to overlook the benefits of water because it is so readily available and inexpensive. See Chapter 2 for more information on hydration.

Moderation, Balance, Dietary Adequacy

There are 3 basic principles to follow when choosing foods for a healthy diet. Moderation refers to eating a wide selection of foods within and among the 5 major food groups daily. No one major food group is more or less important than any other food group. Moderation also refers to choosing appropriate portion sizes. Balance refers to eating more servings from the larger food groups at the bottom of the Food Guide Pyramid and fewer servings from the smaller food groups at the top of the pyramid. Dietary adequacy can be obtained by including a variety of nutrient-dense foods such as grains, fruits, and vegetables. See Chapter 2 for more information on planning a healthy diet.

For peak performance, you need to eat a balanced diet most of the time. Don't be overly concerned with occasional dietary fluctuations or deviations. Obtaining dietary adequacy isn't as hard as the supplement salespeople would have you believe.

The Well-Balanced Diet

The optimum diet contains adequate amounts of each of the 6 essential classes of nutrients. Of the 40 known nutrients, 10 are considered "leader nutrients." If you obtain adequate amounts of leader nutrients from the foods you eat, you'll probably obtain the other 30 nutrients as well.

The 10 leader nutrients are protein, carbohydrates, fat, vitamin A, vitamin C, thiamin, riboflavin, niacin, calcium, and iron. The 5 food groups in the Food Guide Pyramid were developed with these leader nutrients in mind. The foods in the grain group are high in carbohydrates, thiamin, niacin, and iron. The fruit and vegetable groups contain foods high in vitamins A and C. Meat group foods are high in protein, niacin, iron, and thiamin. Foods in the milk group are good sources of calcium, riboflavin, and protein.

Since no one food or food group supplies all the nutrients needed, it's important to choose different foods from each of the 5 groups in the Pyramid. By eating at least the minimum number of servings from each food group daily, you can be reasonably assured you're getting the nutrients you need for optimum performance.

Nutrition Counseling

Beware of self-proclaimed nutrition "experts" who recommend supplements and rigid diets. The title "nutritionist" can be used by anyone, regardless of training. You have more than a 50% chance of finding a person who has phony credentials or delivers false information calling him or herself a "nutritionist." If you want individual nutrition counseling, consult a registered dietitian (R.D.).

A registered dietitian is a healthcare professional who is educated in nutrition and food science. To become an R.D., the American Dietetic Association (ADA) requires that a person take specific course work from an accredited university (minimum of a Bachelor of Science degree), complete a nutrition internship at an approved hospital, and pass a national certification exam. Registered dietitians are required to continue their professional education by attending scientific meetings, or by writing scientific papers and giving lectures to colleagues.

You can find an R.D. by requesting a referral from your physician, or by contacting the nutrition department of a hospital, clinic, or community health agency. You can also check in the phone book under dietitians, nutritionists, and weight control—remember to choose a professional with R.D. behind his or her name.

There are registered dietitians who specialize in sports nutrition. They usually belong to the Sports, Cardiovascular, and Wellness Nutrition Group (abbreviated SCAN) of the American Dietetic Association. You can be referred to SCAN members in your geographic area by calling the American Dietetic Association at 1 (800) 366-1655 or visiting the American Dietetic Association Web site at www.eatright.org.

Appendix 1

Fiber Content of Food

Fiber Content of Foods

Food Group	Serving Size	Grams of Dietary Fiber
Breads and Crackers		
Bran muffin	1 medium	3
Whole-wheat bread	1 slice	2
Oat bran, English muffin	1 muffin	3
Ry-Krisp	0.5 ounce	3
Crispbread, Wasa	1 piece	1–3
Cereals and Pasta		
General Mills Fiber One	1 ounce	13
Kellogg's All-Bran	1 ounce	10
Whole-wheat pasta	1 cup	5
Long-grain brown rice	1 cup	3
Kellogg's Bran Flakes	1 ounce	4
Oatmeal	1 cup	2
Popcorn	1 ounce	2
Fruits and Nuts		
Almonds	¼ cup	5
Dried prunes	3	4
Apple (with skin)	1 medium	3
Banana	1 medium	3
Dried dates	5	3
Nectarine	1 medium	3
Peach (with skin)	1 medium	3
Roasted peanuts	¼ cup	3
Strawberries	1 cup	3
Cantaloupe	¼ cup	2
Orange	1 medium	2
Smooth peanut butter	2 tbsp.	2
Walnut pieces	¼ cup	2
Pistachios	1 ounce	3
Cooked Legumes		
Kidney beans	½ cup	9
Baked beans	½ cup	7
Navy beans	½ cup	5
Pinto beans	½ cup	5
Lentils	½ cup	2

Fiber Content of Foods (continued)

Food Group	Serving Size	Grams of Dietary Fiber
Vegetables		
Cooked frozen peas	½ cup	4
Baked potato (with skin)	1 medium	4
Cooked broccoli tops	½ cup	3
Cooked young carrots	½ cup	3
Cooked corn	½ cup	3
Cooked green beans	½ cup	2

Appendix 2

Tips for Choosing Nutrient-Dense Foods

Tips for Choosing Nutrient-Dense Foods

- Bring boundaries to your meals—watch portions of meals and snacks.
- Remember—nonfat does not mean calorie free!
- Choose nutrient-dense cereals such as Grapenuts, Total, Raisin Bran, and Wheat Chex. Top with bananas, strawberries, peaches, blueberries.
- Make oatmeal with nonfat milk rather than with water. Top with lowfat yogurt or fruit.
- Eat fruit instead of filling up on fruit juices between or with meals.
- Blend your own lowfat milk shakes or fruit smoothies for a meal or snack.
- Choose hearty, dense breads such as sprouted wheat, oat bran, and honey bran. Use thick slices for sandwiches and toast. Stuff with lowfat tuna salad, chicken salad, or veggies and lowfat cream cheese.
- Choose hearty soups such as minestrone, chicken and vegetable, black bean, or lentil.
- Bake or grill chicken, beef, or fish instead of frying. Use lowfat marinades, sauces, and herbs to add flavor in place of cream sauces or gravy.
- Include lower-calorie vegetables such as tomatoes, carrots, cucumbers, green and red peppers, broccoli, cauliflower, spinach, kale on a salad or as a snack.
- Try stir-fry chicken, lean beef, fish, or tofu with vegetables. Make hearty lowfat chili. Serve with brown or white rice.
- Use lowfat fajitas or wraps and add a combination of the following: veggies, chicken, lowfat ground turkey, nonfat refried beans, shrimp, lowfat cheese, nonfat sour cream, salsa, onions.
- Add lowfat cheese, lowfat cottage cheese, garbanzo beans, kidney beans, chopped eggs, and lowfat dressing to mixed-green salads.
- Try nutrient-dense snacks such as oatmeal raisin cookies, lowfat fig bars, lowfat puddings, lowfat frozen yogurt, lowfat fruit breads, lowfat crackers, low-fat granola bars, fruit.

Appendix 3

U.S. Dietary Reference Intakes for Vitamins

U.S. Dietary Reference Intakes for Vitamins

Nutrient	Functions	Sources
Vitamin C	Collagen formation, immunity, antioxidant	Citrus fruits, tomatoes, strawberries, potatoes, broccoli, cabbage
Vitamin B_1 (Thiamin)	Energy production, central nervous system	Meat, whole-grain cereals, milk, beans
Niacin	Energy production, synthesis of fat and amino acids	Peanut butter, whole-grain cereals, greens, meat, poultry, fish
Vitamin B_6	Protein metabolism, hemoglobin synthesis, energy production	Whole-grain cereals, bananas, meat, spinach, cabbage, lima beans
Folacin	New cell growth, red blood cell production	Greens, mushrooms, liver
Vitamin B_{12} (Cobalamin)	Energy metabolism, red blood cell production, central nervous system	Animal foods
Vitamin A	Vision, skin, antioxidant, immunity	Milk, egg yolk, liver, yogurt, carrots, greens
Vitamin D	Formation of bones, aids absorption of calcium	Sunlight, fortified dairy products, eggs, fish
Vitamin E	Antioxidant, protects unsaturated fats in cells from damage	Vegetable oils, margarines, grains
Vitamin K	Blood clotting	Greens, liver

To find the DRI for a specific nutrient, search the National Academies of Sciences web page. The URL is: http://www.4.nationalacademies.org/news.nsf

Appendix 4

U.S. Dietary Reference Intakes for Minerals

U.S. Dietary Reference Intakes for Minerals

Nutrient	Functions	Sources
Calcium	Bone formation, enzyme reactions, muscle contractions	Dairy products, green leafy vegetables, beans
Iron	Hemoglobin formation, muscle growth and function, energy production	Lean meat, beans, dried fruit, some green leafy vegetables
Magnesium	Energy production, muscle relaxation, nerve conduction	Grains, nuts, meats, beans
Sodium	Nerve impulses, muscle action, body fluid balance	Table salt, small amounts in most food except fruit
Potassium	Fluid balance, muscle action, glycogen and protein synthesis	Bananas, orange juice, fruits, vegetables
Zinc	Tissue growth and healing, immunity, gonadal development	Meat, shellfish, oysters, grains
Copper	Hemoglobin formation, energy production, immunity	Whole grains, beans, nuts dried fruit, shellfish
Selenium	Antioxidant, protects against free radicals, enhances vitamin E	Meat, seafood, grains
Chromium	Part of glucose tolerance factor—helps insulin	Whole grains, meat, cheese, beer
Manganese	Bone and tissue development, fat synthesis	Nuts, grains, beans, tea, fruits, vegetables
Iodine	Regulates metabolism	Iodized salt, seafood
Fluoride	Formation of bones and tooth enamel	Tap water, tea, coffee, rice, spinach, lettuce
Phosphorus	Builds bones and teeth, metabolism	Meat, fish, dairy products, carbonated drinks

To find the DRI for a specific nutrient, search the National Academies of Sciences web page. The URL is: http://www.4.nationalacademies.org/news.nsf

Appendix 5

Caloric Expenditures

The following table lists approximate caloric expenditures per minute for various physical activities.

APPROXIMATE CALORIC EXPENDITURE PER MINUTE FOR VARIOUS PHYSICAL ACTIVITIES*

Body Weight in kilograms	45	50	55	59	64	68	73	77	82	86	91	95	100
Body Weight in pounds	**100**	**110**	**120**	**130**	**140**	**150**	**160**	**170**	**180**	**190**	**200**	**210**	**220**
SEDENTARY ACTIVITIES													
Lying quietly	.99	1.1	1.2	1.3	1.4	1.5	1.6	1.7	1.8	1.9	2.0	2.1	2.2
Sitting and writing	1.2	1.4	1.5	1.7	1.8	1.9	2.0	2.2	2.3	2.4	2.5	2.7	2.8
Standing with light work	2.7	3.0	3.3	3.5	3.8	4.1	4.4	4.6	4.9	5.2	5.4	5.7	6.0
PHYSICAL ACTIVITIES													
Archery	3.1	3.5	3.8	4.1	4.5	4.8	5.1	5.4	5.7	6.0	6.4	6.7	7.0
Badminton													
Recreational singles	3.6	4.0	4.4	4.7	5.1	5.4	5.8	6.2	6.6	6.9	7.3	7.6	8.0
Competitive	5.9	6.4	7.0	7.6	8.2	8.8	9.4	10.0	10.16	11.2	11.8	12.4	13.0
Baseball													
Player	3.1	3.4	3.8	4.1	4.4	4.7	5.0	5.3	5.6	5.9	6.3	6.6	6.9
Pitcher	3.9	4.3	4.7	5.1	5.5	5.9	6.3	6.7	7.1	7.4	7.9	8.2	8.6
Basketball													
Recreational	4.9	5.5	6.0	6.5	7.0	7.5	8.0	8.5	9.0	9.5	10.0	10.5	11.0
Vigorous competition	6.5	7.2	7.8	8.5	9.2	9.9	10.5	11.2	11.9	12.5	13.2	13.8	14.5
Bicycling, level													
(mph) (min/mile)													
5 12:00	1.9	2.1	2.3	2.5	2.7	2.9	3.1	3.3	3.5	3.7	3.9	4.1	4.3
10 6:00	4.2	4.6	5.1	5.5	5.9	6.4	6.8	7.2	7.6	8.1	8.5	8.9	9.4
15 4:00	7.3	8.0	8.7	9.5	10.0	10.9	11.6	12.4	13.1	13.8	14.5	15.3	16.0
20 3:00	10.7	11.7	12.8	13.9	14.9	16.0	17.1	18.1	19.2	20.3	21.3	22.4	23.5

APPROXIMATE CALORIC EXPENDITURE PER MINUTE FOR VARIOUS PHYSICAL ACTIVITIES*

Body Weight in kilograms	45	50	55	59	64	68	73	77	82	86	91	95	100
Body Weight in pounds	**100**	**110**	**120**	**130**	**140**	**150**	**160**	**170**	**180**	**190**	**200**	**210**	**220**
PHYSICAL ACTIVITIES													
Canoeing													
(mph) (min/mile)													
2.5 24	1.9	2.1	2.3	2.5	2.7	2.9	3.1	3.3	3.5	3.7	3.9	4.1	4.3
4.0 15	4.4	4.9	5.3	5.8	6.2	6.7	7.1	7.6	8.0	8.5	8.9	9.4	9.8
5.0 12	5.7	6.3	6.9	7.5	8.1	8.7	9.3	9.8	10.4	11.0	11.6	12.2	12.8
Dancing													
Moderately (waltz)	3.1	3.5	3.8	4.1	4.5	4.8	5.1	5.4	5.7	6/0	6.4	6.7	7.0
Active (square, disco)	4.5	5.0	5.4	5.9	6.3	6.8	7.3	7.7	8.2	8.6	9.1	9.5	10.0
Aerobic (vigorously)	6.0	6.7	7.3	7.9	8.5	9.1	9.7	10.3	10.9	11.5	12.1	12.7	13.3
Fencing													
Moderately	3.3	3.6	4.0	4.3	4.6	5.0	5.3	5.7	6.0	6.3	6.7	7.0	7.3
Vigorously	6.6	7.3	8.0	8.7	9.4	10.0	10.7	11.4	12.1	12.7	13.4	14.1	14.8
Football													
Moderate	3.3	3.6	4.0	4.3	4.6	5.0	5.3	5.7	6.0	6.3	6.7	7.0	7.3
Touch, vigorous	5.5	6.1	6.6	7.2	7.8	8.3	8.9	9.4	10.0	101.6	11.1	11.7	12.2
Golf													
Twosome (carry clubs)	3.6	4.0	4.4	4.7	5.1	5.4	5.8	6.2	6.6	6.9	7.3	7.6	8.0
Foursome (carry clubs)	2.7	3.0	3.3	3.5	3.8	4.1	4.4	4.6	4.9	5.2	5.4	5.7	6.0
Power-cart	1.9	2.1	2.3	2.5	2.7	2.9	3.1	3.3	3.5	3.7	3.9	4.1	4.3
Handball													
Moderate	6.5	7.2	7.8	8.5	9.2	9.9	10.5	11.2	11.9	12.5	13.2	13.8	14.5
Competitive	7.7	8.4	9.1	10.0	10.8	11.5	12.3	13.1	13.9	14.7	15.4	16.2	17.0

APPROXIMATE CALORIC EXPENDITURE PER MINUTE FOR VARIOUS PHYSICAL ACTIVITIES*

Body Weight in kilograms	**45**	**50**	**55**	**59**	**64**	**68**	**73**	**77**	**82**	**86**	**91**	**95**	**100**
Body Weight in pounds	**100**	**110**	**120**	**130**	**140**	**150**	**160**	**170**	**180**	**190**	**200**	**210**	**220**
PHYSICAL ACTIVITIES													
Hiking, pack (3 mph)	4.5	5.0	5.4	5.9	6.3	6.8	7.3	7.7	8.2	8.6	9.1	9.5	10.0
Hockey, field	5.0	6.7	7.3	7.9	8.5	9.1	9.7	10.3	10.9	11.5	12.1	12.7	13.3
Hockey, ice	6.6	7.3	8.0	8.7	9.4	10.0	10.7	11.4	12.1	12.7	13.4	14.1	14.8
Horseback riding													
Walk	1.9	2.1	2.3	2.5	2.7	2.9	3.1	3.3	3.5	3.7	3.9	4.1	4.3
Sitting to trot	2.7	3.0	3.3	3.5	3.8	4.1	4.4	4.6	4.9	5.2	5.4	5.7	6.0
Posting to trot	4.2	4.6	5.1	5.5	5.9	6.4	6.8	7.2	7.6	8.1	8.5	8.9	9.4
Gallop	5.7	6.3	6.9	7.5	8.1	8.7	9.3	9.8	10.4	11.0	11.6	12.2	12.8
Jogging (see Running)													
Judo	8.5	9.3	10.2	11.0	11.9	12.8	13.6	14.5	15.4	16.2	17.1	17.9	18.8
Karate	8.5	9.3	10.2	11.0	11.9	12.8	13.6	14.5	15.4	16.2	17.1	17.9	18.8
Mountain climbing	6.5	7.2	7.8	8.5	9.2	9.8	10.5	11.2	11.8	12.5	13.1	13.8	14.5
Paddle ball	5.7	6.3	6.9	7.5	8.1	8.7	9.3	9.8	10.4	11.0	11.6	12.2	12.8
Racketball	6.5	7.1	7.8	8.4	9.1	9.8	10.4	11.1	11.7	12.4	13.0	13.7	14.4
Roller skating (9 mph)	4.2	4.6	5.1	5.5	5.9	6.4	6.8	7.2	7.6	8.1	8.5	8.9	9.4
Running (steady state)													
(mph) (min/mile)													
5.0 12:00	6.0	6.6	7.3	7.9	8.5	9.1	9.7	10.3	10.9	11.6	12.2	12.8	13.4
5.5 10:55	6.7	7.3	8.0	8.7	9.4	10.0	10.7	11.4	12.1	12.8	13.4	14.1	14.8
6.0 10:00	7.2	8.0	8.7	9.5	10.2	10.9	11.7	12.4	13.1	13.8	14.6	15.4	16.1
7.0 8:35	8.5	9.3	10.2	11.0	11.9	12.8	13.6	14.5	15.4	16.2	17.1	17.9	18.8
8.0 7:30	9.7	10.7	11.6	12.6	13.6	14.6	15.6	16.6	17.6	18.5	19.5	20.5	21.5

APPROXIMATE CALORIC EXPENDITURE PER MINUTE FOR VARIOUS PHYSICAL ACTIVITIES*

Body Weight in kilograms	45	50	55	59	64	68	73	77	82	86	91	95	100
Body Weight in pounds	100	110	120	130	140	150	160	170	180	190	200	210	220
PHYSICAL ACTIVITIES													
Running (steady state) (continued)													
(mph) (min/mile)													
9.0 6:40	10.8	11.9	12.9	14.0	15.1	16.2	17.3	18.4	19.5	20.6	21.7	22.8	23.9
10.0 6:00	12.1	13.3	14.5	15.7	17.0	18.2	19.4	20.7	21.9	23.1	24.2	25.4	26.7
11.0 5:28	13.3	14.6	16.0	17.3	18.7	20.0	21.4	22.7	24.1	25.4	26.8	28.1	29.5
12.0 5:00	14.5	16.0	17.4	18.9	20.4	21.9	23.3	24.8	26.3	27.8	29.2	30.7	32.2
Skating, ice (9 mph)	4.2	4.6	5.1	5.5	5.9	6.4	6.8	7.2	7.6	8.1	8.5	8.9	9.4
Skiing, cross-country													
(mph) (min/mile)													
2.5 24:00	5.0	5.5	6.0	6.5	7.0	7.5	8.0	8.5	9.0	9.5	10.0	10.6	11.1
4.0 15:00	6.5	7.2	7.8	8.5	9.2	9.9	10.5	11.2	11.9	12.5	13.2	13.8	14.5
5.0 12:00	7.7	8.4	9.2	10.0	10.8	11.5	12.3	13.1	13.9	14.7	15.4	16.2	17.0
Skiing, downhill	6.5	7.2	7.8	8.5	9.2	9.9	10.5	11.2	11.9	12.5	13.2	13.8	14.5
Soccer	5.9	6.6	7.2	7.8	8.4	9.0	9.6	10.2	10.8	11.4	12.0	12.6	13.2
Squash													
Normal	6.7	7.3	8.0	8.7	9.5	10.1	10.8	11.5	12.2	12.9	13.5	14.2	14.9
Competition	7.7	8.4	9.2	10.0	10.8	11.5	12.3	13.1	13.9	14.7	15.4	16.2	17.0
Swimming (yards/mi)													
Backstroke													
25	2.5	2.8	3.0	3.3	3.5	3.8	4.0	4.3	4.5	4.8	5.1	5.3	5.6
30	3.5	3.9	4.2	4.6	4.9	5.3	5.6	6.0	6.4	6.7	7.1	7.4	7.8
35	4.5	5.0	5.4	5.9	6.3	6.8	7.3	7.7	8.2	8.6	9.1	9.5	10.0
40	5.5	6.1	6.6	7.2	7.8	8.3	8.9	9.4	10.0	10.6	11.1	11.7	12.2

APPROXIMATE CALORIC EXPENDITURE PER MINUTE FOR VARIOUS PHYSICAL ACTIVITIES*

Body Weight in kilograms	**45**	**50**	**55**	**59**	**64**	**68**	**73**	**77**	**82**	**86**	**91**	**95**	**100**
Body Weight in pounds	**100**	**110**	**120**	**130**	**140**	**150**	**160**	**170**	**180**	**190**	**200**	**210**	**220**
PHYSICAL ACTIVITIES													
Swimming (yards/mi)													
Breaststroke													
20	3.1	3.5	3.8	4.1	4.5	4.8	5.1	5.4	5.7	6.0	6.4	6.7	7/0
30	4.7	5.2	5.7	6.2	6.7	7.1	7.6	8.1	8.6	9.1	9.5	10.0	10.5
40	6.3	7.0	7.6	8.3	8.9	9.6	10.2	10.9	11.5	12.2	12.8	13.5	14.1
Front crawl													
20	3.1	3.5	3.8	4.1	4.5	4.8	5.1	5.4	5.7	6.0	6.4	6.7	7.0
25	4.0	4.4	4.8	5.2	5.6	6.0	6.4	6.8	7.2	7.6	8.0	8.4	8.8
35	4.8	5.4	5.9	6.4	6.8	7.3	7.8	8.3	8.8	9.2	9.7	10.2	10.7
45	5.7	6.3	6.9	7.5	8.1	8.7	9.3	9.8	10.4	11.0	11.6	12.2	12.8
50	7.0	7.7	8.5	9.2	9.9	10.6	11.3	12.0	12.8	13.5	14.2	14.9	15.6
Table tennis	3.4	3.8	4.1	4.5	4.8	5.2	5.5	5.9	6.3	6.6	7.0	7.3	7.7
Tennis													
Singles (recreational)	5.0	5.5	6.0	6.5	7.0	7.5	8.0	8.5	9.0	9.5	10.0	10.6	11.1
Competition	6.4	7.1	7.7	8.4	9.1	9.8	10.4	11.1	11.8	12.4	13.1	13.7	14.4
Volleyball													
Moderate recreational	2.9	3.2	3.5	3.8	4.1	4.4	4.7	5.0	5.3	5.6	5.9	6.1	6.4
Vigorous, competition	6.5	7.1	7.8	8.4	9.1	9.8	10.4	11.1	11.7	12.4	13.0	13.7	14.4
Walking													
(mph) (min/mile)													
2.0 30:00	2.1	2.3	2.5	2.8	3.0	3.2	3.4	3.6	3.9	4.1	4.3	4.5	4.7
3.0 20:00	2.7	3.0	3.3	3.5	3.8	4.1	4.4	4.6	4.9	5.2	5.4	5.7	6.0

APPROXIMATE CALORIC EXPENDITURE PER MINUTE FOR VARIOUS PHYSICAL ACTIVITIES*

Body Weight in kilograms		45	50	55	59	64	68	73	77	82	86	91	95	100
Body Weight in pounds		100	110	120	130	140	150	160	170	180	190	200	210	220
PHYSICAL ACTIVITIES														
Walking														
(mph)	(min/mile)													
3.5	17:10	3.3	3.7	4.0	4.4	4.7	5.1	5.4	5.8	6.2	6.5	6.9	7.2	7.6
4.0	15:00	4.2	4.6	5.1	5.5	5.9	6.4	6.8	7.2	7.6	8.1	8.5	8.9	9.4
4.5	13:20	4.7	5.2	5.7	6.2	6.7	7.1	7.6	8.1	8.6	9.1	9.5	10.0	10.5
5.0	12:00	5.4	6.0	6.5	7.1	7.7	8.2	8.7	9.2	9.8	10.4	10.9	11.5	12.0
5.4	11:10	6.2	6.9	7.5	8.2	8.8	9.5	10.1	10.3	11.4	12.1	12.7	13.4	14.0
5.8	10:20	7.7	8.4	9.2	10.0	10.8	11.5	12.3	13.1	13.9	14.7	15.4	16.2	17.0
Water skiing		5.0	5.5	6.0	6.5	7.0	7.5	8.0	8.5	9.0	9.5	10.0	10.6	11.1
Weight training		5.2	5.7	6.2	6.8	7.3	7.8	8.3	8.9	9.4	9.9	10.5	11.0	11.5
Wrestling		8.5	9.3	10.2	11.0	11.9	12.8	13.6	14.5	15.4	16.2	17.1	17.9	18.8

*Adapted from Williams, M. H. *Nutrition for Fitness and Sport*, 3rd ed. Wm. C. Brown Publishers, 1992.

Note: The energy cost, in calories, will vary for different physical activities in a given individual depending on several factors. For example, the caloric cost of bicycling will vary depending on the type of bicycle, going uphill or downhill, and wind resistance. Walking with hand weights or ankle weights will increase energy output. Thus, the values expressed here are approximations and may be increased or decreased depending upon factors that influence energy cost.

Appendix 6

BMI Values

BMI	17	17.5	18	18.5	19	20	21	22	23	24	24.9	25	26	27	28	29	29.9	30	35	40
4' 10"	81	84	86	89	91	96	101	105	110	115	119	120	124	129	134	139	143	144	168	192
4' 11"	84	87	89	92	94	99	104	109	114	119	123	124	129	134	139	144	148	149	173	198
5'	87	90	92	95	97	102	108	113	118	123	128	128	133	138	143	149	153	154	179	205
5' 1"	90	93	95	98	101	106	111	117	122	127	132	132	138	143	148	154	158	159	185	212
5' 2"	93	96	98	101	104	109	115	120	126	131	136	137	142	148	153	159	164	164	191	219
5' 3"	96	99	102	105	107	113	119	124	130	136	141	141	147	153	158	164	169	169	198	226
5' 4"	99	102	105	108	111	117	122	128	134	140	145	146	152	157	163	169	174	175	204	233
5' 5"	102	105	108	111	114	120	126	132	138	144	150	150	156	162	168	174	180	180	210	241
5' 6"	105	108	112	115	118	124	130	136	143	149	154	155	161	167	174	180	185	186	217	248
5' 7"	109	112	115	118	121	128	134	141	147	153	159	160	166	173	179	185	191	192	224	256
5' 8"	112	115	118	122	125	132	138	145	151	158	164	165	171	178	184	191	197	197	230	263
5' 9"	115	119	122	125	129	136	142	149	156	163	169	169	176	183	190	197	203	203	237	271
5' 10"	119	122	126	129	133	139	146	153	160	167	174	174	181	188	195	202	209	209	244	279
5' 11"	122	126	129	133	136	143	151	158	165	172	179	179	187	194	201	208	215	215	251	287
6'	125	129	133	137	140	148	155	162	170	177	184	184	192	199	207	214	221	221	258	295
6' 1"	129	133	137	140	144	152	159	167	174	182	189	190	197	205	212	220	227	228	265	303
6' 2"	132	136	140	144	148	156	164	171	179	187	194	195	203	210	218	226	233	234	273	312
6' 3"	136	140	144	148	152	160	168	176	184	192	199	200	208	216	224	232	239	240	280	320
6' 4"	140	144	148	152	156	164	173	181	189	197	205	206	214	222	230	238	246	247	288	329

Index

C

D

E

F

G